THE SEVEN DEADLY SINS

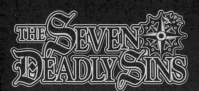

nakaba suzuki presents

34

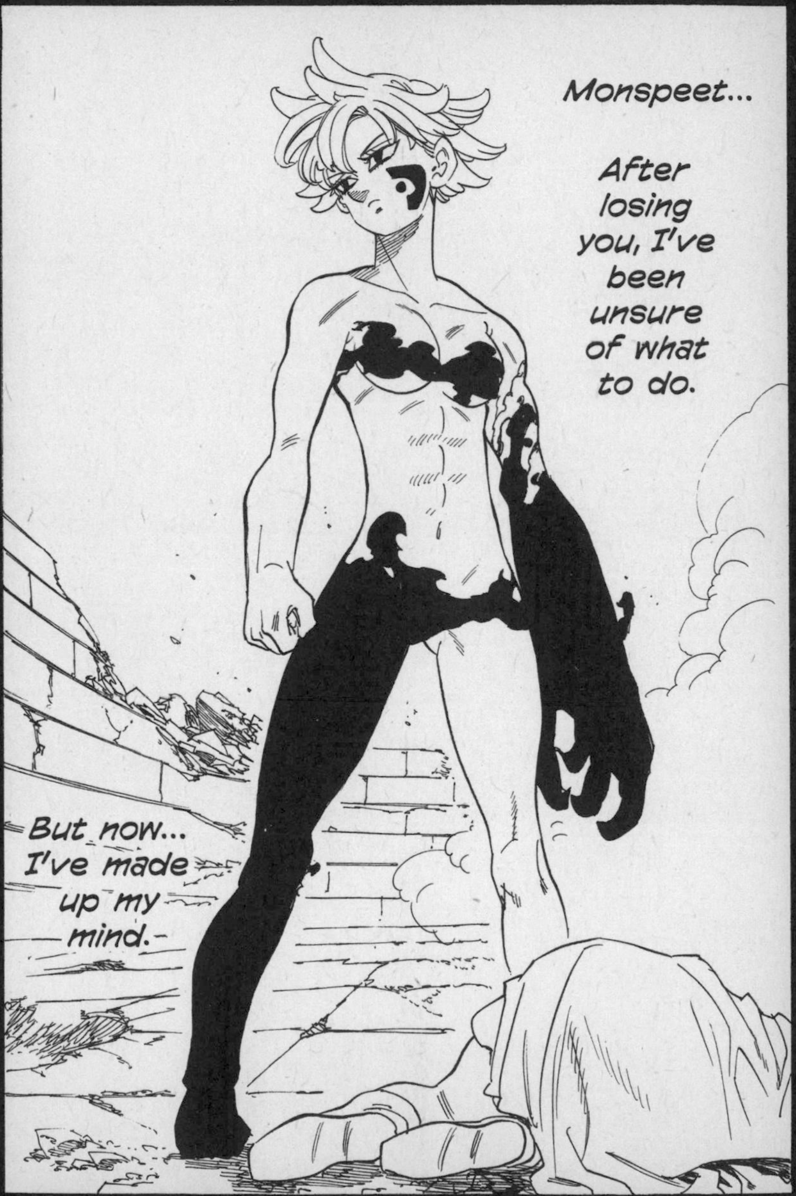
Monspeet...
After losing you, I've been unsure of what to do.
But now... I've made up my mind.

C O N T E N T S

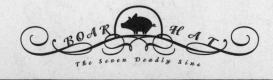

BOAR HAT

The Seven Deadly Sins

Chapter 276 - The Tragic Strike

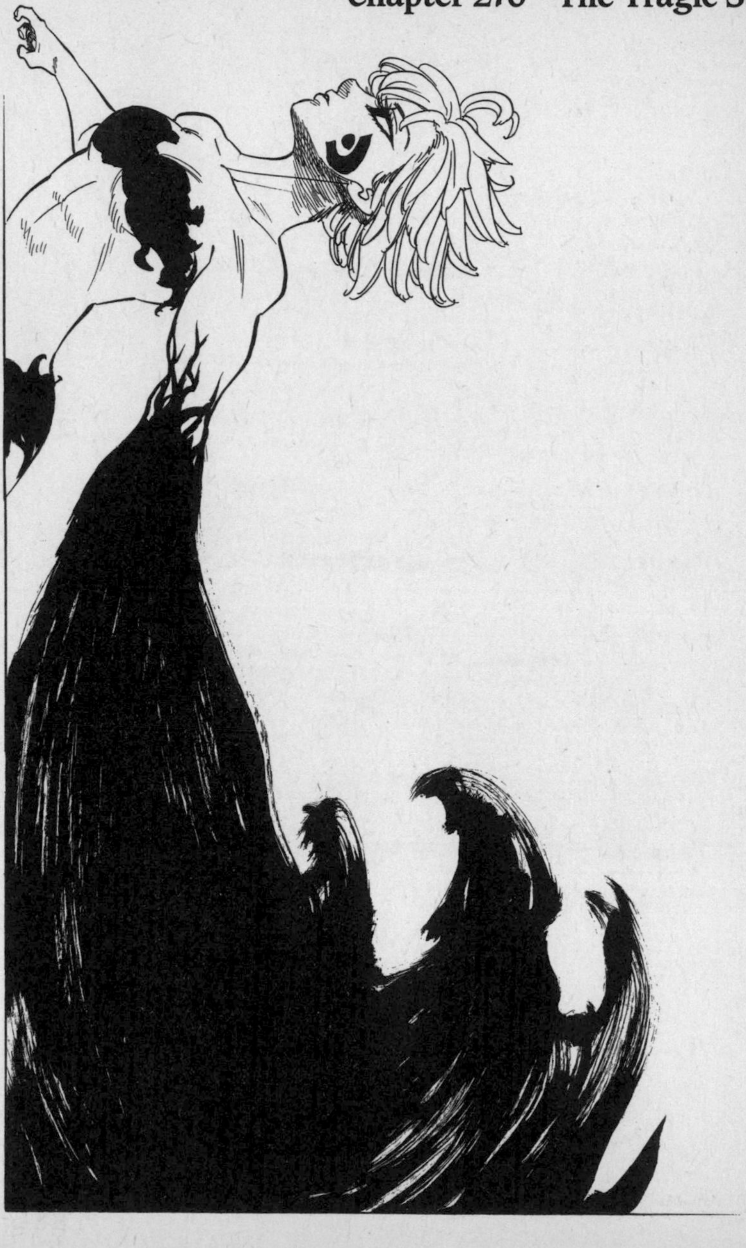

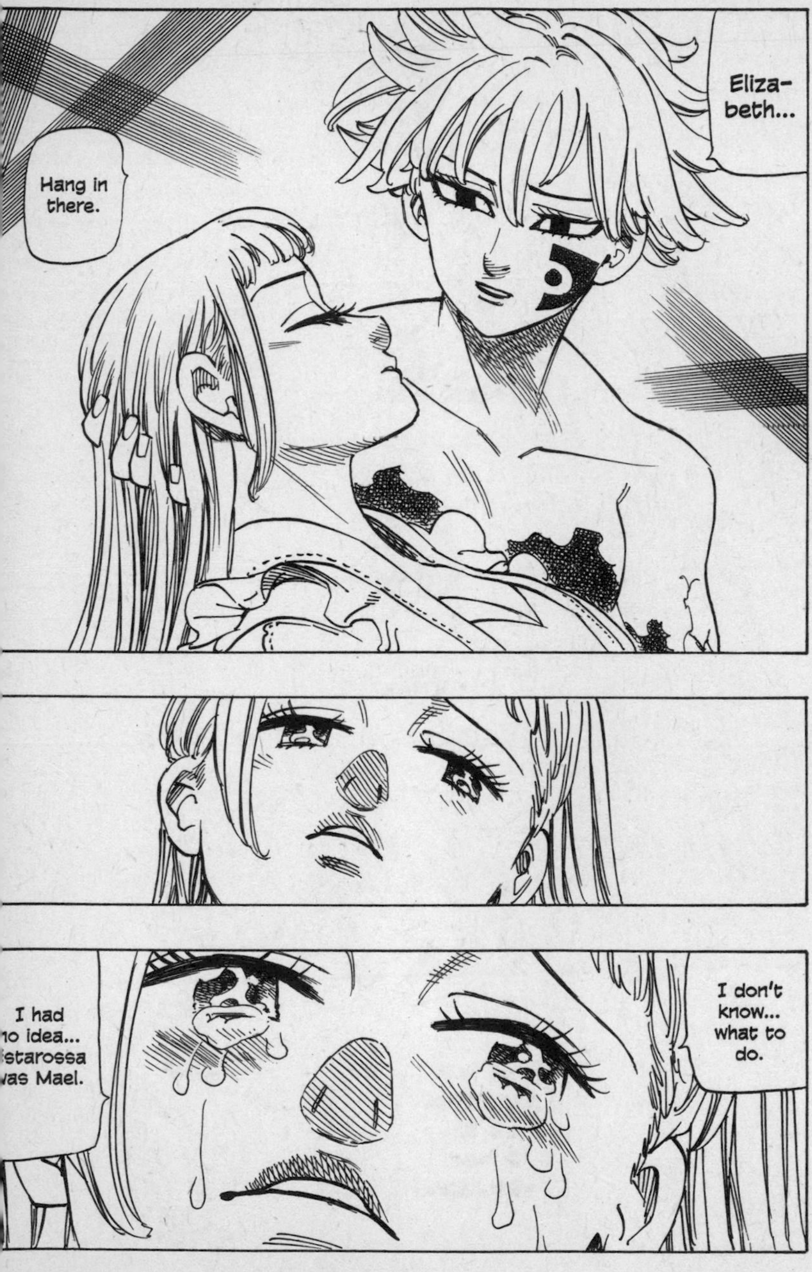
Eliza-
beth...
Hang in there.
I don't know... what to do.
I had o idea... starossa as Mael.

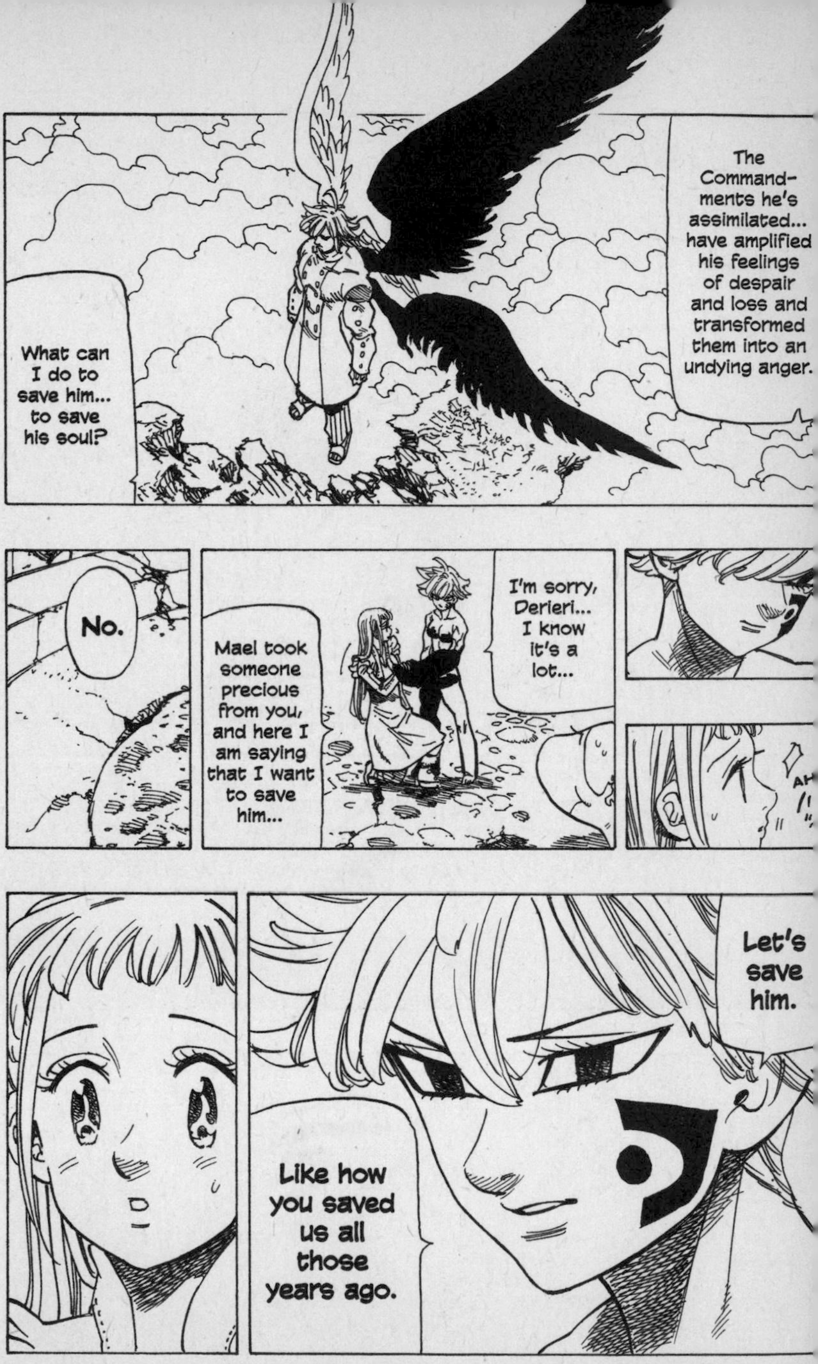
The Commandments he's assimilated... have amplified his feelings of despair and loss and transformed them into an undying anger.
What can I do to save him... to save his soul?
AH!!
I'm sorry, Derieri... I know it's a lot...
Mael took someone precious from you, and here I am saying that I want to save him...
No.
Let's save him.
Like how you saved us all those years ago.

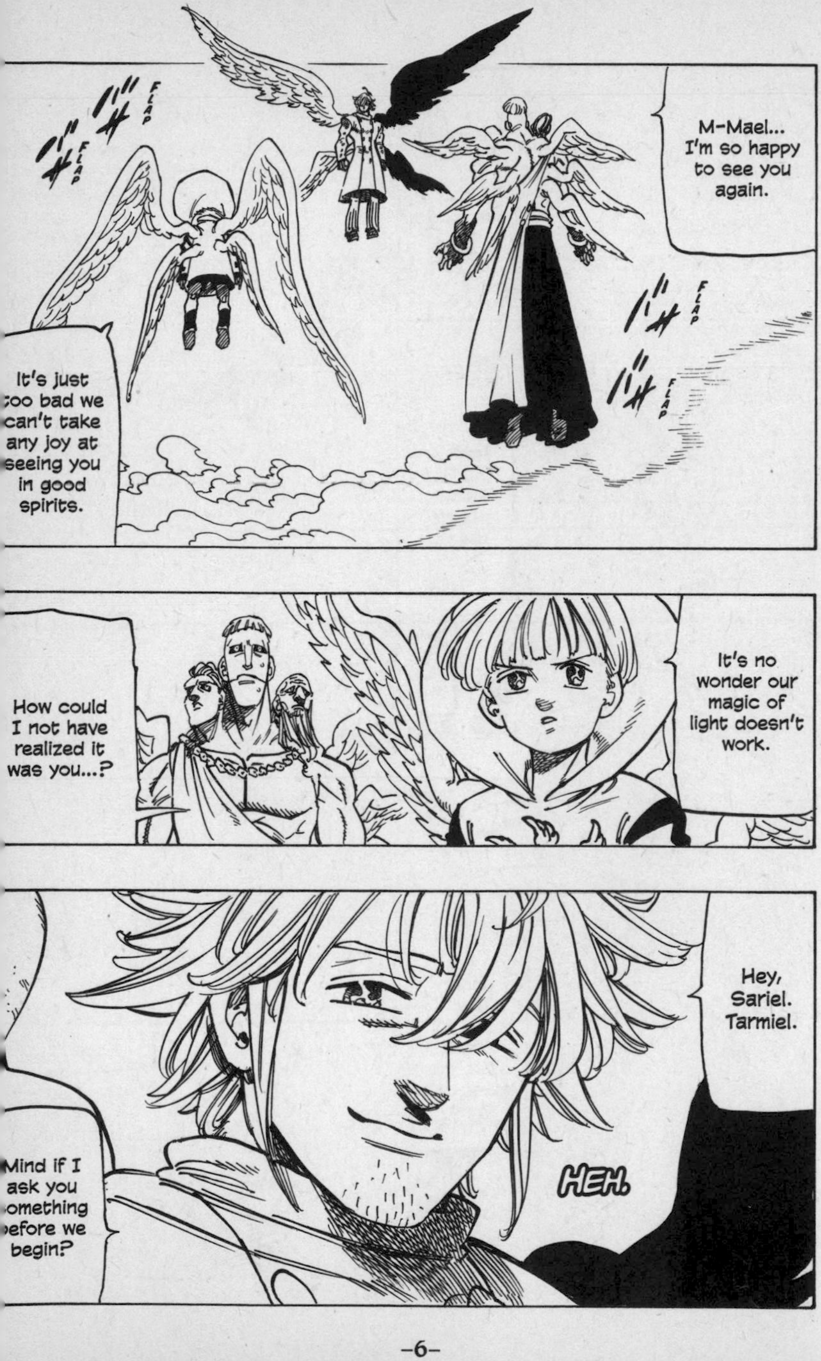
M-Mael... I'm so happy to see you again.
FLAP
FLAP
FLAP
FLAP
It's just oo bad we can't take any joy at seeing you in good spirits.
It's no wonder our magic of light doesn't work.
How could I not have realized it was you...?
Hey, Sariel. Tarmiel.
HEH.
Mind if I ask you omething efore we begin?

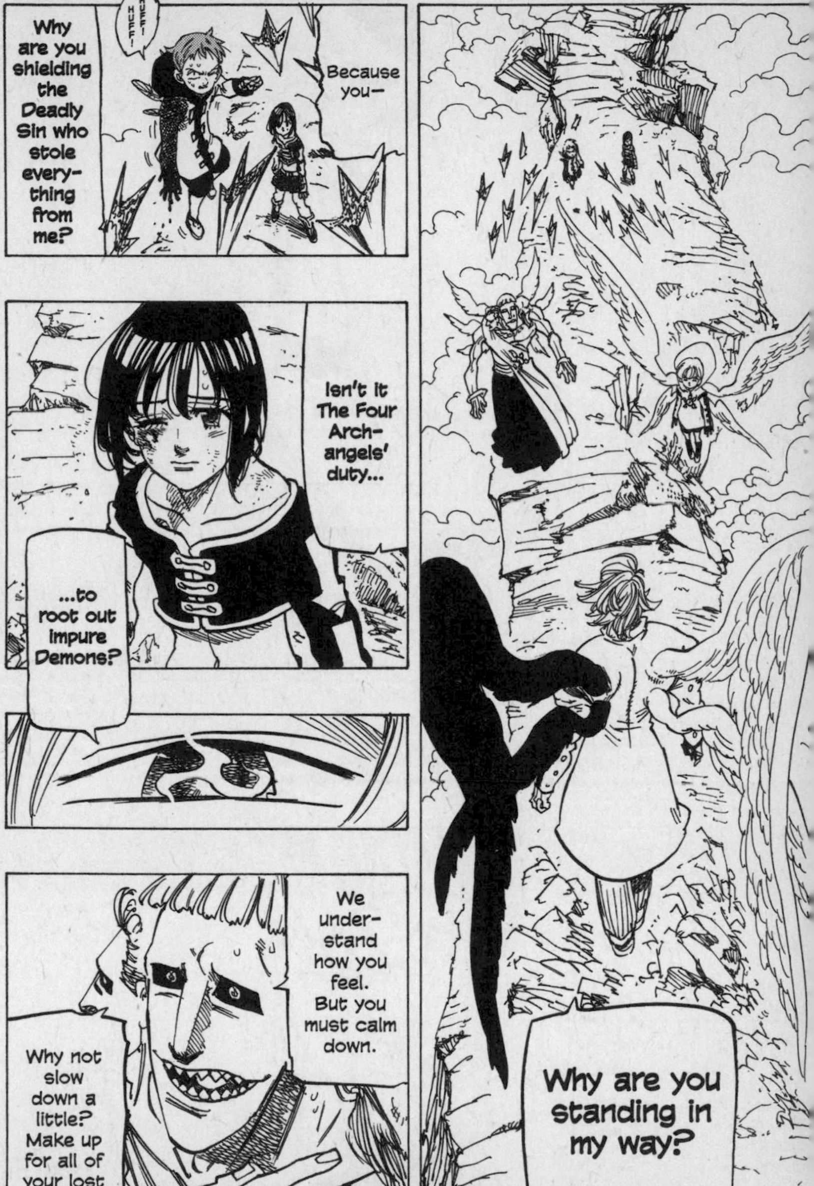
HUFF! HUFF!
Why are you shielding the Deadly Sin who stole everything from me?
Because you—
Isn't it The Four Archangels' duty...
...to root out impure Demons?
We understand how you feel. But you must calm down.
Why not slow down a little? Make up for all of your lost time?
Why are you standing in my way?

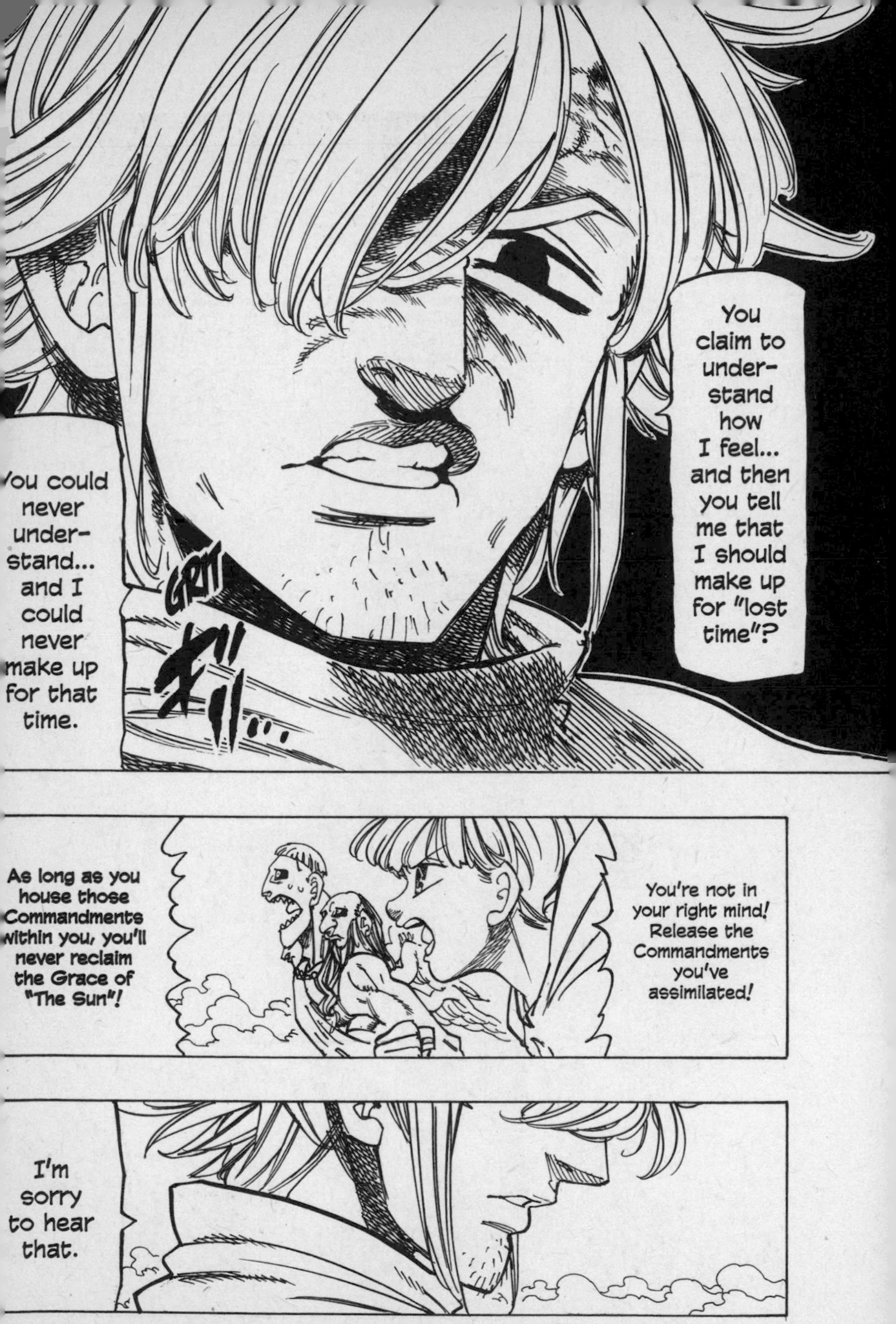
You claim to under-stand how I feel... and then you tell me that I should make up for "lost time"?
You could never under-stand... and I could never make up for that time.
GRIT
You're not in your right mind! Release the Commandments you've assimilated!
As long as you house those Commandments within you, you'll never reclaim the Grace of "The Sun"!
I'm sorry to hear that.

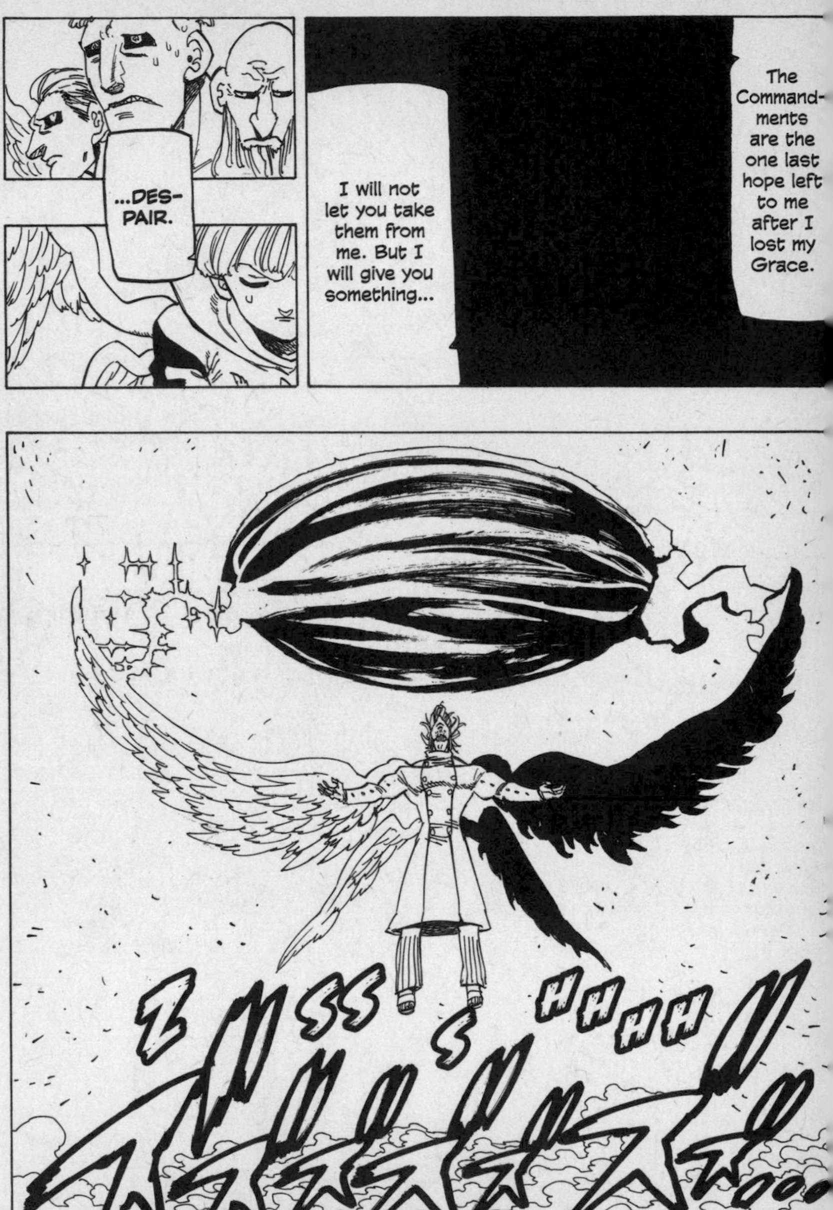
The Commandments are the one last hope left to me after I lost my Grace.
I will not let you take them from me. But I will give you something...
...DESPAIR.
ZSSSHHHH

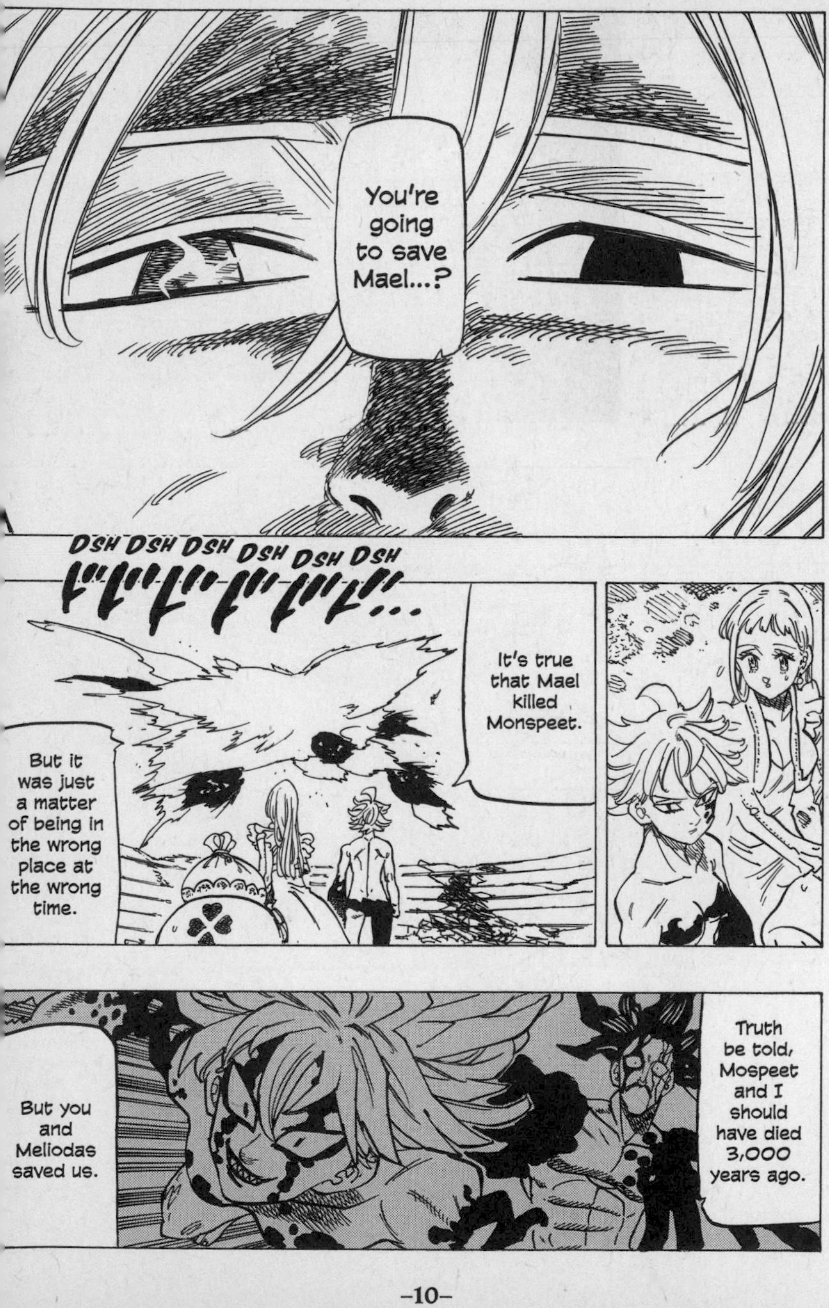
You're going to save Mael...?
It's true that Mael killed Monspeet.
DSH DSH DSH DSH DSH DSH
But it was just a matter of being in the wrong place at the wrong time.
Truth be told, Mospeet and I should have died 3,000 years ago.
But you and Meliodas saved us.

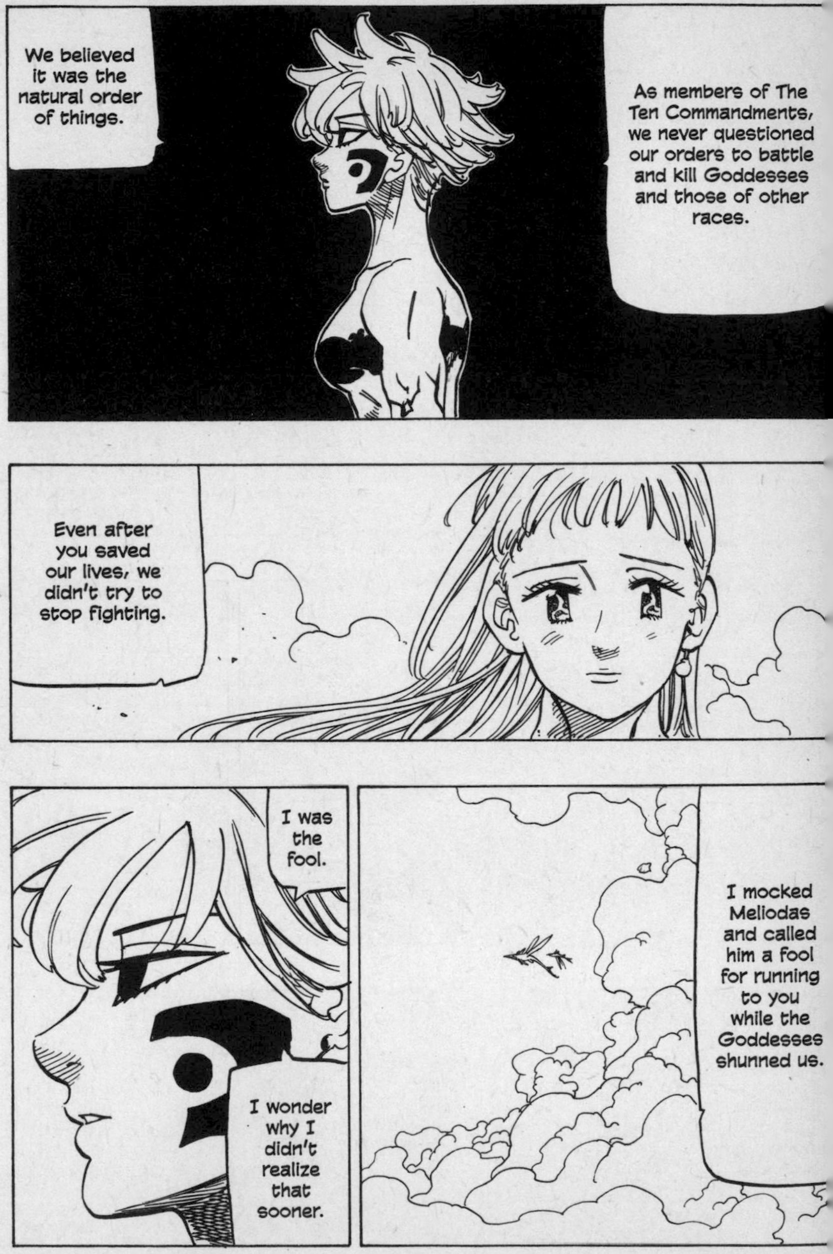
As members of The Ten Commandments, we never questioned our orders to battle and kill Goddesses and those of other races.
We believed it was the natural order of things.
Even after you saved our lives, we didn't try to stop fighting.
I mocked Meliodas and called him a fool for running to you while the Goddesses shunned us.
I was the fool.
I wonder why I didn't realize that sooner.

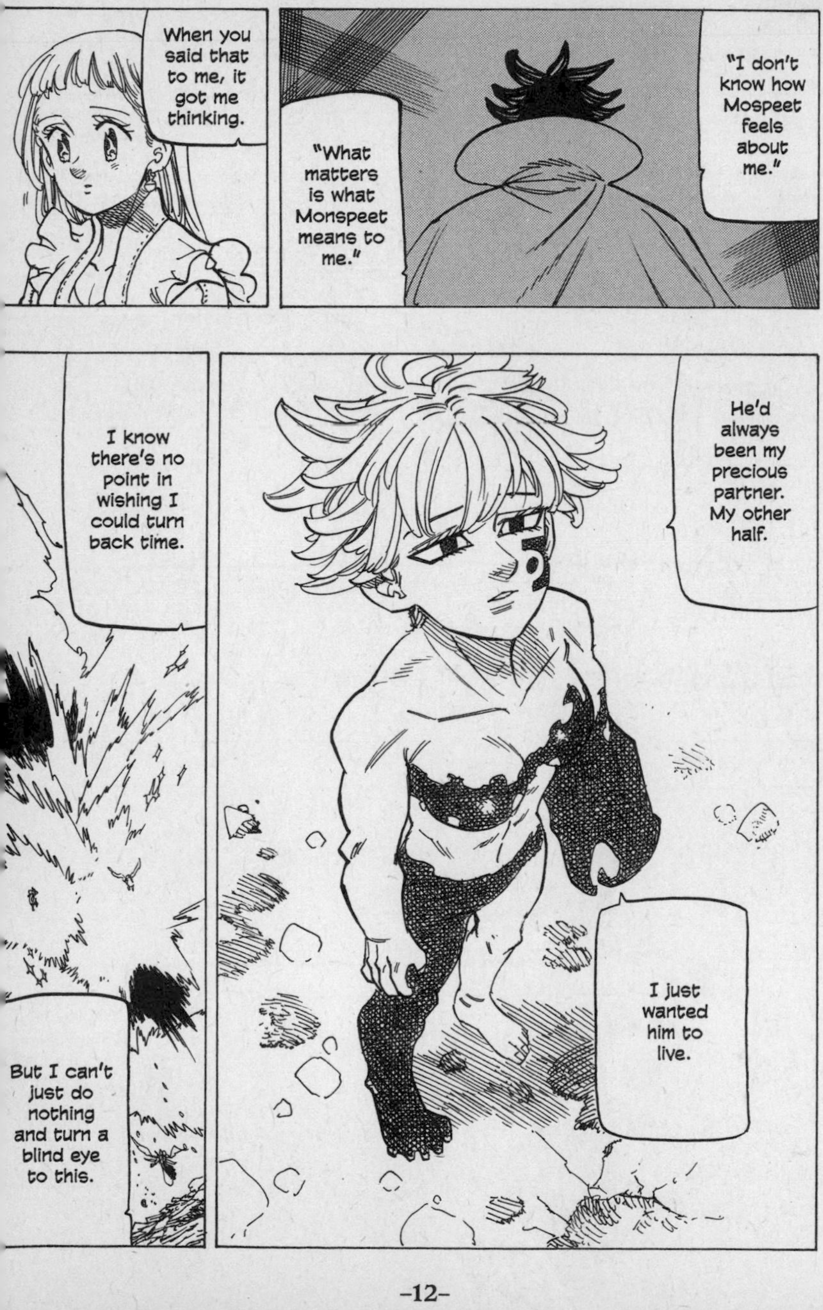
"I don't know how Mospeet feels about me."
"What matters is what Monspeet means to me."
When you said that to me, it got me thinking.
He'd always been my precious partner. My other half.
I just wanted him to live.
I know there's no point in wishing I could turn back time.
But I can't just do nothing and turn a blind eye to this.

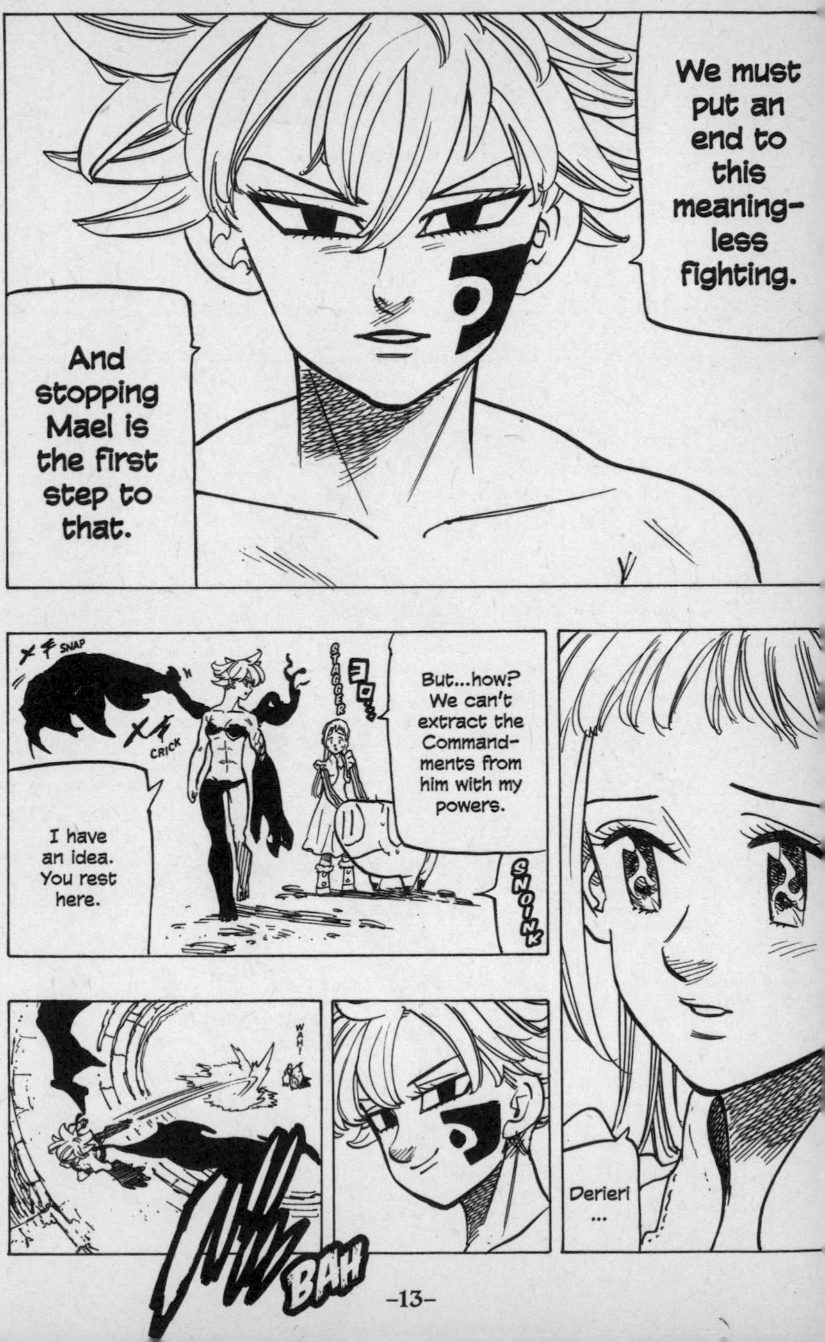
We must put an end to this meaningless fighting.
And stopping Mael is the first step to that.
Derieri ...
But...how? We can't extract the Commandments from him with my powers.
STAGGER
SNOINK
SNAP
CRICK
I have an idea. You rest here.
WAH!
BAH

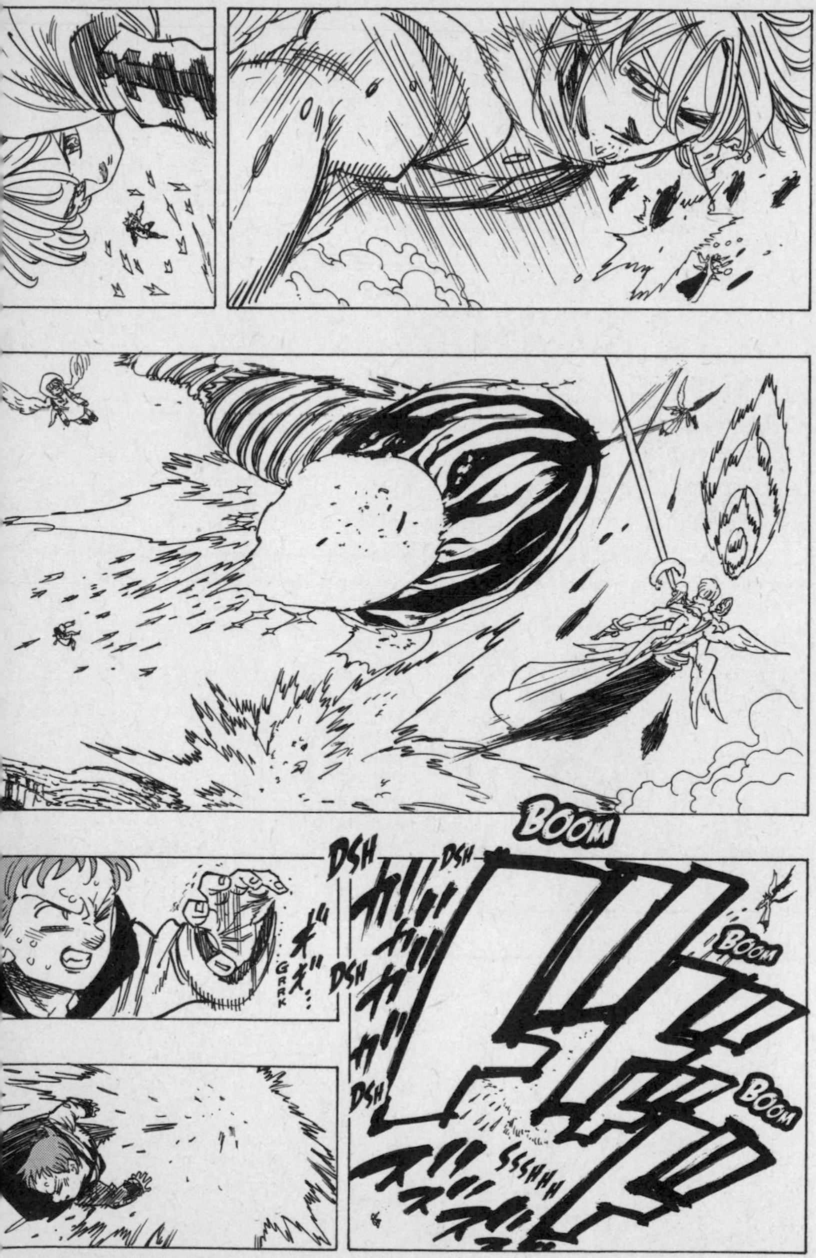
BOOM
DSH
DSH
BOOM
BOOM
DSH
DSH
SSSHHN
GRRK

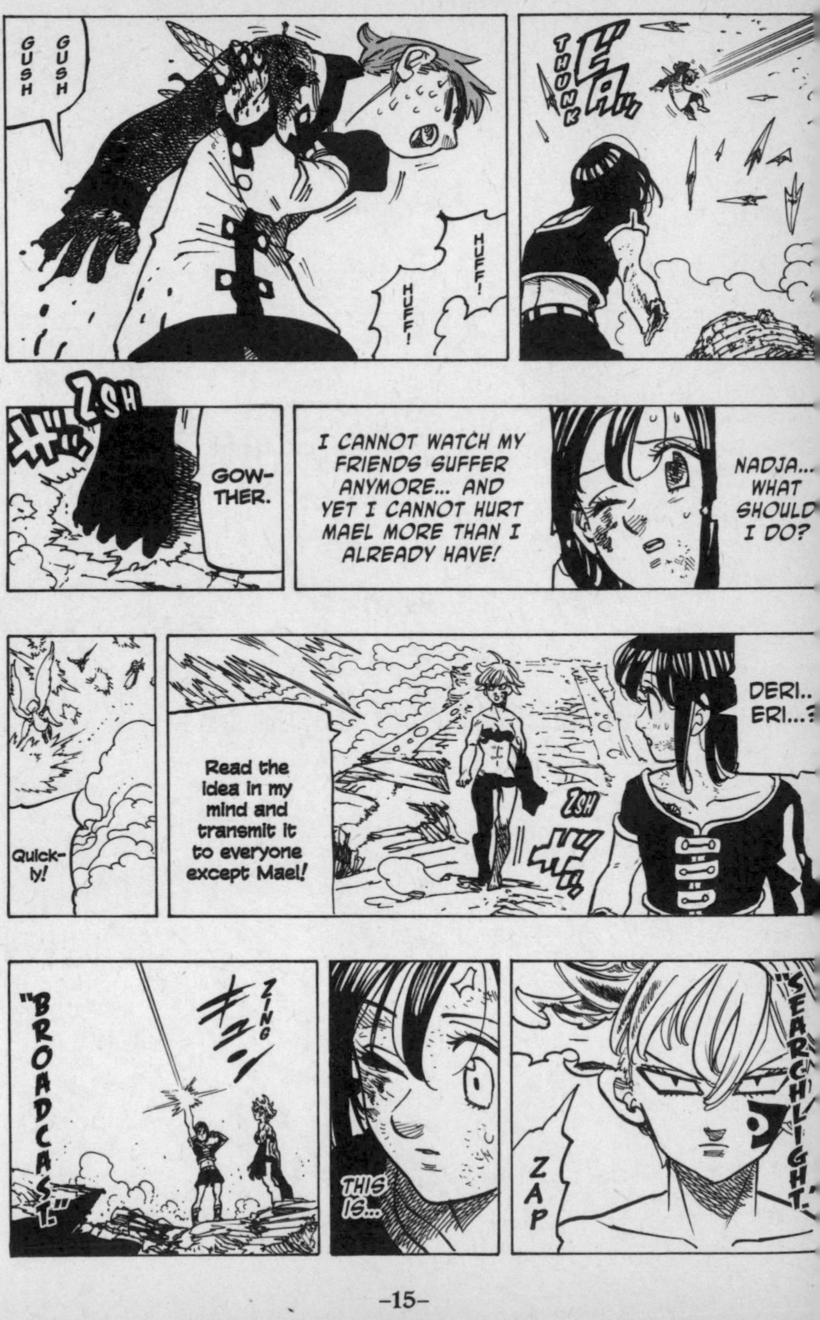
THUNK
GUSH GUSH
HUFF! HUFF!
NADJA... WHAT SHOULD I DO?
I CANNOT WATCH MY FRIENDS SUFFER ANYMORE... AND YET I CANNOT HURT MAEL MORE THAN I ALREADY HAVE!
GOW-THER.
ZSH
DERI.. ERI...?!
ZSH
Read the idea in my mind and transmit it to everyone except Mael!
Quick-ly!
"SEARCHLIGHT."
ZAP
THIS IS...
ZING
"BROADCAST."

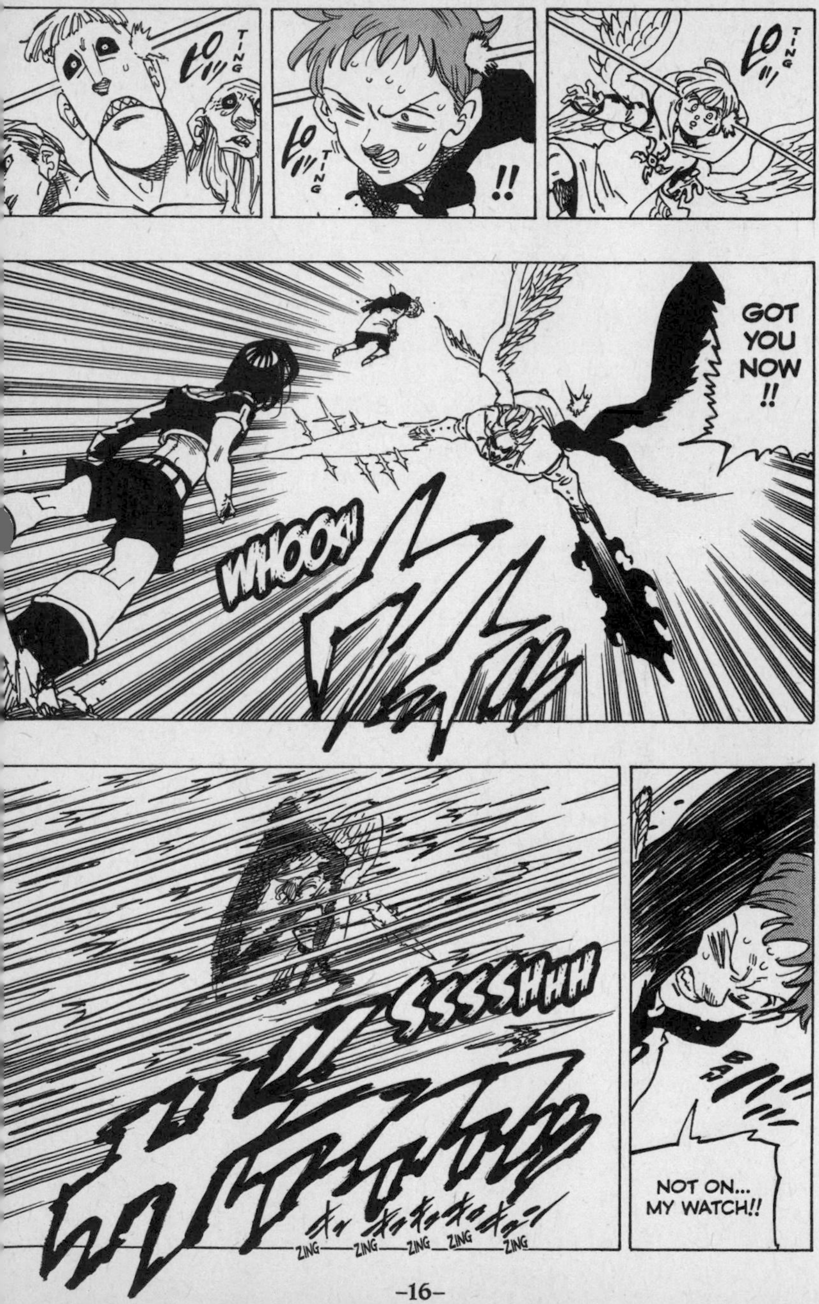
TING
TING
!!
TING
GOT YOU NOW!!
WHOOSH
NOT ON... MY WATCH!!
SSSSHHH
ZING
ZING
ZING
ZING
ZING

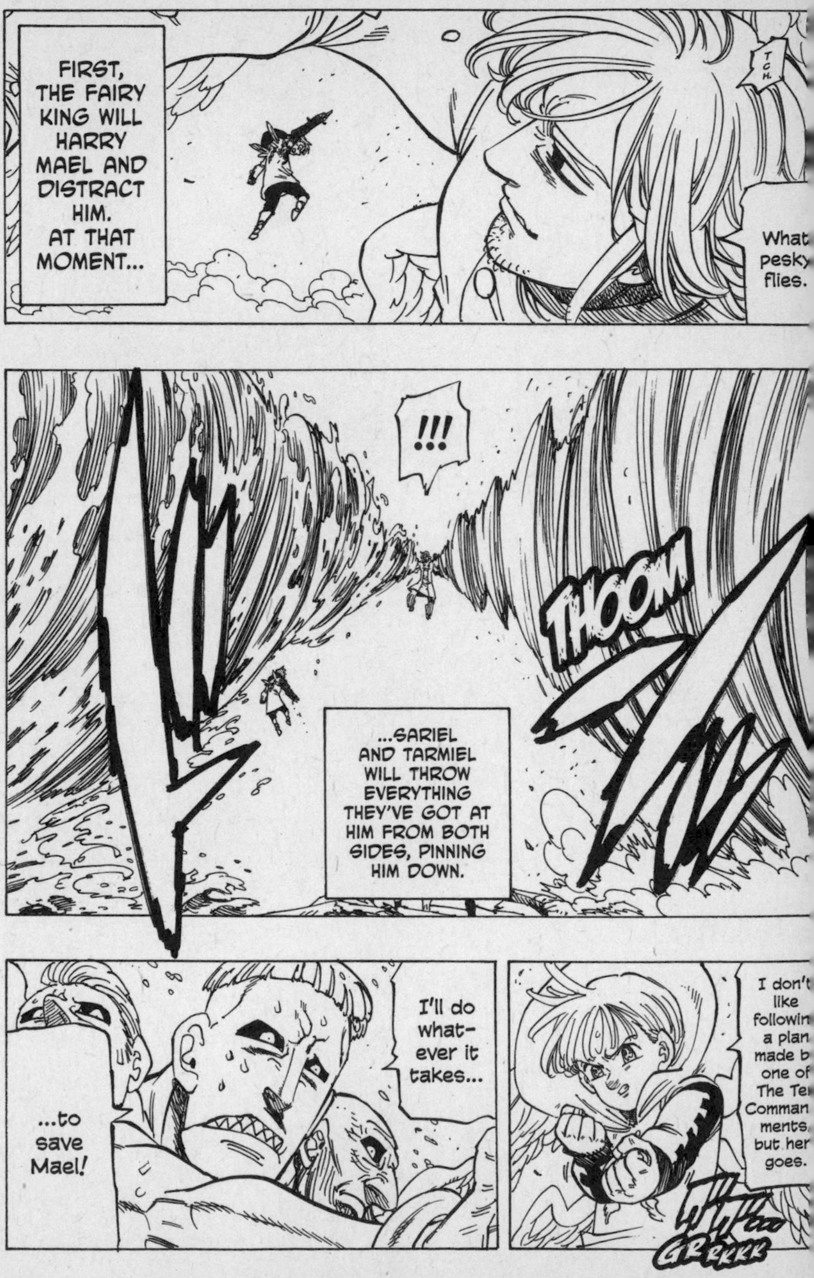
TCH.
What pesky flies.
FIRST, THE FAIRY KING WILL HARRY MAEL AND DISTRACT HIM. AT THAT MOMENT...
!!!
THOOM
...SARIEL AND TARMIEL WILL THROW EVERYTHING THEY'VE GOT AT HIM FROM BOTH SIDES, PINNING HIM DOWN.
I don't like followin a plan made b one of The Te Comman ments, but her goes.
GRRRRK
I'll do whatever it takes...
...to save Mael!

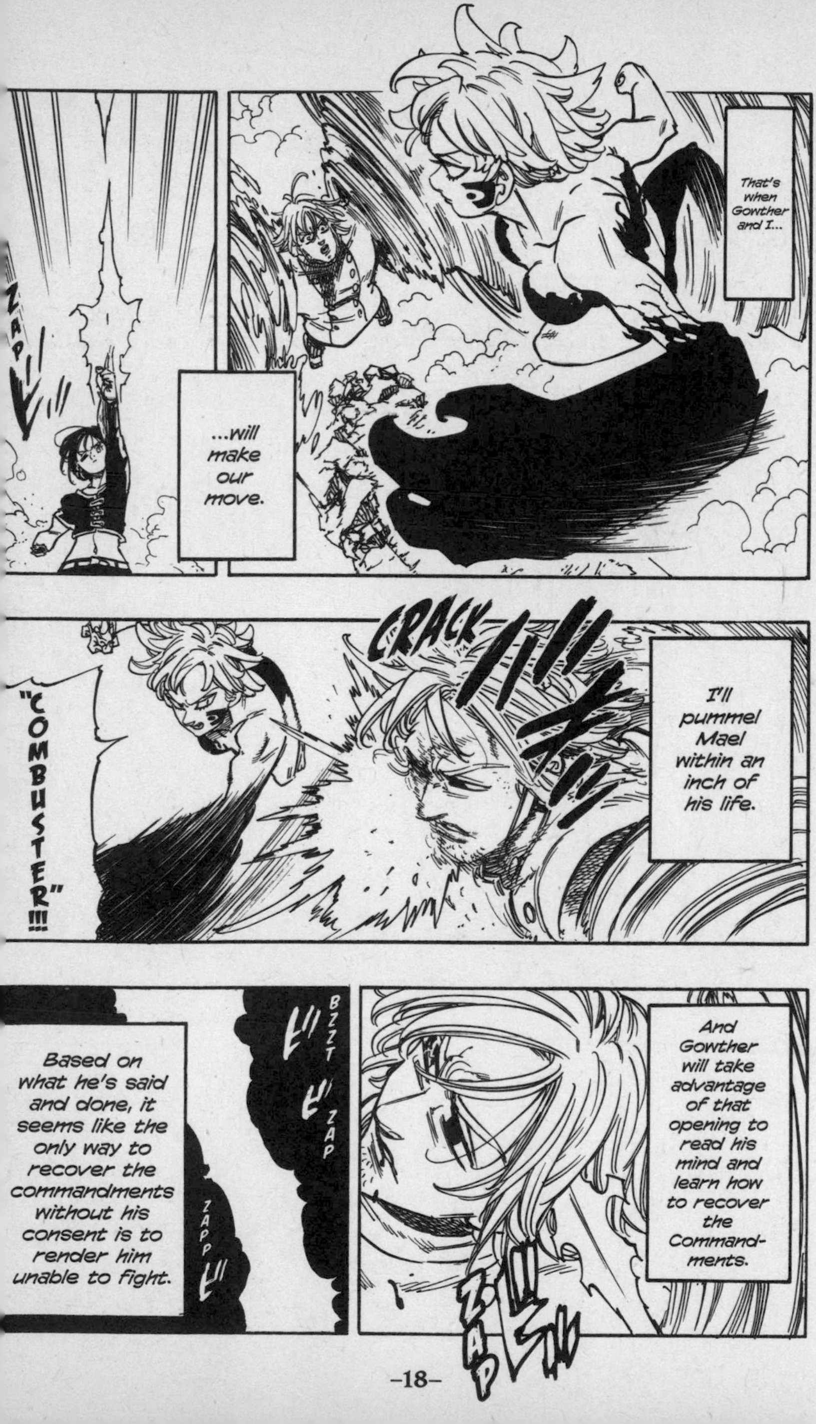
That's when Gowther and I...
...will make our move.
ZAP!
CRACK
I'll pummel Mael within an inch of his life.
"COMBUSTER"!!!
And Gowther will take advantage of that opening to read his mind and learn how to recover the Commandments.
ZAP
BZZT
ZAP
ZAPP
Based on what he's said and done, it seems like the only way to recover the commandments without his consent is to render him unable to fight.

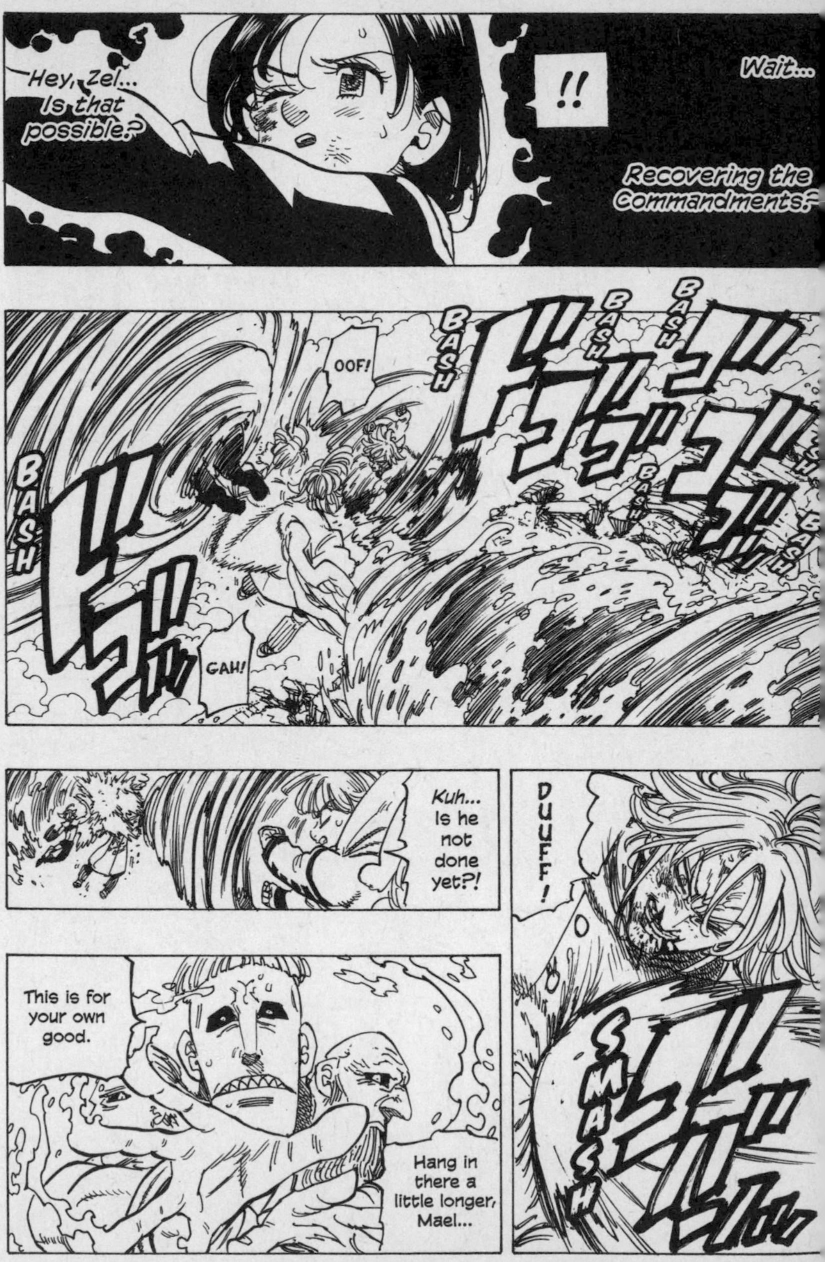

Wait...
Recovering the Commandments?
!!
Hey, Zel... Is that possible?
BASH
BASH
BASH
OOF!
BASH
BASH
BASH
GAH!
DUUFF!
SMASH
Kuh... Is he not done yet?!
This is for your own good.
Hang in there a little longer, Mael...

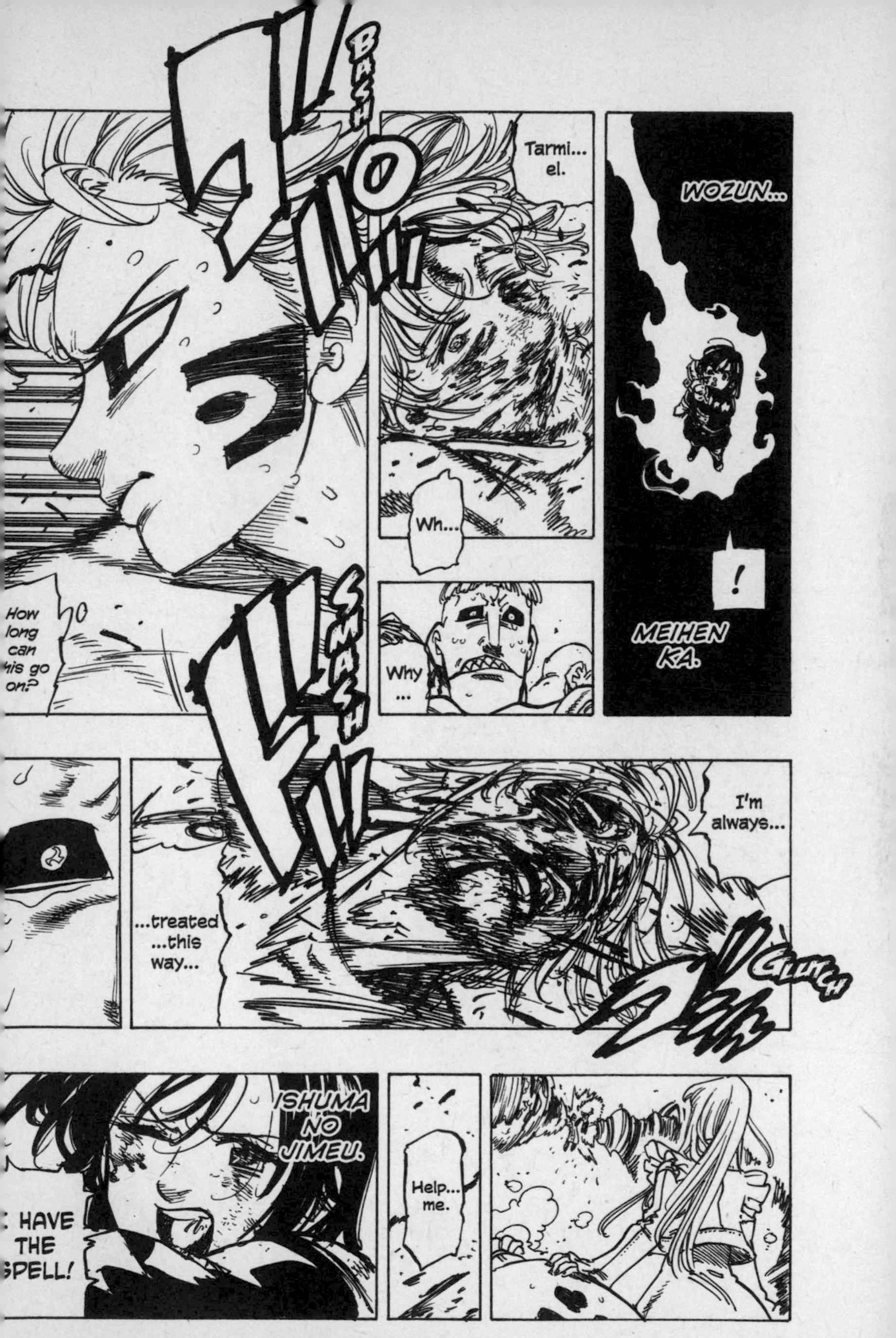
WOZUN...
!
MEIHEN KA.
Tarmi... el.
Wh...
Why ...
BASH
How long can his go on?
SMASH
I'm always...
GLURCH
...treated ...this way...
Help... me.
ISHUMA NO JIMEU.
HAVE THE SPELL!

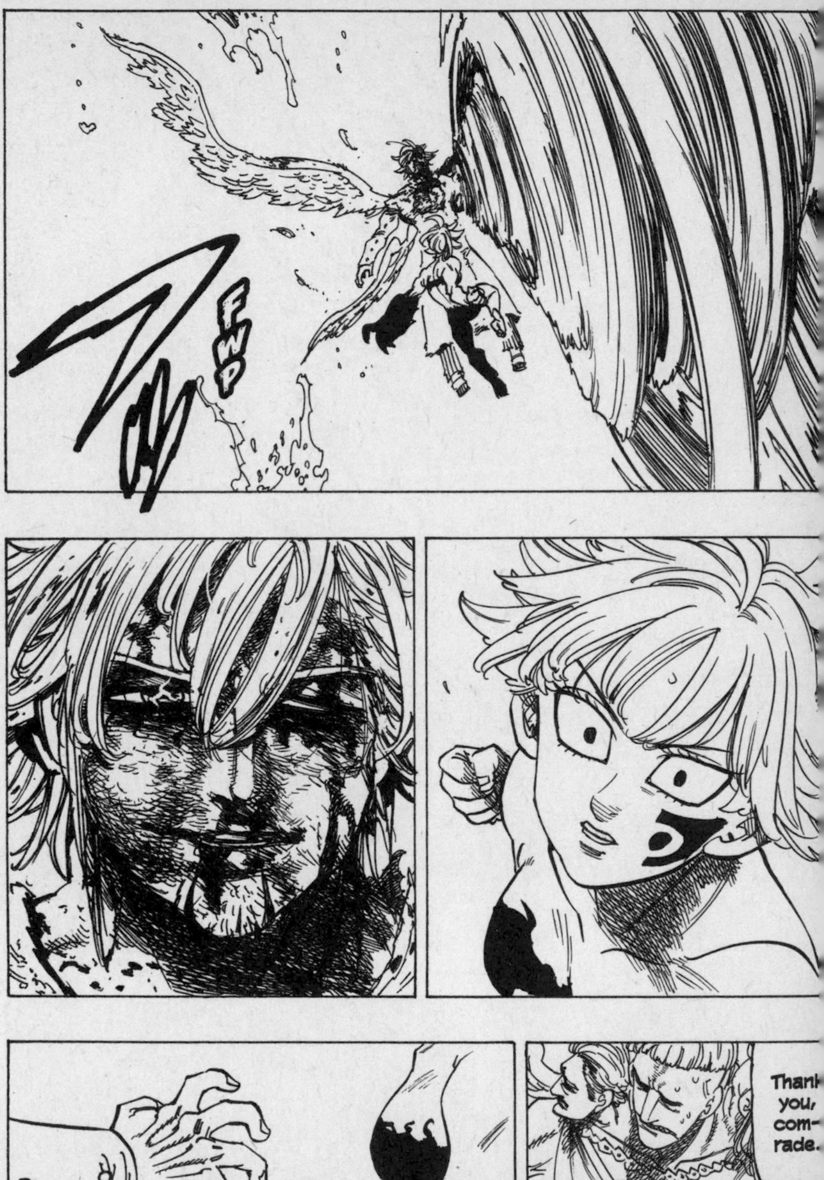
FWP
Thank you, com- rade.

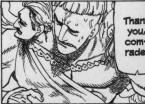

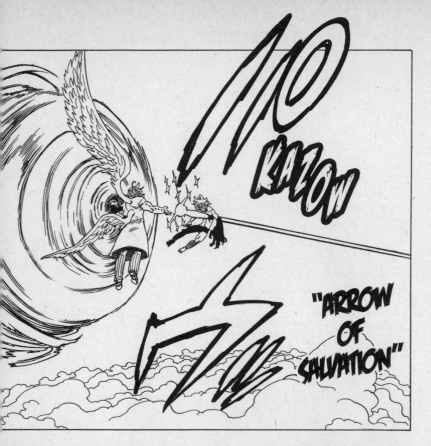

KAZOW

"ARROW
OF
SALVATION"

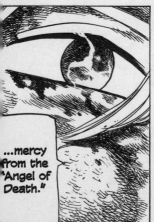

...mercy
from the
"Angel of
Death."

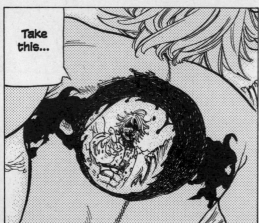

Take
this...

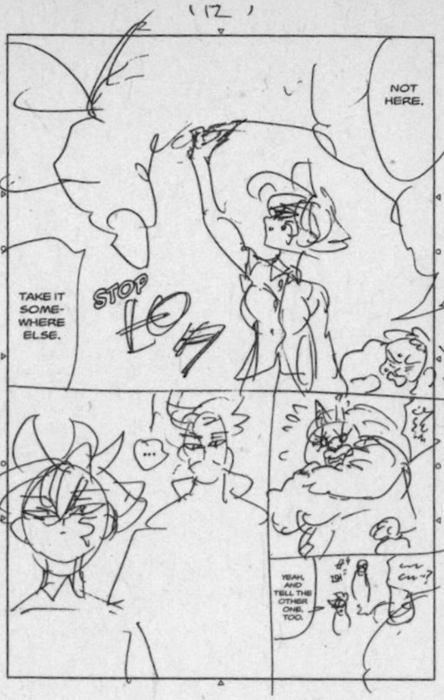
'12'
NOT HERE.
TAKE IT SOMEWHERE ELSE.
STOP
YEAH, AND TELL THE OTHER ONE, TOO.

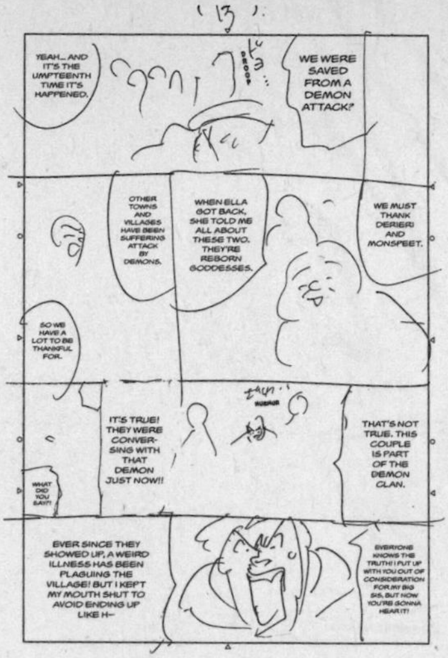
'13'
WE WERE SAVED FROM A DEMON ATTACK!?
YEAH... AND IT'S THE UMPTEENTH TIME IT'S HAPPENED.
WE MUST THANK DERIERI AND MONSPEET.
WHEN ELLA GOT BACK, SHE TOLD ME ALL ABOUT THESE TWO. THEY'RE REBORN GODDESSES.
OTHER TOWNS AND VILLAGES HAVE BEEN SUFFERING ATTACK BY DEMONS.
SO WE HAVE A LOT TO BE THANKFUL FOR.
THAT'S NOT TRUE. THIS COUPLE IS PART OF THE DEMON CLAN.
HUBBUB
IT'S TRUE! THEY WERE CONVERSING WITH THAT DEMON JUST NOW!!
WHAT DID YOU SAY!?
EVERYONE KNOWS THE TRUTH! I PUT UP WITH YOU OUT OF CONSIDERATION FOR MY BIG SIS, BUT NOW YOU'RE GONNA HEAR IT!
EVER SINCE THEY SHOWED UP, A WEIRD ILLNESS HAS BEEN PLAGUING THE VILLAGE! BUT I KEPT MY MOUTH SHUT TO AVOID ENDING UP LIKE H—

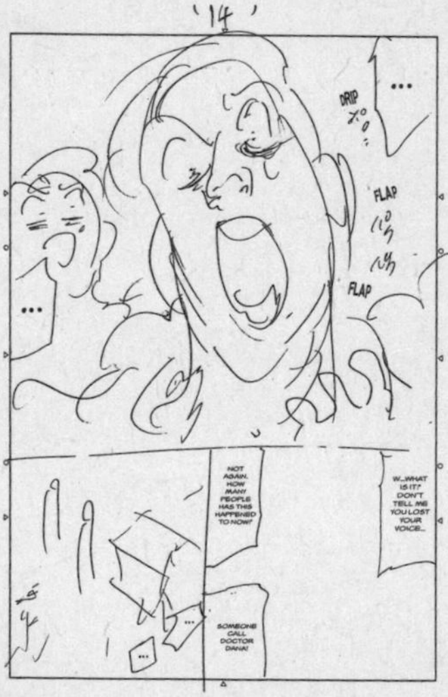
'14'
...
DRIP
FLAP
FLAP
...
W...WHAT IS IT? DON'T TELL ME YOU LOST YOUR VOICE...
NOT AGAIN. HOW MANY PEOPLE HAS THIS HAPPENED TO NOW?
SOMEONE CALL DOCTOR DANA!
...
...

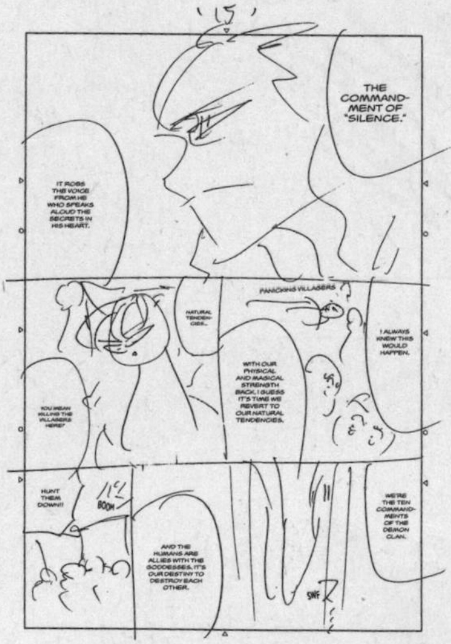
'15'
THE COMMANDMENT OF "SILENCE."
IT ROBS THE VOICE FROM HE WHO SPEAKS ALOUD THE SECRETS IN HIS HEART.
PANICKING VILLAGERS
I ALWAYS KNEW THIS WOULD HAPPEN.
WITH OUR PHYSICAL AND MAGICAL STRENGTH BACK, I GUESS IT'S TIME WE REVERT TO OUR NATURAL TENDENCIES.
NATURAL TENDENCIES...
YOU MEAN KILLING THE VILLAGERS HERE?
WE'RE THE TEN COMMANDMENTS OF THE DEMON CLAN.
SNIF
AND THE HUMANS ARE ALLIES WITH THE GODDESSES. IT'S OUR DESTINY TO DESTROY EACH OTHER.
BOOM
HUNT THEM DOWN!!

This is part of a mystery sketch that I'd drawn before chapter 260. The premise was "Derieri and company save villagers being attacked by Demons but are also feared and rejected by those same villagers. And then just as they're trying to find the right path they should take, someone appears before them."

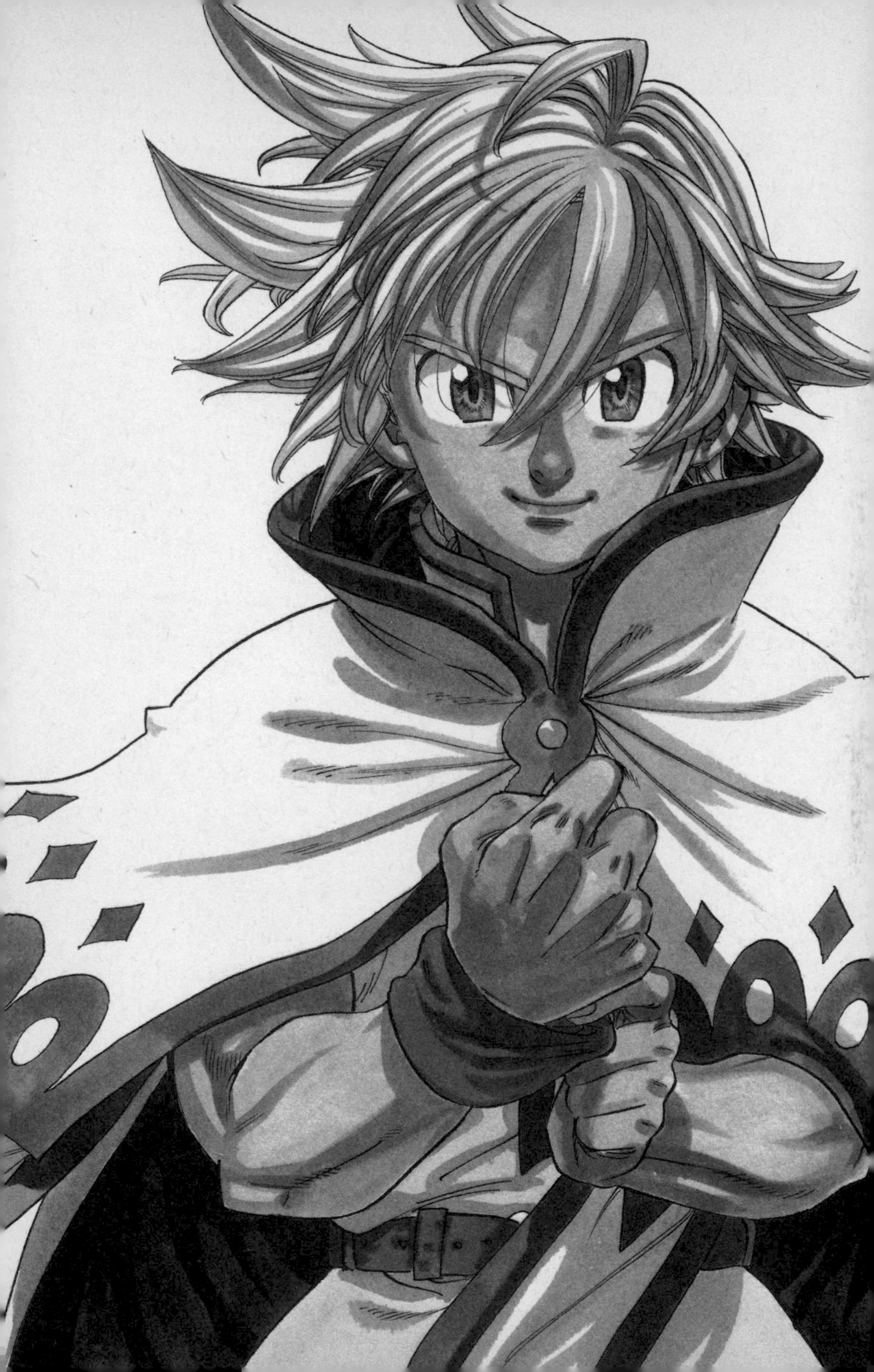

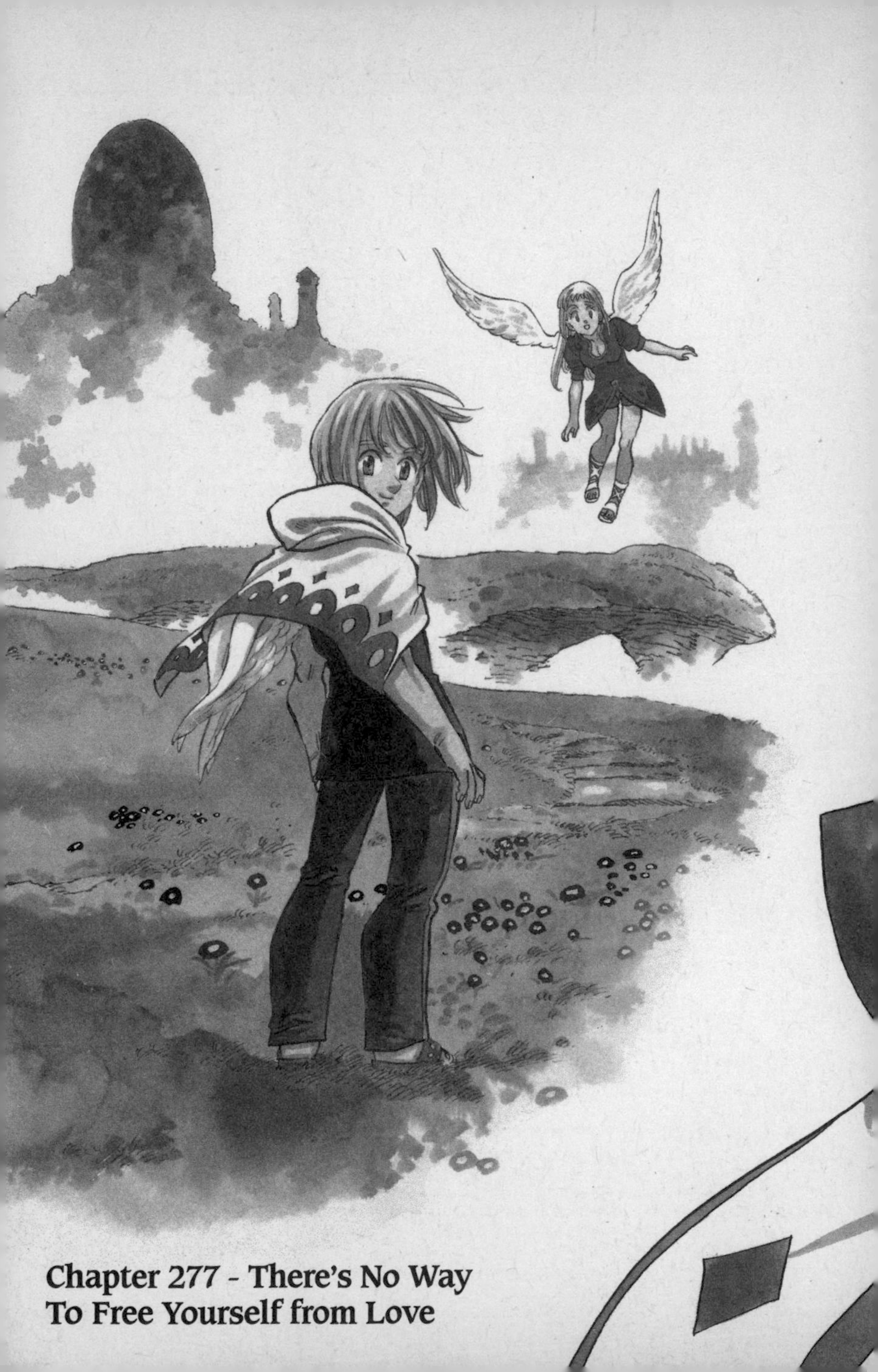

Chapter 277 - There's No Way To Free Yourself from Love

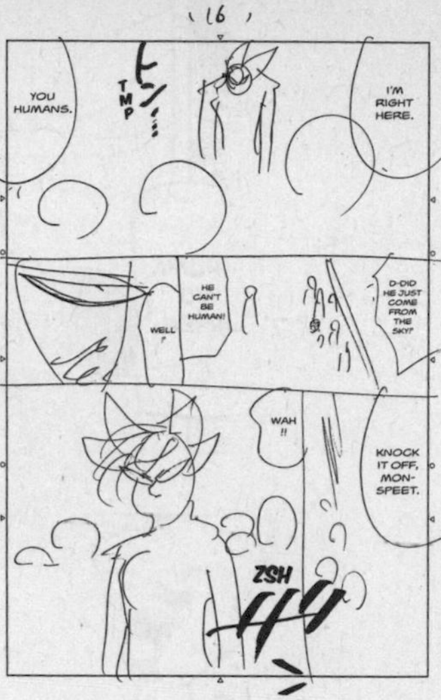
I'M RIGHT HERE.
TMP
YOU HUMANS.
D-DID HE JUST COME FROM THE SKY?
HE CAN'T BE HUMAN!
WELL
KNOCK IT OFF, MON-SPEET.
WAH !!
ZSH

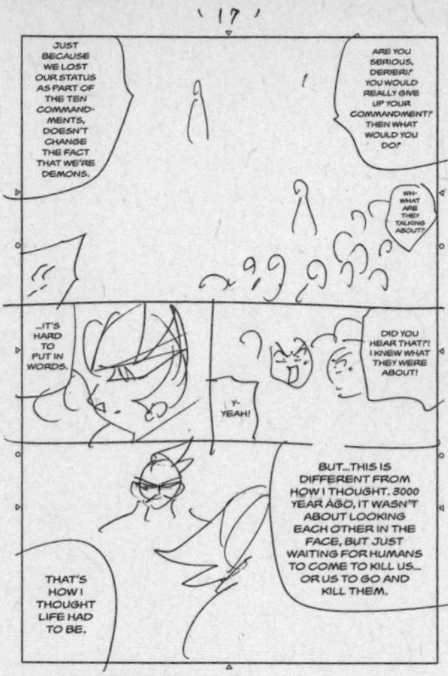
ARE YOU SERIOUS, DERIERI?! YOU WOULD REALLY GIVE UP YOUR COMMANDMENT?! THEN WHAT WOULD YOU DO?
JUST BECAUSE WE LOST OUR STATUS AS PART OF THE TEN COMMAND-MENTS, DOESN'T CHANGE THE FACT THAT WE'RE DEMONS.
WH-WHAT ARE THEY TALKING ABOUT?!
DID YOU HEAR THAT?! I KNEW WHAT THEY WERE ABOUT!
Y-YEAH!
...IT'S HARD TO PUT IN WORDS.
BUT...THIS IS DIFFERENT FROM HOW I THOUGHT. 3000 YEAR AGO, IT WASN'T ABOUT LOOKING EACH OTHER IN THE FACE, BUT JUST WAITING FOR HUMANS TO COME TO KILL US... OR US TO GO AND KILL THEM.
THAT'S HOW I THOUGHT LIFE HAD TO BE.

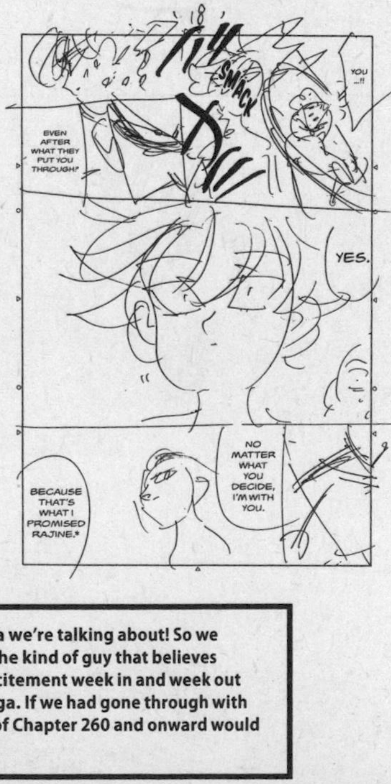
YOU ...!!
SMACK
EVEN AFTER WHAT THEY PUT YOU THROUGH?
YES.
NO MATTER WHAT YOU DECIDE, I'M WITH YOU.
BECAUSE THAT'S WHAT I PROMISED RAJINE.*

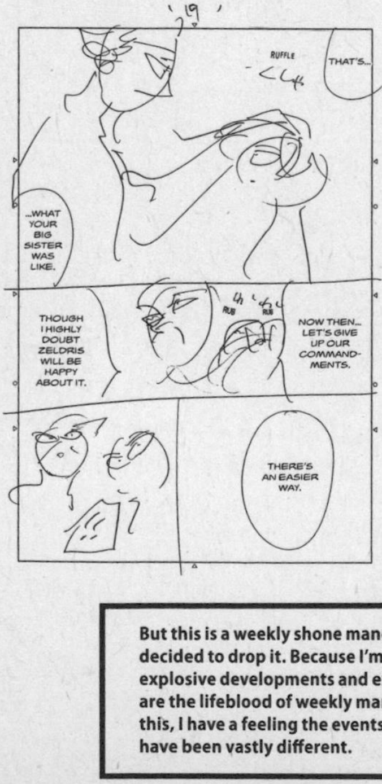
THAT'S...
RUFFLE
...WHAT YOUR BIG SISTER WAS LIKE.
NOW THEN... LET'S GIVE UP OUR COMMAND-MENTS.
RUB RUB
THOUGH I HIGHLY DOUBT ZELDRIS WILL BE HAPPY ABOUT IT.
THERE'S AN EASIER WAY.

***Rajine…The name of Derieri's older sister.**

But this is a weekly shone manga we're talking about! So we decided to drop it. Because I'm the kind of guy that believes explosive developments and excitement week in and week out are the lifeblood of weekly manga. If we had gone through with this, I have a feeling the events of Chapter 260 and onward would have been vastly different.

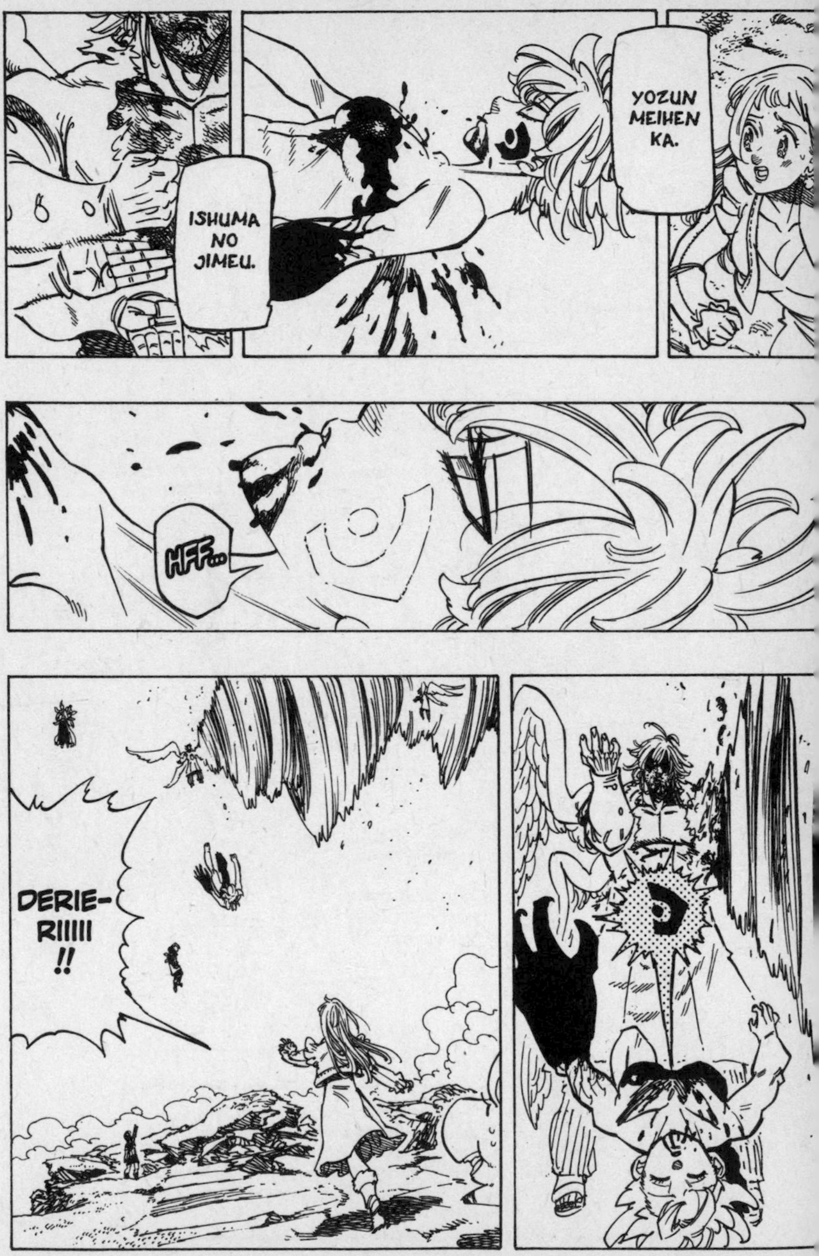
YOZUN MEIHEN KA.
ISHUMA NO JIMEU.
HFF...
DERIE-RIIIII !!

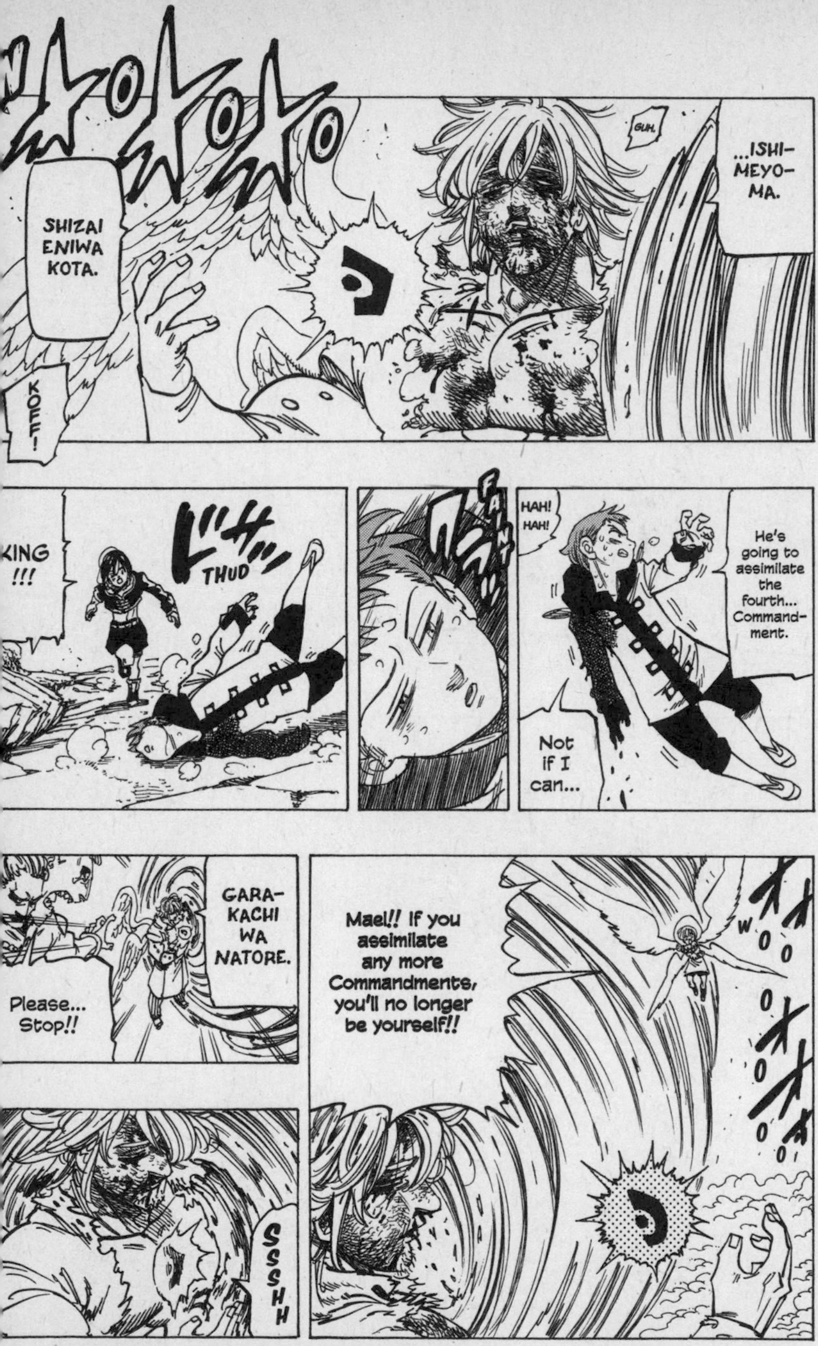

GUH.
...ISHI-MEYO-MA.
SHIZAI ENIWA KOTA.
KOFF!
HAH! HAH!
He's going to assimilate the fourth... Commandment.
Not if I can...
FAINT
THUD
KING !!!
WOOOOOOO
Mael!! If you assimilate any more Commandments, you'll no longer be yourself!!
GARA-KACHI WA NATORE.
Please... Stop!!
SSSHH

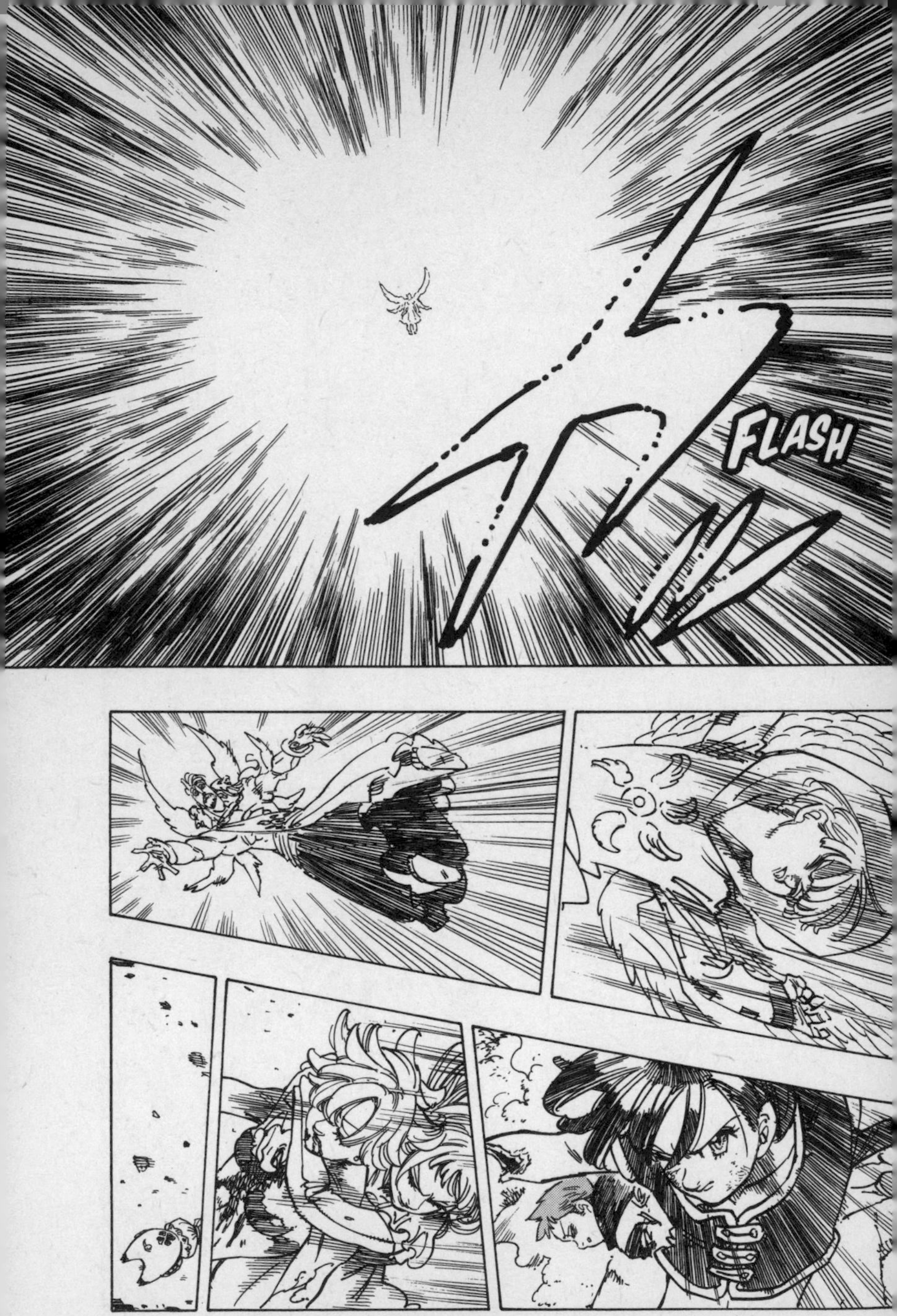
FLASH

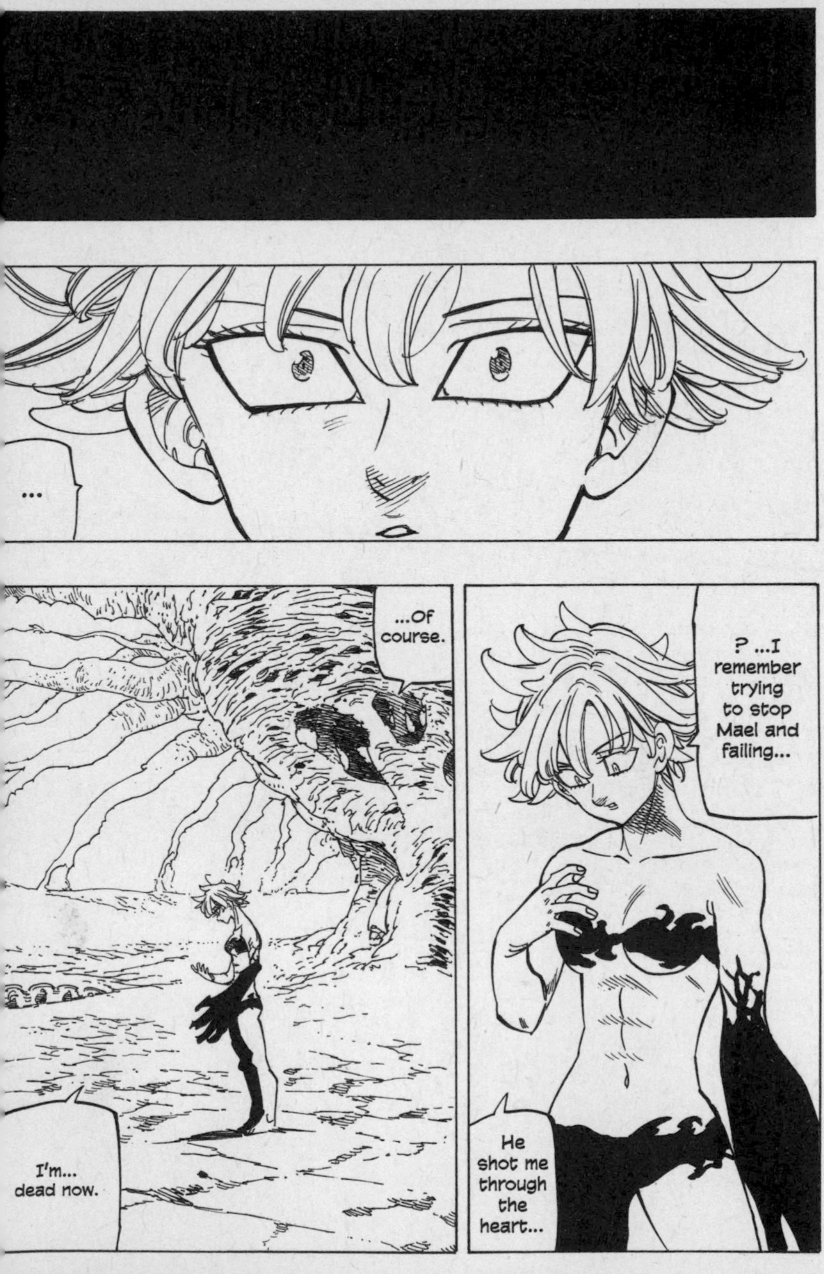
...
? ...I remember trying to stop Mael and failing...
He shot me through the heart...
...Of course.
I'm... dead now.

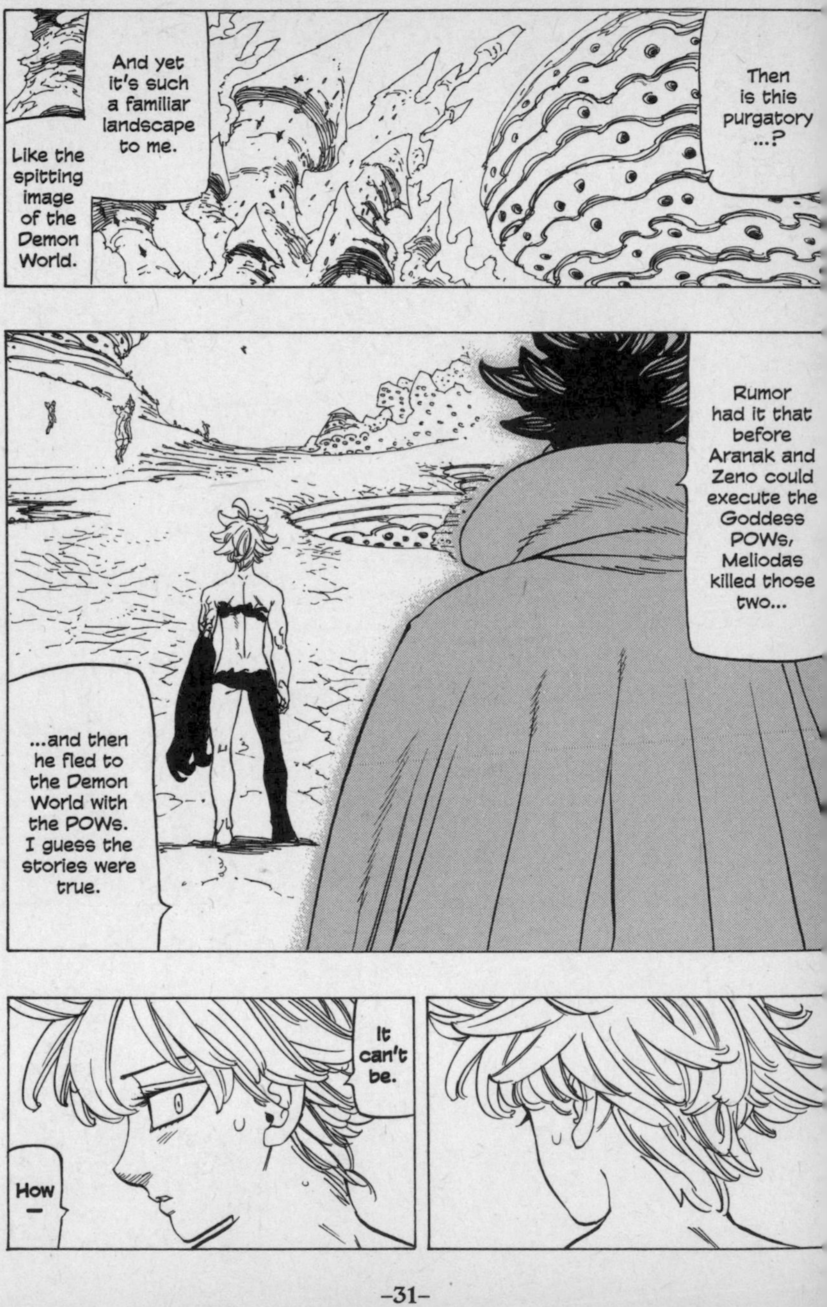
Then is this purgatory ...?
And yet it's such a familiar landscape to me.
Like the spitting image of the Demon World.
Rumor had it that before Aranak and Zeno could execute the Goddess POWs, Meliodas killed those two...
...and then he fled to the Demon World with the POWs. I guess the stories were true.
It can't be.
How—

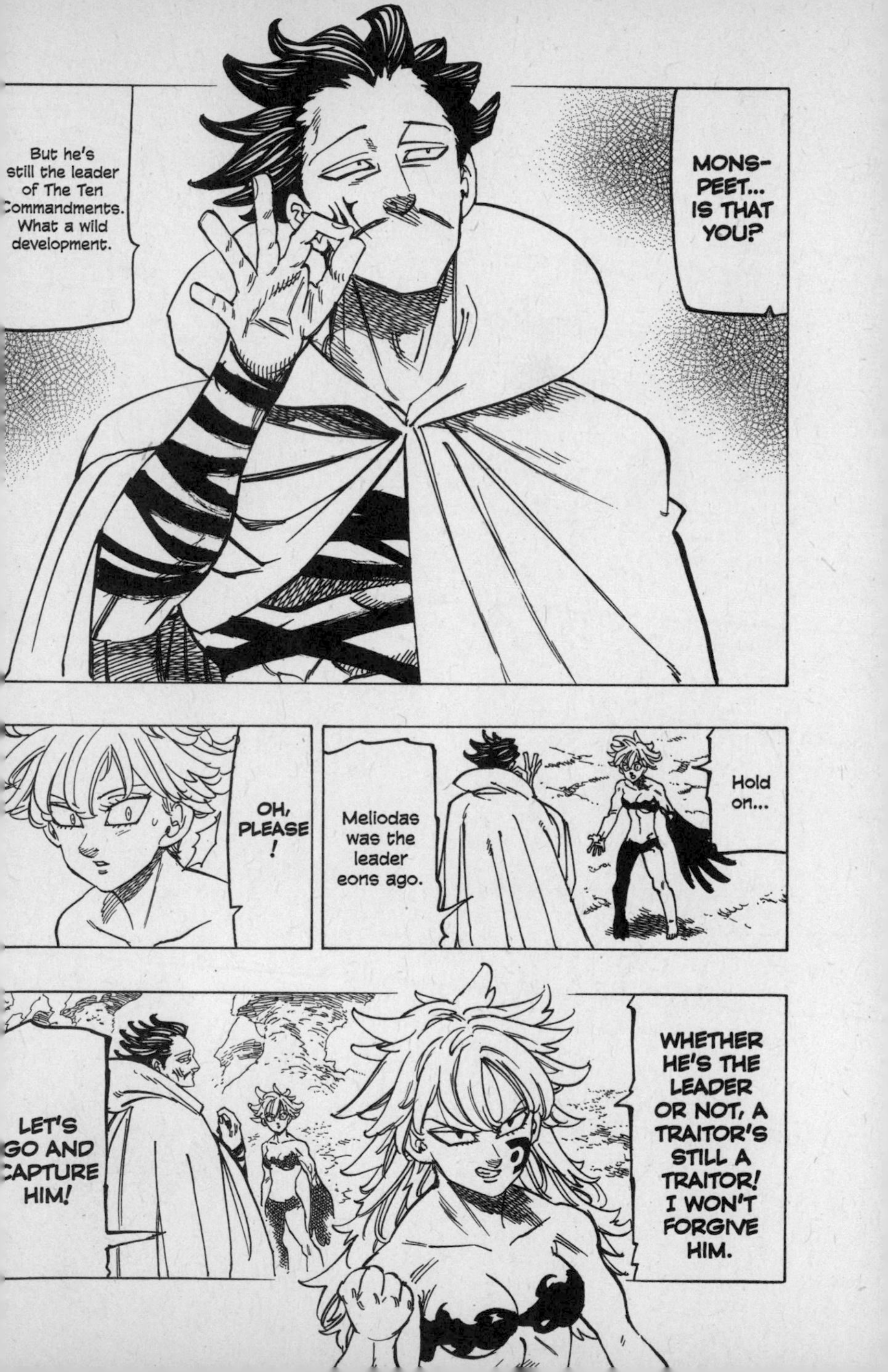

MONS-PEET... IS THAT YOU?
But he's still the leader of The Ten Commandments. What a wild development.
Hold on...
Meliodas was the leader eons ago.
OH, PLEASE!
WHETHER HE'S THE LEADER OR NOT, A TRAITOR'S STILL A TRAITOR! I WON'T FORGIVE HIM.
LET'S GO AND CAPTURE HIM!

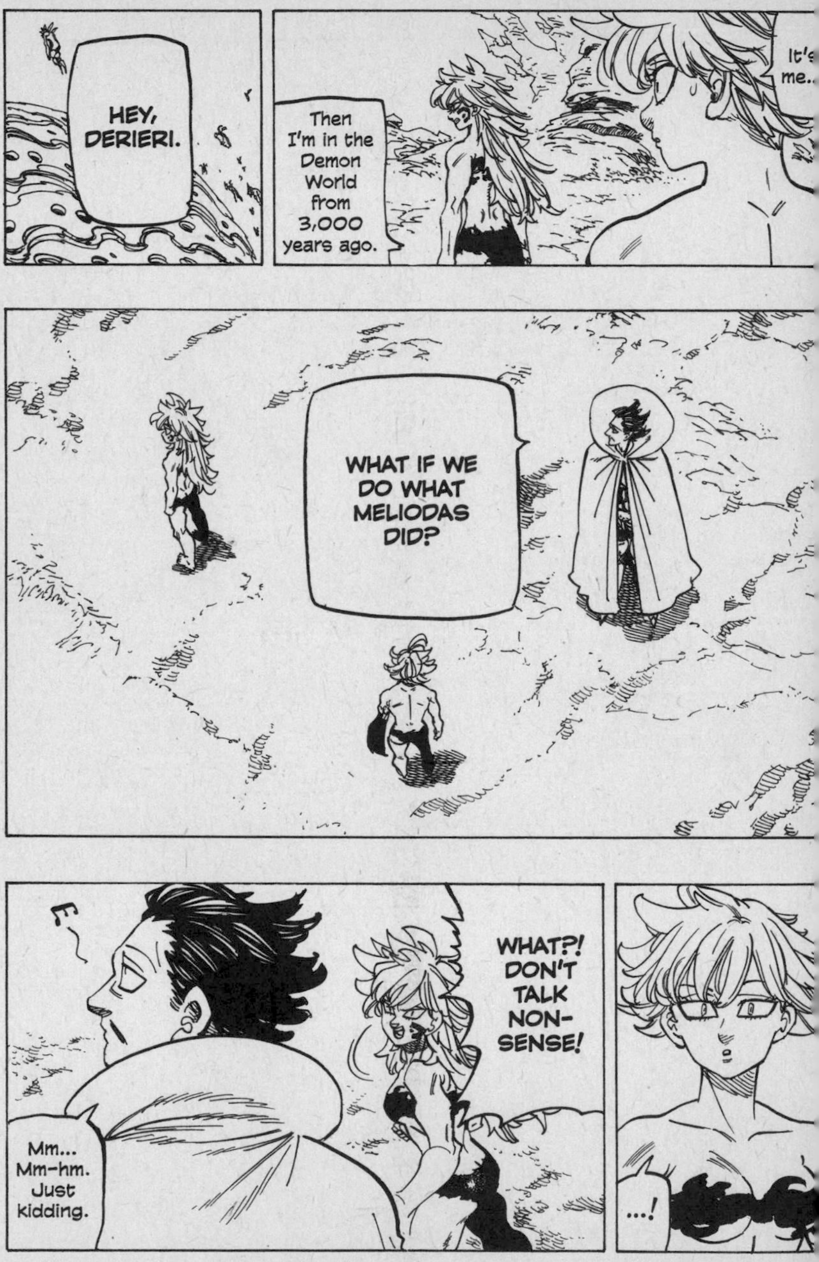
It's me...
Then I'm in the Demon World from 3,000 years ago.
HEY, DERIERI.
WHAT IF WE DO WHAT MELIODAS DID?
...!
WHAT?! DON'T TALK NON-SENSE!
Mm... Mm-hm. Just kidding.

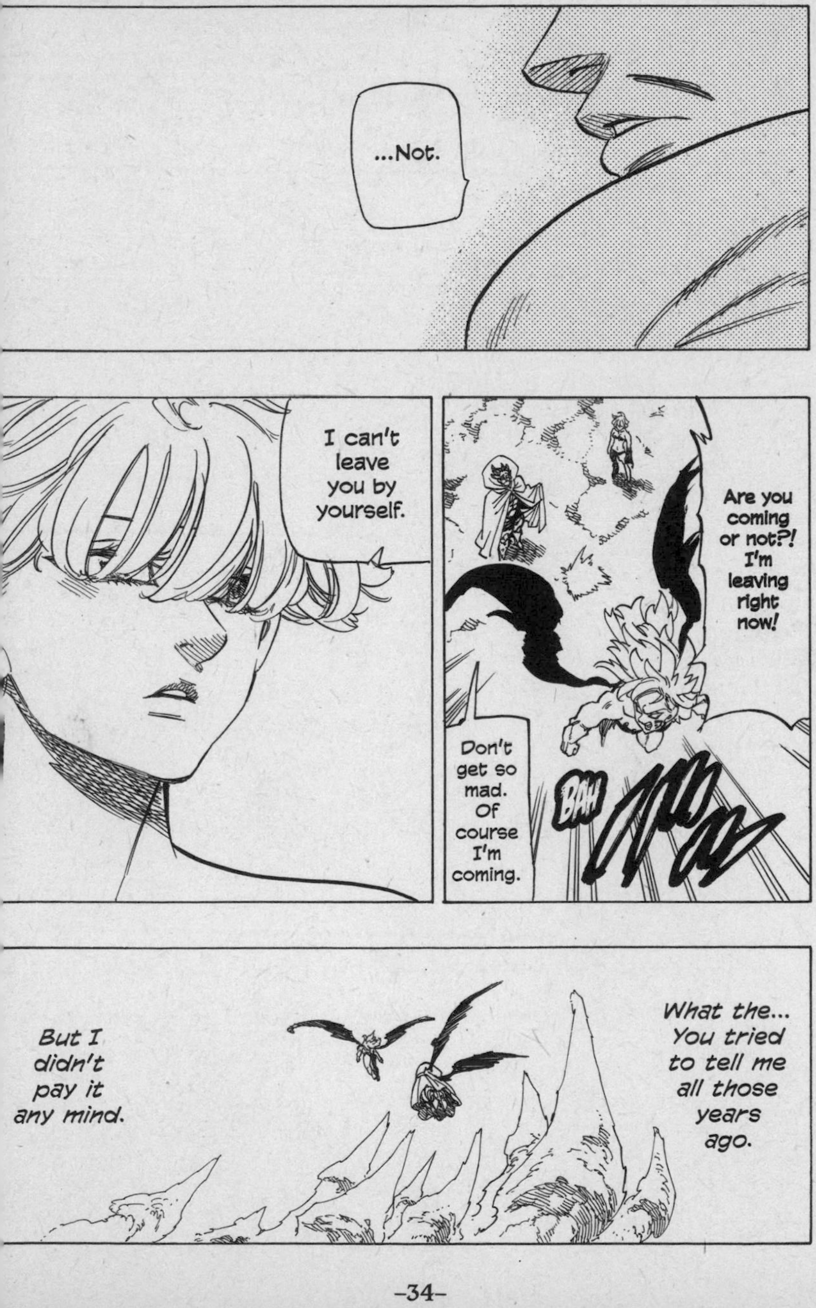
...Not.
Are you coming or not?! I'm leaving right now!
Don't get so mad. Of course I'm coming.
BAH
I can't leave you by yourself.
What the... You tried to tell me all those years ago.
But I didn't pay it any mind.

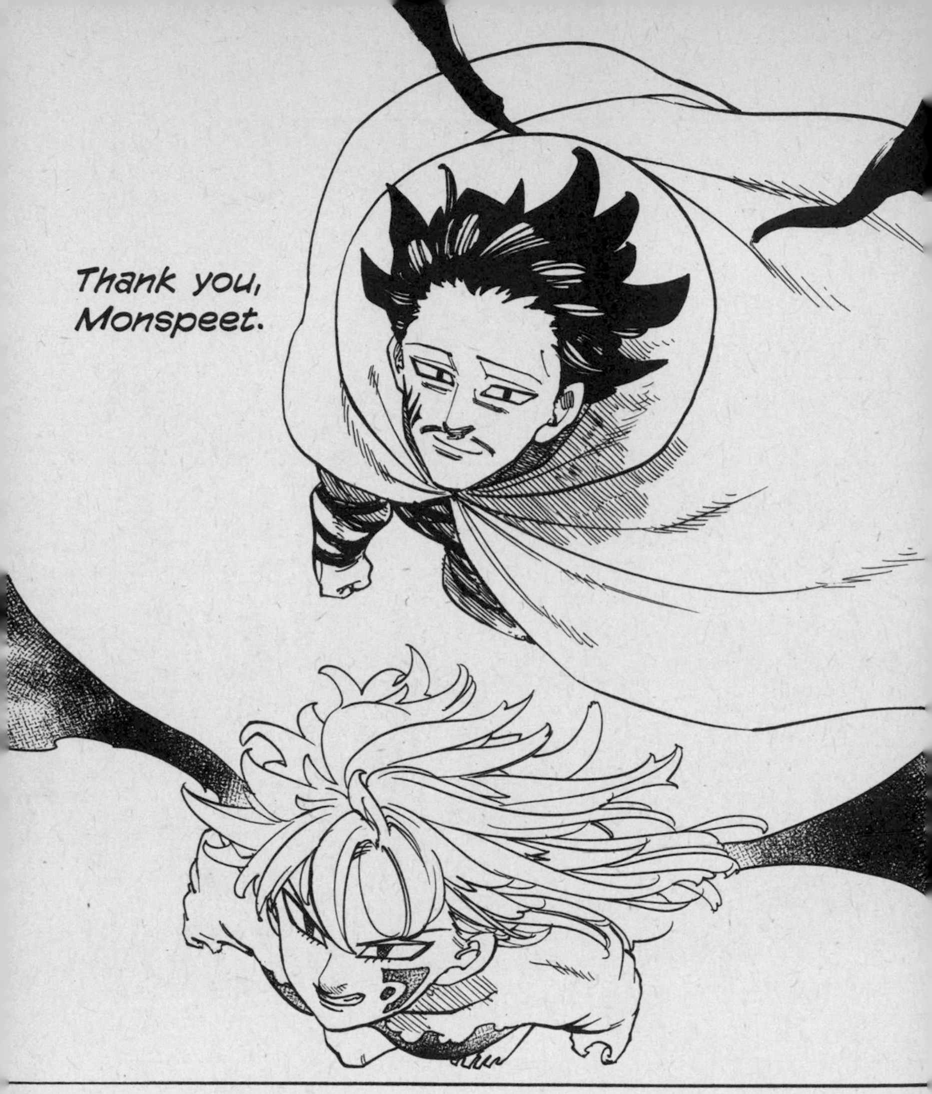
Thank you, Monspeet.

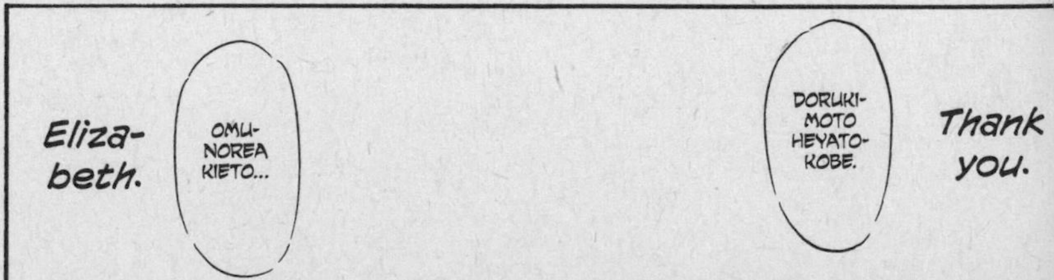
Thank you.
DORUKI-MOTO HEYATO-KOBE.
OMU-NOREA KIETO...
Eliza-beth.

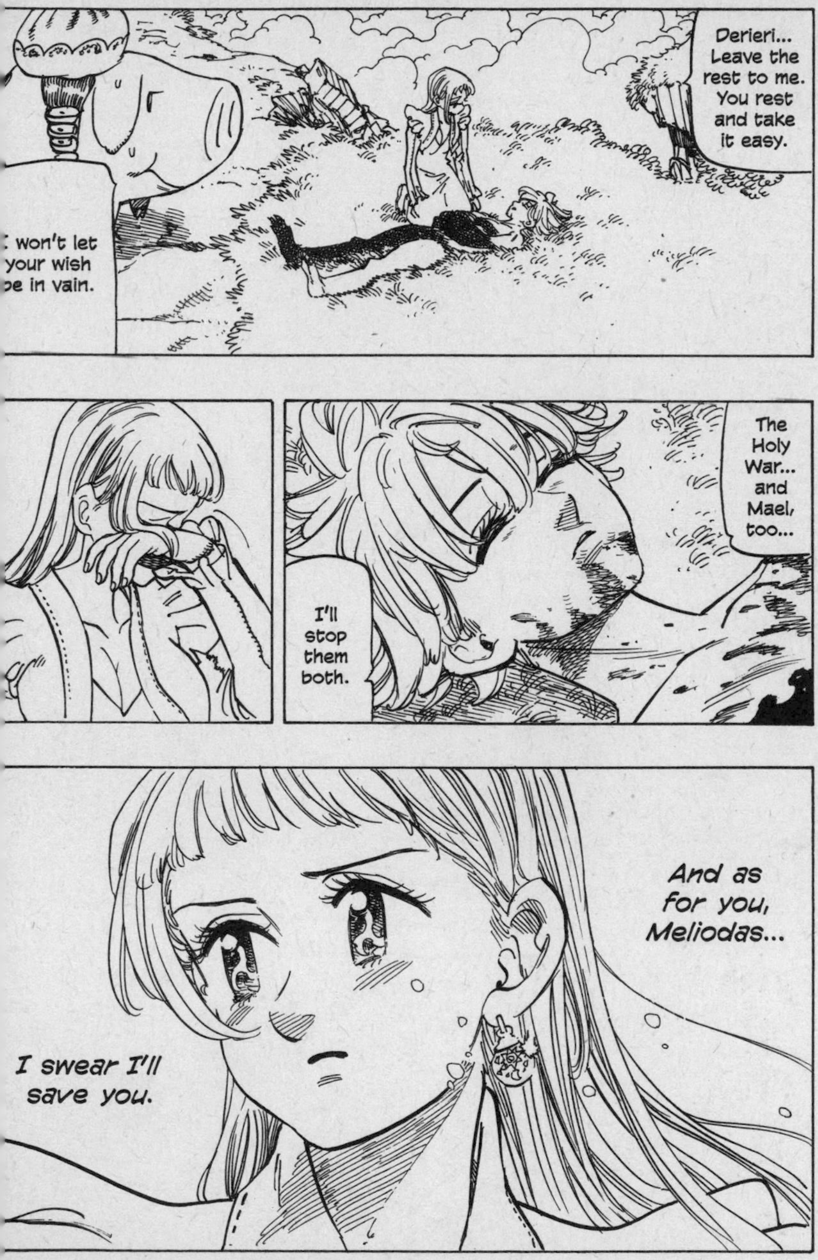
Derieri... Leave the rest to me. You rest and take it easy.
won't let your wish e in vain.
The Holy War... and Mael, too...
I'll stop them both.
And as for you, Meliodas...
I swear I'll save you.

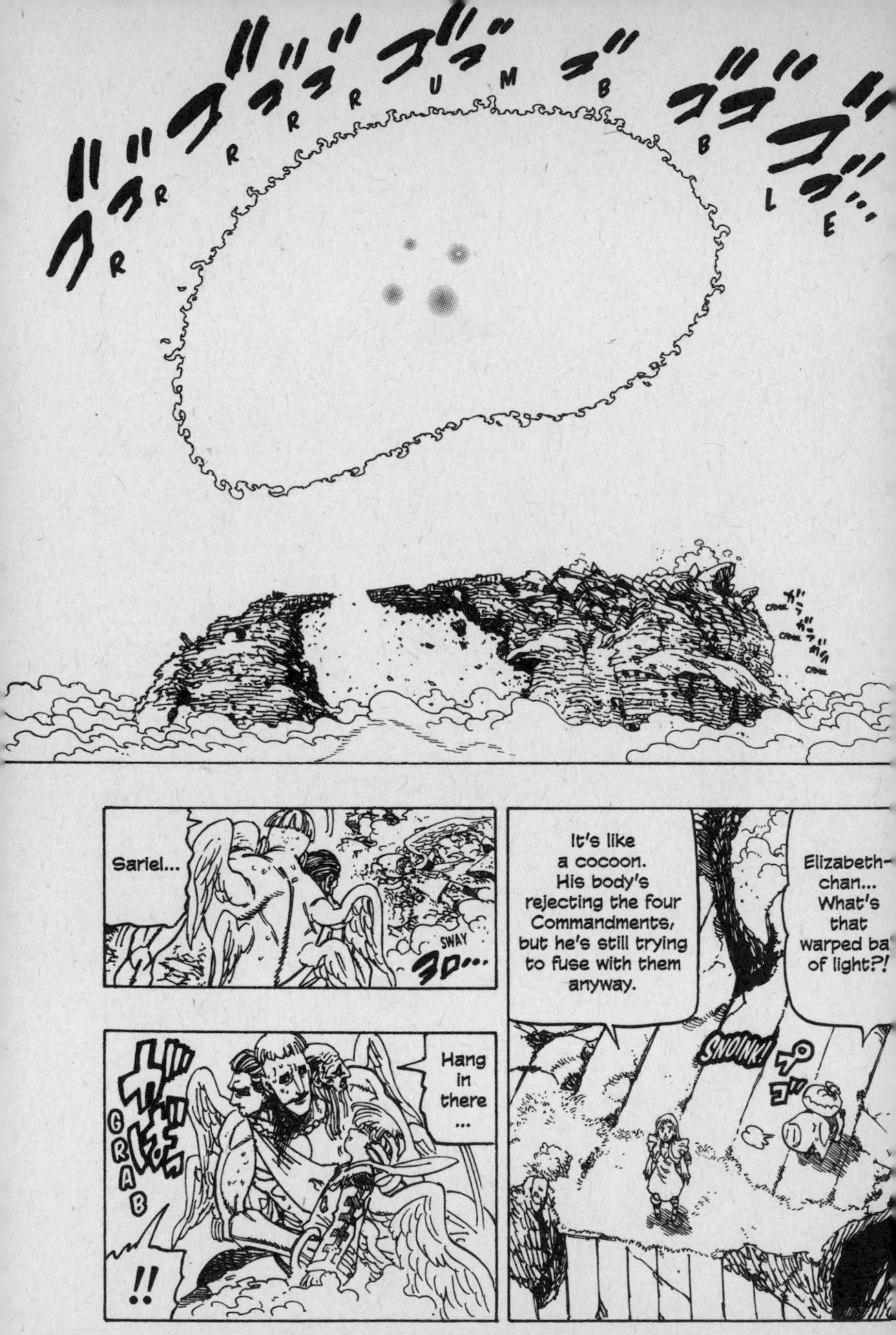

RRRRRUMBBLE...
CRAWL
CRAWL
CRAWL
Elizabeth-chan... What's that warped ba of light?!
It's like a cocoon. His body's rejecting the four Commandments, but he's still trying to fuse with them anyway.
SNOINK!
Sariel...
SWAY
Hang in there ...
GRAB
!!

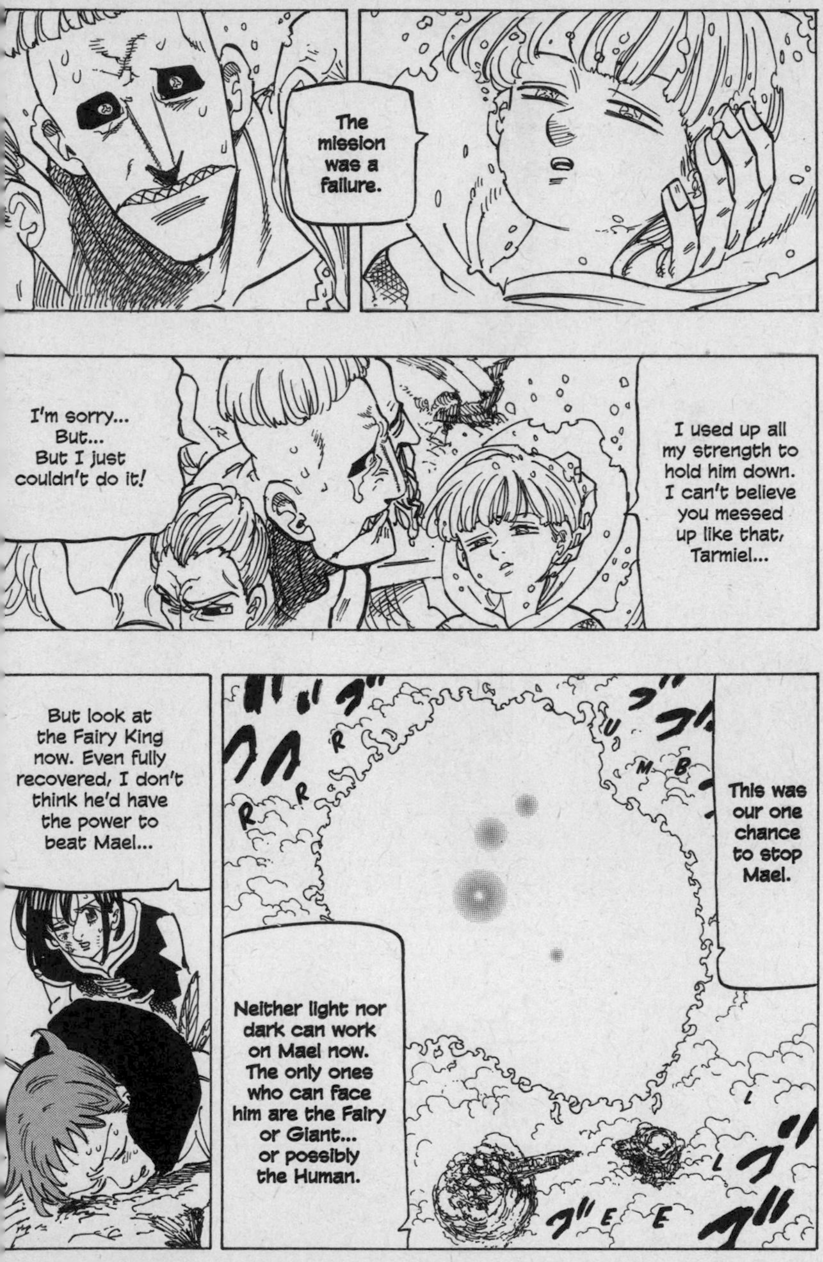
The mission was a failure.
I used up all my strength to hold him down. I can't believe you messed up like that, Tarmiel...
I'm sorry... But... But I just couldn't do it!
This was our one chance to stop Mael.
Neither light nor dark can work on Mael now. The only ones who can face him are the Fairy or Giant... or possibly the Human.
But look at the Fairy King now. Even fully recovered, I don't think he'd have the power to beat Mael...

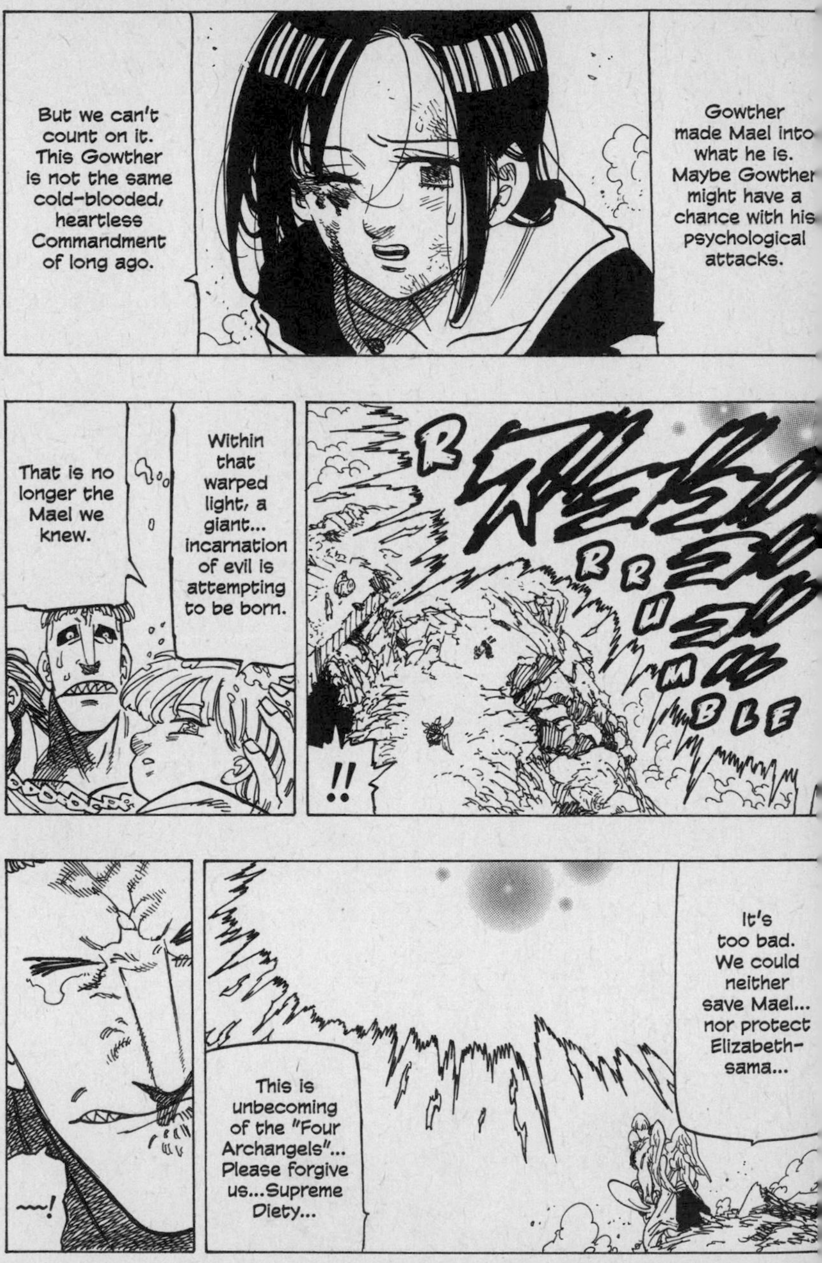
Gowther made Mael into what he is. Maybe Gowther might have a chance with his psychological attacks.
But we can't count on it. This Gowther is not the same cold-blooded, heartless Commandment of long ago.
RRRUMBLE
!!
Within that warped light, a giant... incarnation of evil is attempting to be born.
That is no longer the Mael we knew.
It's too bad. We could neither save Mael... nor protect Elizabeth-sama...
This is unbecoming of the "Four Archangels"... Please forgive us...Supreme Diety...
~~!

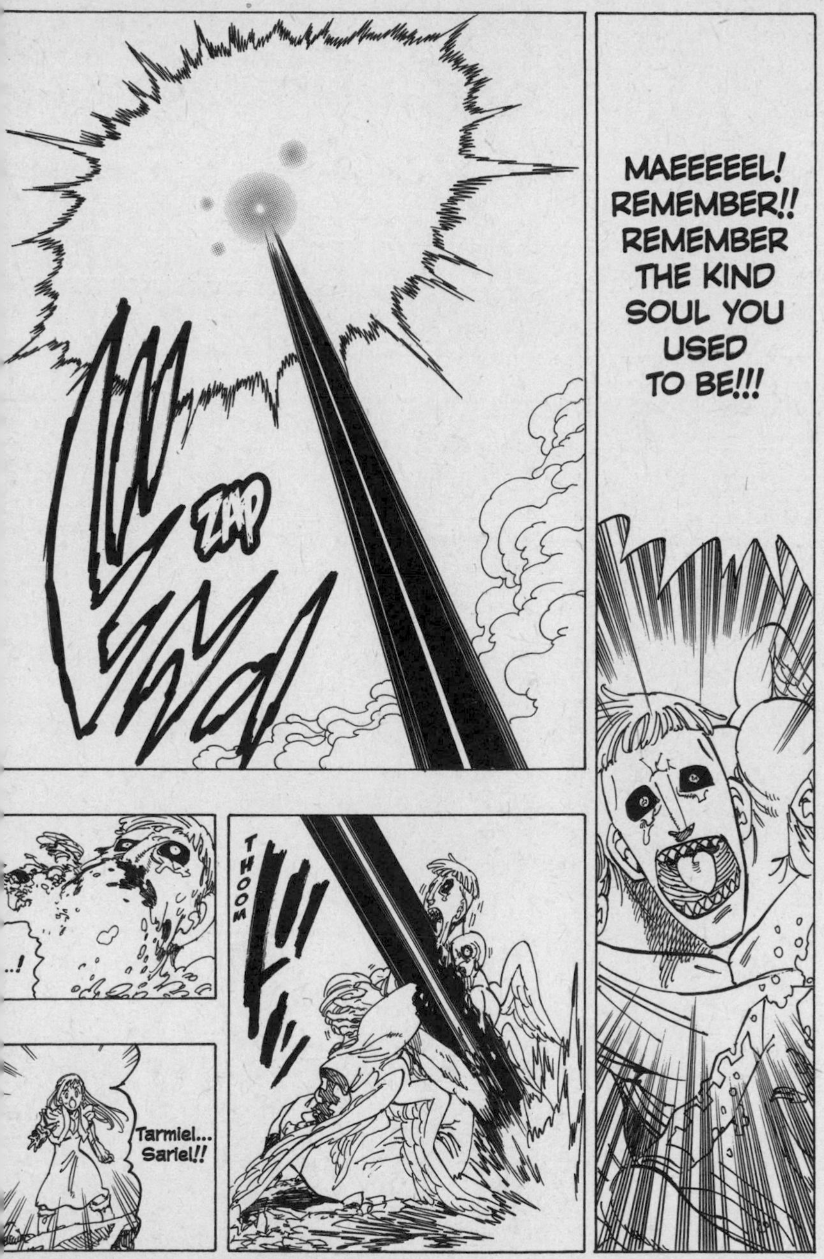
MAEEEEEL! REMEMBER!! REMEMBER THE KIND SOUL YOU USED TO BE!!!
ZAP
THOOM
..!
Tarmiel... Sariel!!

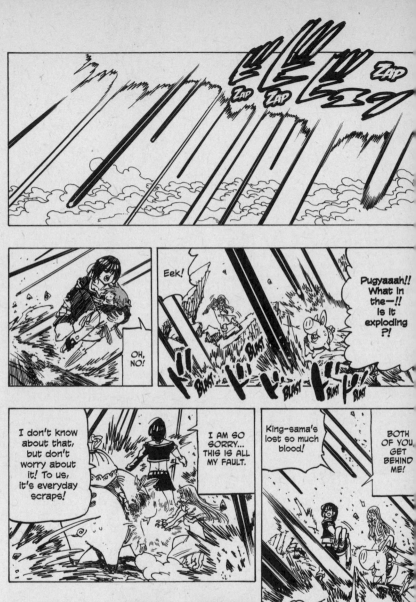

ZAP ZAP ZAP ZAP

OH, NO!

Eek!

Pugyaaah!! What in the—!! Is it exploding?!

I don't know about that, but don't worry about it! To us, it's everyday scraps!

I AM SO SORRY... THIS IS ALL MY FAULT.

King-sama's lost so much blood!

BOTH OF YOU GET BEHIND ME!

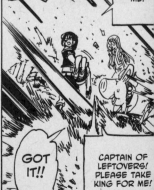

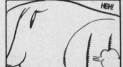

HEH!

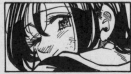

GOT IT!!

CAPTAIN OF LEFTOVERS! PLEASE TAKE KING FOR ME!

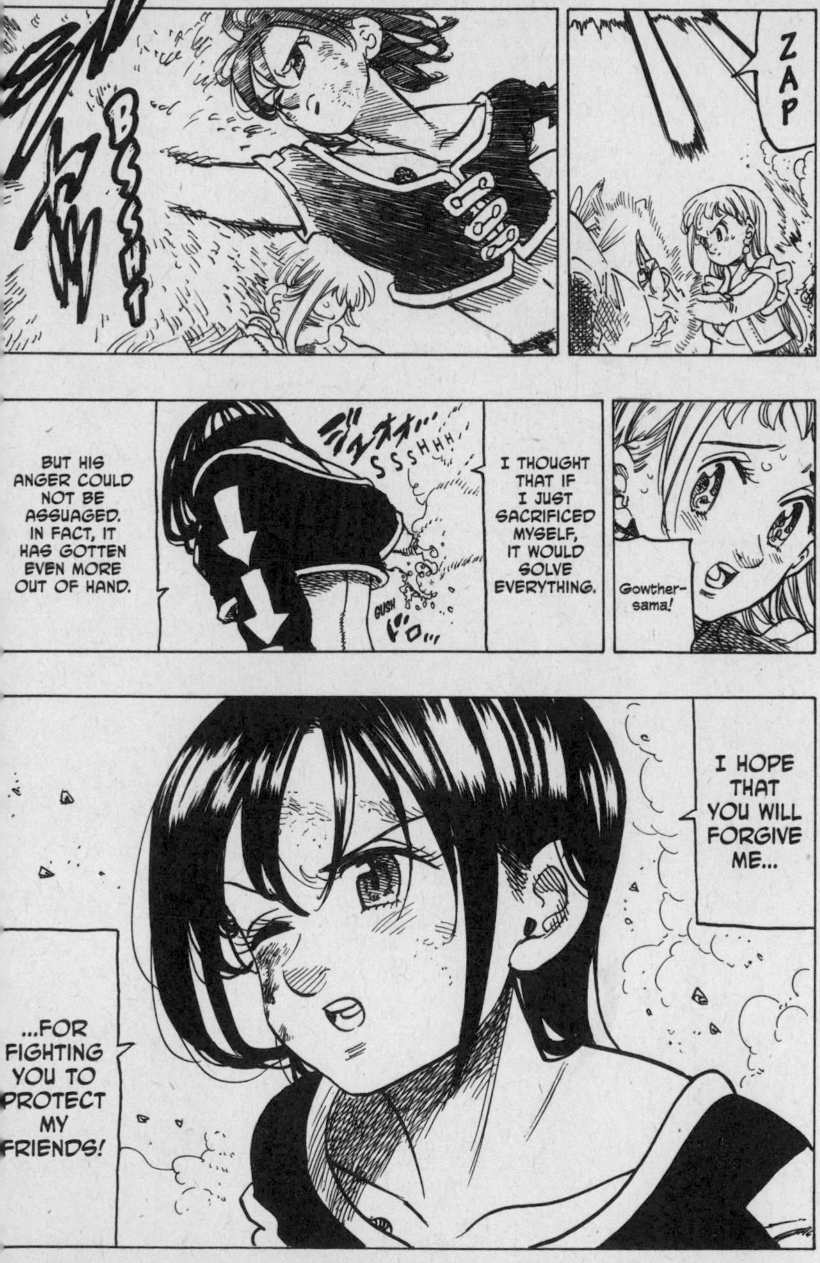
ZAP
BSSHT
Gowther-sama!
I THOUGHT THAT IF I JUST SACRIFICED MYSELF, IT WOULD SOLVE EVERYTHING.
SSSHHH
GUSH
BUT HIS ANGER COULD NOT BE ASSUAGED. IN FACT, IT HAS GOTTEN EVEN MORE OUT OF HAND.
I HOPE THAT YOU WILL FORGIVE ME...
...FOR FIGHTING YOU TO PROTECT MY FRIENDS!

Chapter 278 - Confront Despair!!

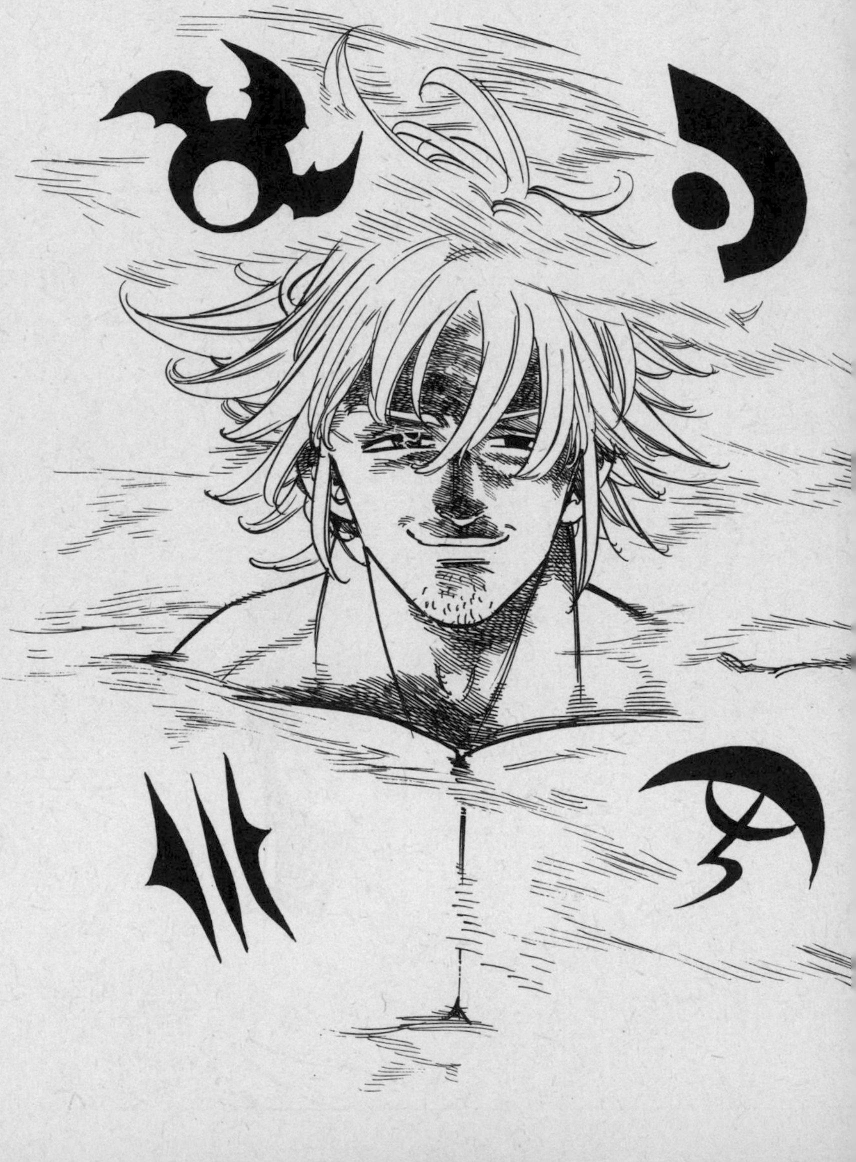

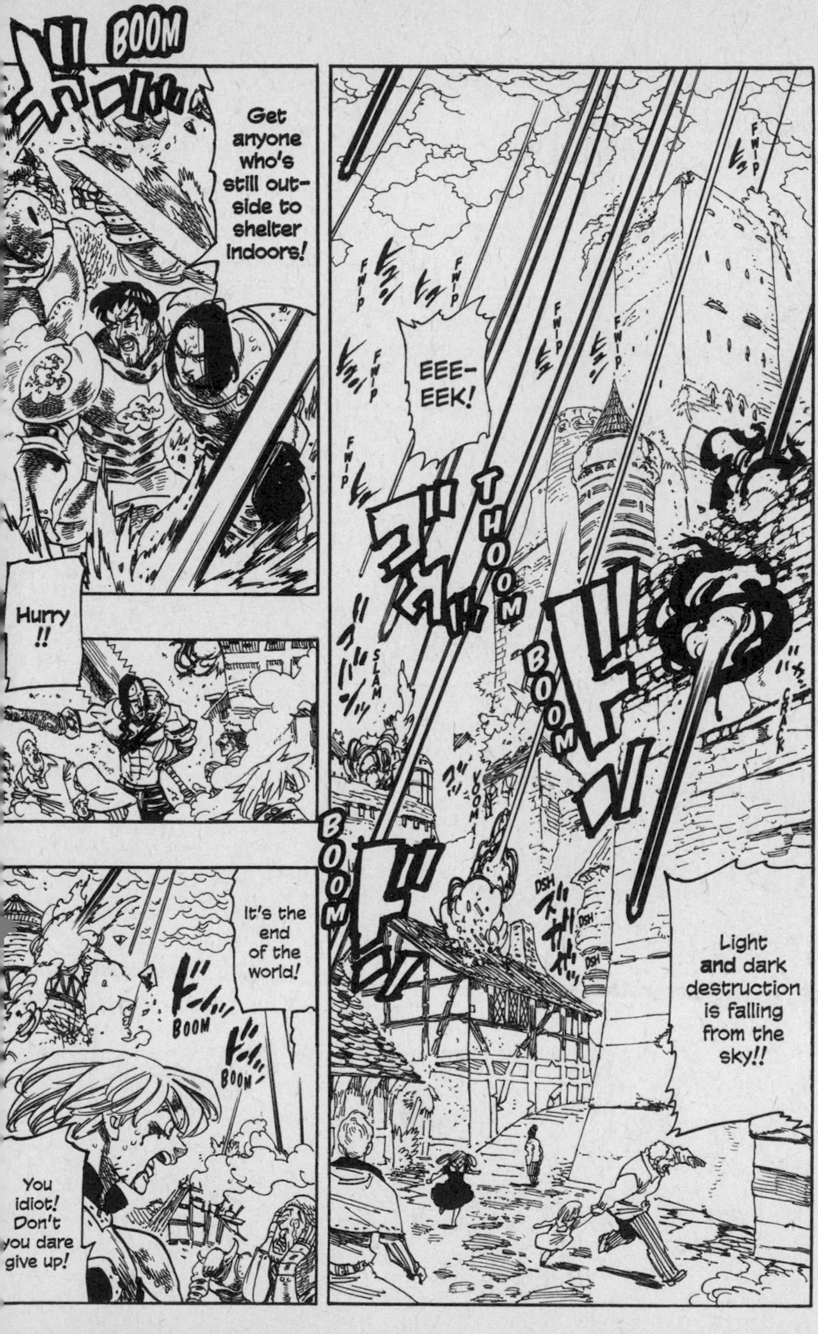
FWIP
FWIP
FWIP
FWIP
FWIP
FWIP
FWIP
EEE-
EEK!
THOOM
SLAM
BOOM
CRACK
VOOM
BOOM
DSH
DSH
DSH
Light and dark destruction is falling from the sky!!
BOOM
Get anyone who's still outside to shelter indoors!
Hurry!!
It's the end of the world!
BOOM
BOOM
You idiot! Don't you dare give up!

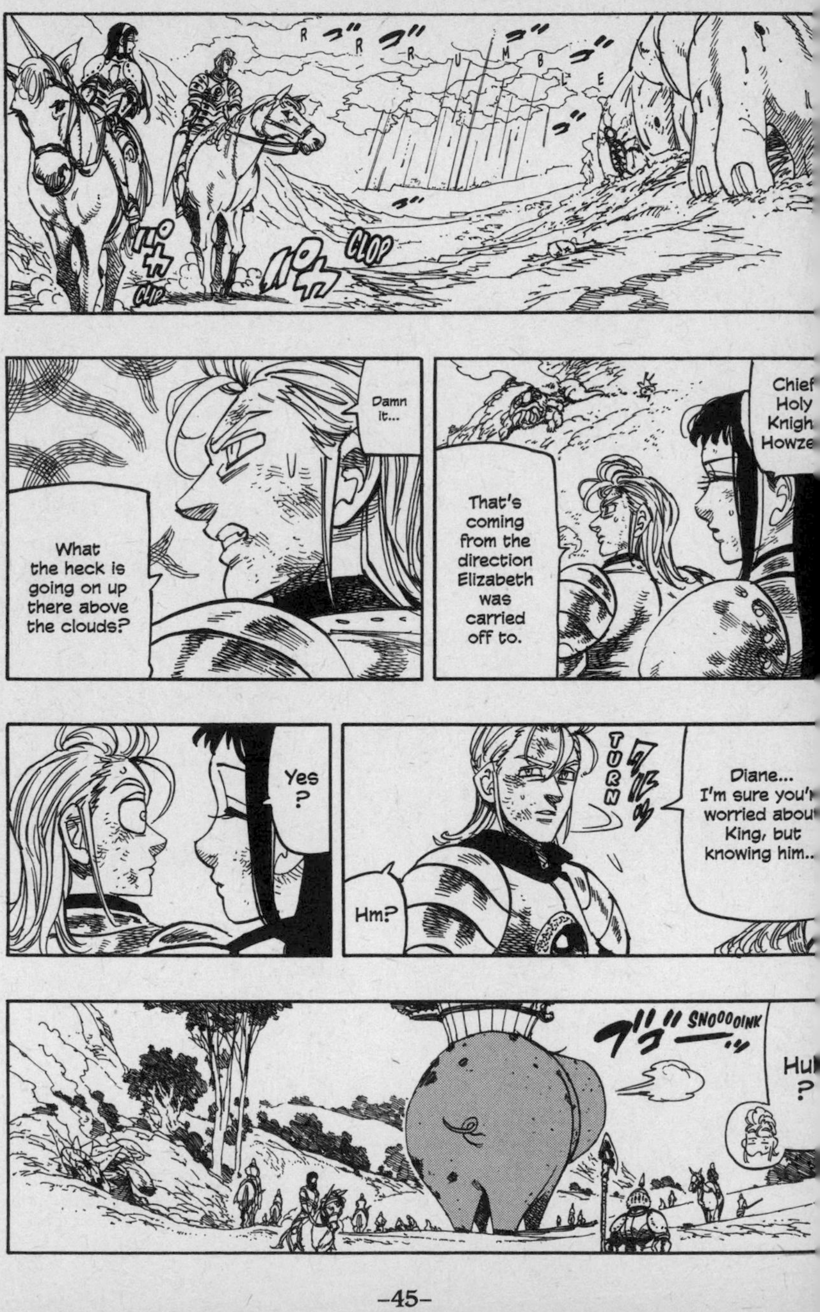
RRUMBLE
CLOP
CLIP
Chief Holy Knigh Howze
That's coming from the direction Elizabeth was carried off to.
Damn it...
What the heck is going on up there above the clouds?
Diane... I'm sure you'r worried abou King, but knowing him..
TURN
Hm?
Yes ?
SNOOOOINK
Hu ?

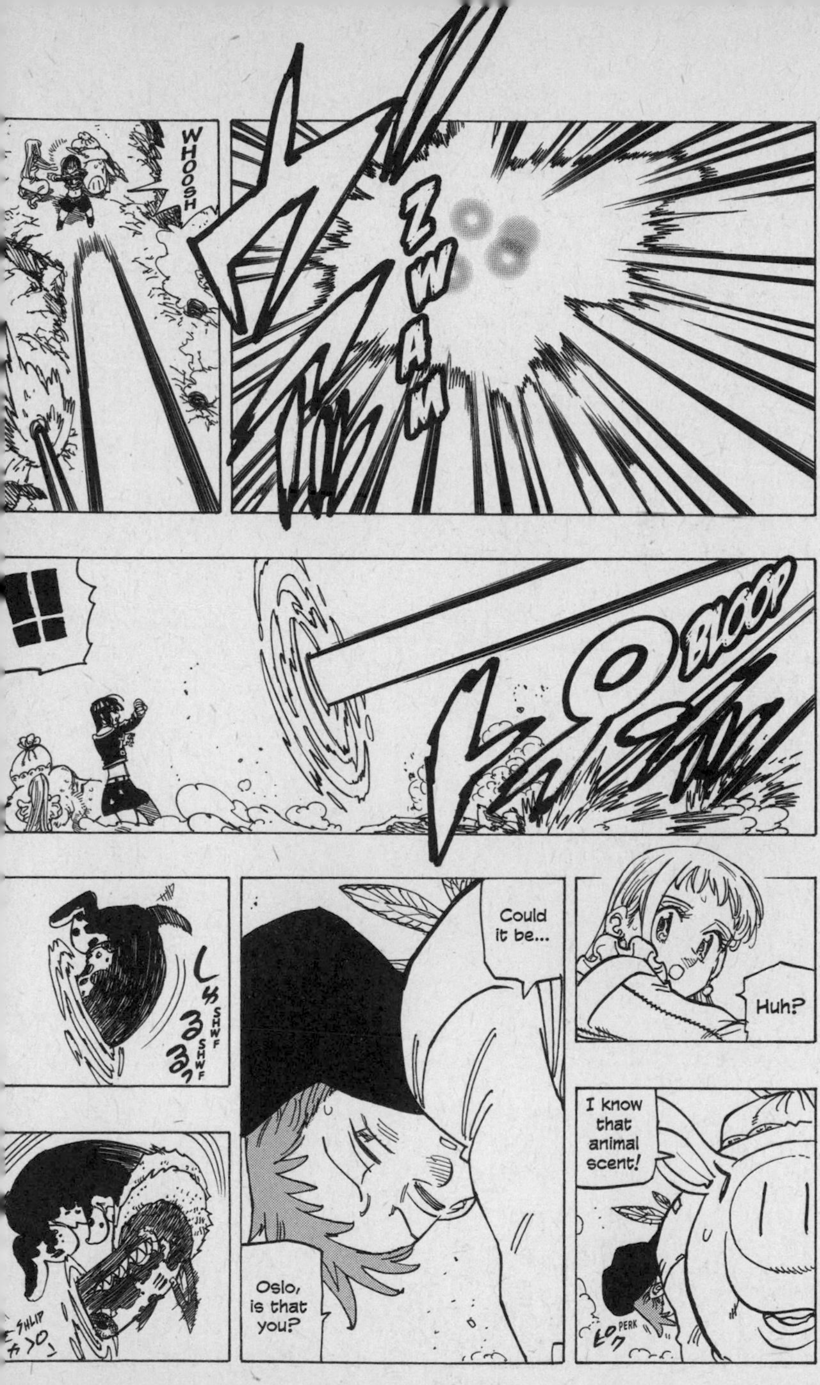
ZWAM
WHOOSH
BLOOP
!!
Huh?
Could it be...
Oslo, is that you?
SHWF
SHWF
I know that animal scent!
PERK
SHLIP

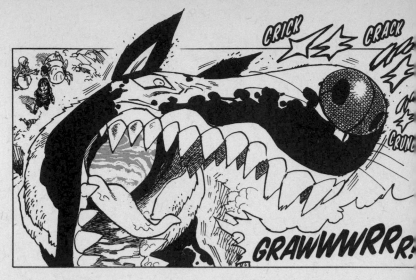

CRICK CRACK

CRUN

GRAWWWRRr!

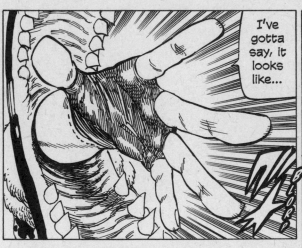

I've gotta say, it looks like...

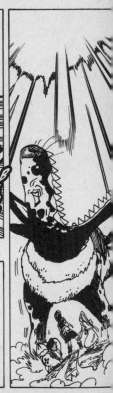

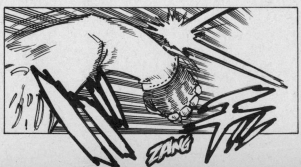

ZANG

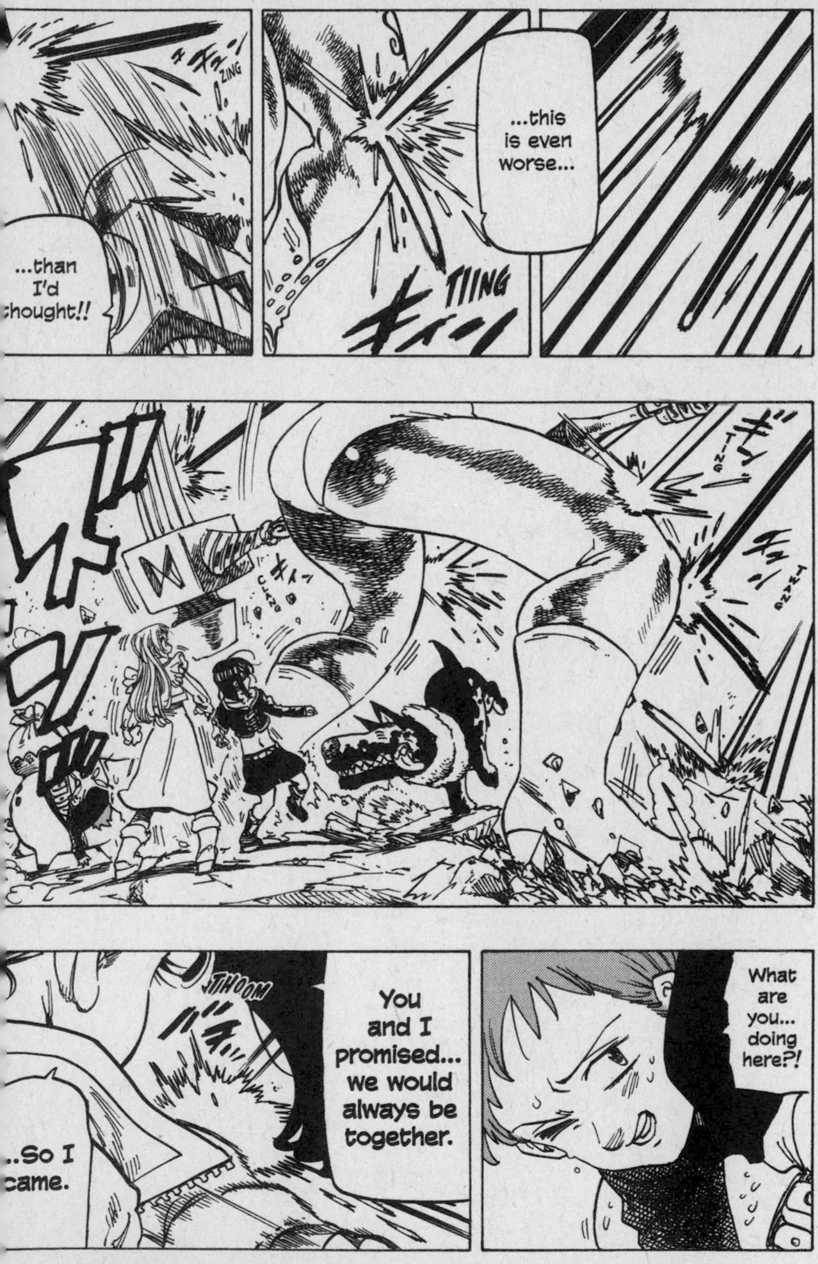

...this is even worse...
TIING
ZING
...than I'd thought!!
TING
TWANG
CLANG
What are you... doing here?!
THOOM
You and I promised... we would always be together.
..So I came.

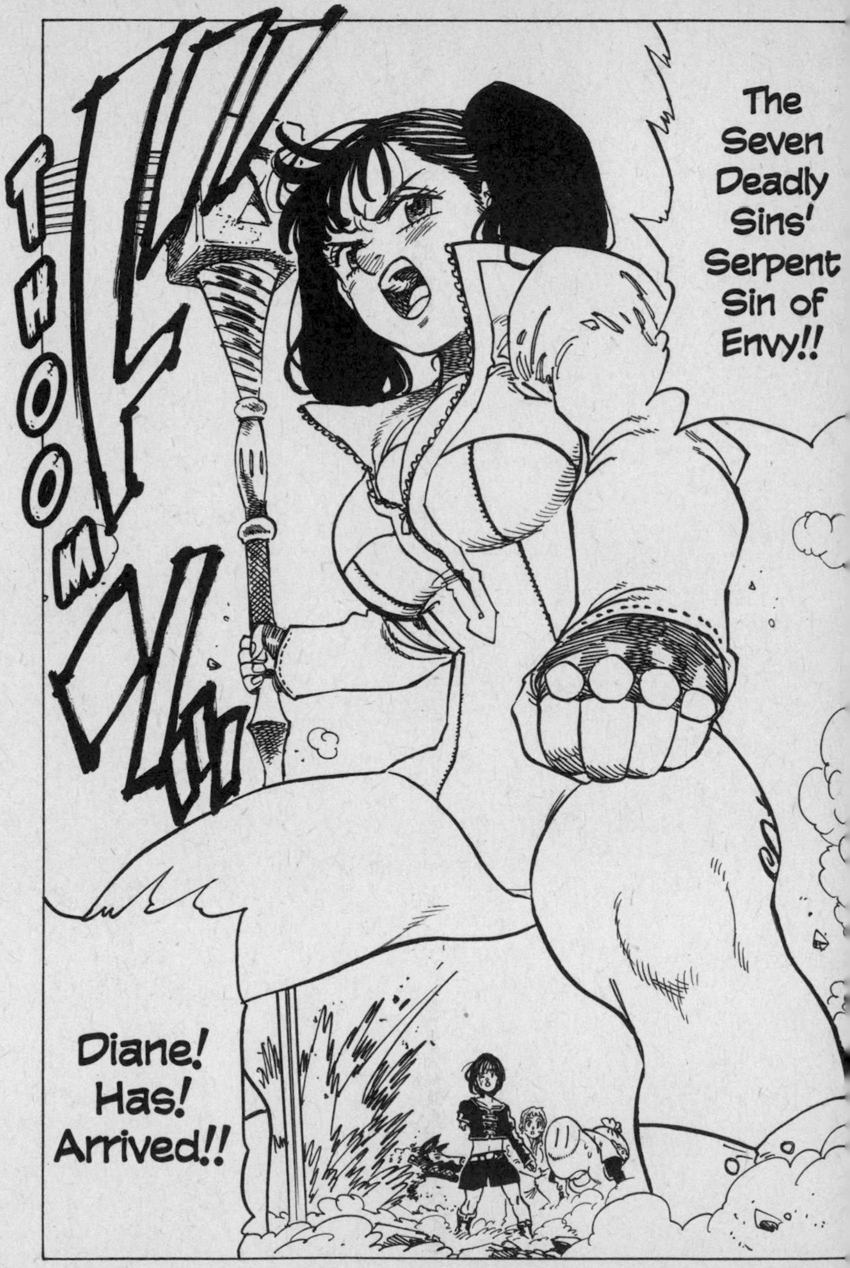
THOOM
The Seven Deadly Sins' Serpent Sin of Envy!!
Diane! Has! Arrived!!

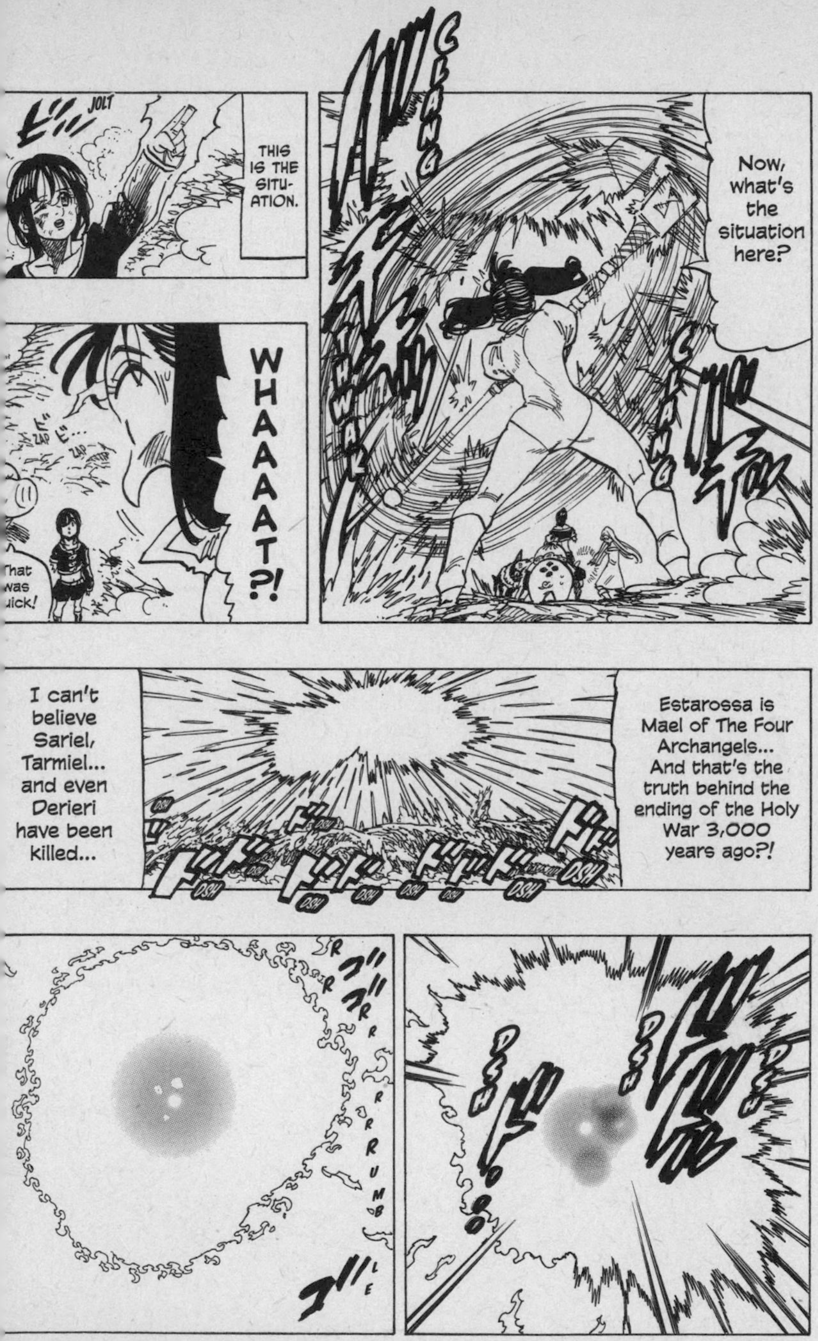
CLANG
Now, what's the situation here?
THWAK
CLANG
JOLT
THIS IS THE SITUATION.
WHAAAAAT?!
ZAP
ZAP
That was uick!
Estarossa is Mael of The Four Archangels... And that's the truth behind the ending of the Holy War 3,000 years ago?!
I can't believe Sariel, Tarmiel... and even Derieri have been killed...
DOSH
DOSH
DOSH
RRRRRRRRUMBLE

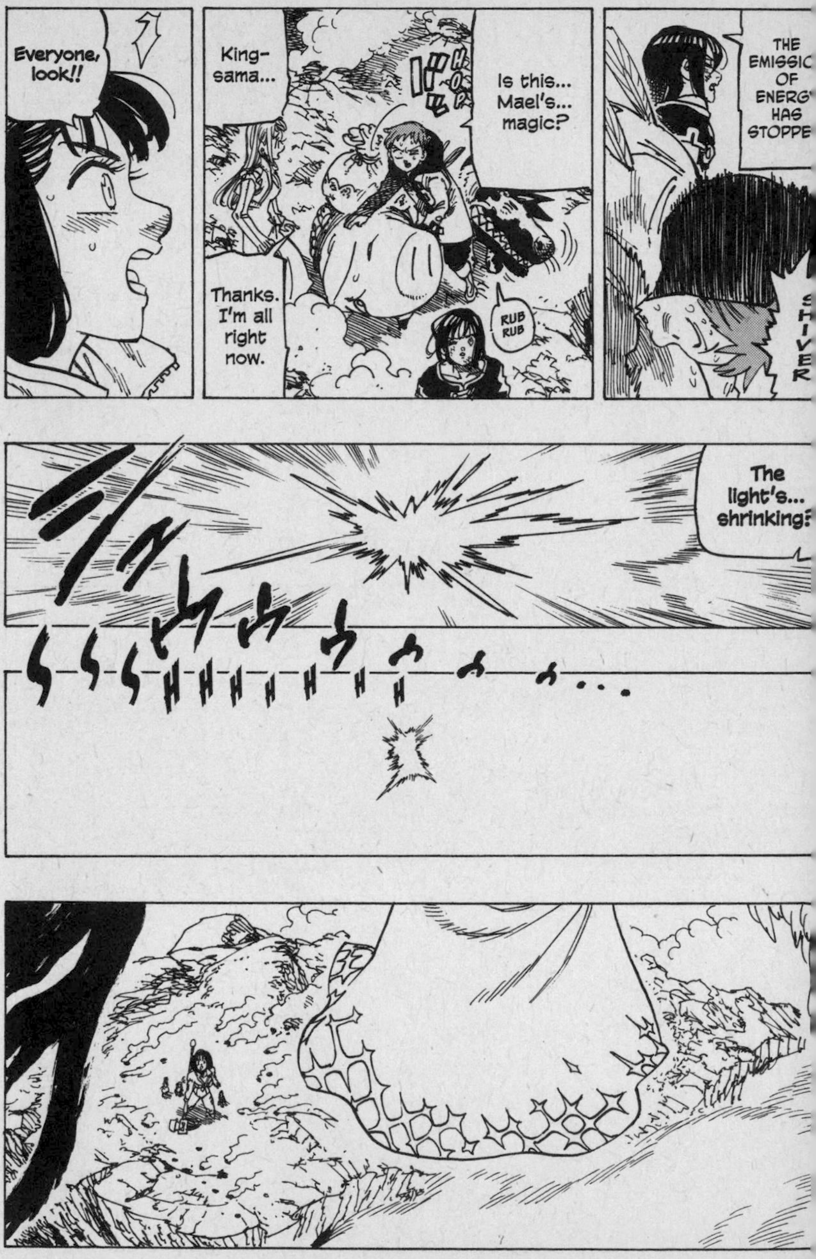
THE EMISSIC OF ENERG HAS STOPPE
SHIVER
Is this... Mael's... magic?
King-sama...
HOP
Thanks. I'm all right now.
RUB RUB
Everyone, look!!
The light's... shrinking!?

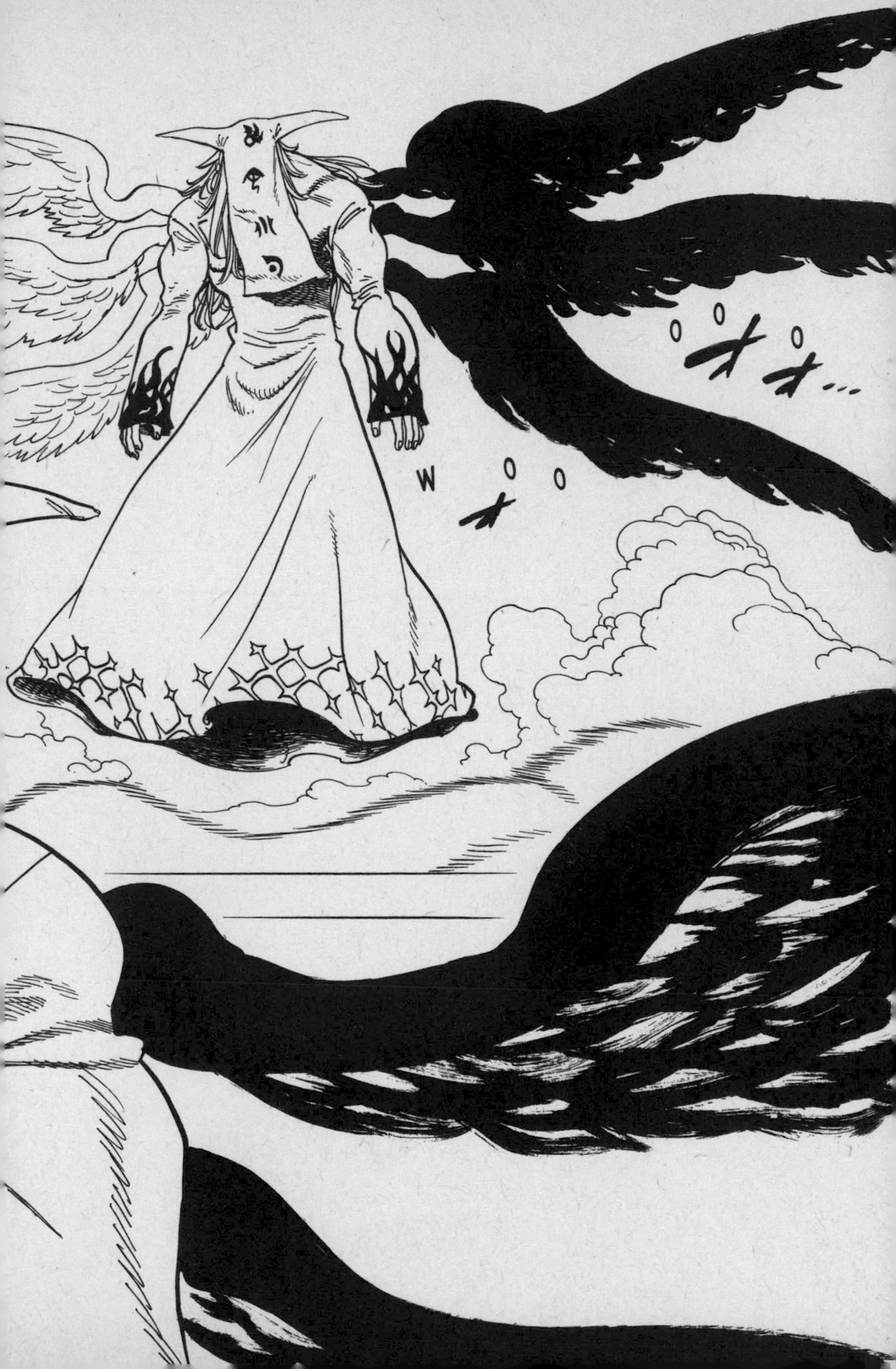
OOO
オオオ…
WOO
オ

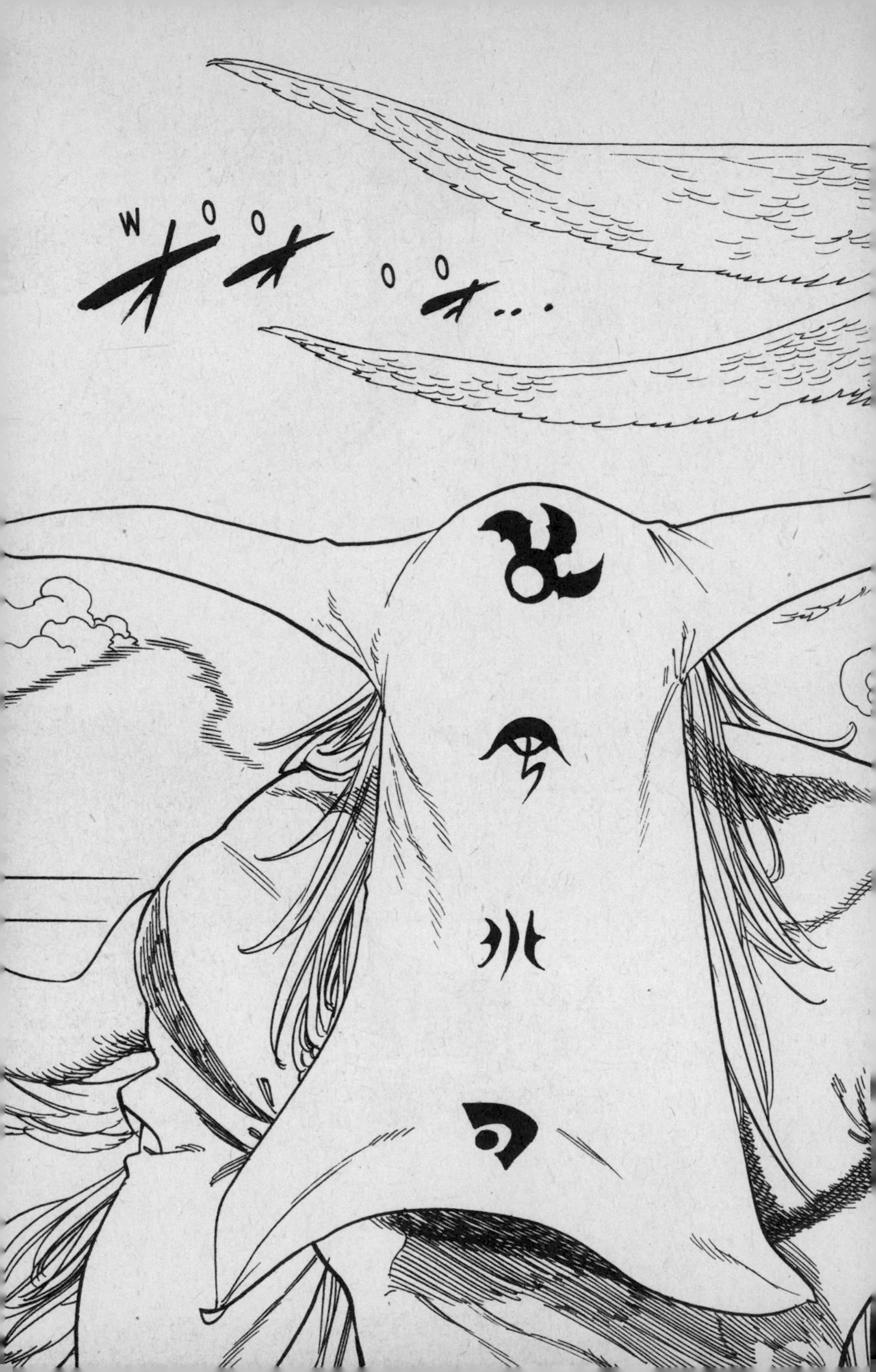
WOOOO
オオォ…

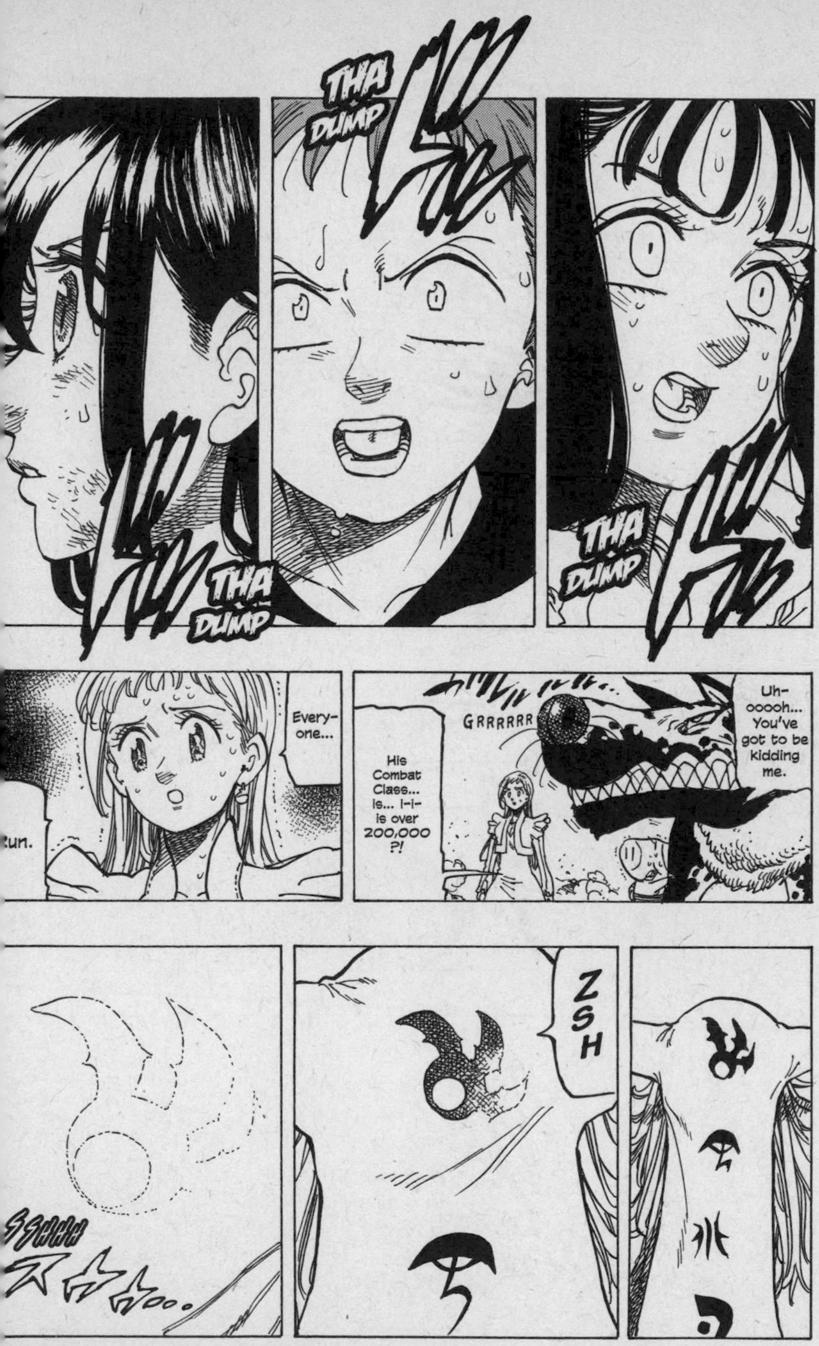
THA DUMP
THA DUMP
THA DUMP
Uh-ooooh... You've got to be kidding me.
GRRRRRRR
His Combat Class... is... i-i-is over 200,000 ?!
Every-one...
ZSH

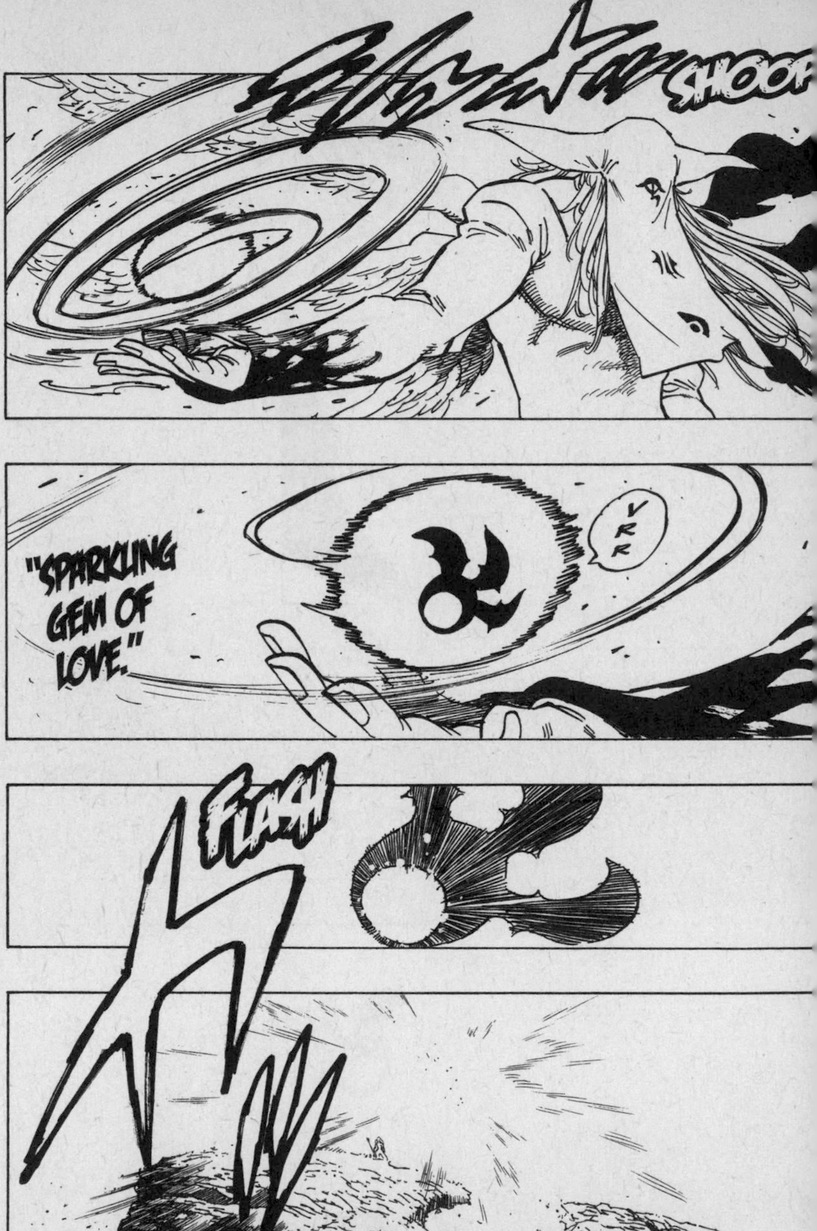
SHOOP
"SPARKLING GEM OF LOVE."
VRR
FLASH

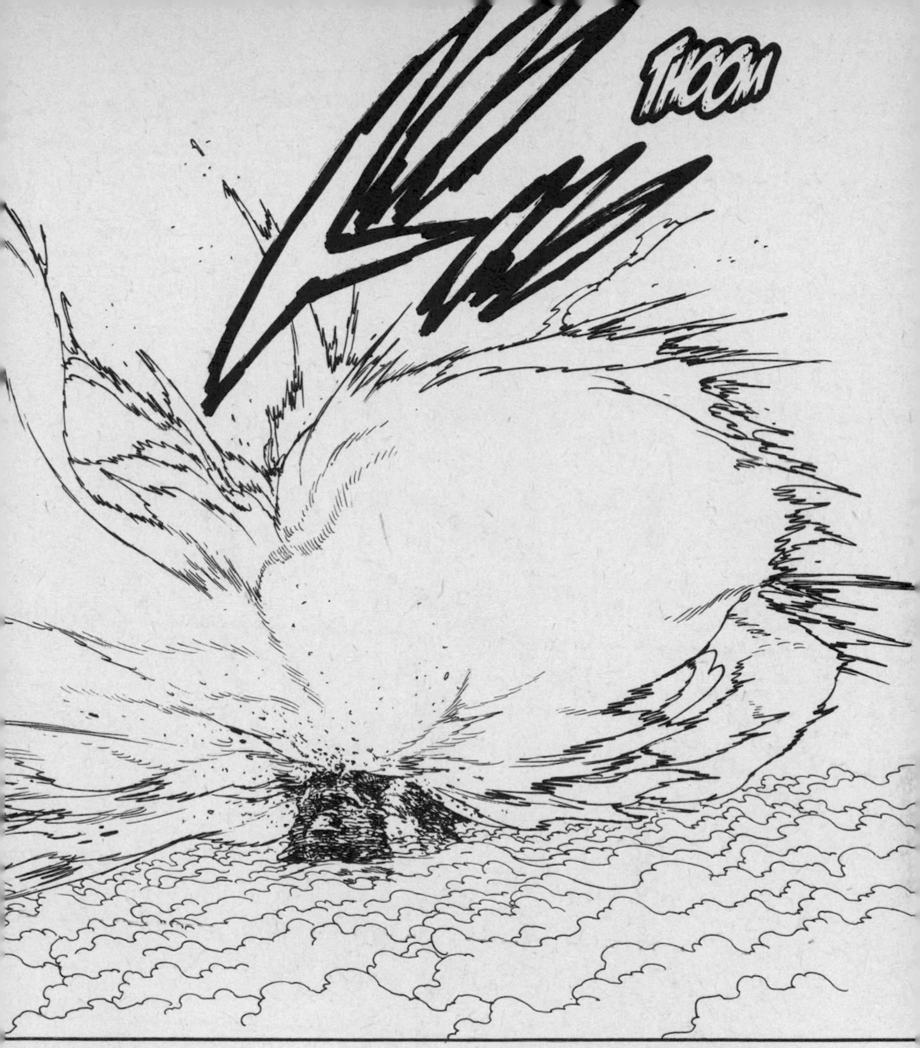
THOOM
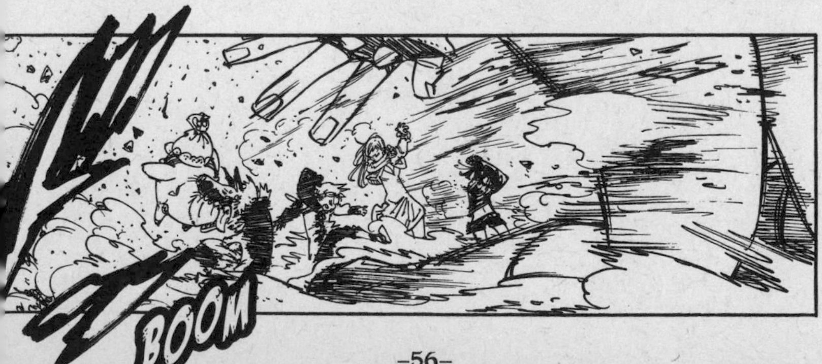
BOOM

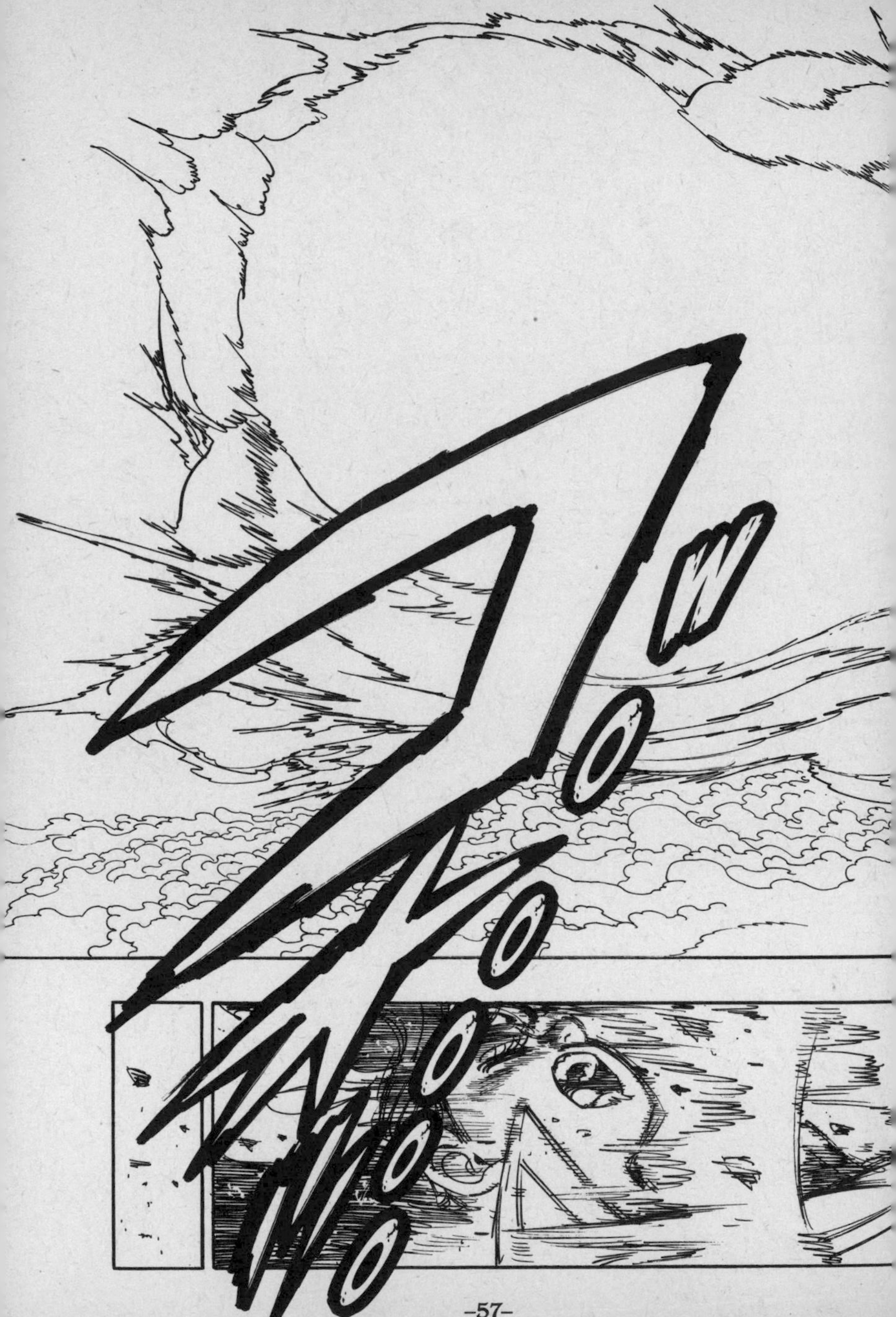

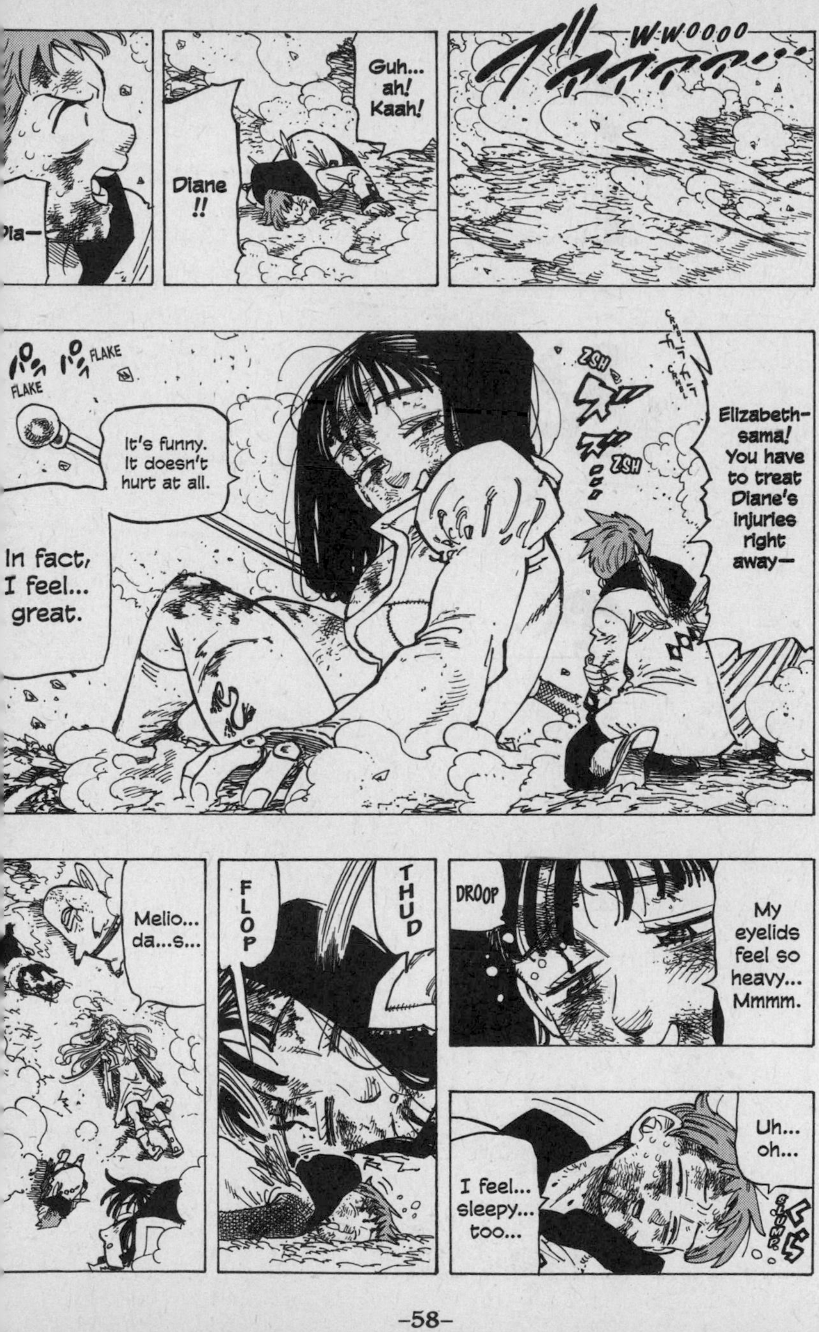
W-W-O-O-O-O
Guh... ah! Kaah!
Diane !!
Dia—
Elizabeth-sama! You have to treat Diane's injuries right away—
ZSH
ZSH
FLAKE
FLAKE
It's funny. It doesn't hurt at all.
In fact, I feel... great.
DROOP
My eyelids feel so heavy... Mmmm.
Uh... oh...
I feel... sleepy... too...
THUD
FLOP
Melio... da...s...

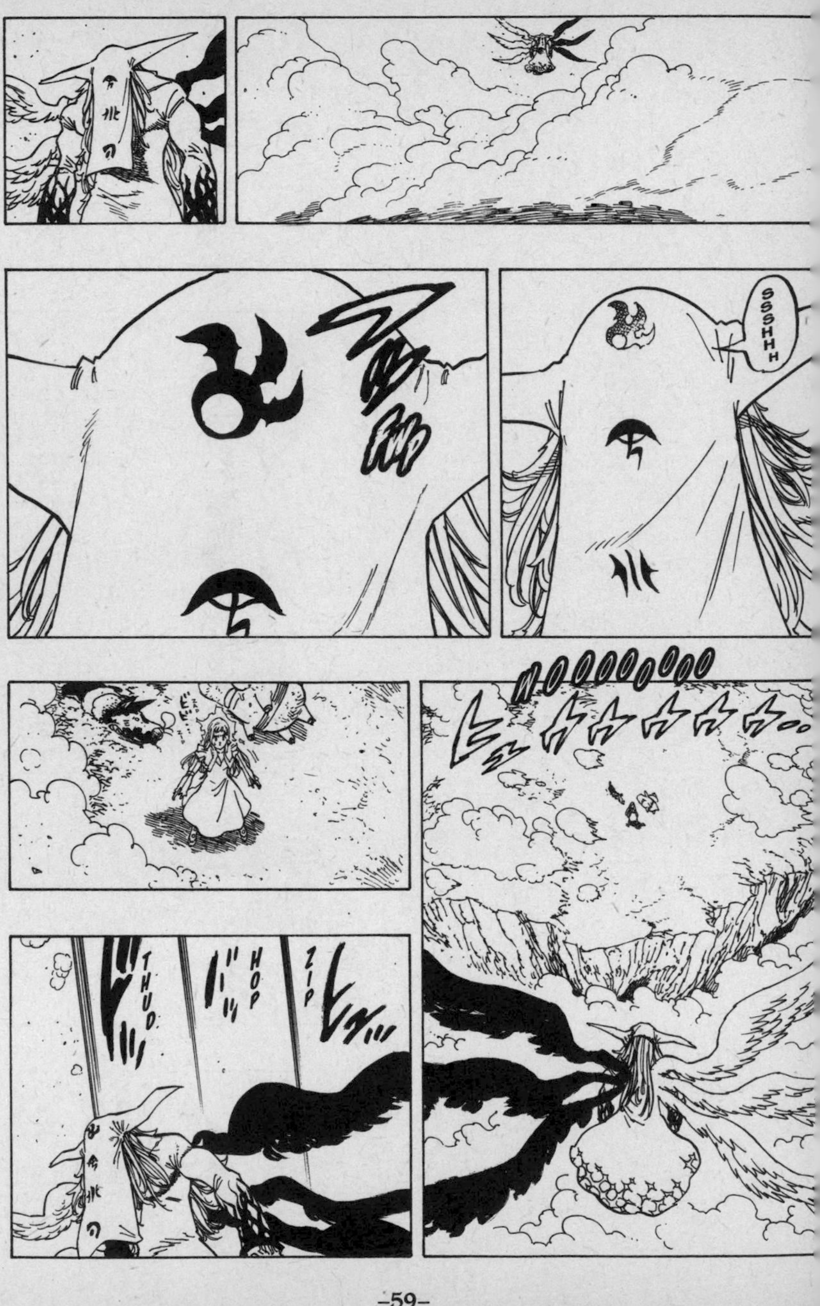
SSSHHH
NOOOOOOOO
ZAP
ZIP
ZIP
HOP
THUD

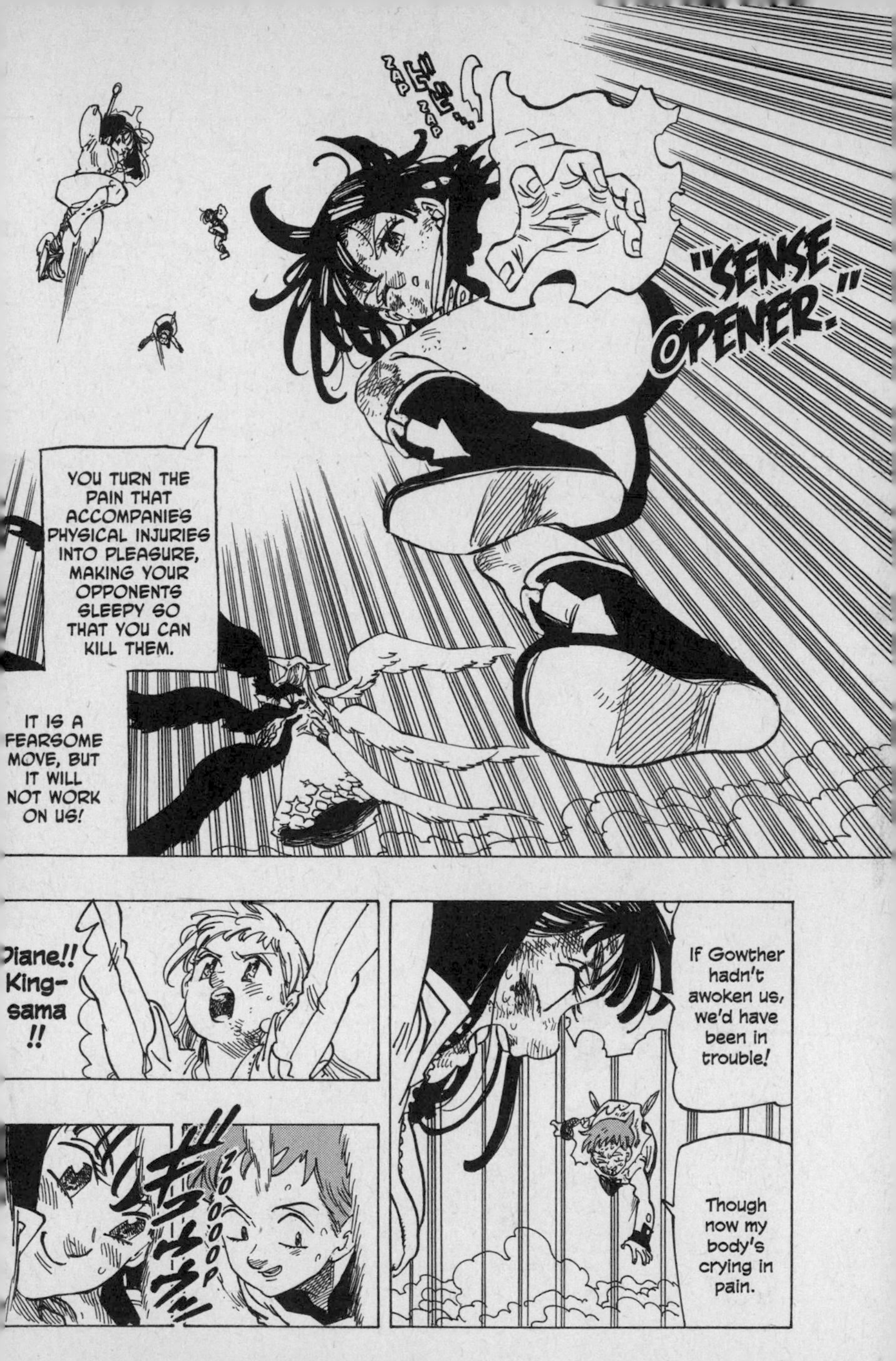
ZAP
ZAP ZAP
"SENSE OPENER."
YOU TURN THE PAIN THAT ACCOMPANIES PHYSICAL INJURIES INTO PLEASURE, MAKING YOUR OPPONENTS SLEEPY SO THAT YOU CAN KILL THEM.
IT IS A FEARSOME MOVE, BUT IT WILL NOT WORK ON US!
If Gowther hadn't awoken us, we'd have been in trouble!
Though now my body's crying in pain.
Diane!! King-sama!!
ZOOOOOP

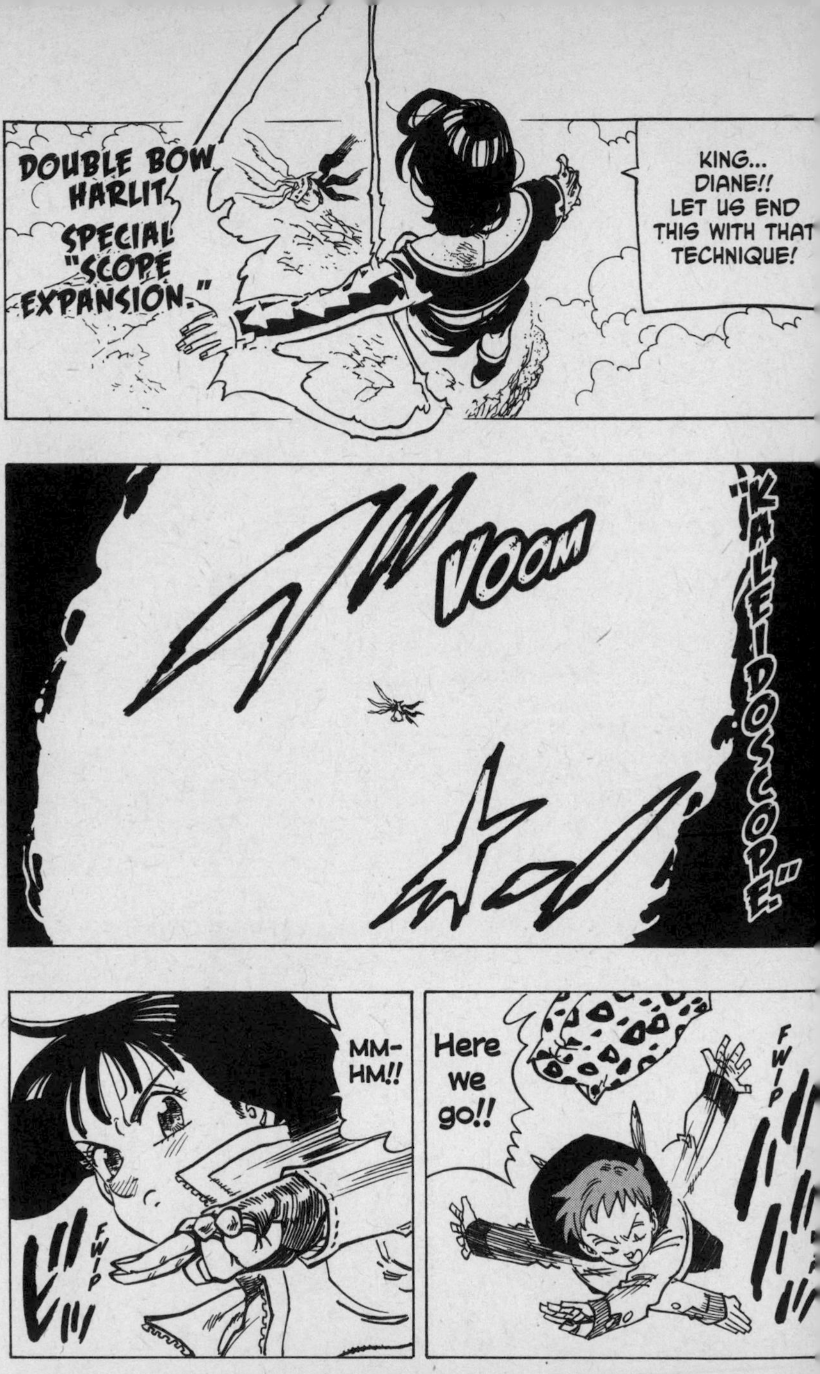
KING... DIANE!! LET US END THIS WITH THAT TECHNIQUE!
DOUBLE BOW HARLIT SPECIAL "SCOPE EXPANSION."
"KALEIDOSCOPE."
VOOM
FWIP
Here we go!!
MM-HM!!
FWIP

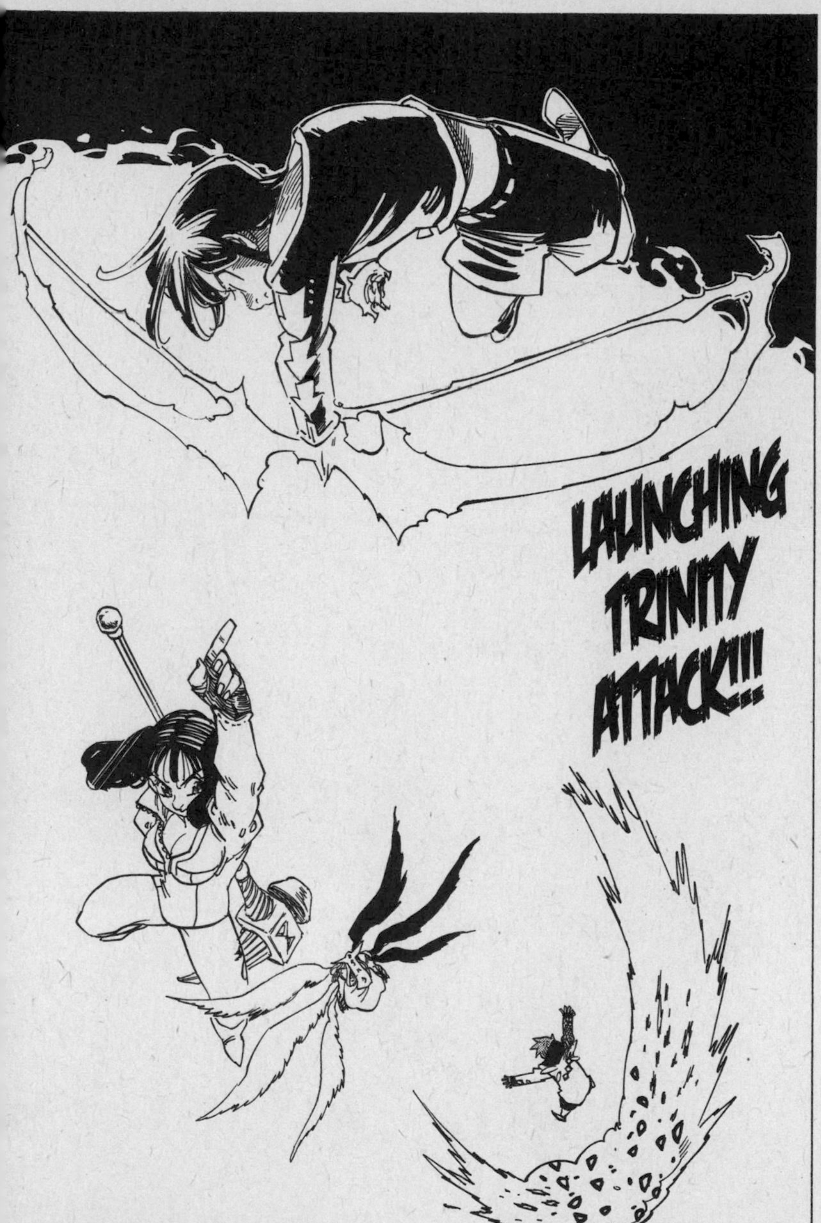
LAUNCHING TRINITY ATTACK!!!

Chapter 279 - The Tolling of the Victory Bel

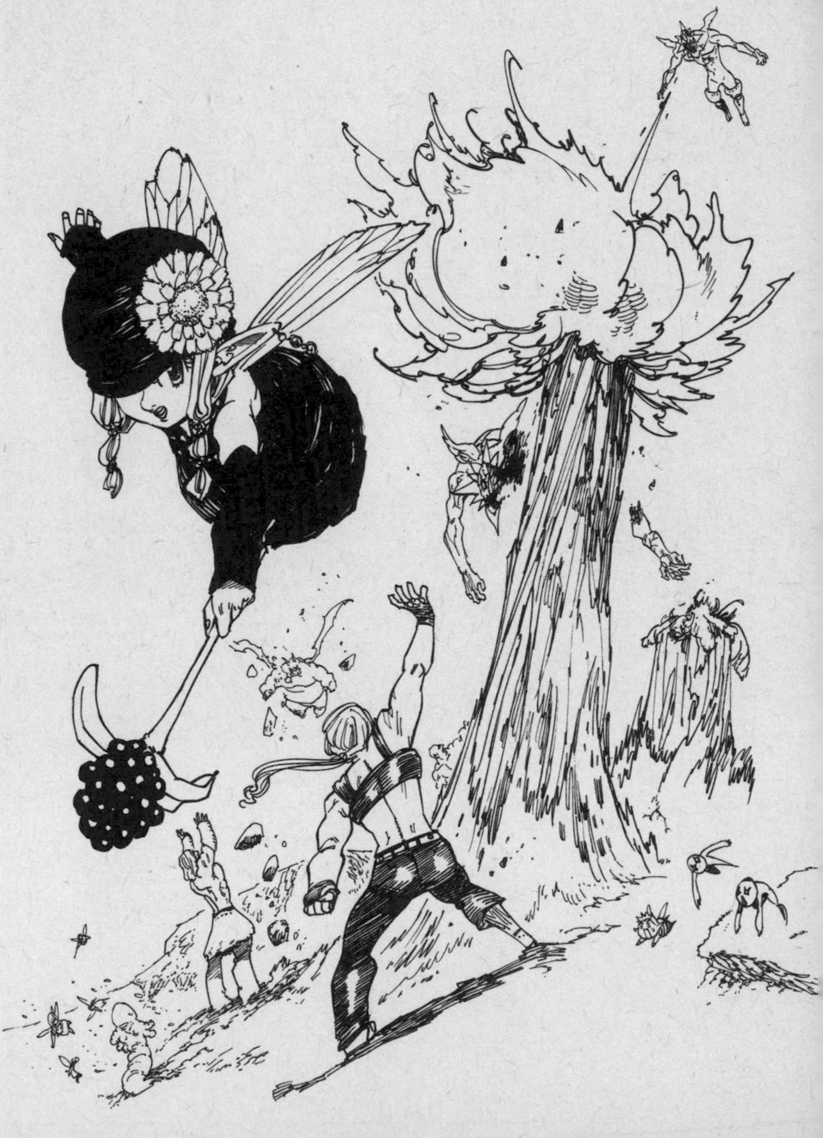

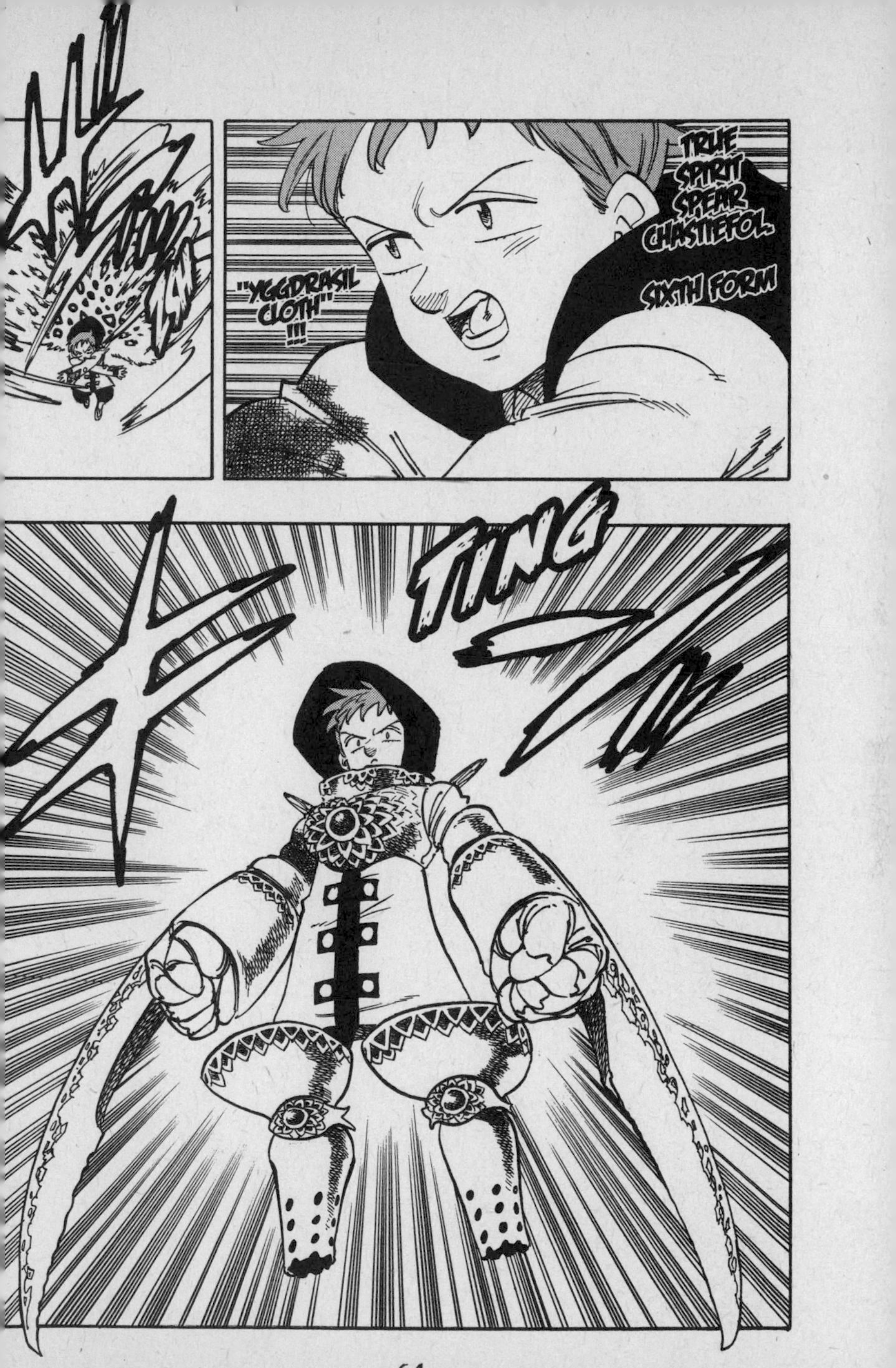
TRUE SPIRIT SPEAR CHASTIEFOL
SIXTH FORM
"YGGDRASIL CLOTH"!!!
TING

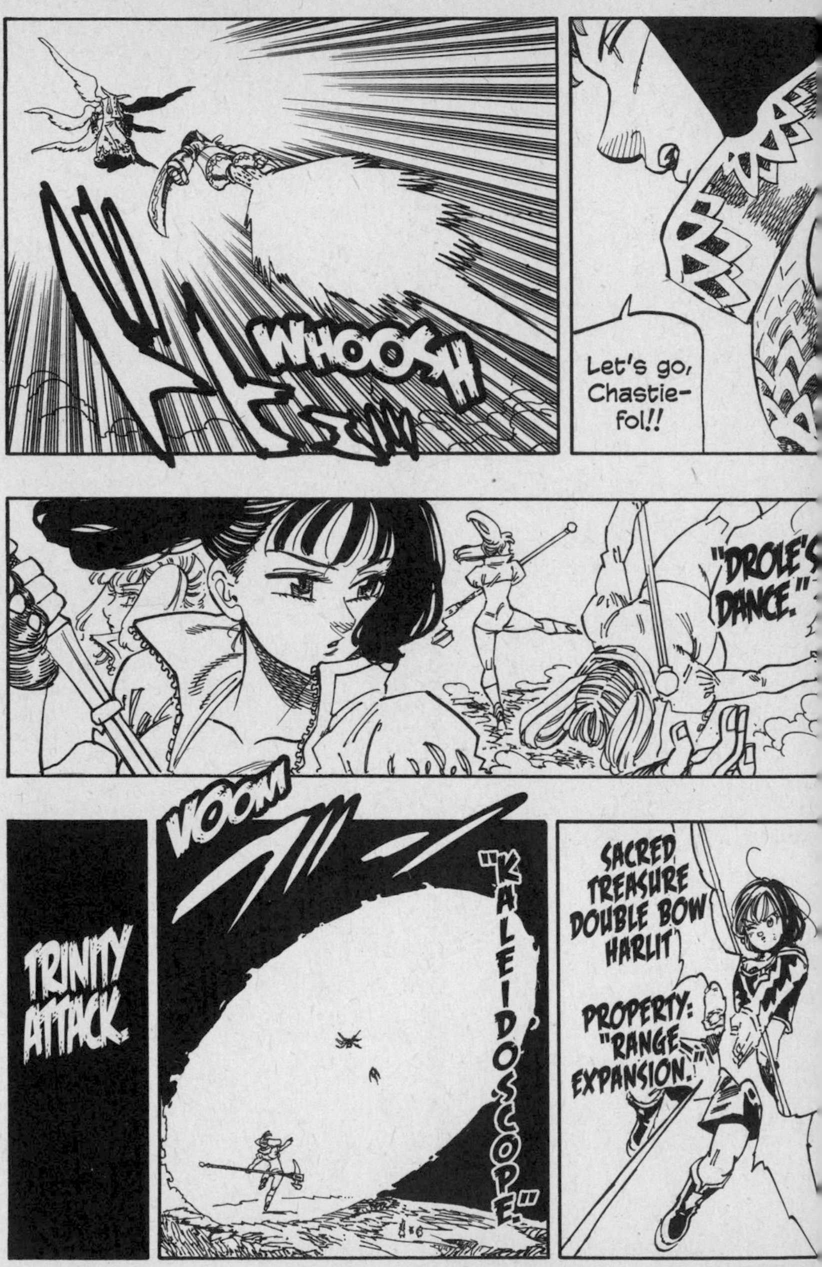
Let's go, Chastie-fol!!
WHOOSH
"DROLE'S DANCE."
SACRED TREASURE DOUBLE BOW HARLIT
PROPERTY: "RANGE EXPANSION."
VOOM
"KALEIDOSCOPE"
TRINITY ATTACK

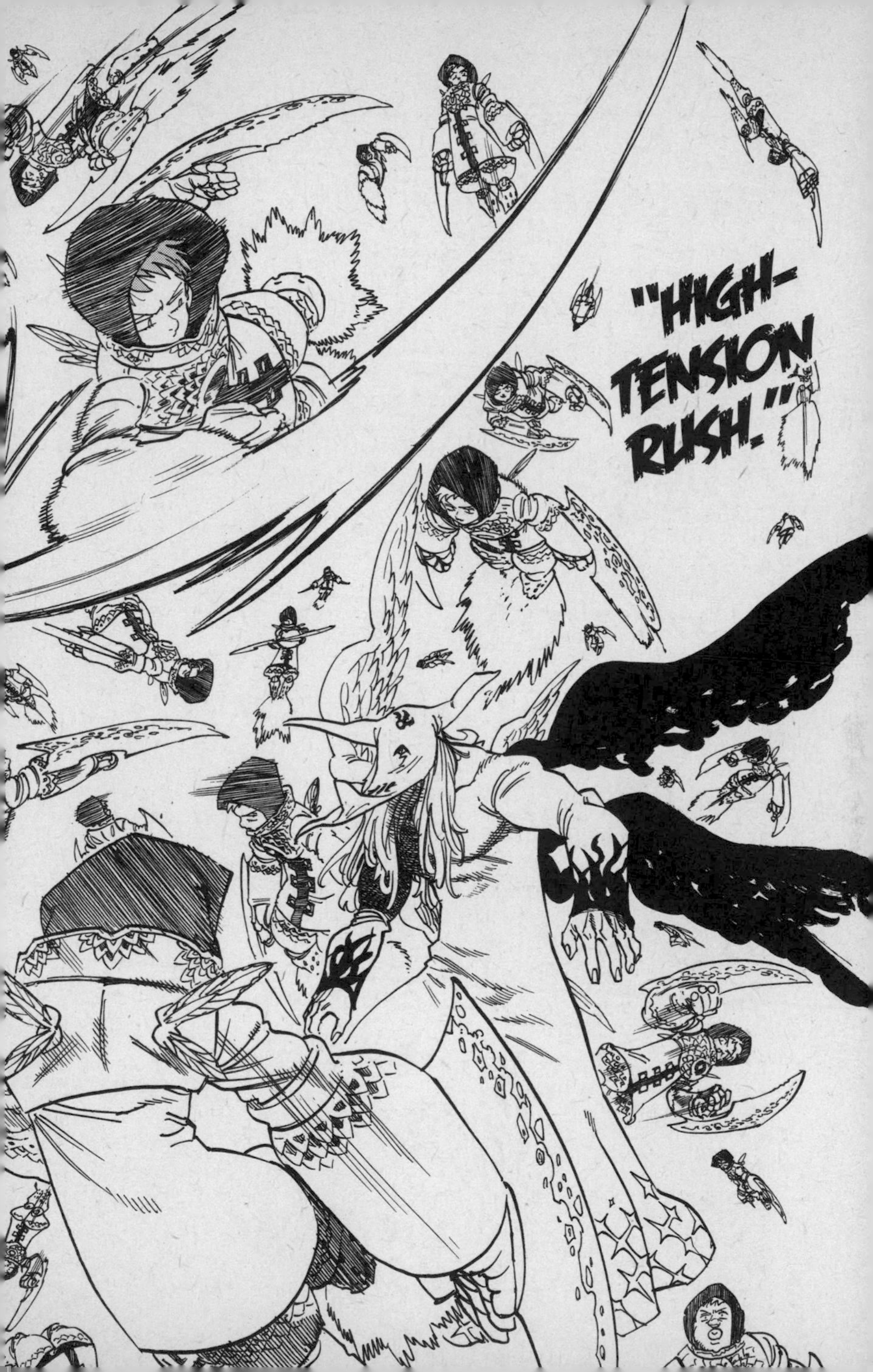
"HIGH-TENSION RUSH."

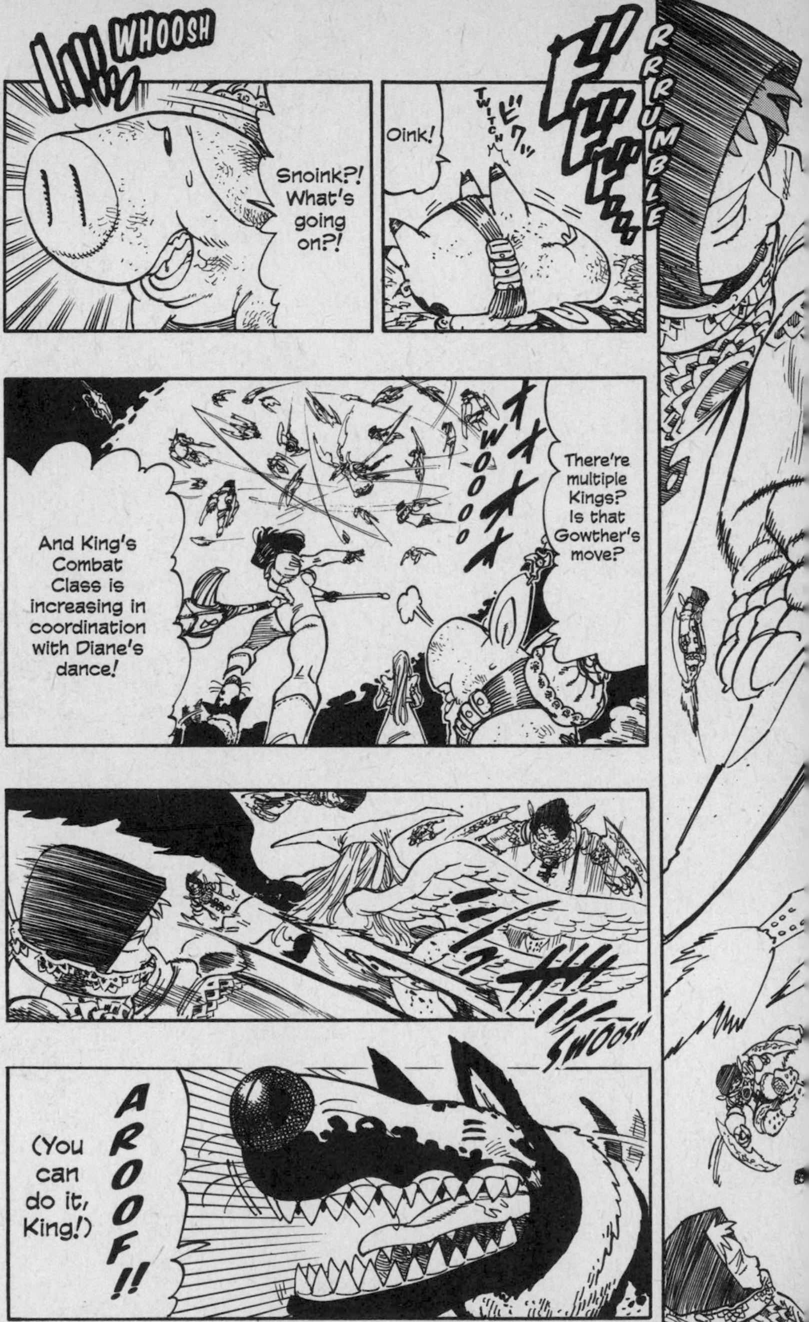
RRRUMBLE
TWITCH
Oink!
WHOOSH
Snoink?! What's going on?!
WOOOOO
There're multiple Kings? Is that Gowther's move?
And King's Combat Class is increasing in coordination with Diane's dance!
SWOOSH
AROOOF!!
(You can do it, King!)

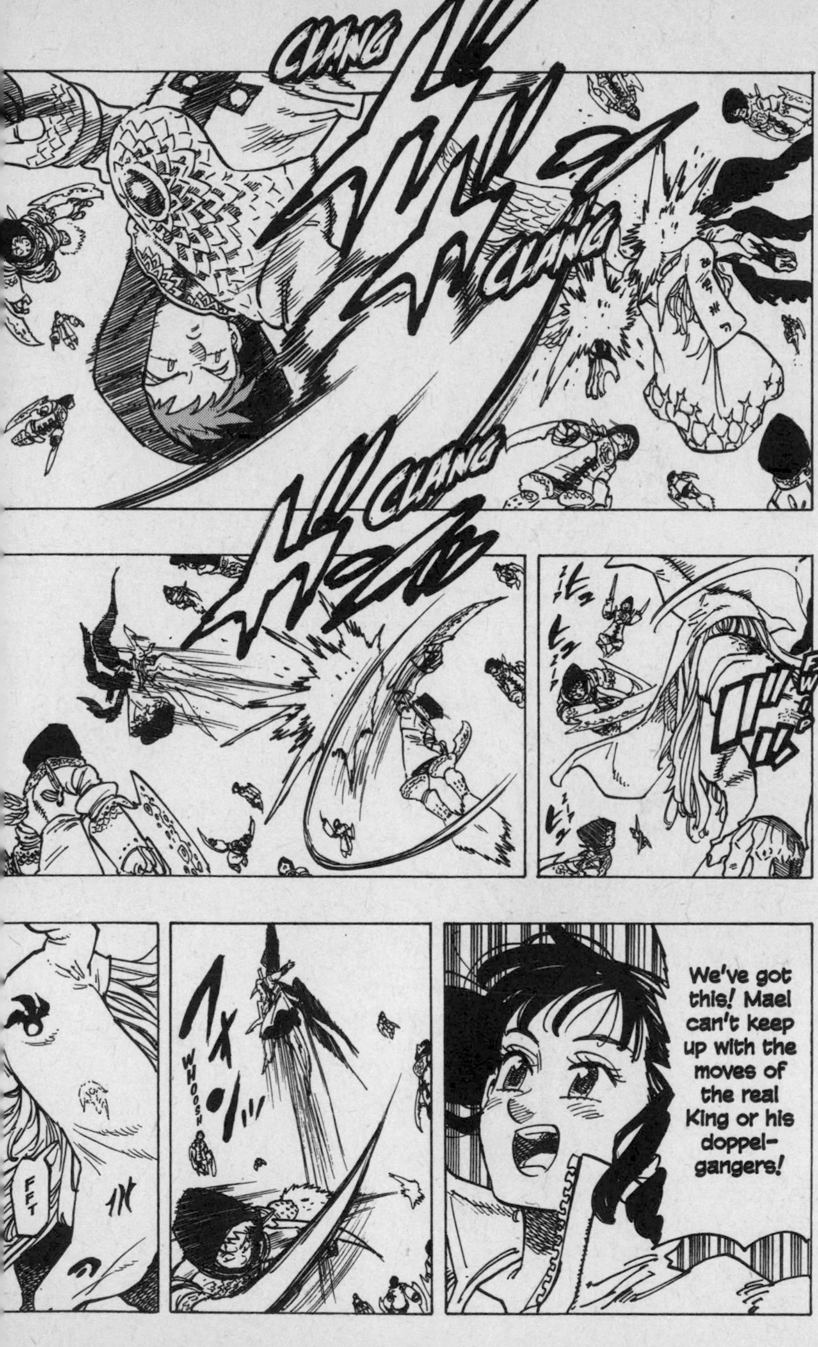
CLANG
CLANG
FWIP
CLANG
We've got this! Mael can't keep up with the moves of the real King or his doppel-gangers!
WHOOSH
FFT

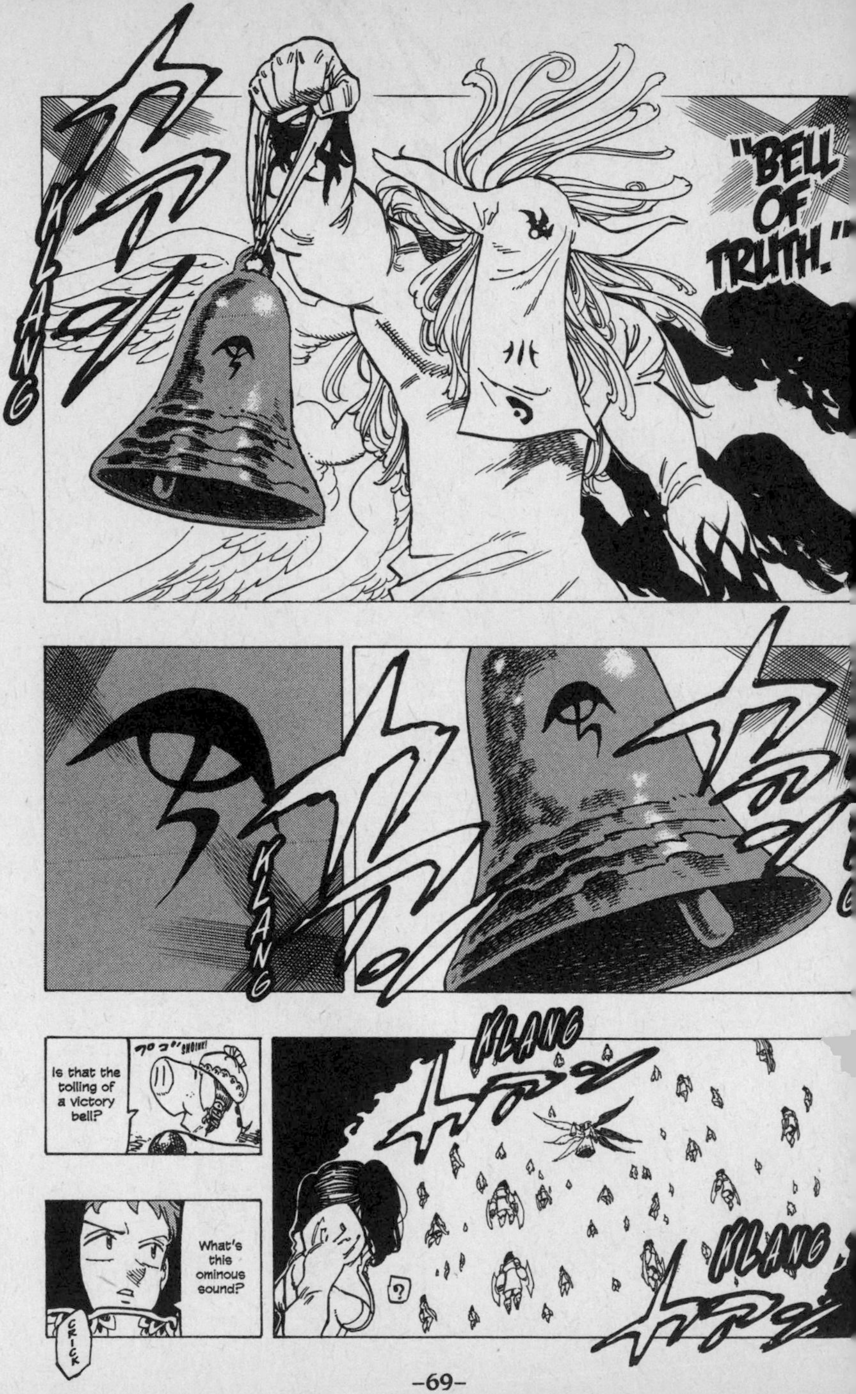
"BELL OF TRUTH."
KLANG
KLANG
KLANG
KLANG
KLANG
SNOINK!
Is that the tolling of a victory bell?
What's this ominous sound?
CRICK
?

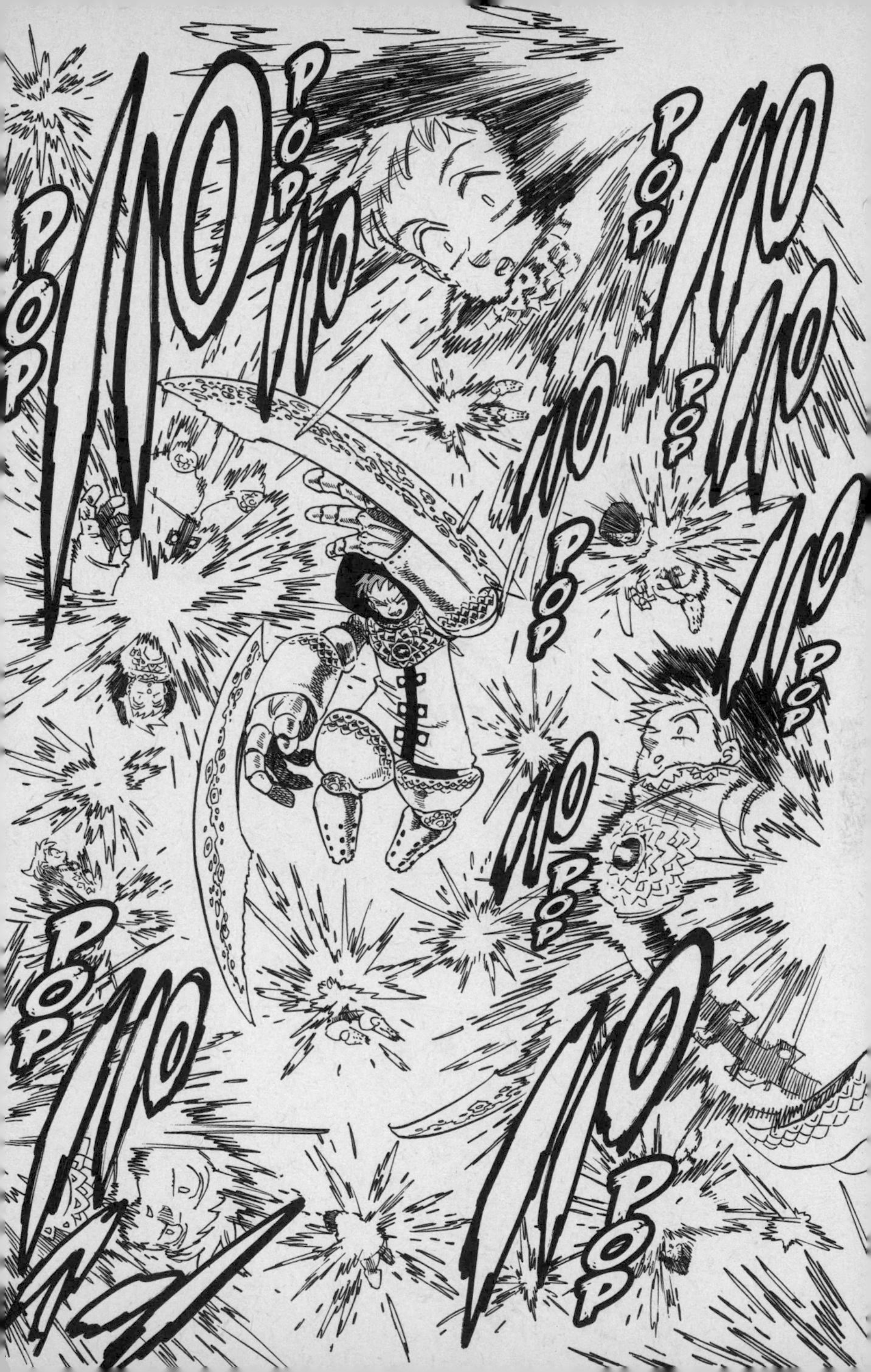
POP
POP
POP
POP
POP
POP
POP
POP
POP

HE'S GIVING THE COMMANDMENTS PHYSICAL FORM. NO SUPERFICIAL MAGIC CANNOT COMPETE WITH IT.

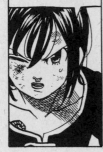

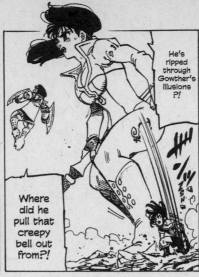

He's ripped through Gowther's illusions?!

Where did he pull that creepy bell out from?!

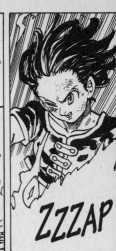

ZZZAP

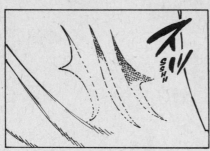

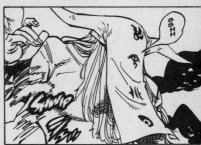

SSHH

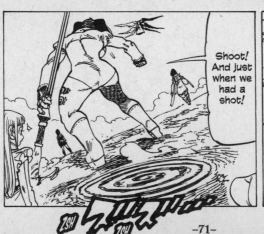

Shoot! And just when we had a shot!

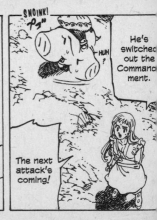

SNOINK!

HUH

He's switched out the Commandment.

The next attack's coming!

x

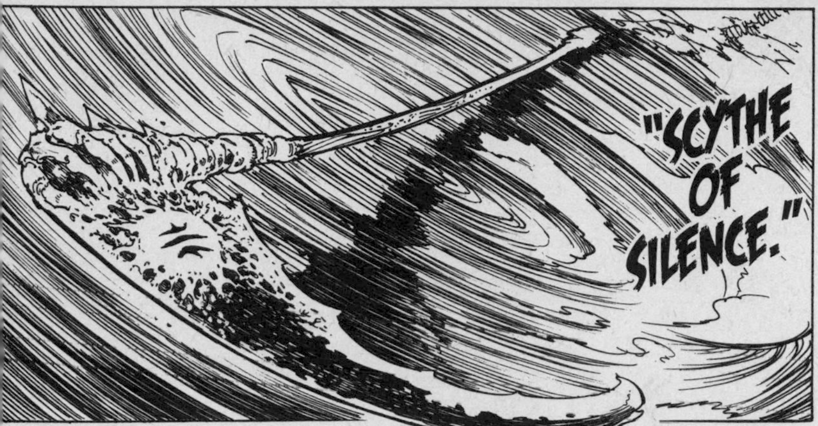
"SCYTHE OF SILENCE."
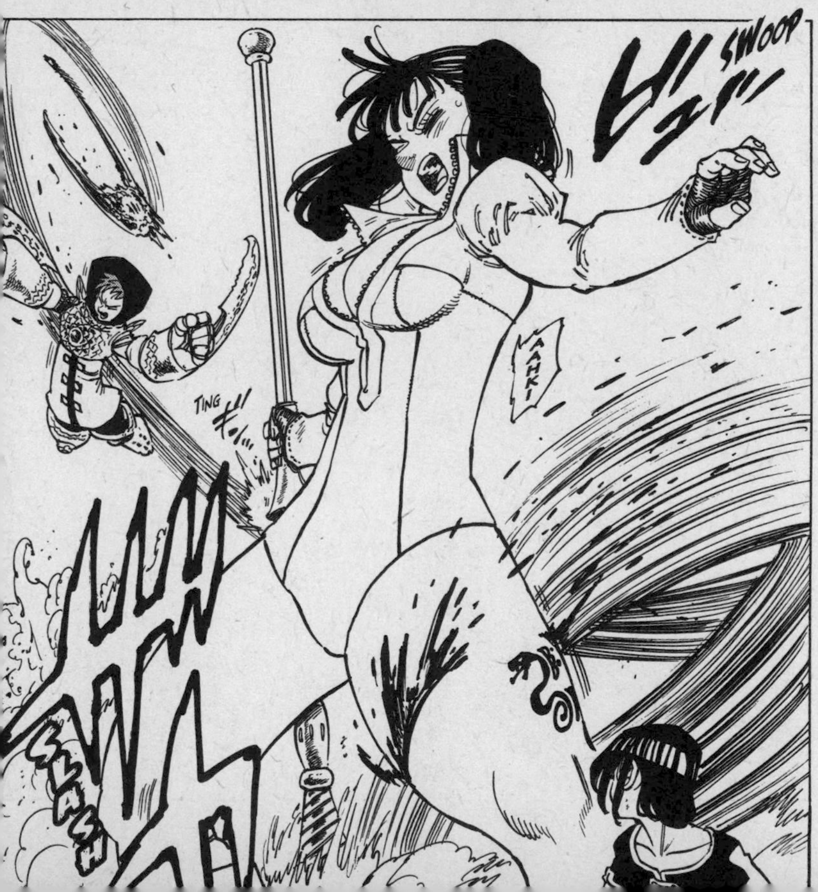
SWOOP
AAHK!
TING
SLAM

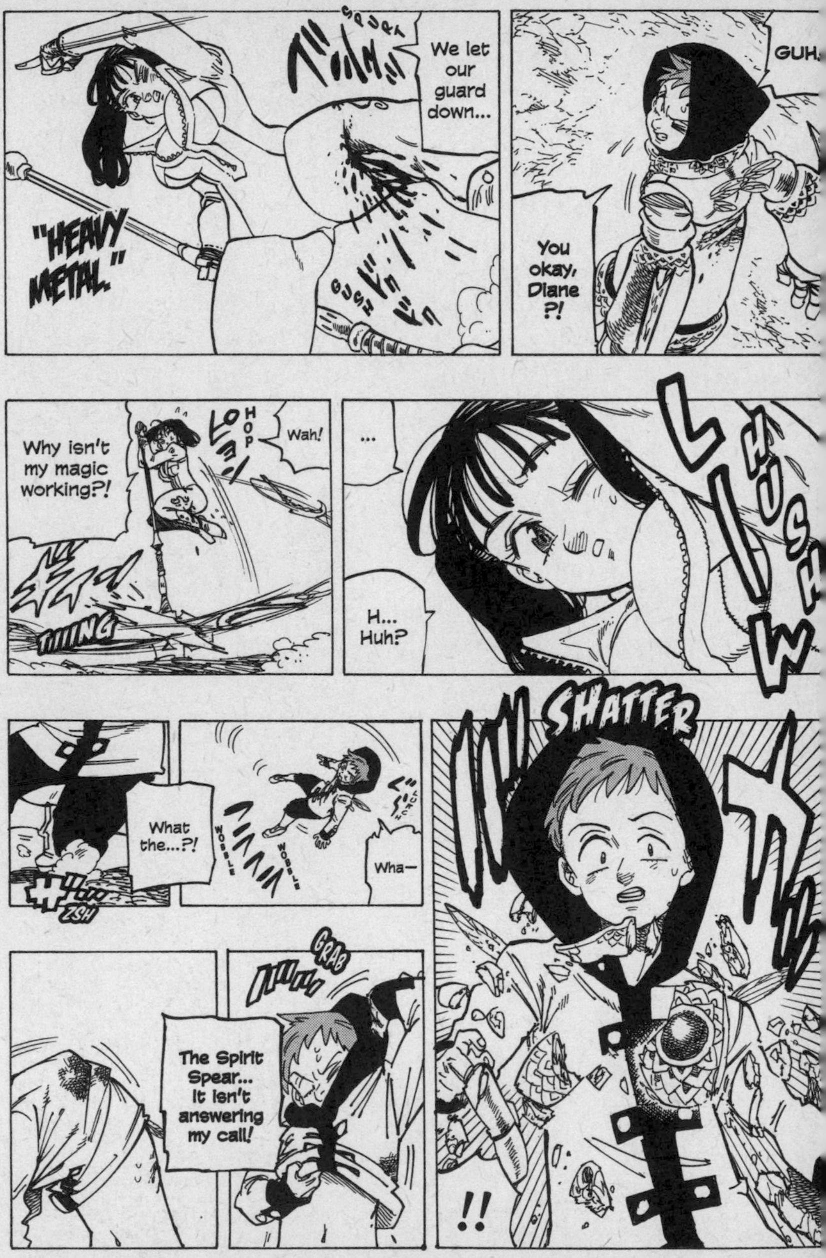

GUH.
You okay, Diane ?!
We let our guard down...
"HEAVY METAL."
...
H... Huh?
Wah!
HOP
Why isn't my magic working?!
TIIIING
SHATTER
!!
Wha–
WOBBLE
WOBBLE
What the...?!
ZSH
GRAB
The Spirit Spear... It isn't answering my call!

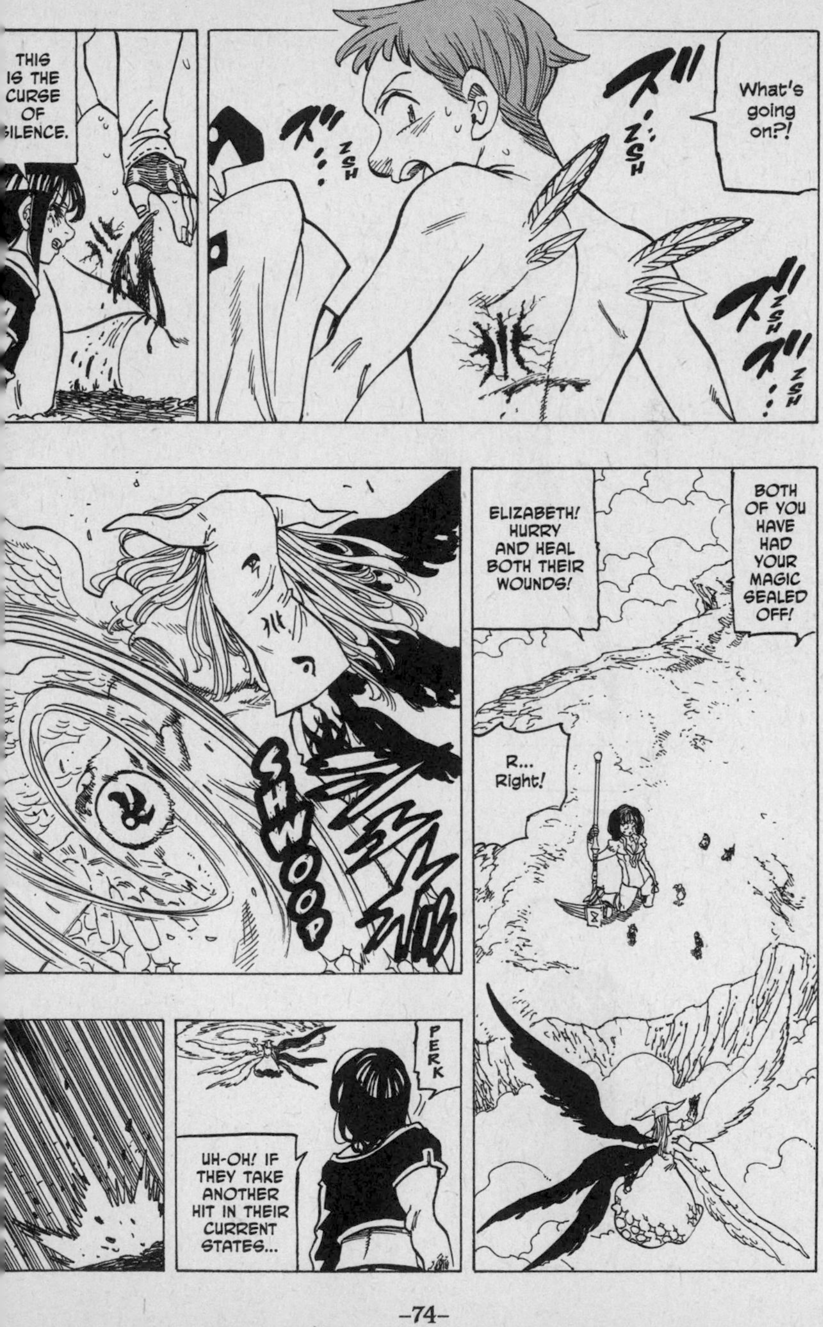
ZSH
What's going on?!
ZSH
ZSH
ZSH
THIS IS THE CURSE OF SILENCE.
BOTH OF YOU HAVE HAD YOUR MAGIC SEALED OFF!
ELIZABETH! HURRY AND HEAL BOTH THEIR WOUNDS!
R... Right!
SHWOOP
PERK
UH-OH! IF THEY TAKE ANOTHER HIT IN THEIR CURRENT STATES...

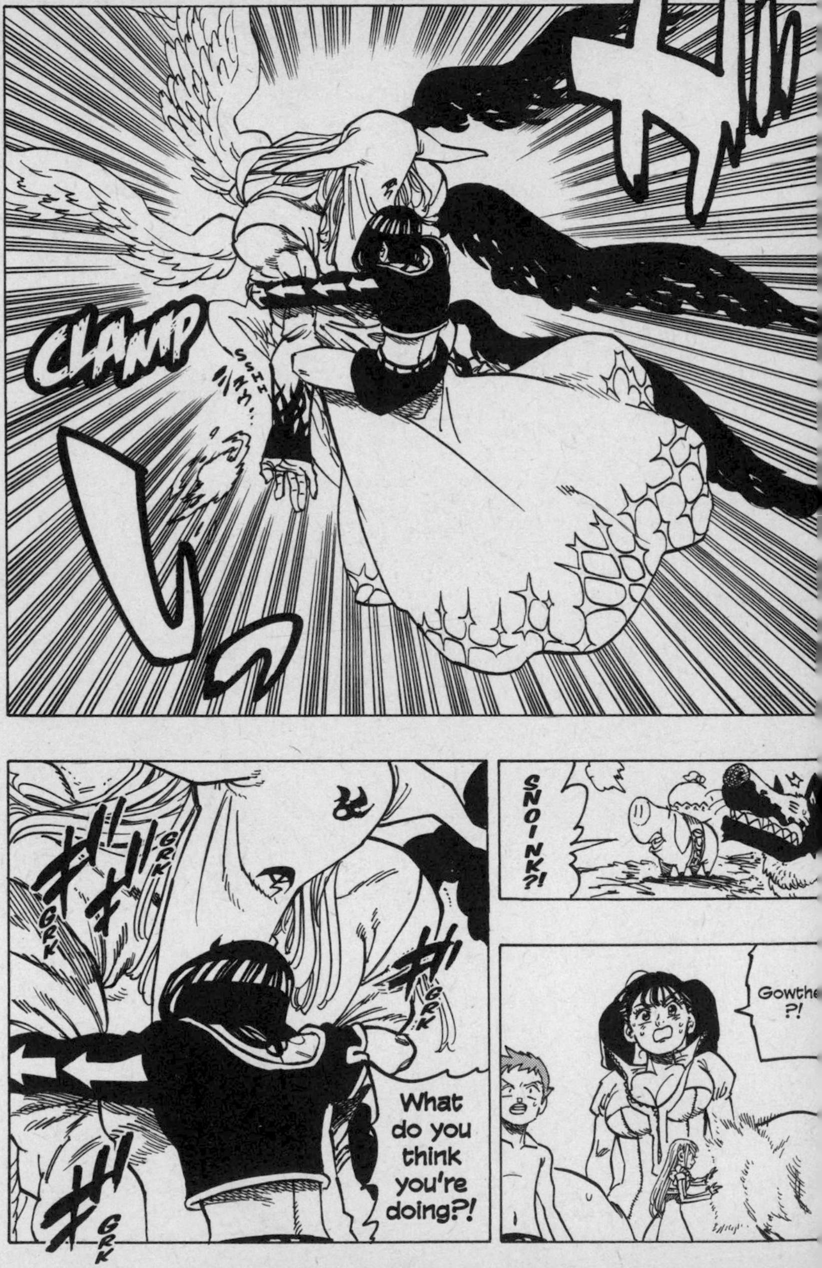
CLAMP
SSHH
SNOINK?!
Gowthe ?!
GRK
GRK
GRK
GRK
What do you think you're doing?!

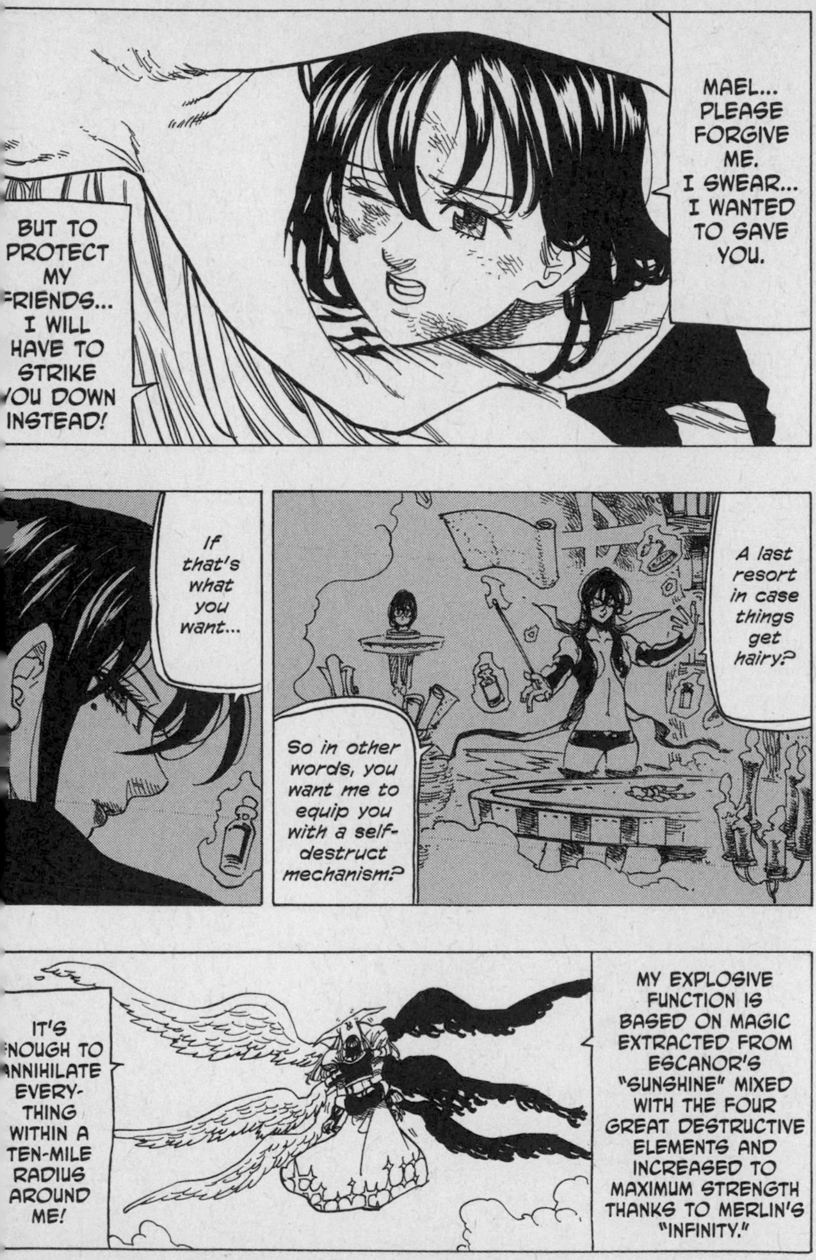
MAEL... PLEASE FORGIVE ME. I SWEAR... I WANTED TO SAVE YOU.
BUT TO PROTECT MY FRIENDS... I WILL HAVE TO STRIKE YOU DOWN INSTEAD!
A last resort in case things get hairy?
So in other words, you want me to equip you with a self-destruct mechanism?
If that's what you want...
MY EXPLOSIVE FUNCTION IS BASED ON MAGIC EXTRACTED FROM ESCANOR'S "SUNSHINE" MIXED WITH THE FOUR GREAT DESTRUCTIVE ELEMENTS AND INCREASED TO MAXIMUM STRENGTH THANKS TO MERLIN'S "INFINITY."
IT'S ENOUGH TO ANNIHILATE EVERY-THING WITHIN A TEN-MILE RADIUS AROUND ME!

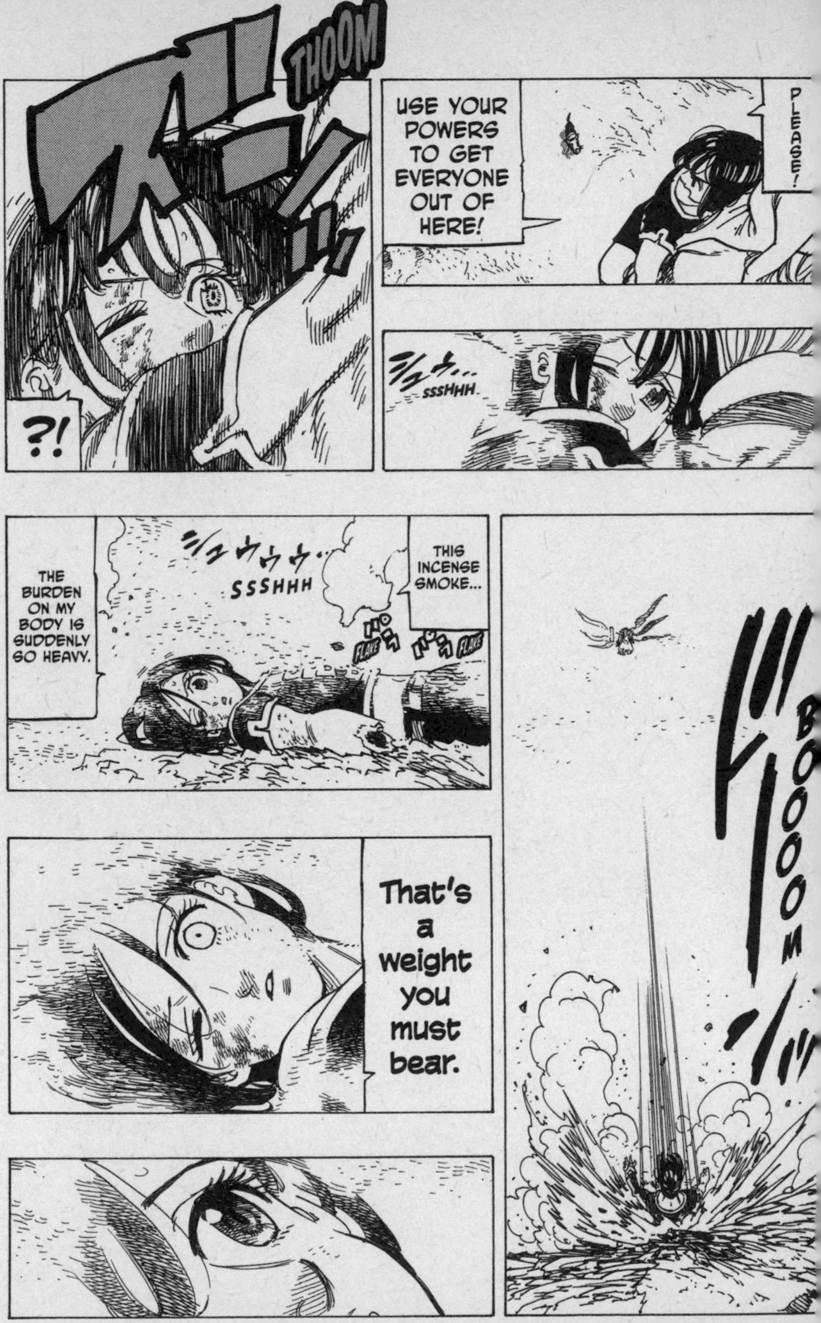
PLEASE!
USE YOUR POWERS TO GET EVERYONE OUT OF HERE!
SSSHHH
THOOM
?!
BOOOOOM
THIS INCENSE SMOKE...
SSSHHH
FLAKE
FLAKE
THE BURDEN ON MY BODY IS SUDDENLY SO HEAVY.
That's a weight you must bear.

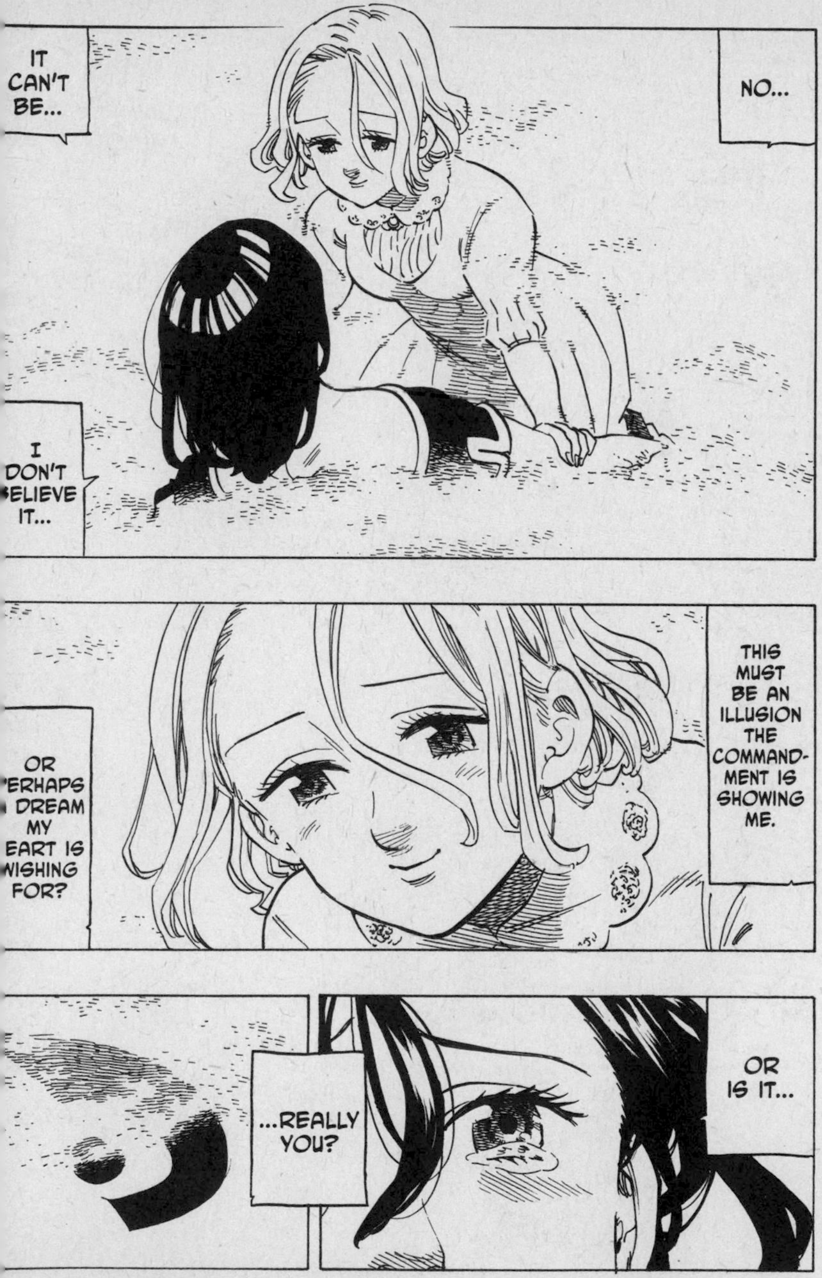
NO...
IT CAN'T BE...
I DON'T ELIEVE IT...
THIS MUST BE AN ILLUSION THE COMMAND-MENT IS SHOWING ME.
OR ERHAPS DREAM MY EART IS WISHING FOR?
OR IS IT...
...REALLY YOU?

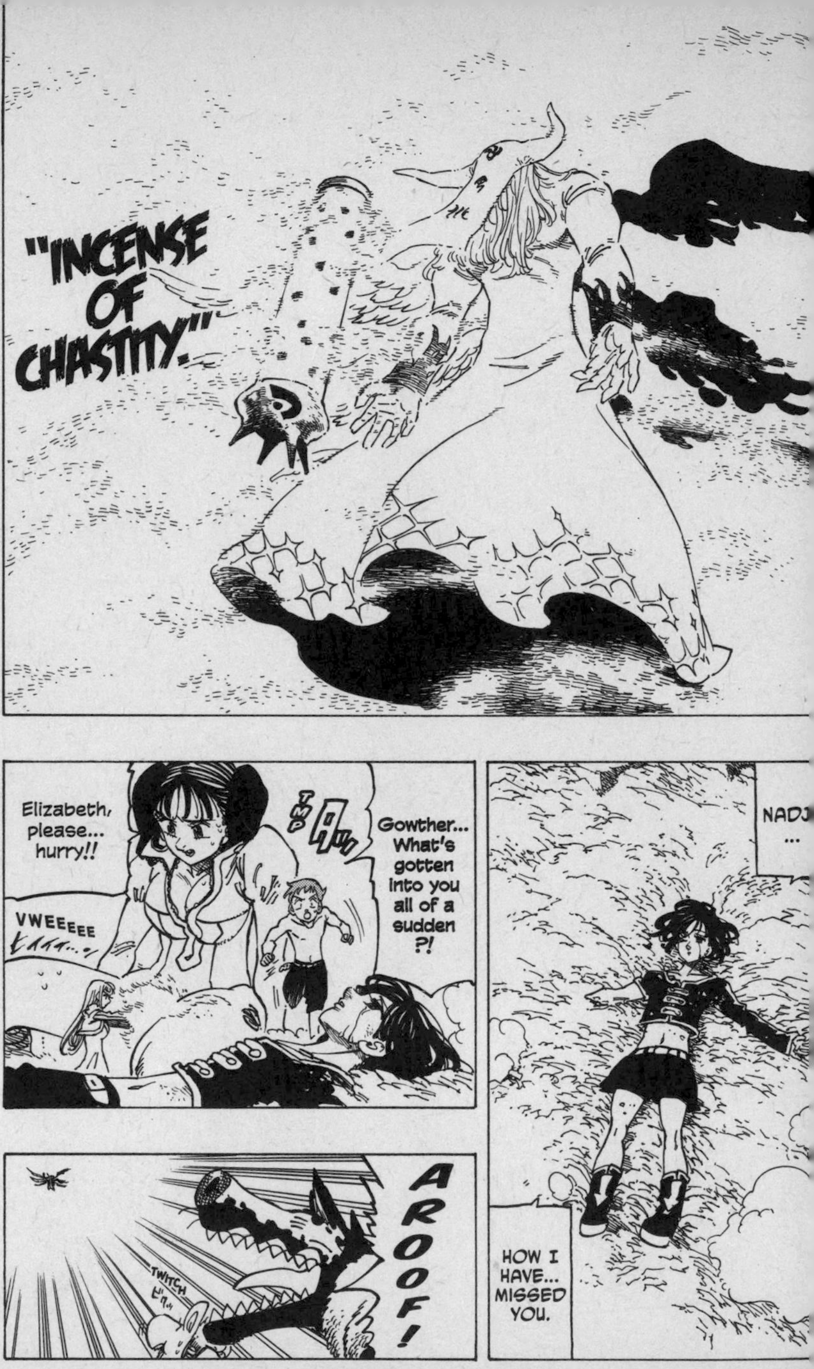
"INCENSE OF CHASTITY."
NADJ...
HOW I HAVE... MISSED YOU.
TMP
Gowther... What's gotten into you all of a sudden?!
Elizabeth, please... hurry!!
VWEEEEE
AROOF!
TWITCH

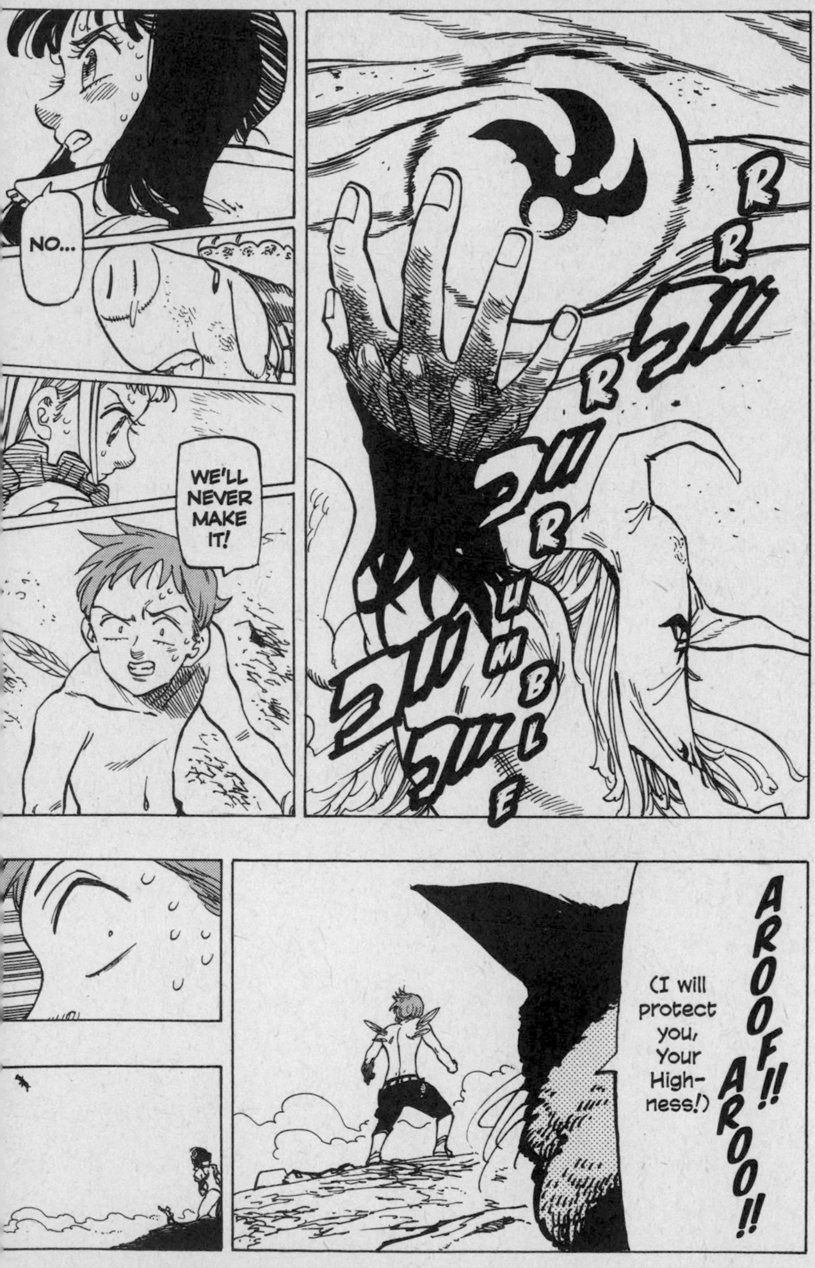
RRRR
RUMBLE
NO...
WE'LL NEVER MAKE IT!
AROOOF!! AROOO!!
(I will protect you, Your Highness!)

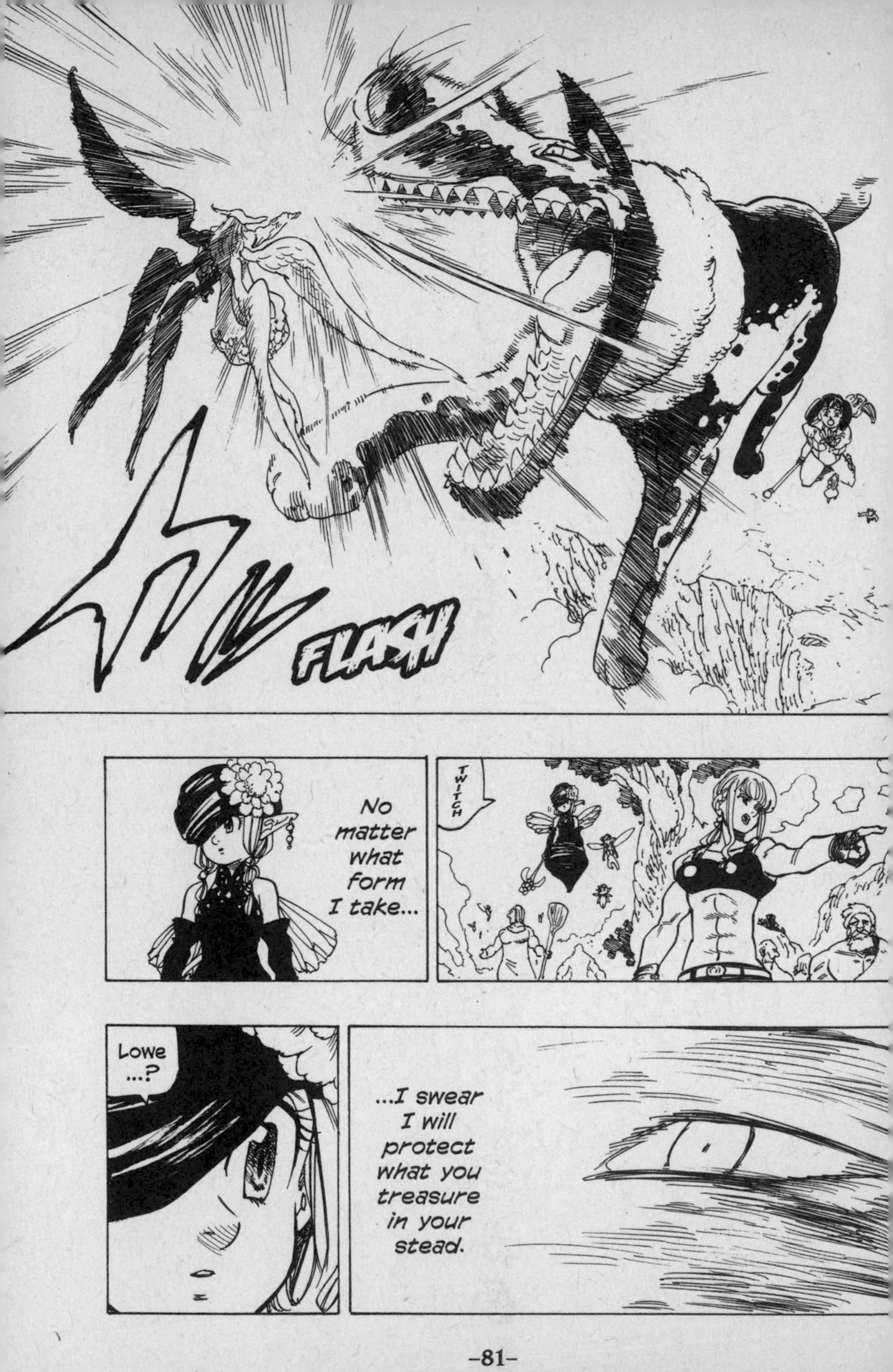
FLASH
TWITCH
No matter what form I take...
Lowe ...?
...I swear I will protect what you treasure in your stead.

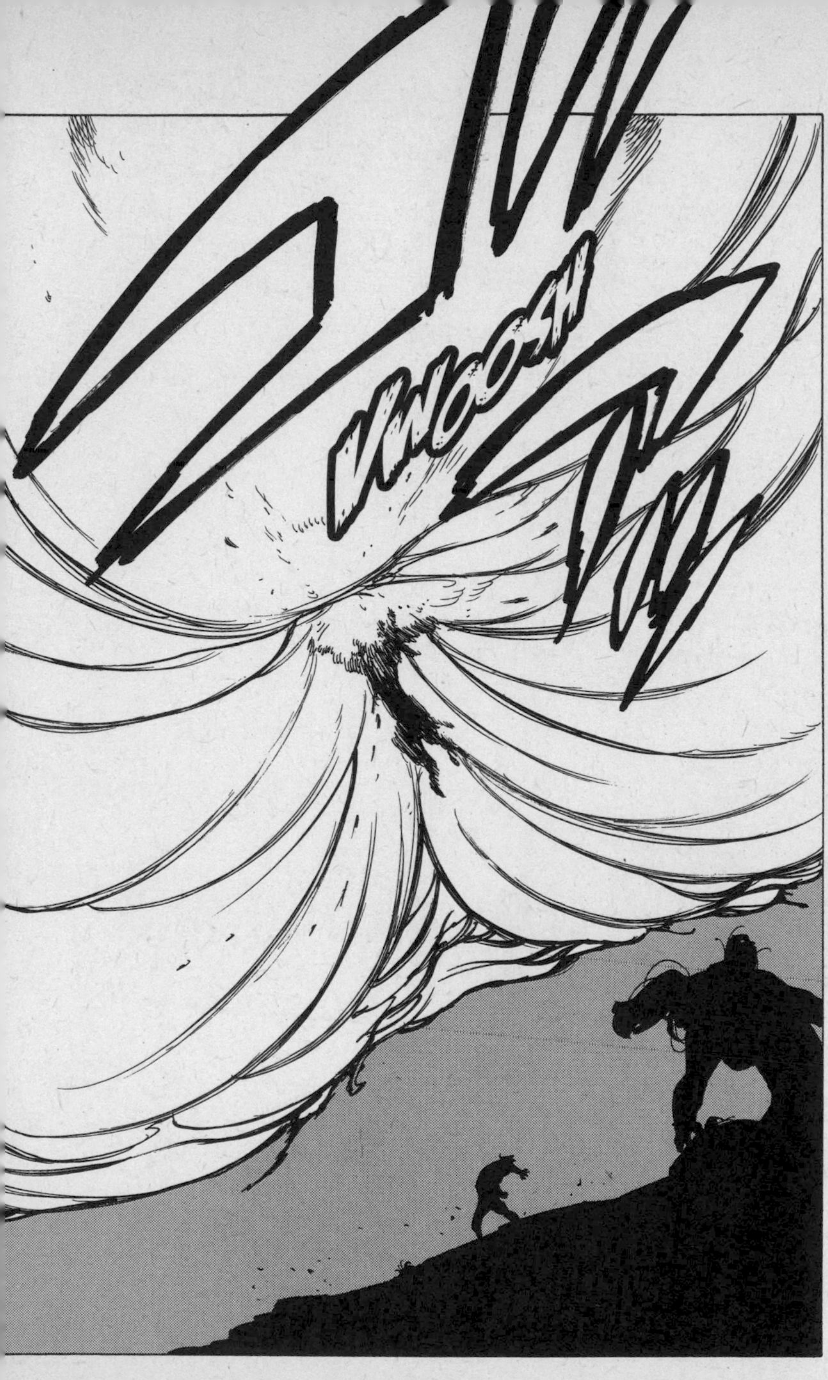
WOOSH

THE SEVEN DEADLY SINS

Chapter 280 - Collapse

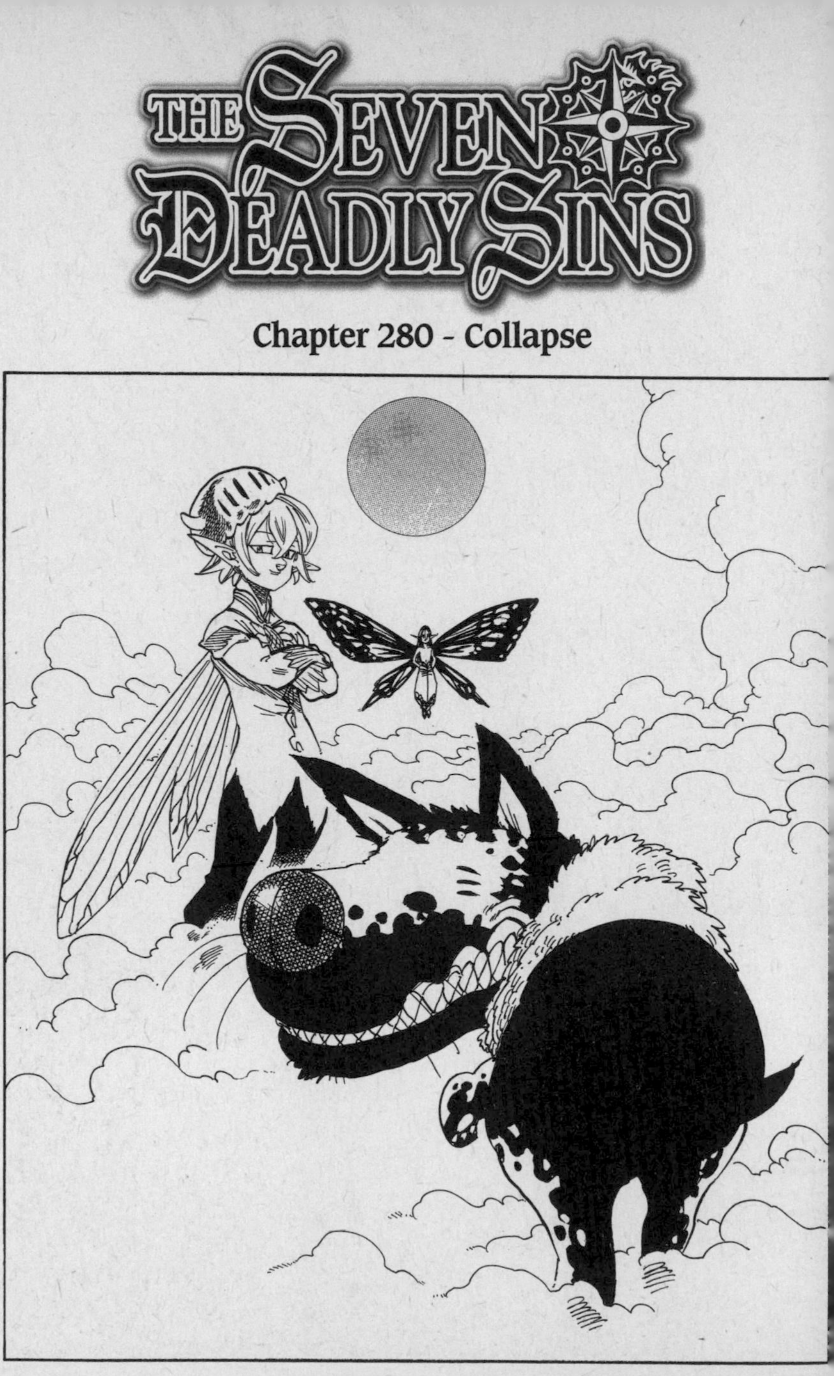

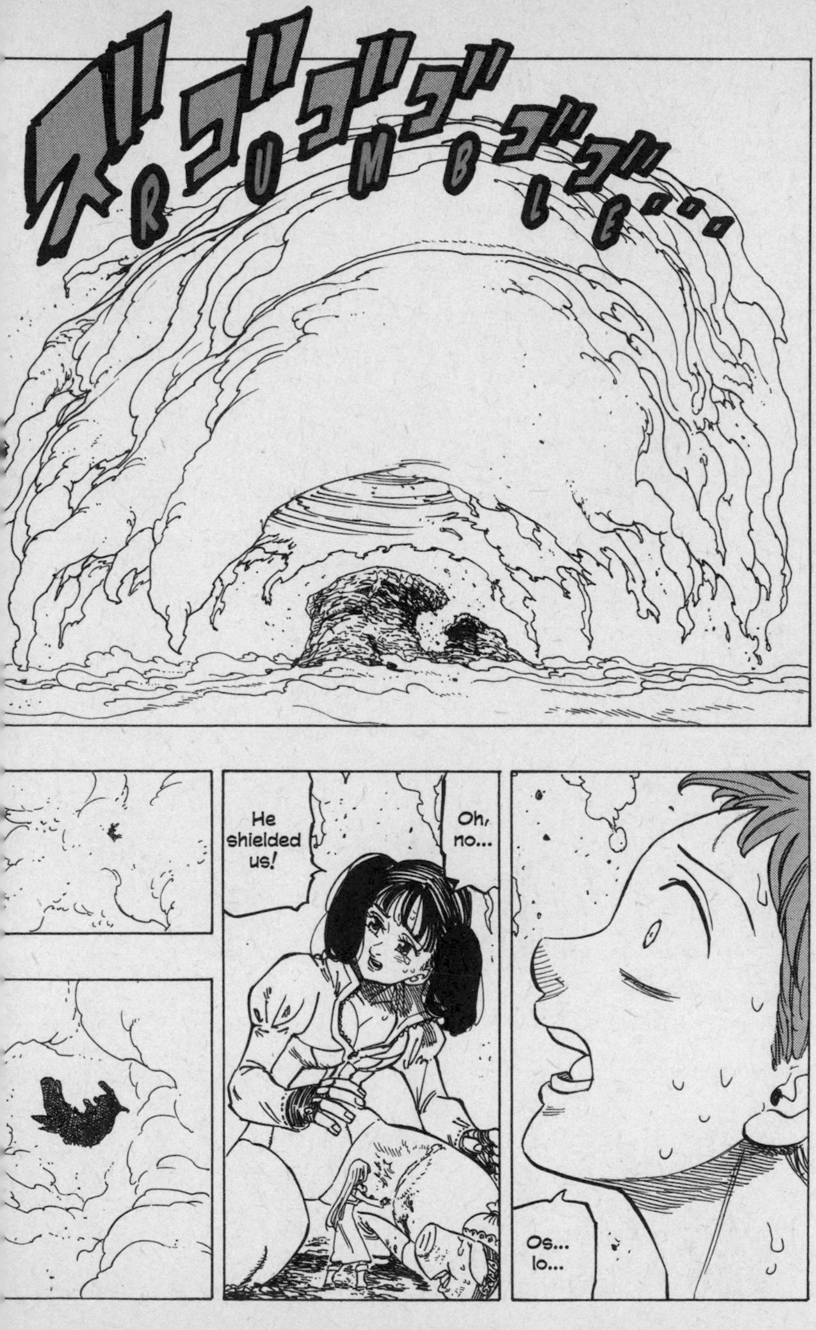
RUMBLE...
Os... lo...
Oh, no...
He shielded us!

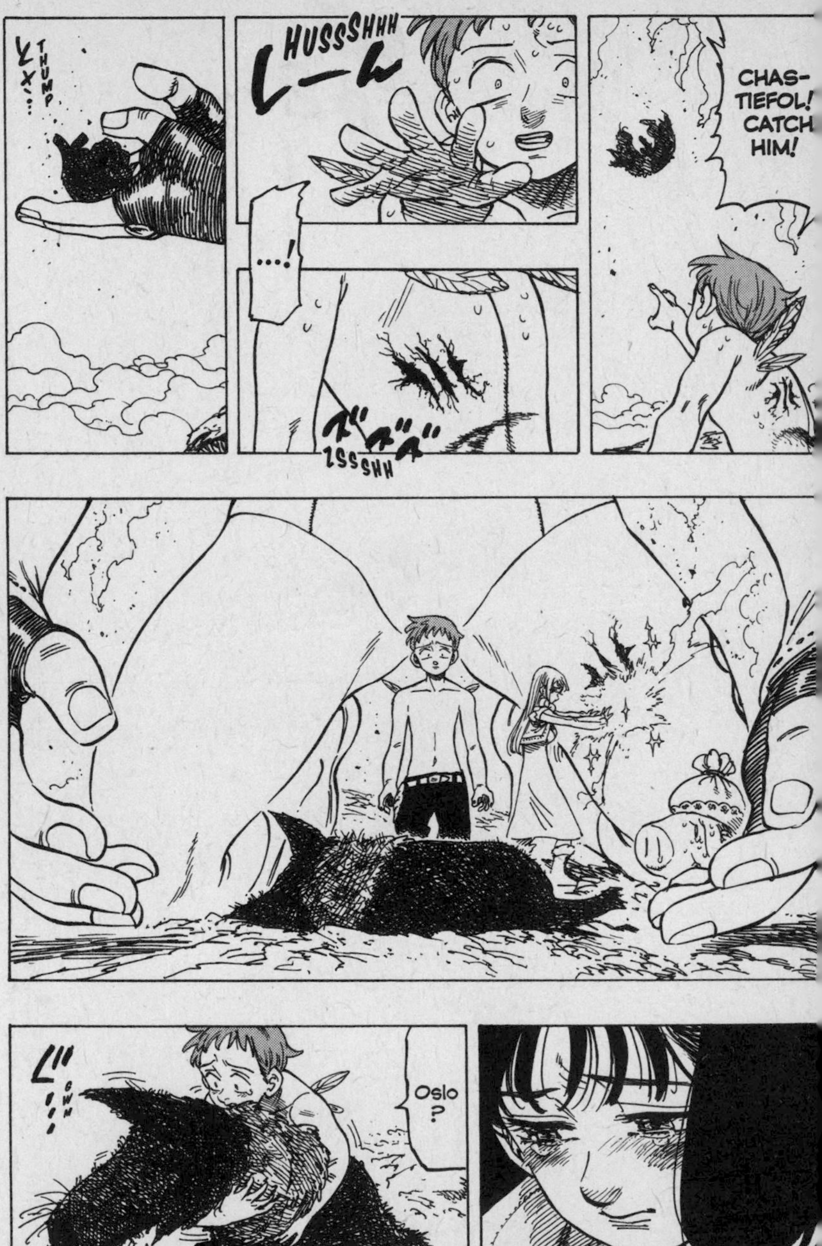
CHASTIEFOL! CATCH HIM!
HUSSSHHH
...!
ZSSSHH
THUMP
Oslo ?
GWN

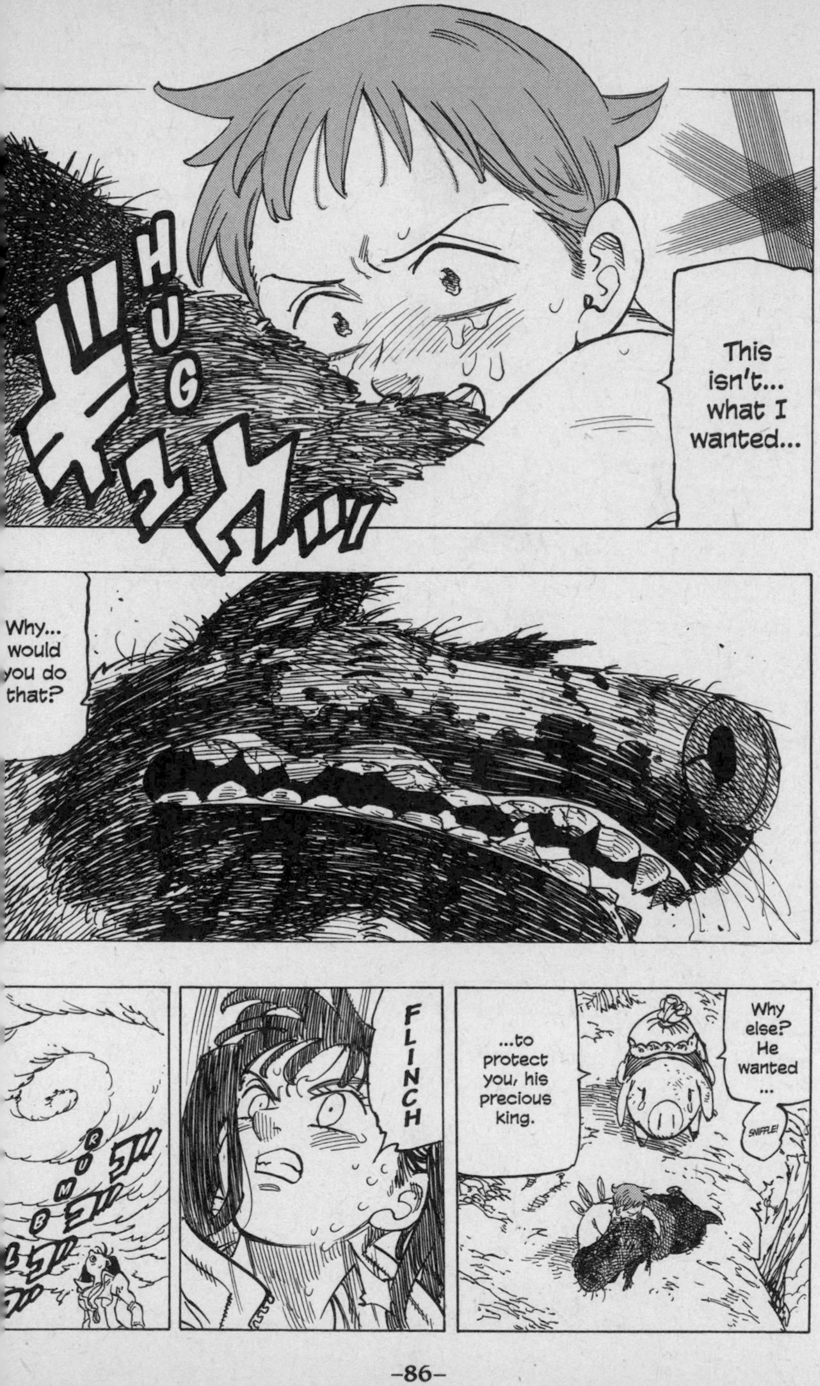
HUG
This isn't... what I wanted...
Why... would you do that?
Why else? He wanted ...
SNIFFLE!
...to protect you, his precious king.
FLINCH
RUMBLE

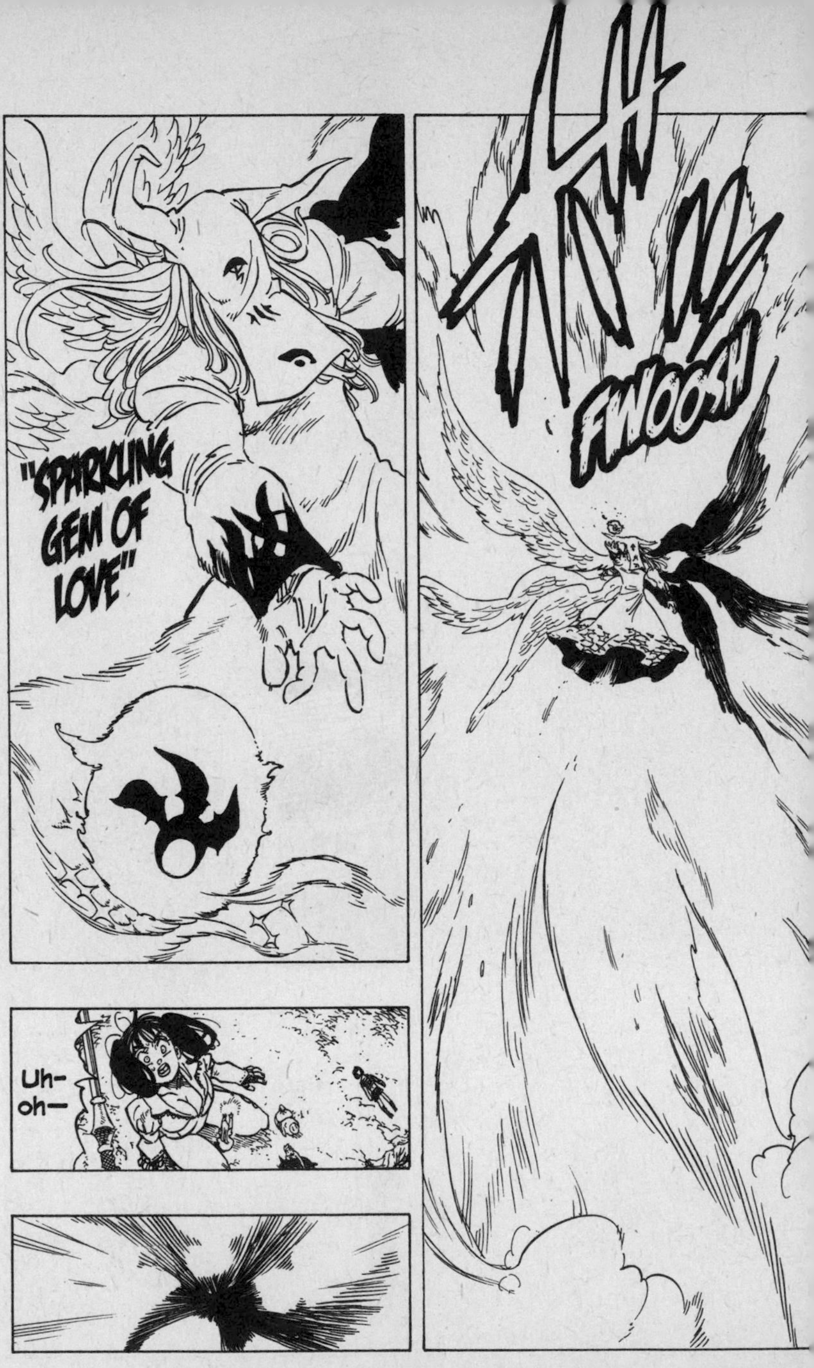
FWOOSH
"SPARKLING GEM OF LOVE"
Uh-oh—

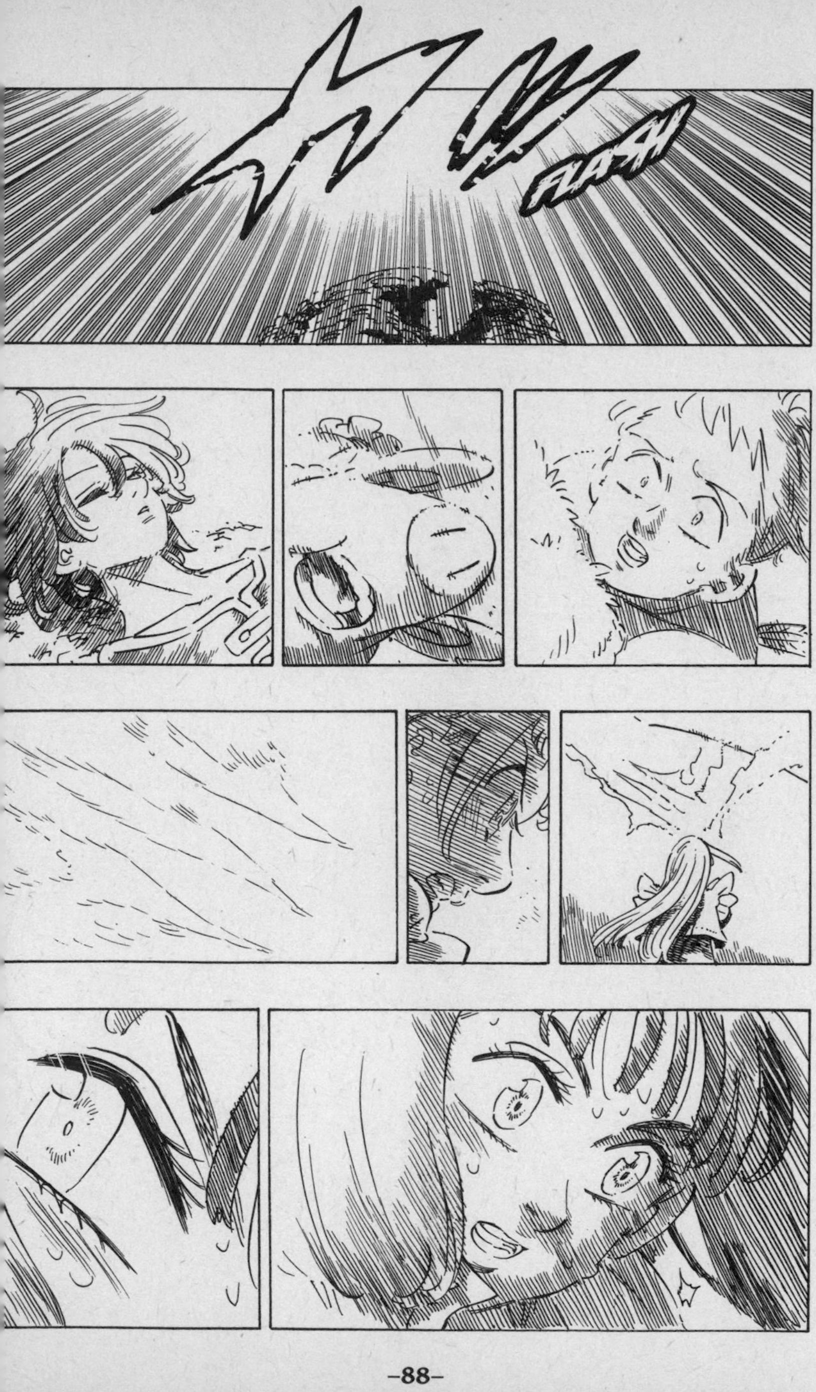
FLASH

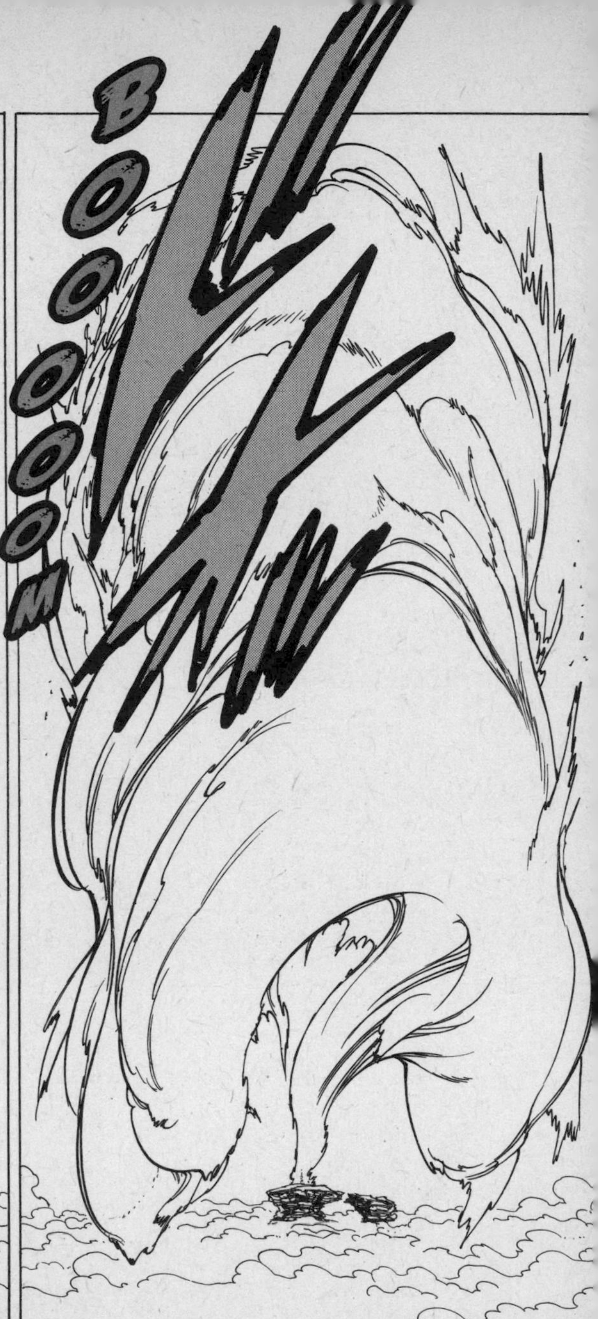
BOOOOOM

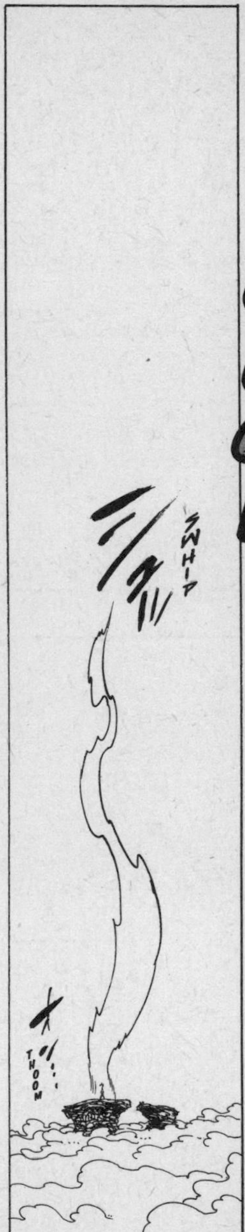
SWHIP
THOOM

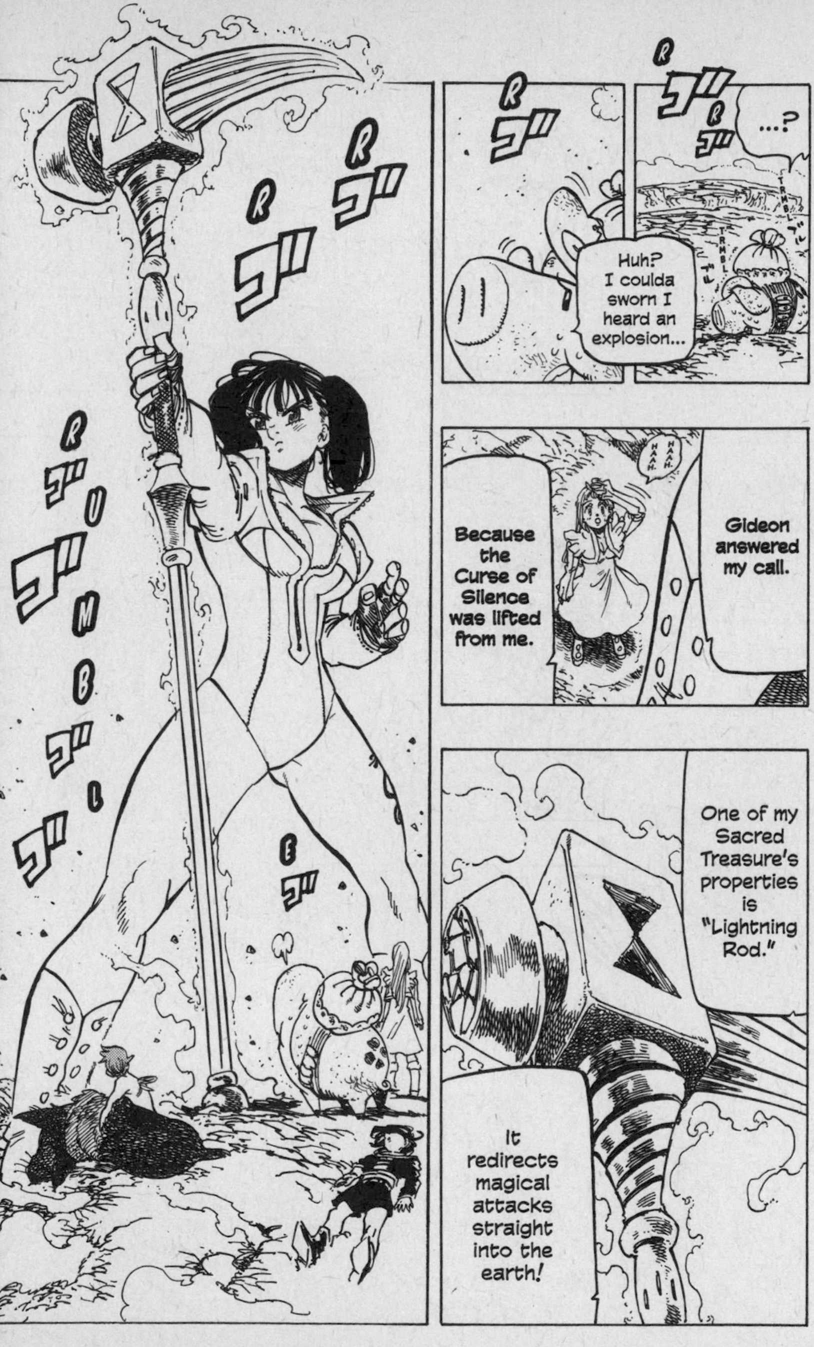
R
...?
TRMBL
TRMBL
R
Huh? I coulda sworn I heard an explosion...
Gideon answered my call.
HAAH. HAAH.
Because the Curse of Silence was lifted from me.
One of my Sacred Treasure's properties is "Lightning Rod."
It redirects magical attacks straight into the earth!
R
R
RUMBLE
E

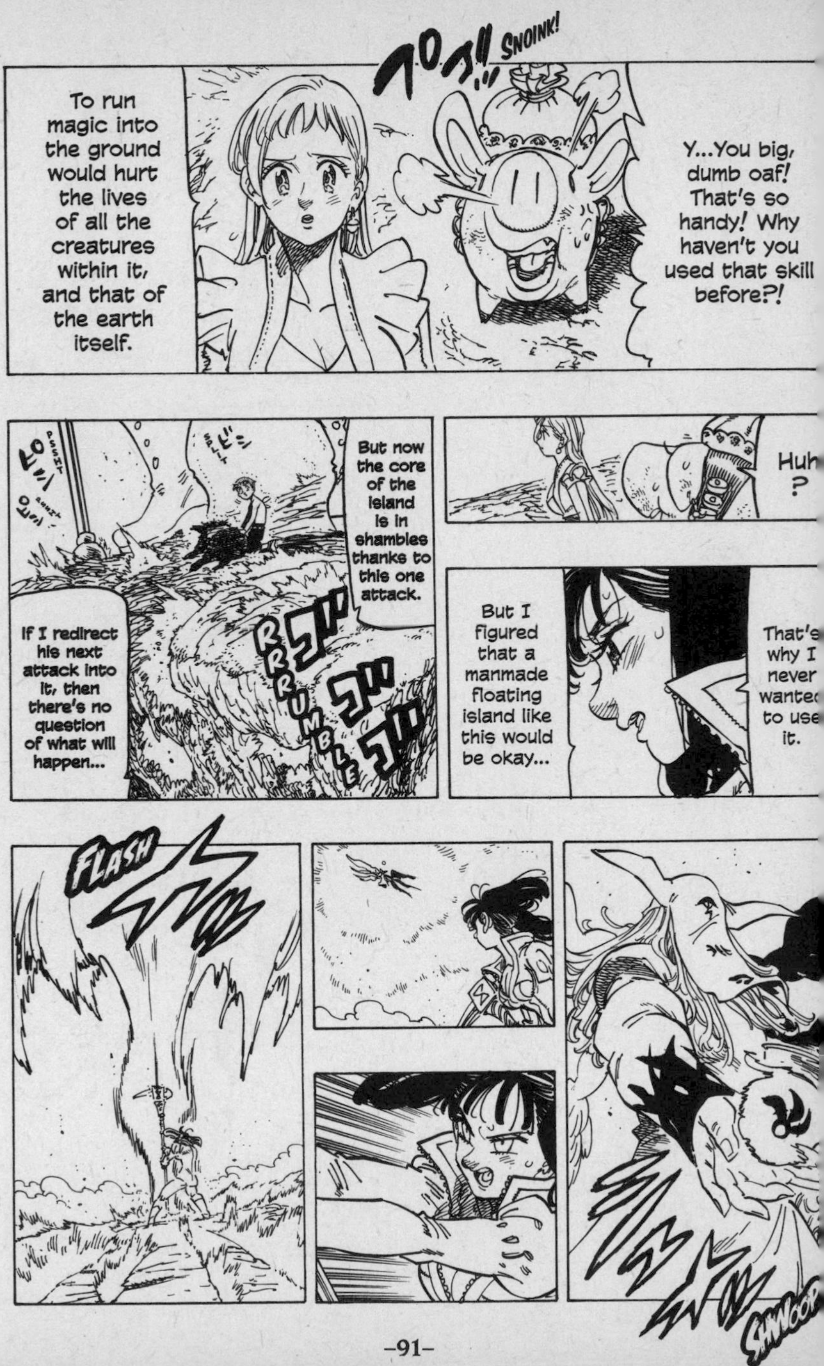
SNOINK!
Y...You big, dumb oaf! That's so handy! Why haven't you used that skill before?!
To run magic into the ground would hurt the lives of all the creatures within it, and that of the earth itself.
Huh?
That's why I never wanted to use it.
But I figured that a manmade floating island like this would be okay...
PSSHT
SPLIT
But now the core of the island is in shambles thanks to this one attack.
RRRUMBLE
If I redirect his next attack into it, then there's no question of what will happen...
SHWOOP
FLASH

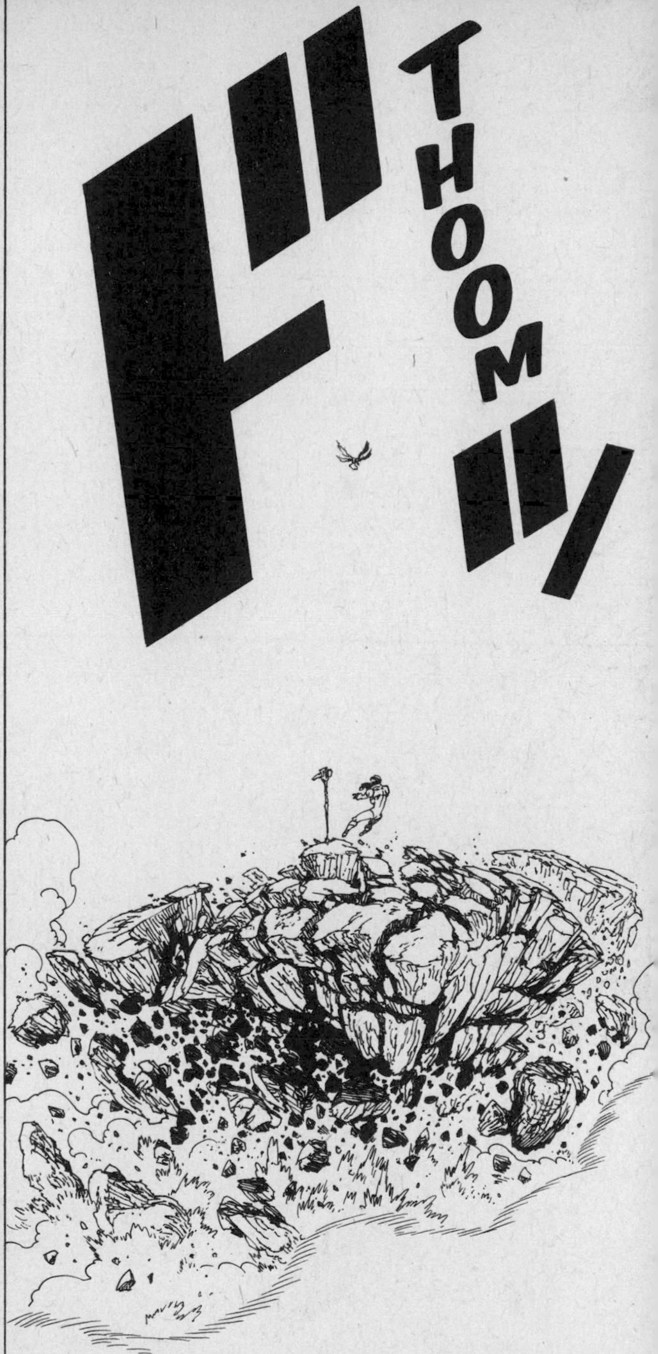
THOOM
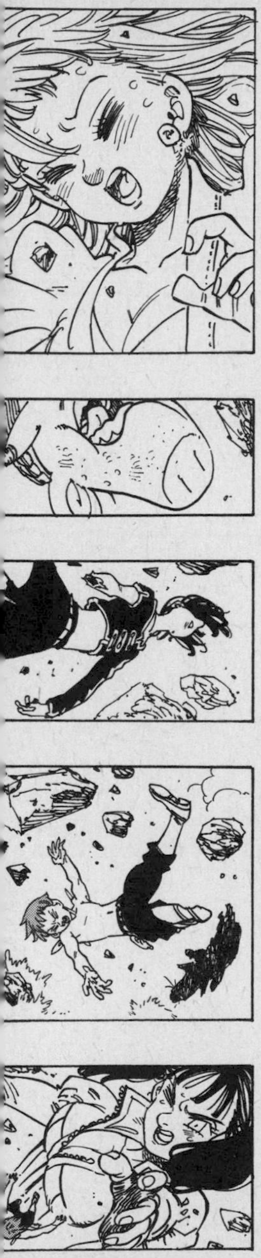

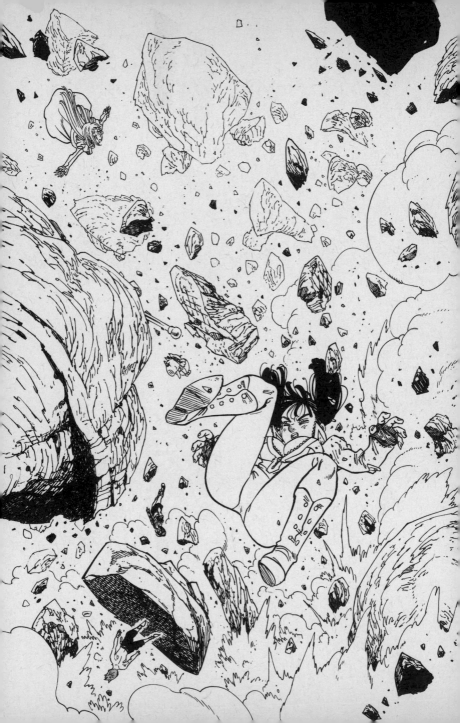

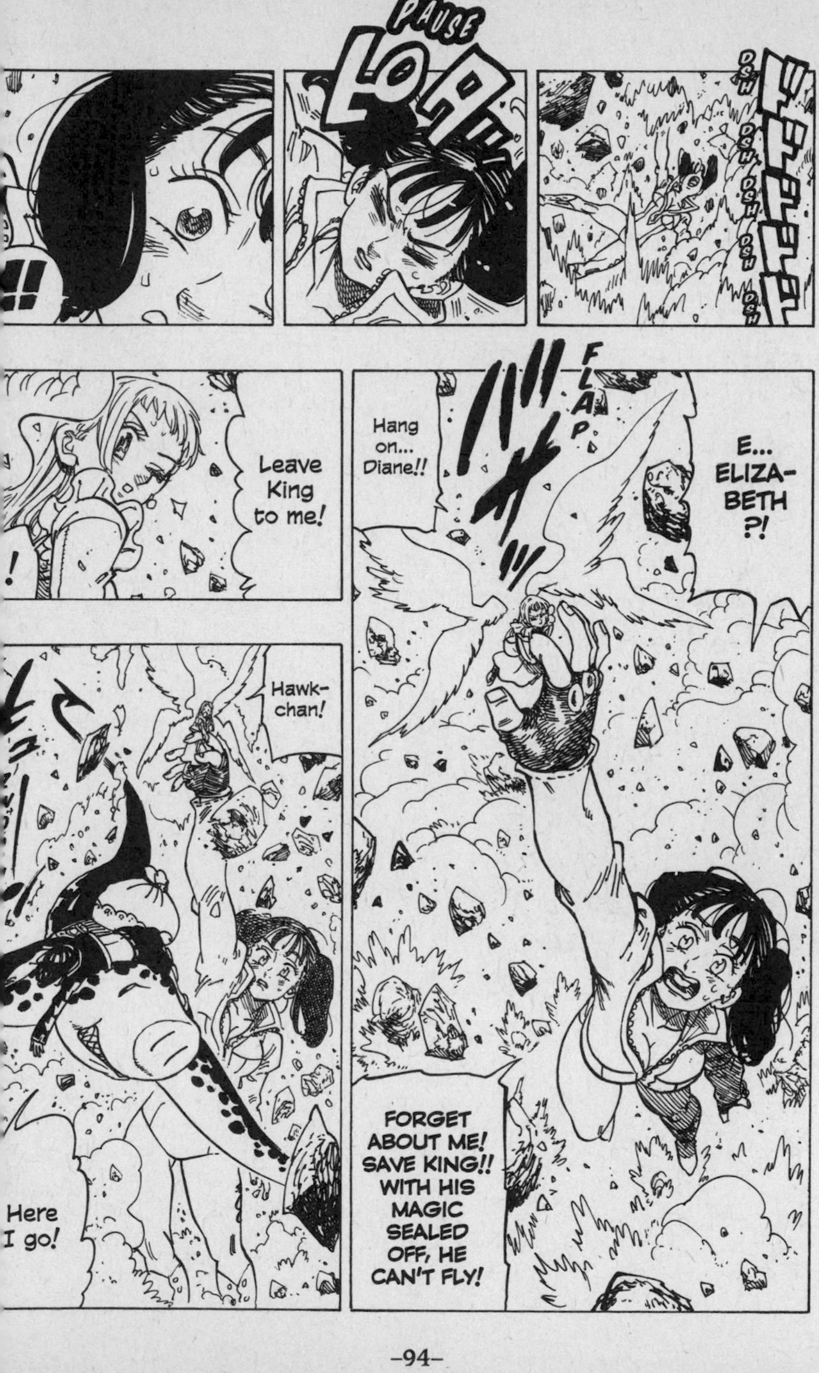
DSH DSH DSH DSH DSH
PAUSE
E... ELIZABETH?!
FLAP
Hang on... Diane!!
FORGET ABOUT ME! SAVE KING!! WITH HIS MAGIC SEALED OFF, HE CAN'T FLY!
Leave King to me!
Hawk-chan!
Here I go!

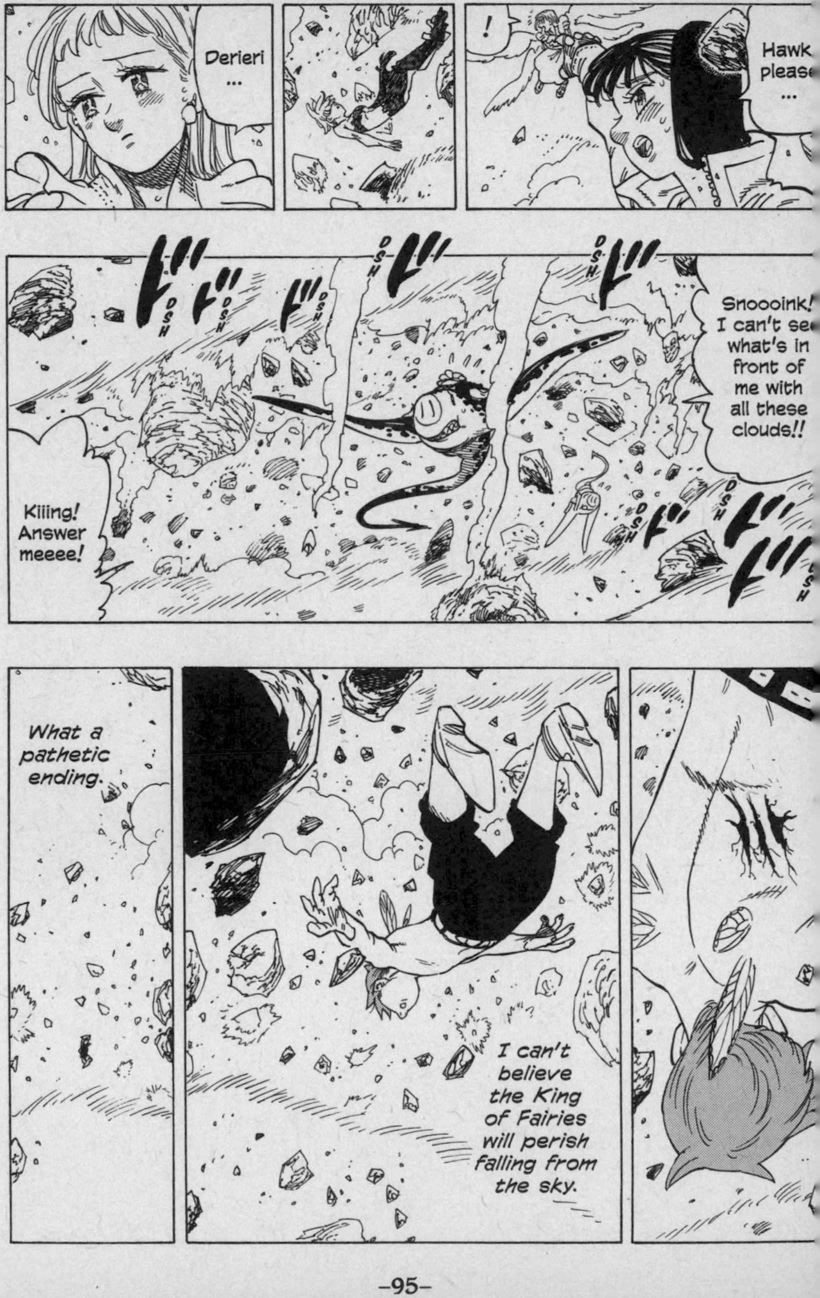
!
Hawk please ...
Derieri ...
Snoooink! I can't se what's in front of me with all these clouds!!
DSH
DSH
DSH
DSH
DSH
DSH
DSH
DSH
DSH
Kiiing! Answer meeee!
I can't believe the King of Fairies will perish falling from the sky.
What a pathetic ending.

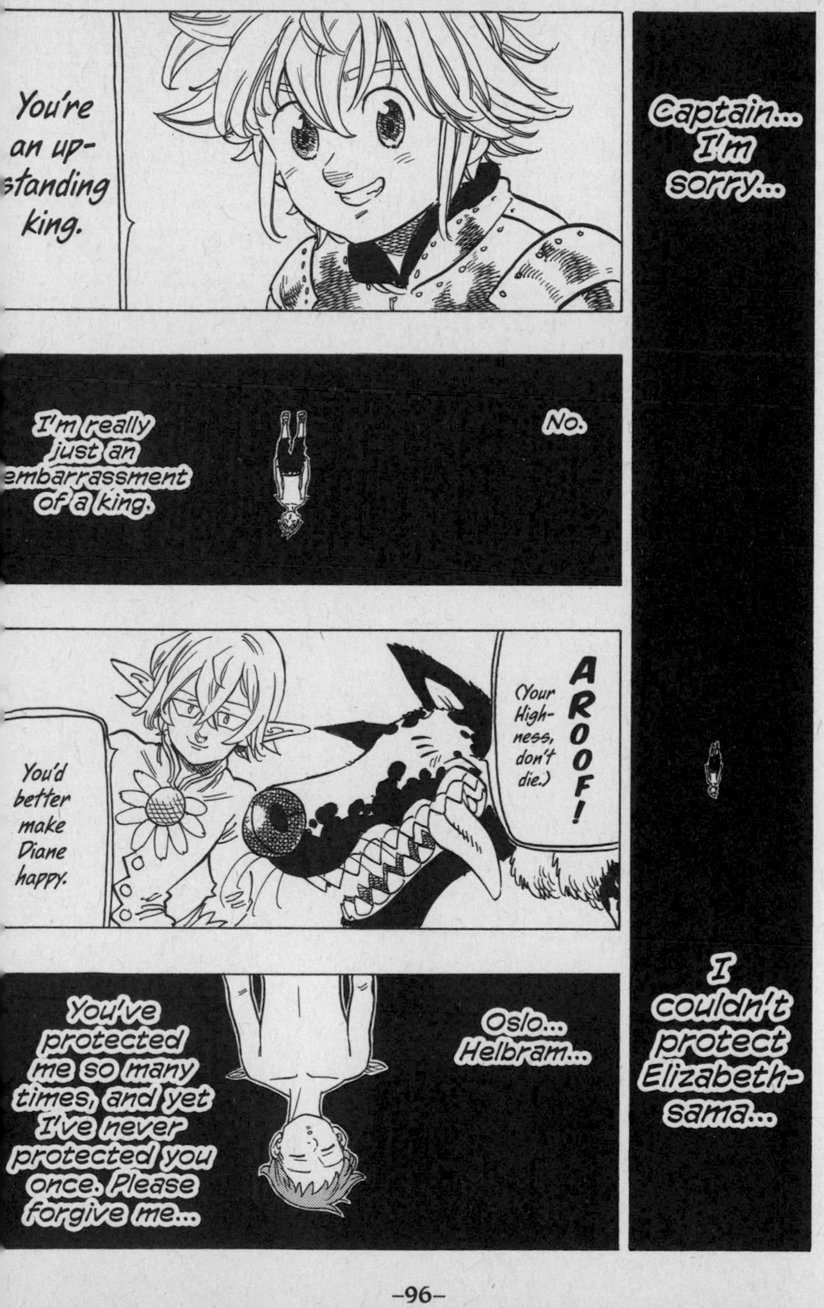
Captain... I'm sorry...
I couldn't protect Elizabeth-sama...
You're an up-standing king.
No.
I'm really just an embarrassment of a king.
AROOF!
(Your Highness, don't die.)
You'd better make Diane happy.
Oslo... Helbram...
You've protected me so many times, and yet I've never protected you once. Please forgive me...

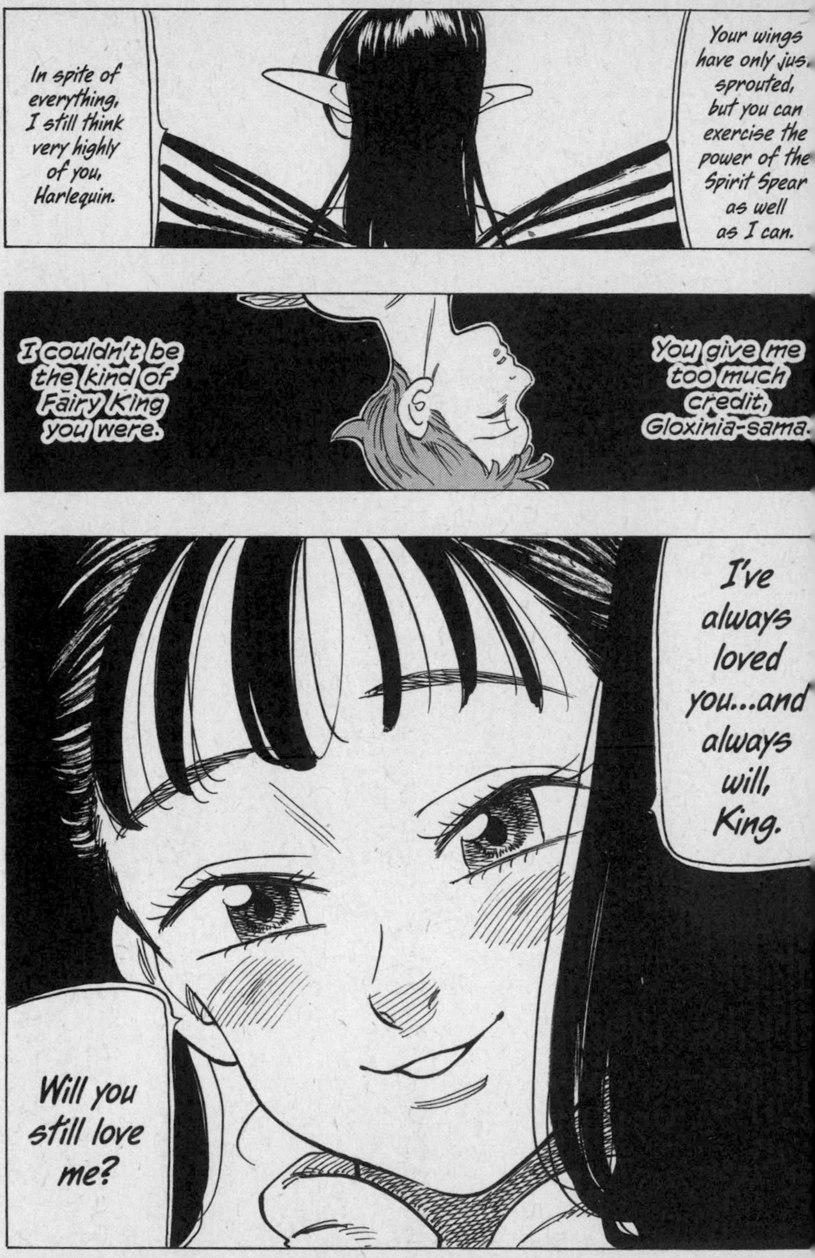

Your wings have only jus sprouted, but you can exercise the power of the Spirit Spear as well as I can.
In spite of everything, I still think very highly of you, Harlequin.
You give me too much credit, Gloxinia-sama.
I couldn't be the kind of Fairy King you were.
I've always loved you...and always will, King.
Will you still love me?

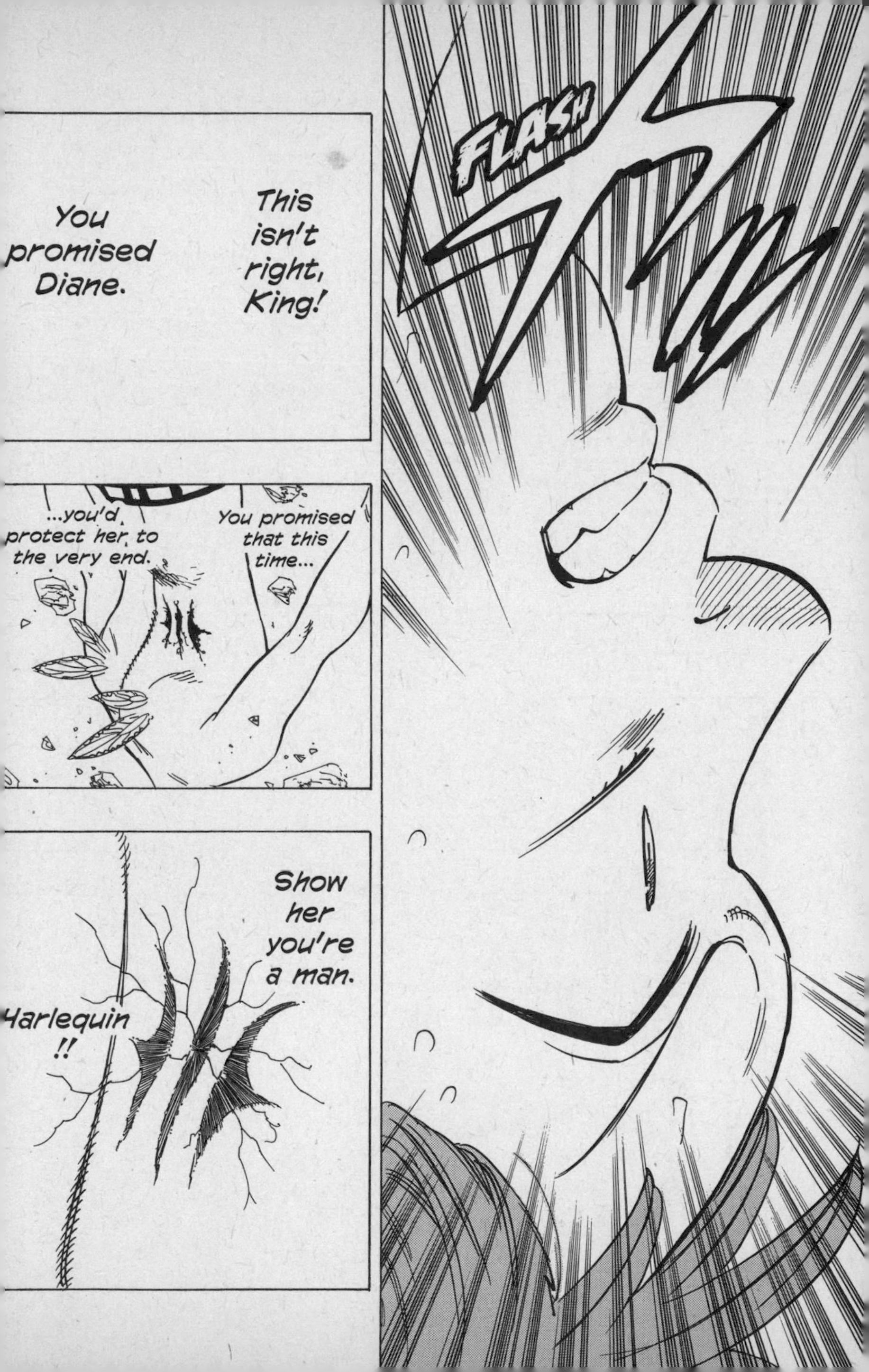
FLASH
This isn't right, King!
You promised Diane.
You promised that this time...
...you'd protect her to the very end.
Show her you're a man.
Harlequin!!

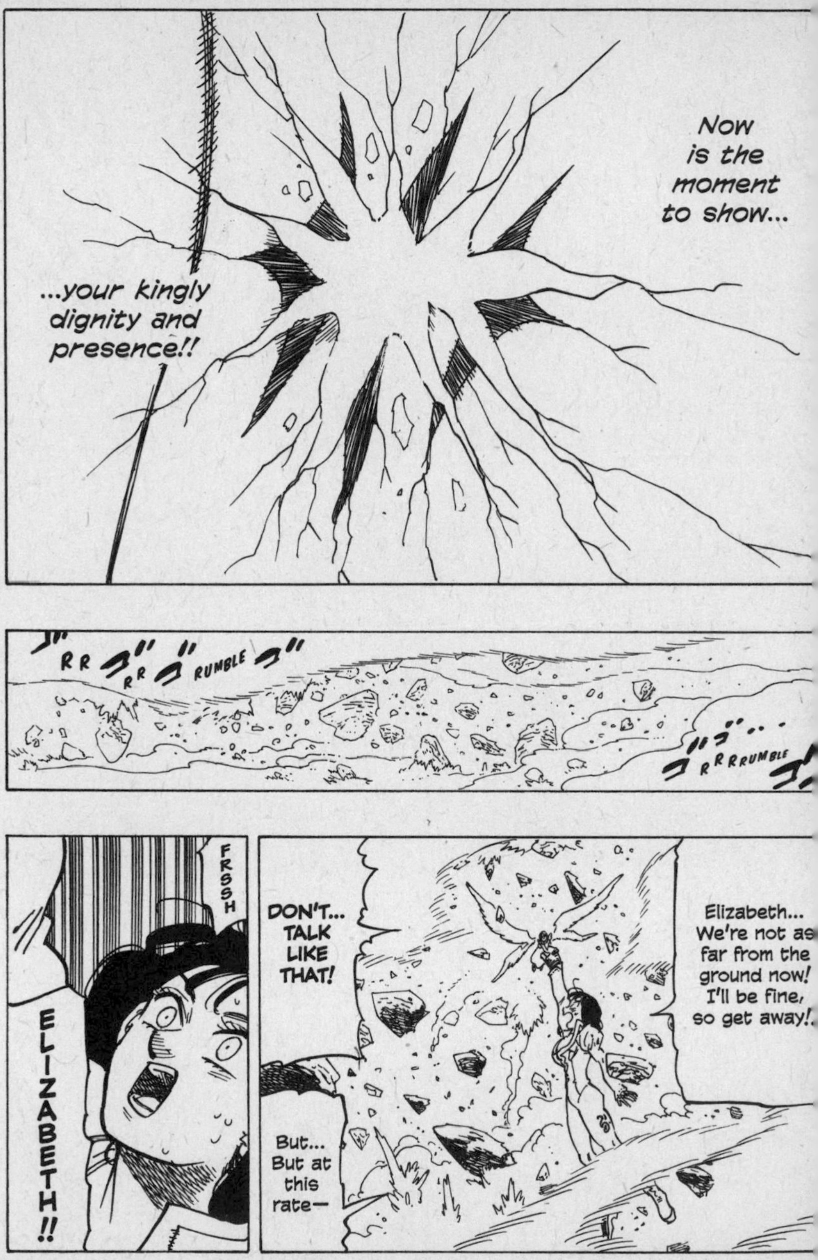
Now is the moment to show...
...your kingly dignity and presence!!
RRRRUMBLE
RR RR RUMBLE
Elizabeth... We're not as far from the ground now! I'll be fine, so get away!.
DON'T... TALK LIKE THAT!
But... But at this rate—
FRSSH
ELIZABETH!!

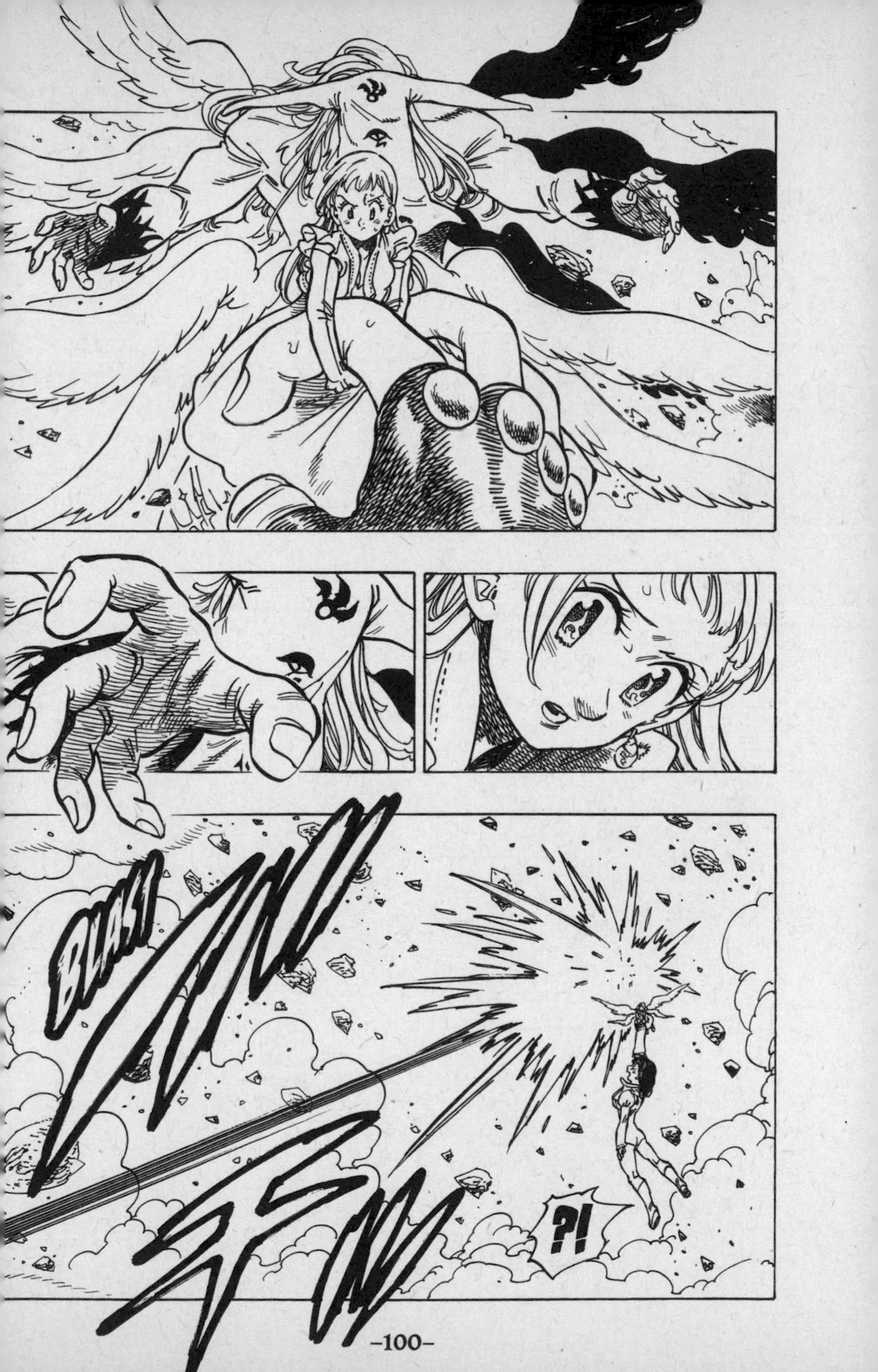
BLAST
?!

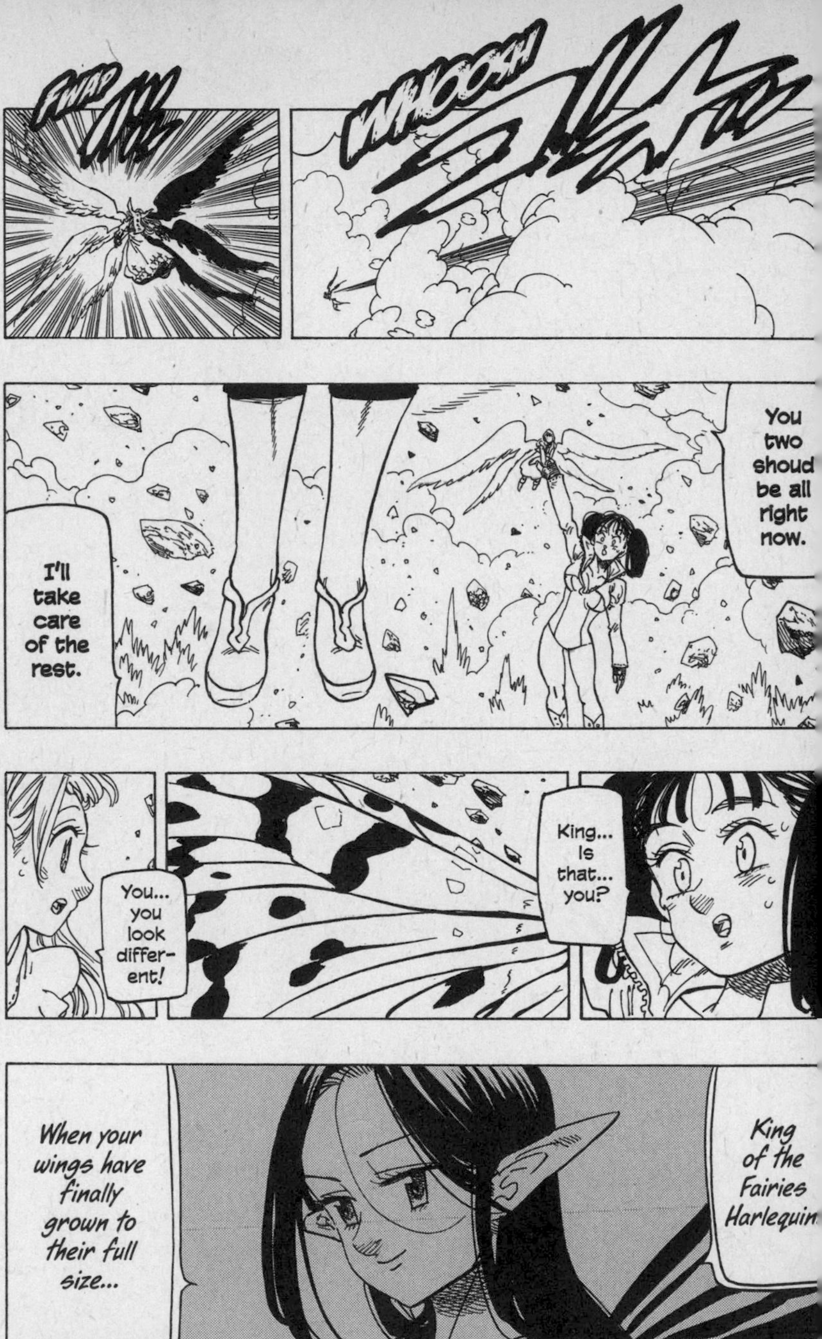
WHOOSH
FWAP
You two shoud be all right now.
I'll take care of the rest.
King... Is that... you?
You... you look different!
King of the Fairies Harlequin
When your wings have finally grown to their full size...

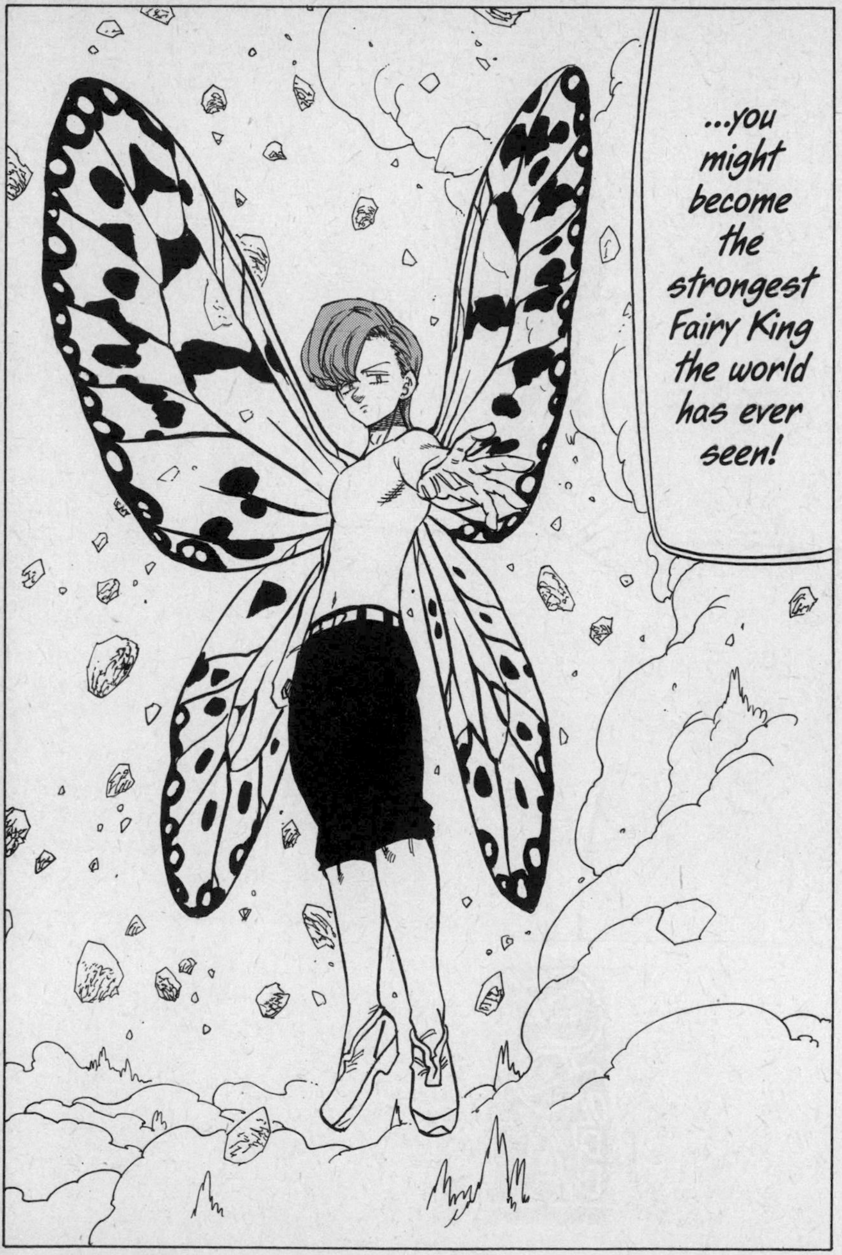
...you might become the strongest Fairy King the world has ever seen!

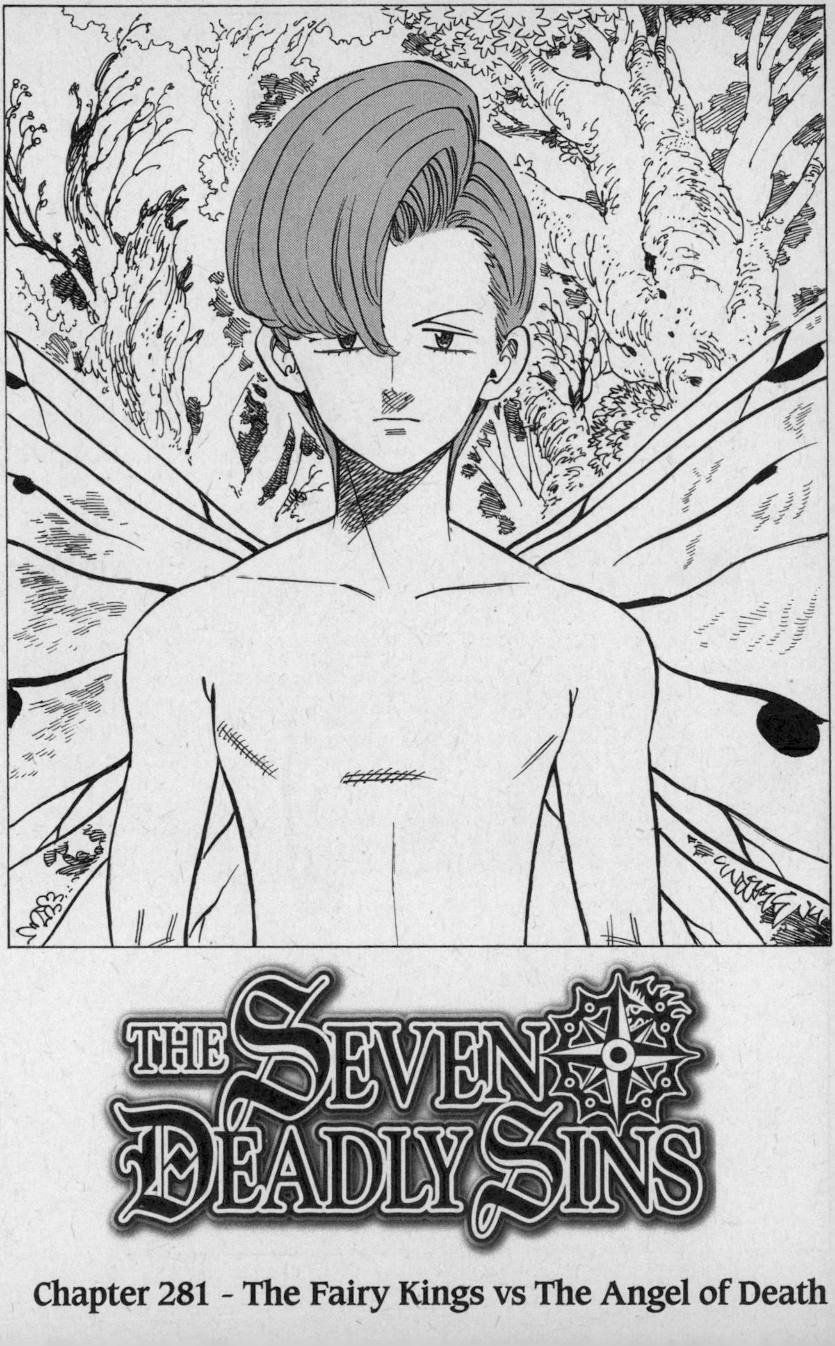

THE SEVEN DEADLY SINS

Chapter 281 - The Fairy Kings vs The Angel of Death

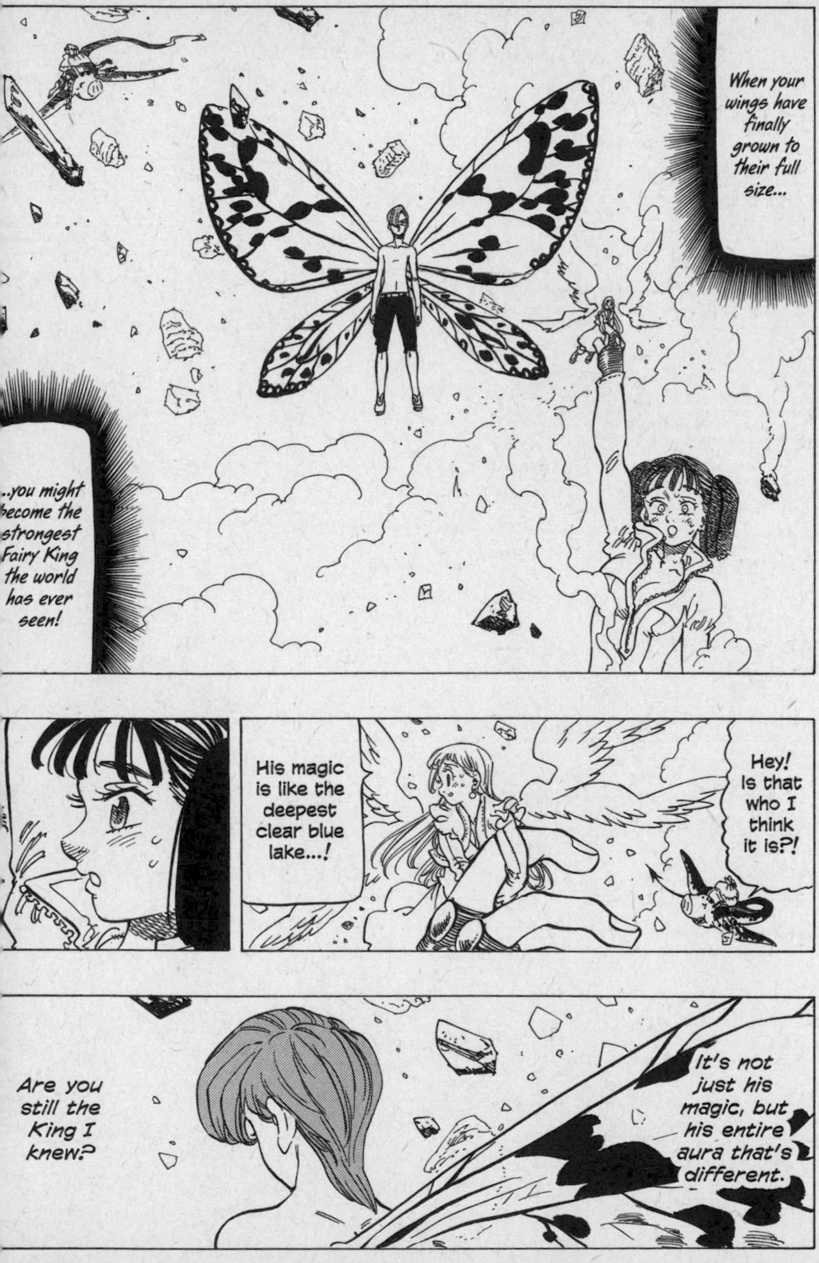
When your wings have finally grown to their full size...
..you might become the strongest Fairy King the world has ever seen!
Hey! Is that who I think it is?!
His magic is like the deepest clear blue lake...!
It's not just his magic, but his entire aura that's different.
Are you still the King I knew?

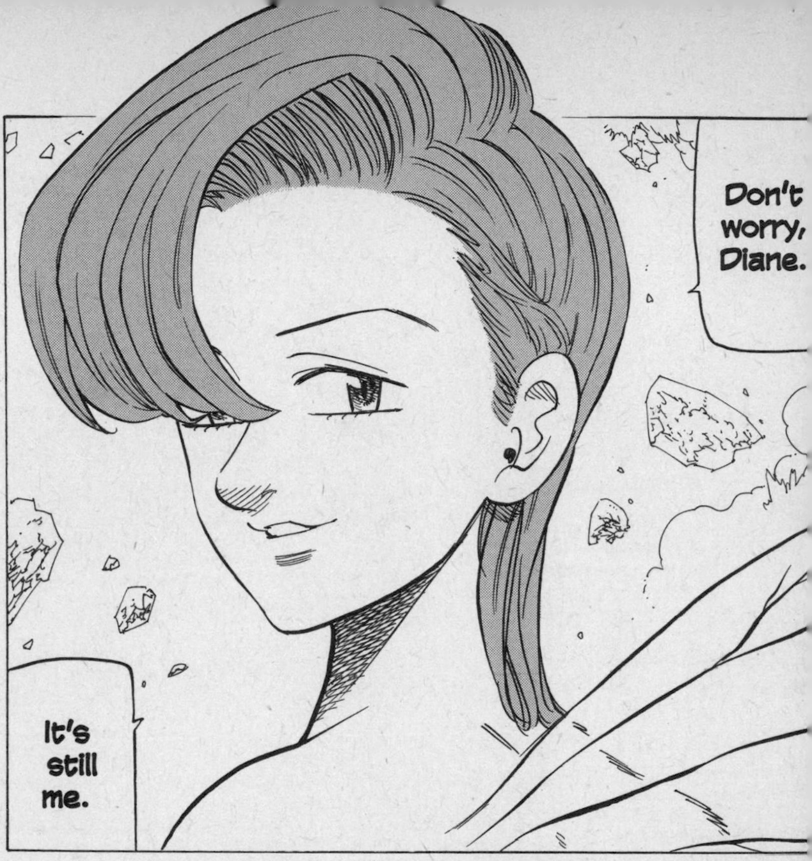
Don't worry, Diane.
It's still me.

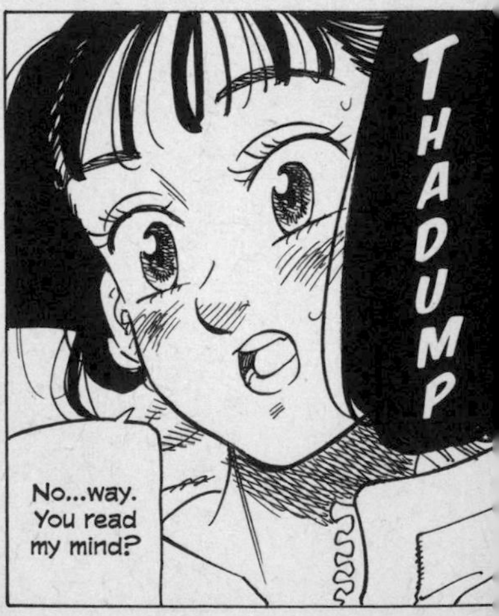
THADUMP
No...way. You read my mind?

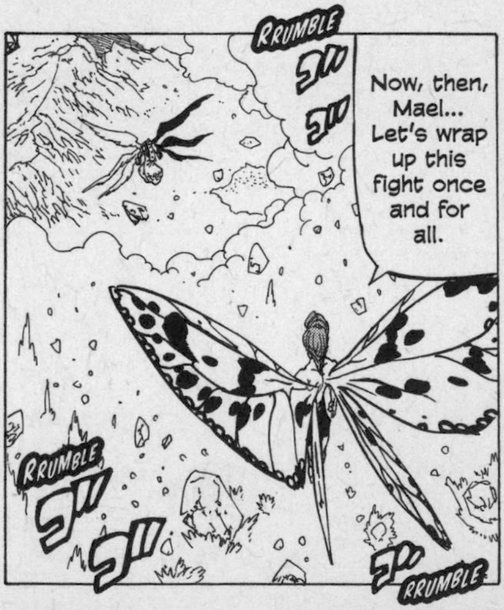
RRUMBLE
Now, then, Mael... Let's wrap up this fight once and for all.
RRUMBLE
RRUMBLE

DON'T INTERFERE:
MY SINS... CANNOT BE FORGIVEN.
WHAT HAVE I DONE? WHAT HAVE I DONE...
I HATE MYSELF.
NOW FEEL THE HUMILIATION... AND PAIN I HAVE FELT.
STAY OUT OF THIS.
ELIZA-BETH.
ELIZA-BETH...
ELIZA-BETH.
I HATE YOU.
WHY ME?
I WILL ONCE AGAIN... MAKE US WHOLE.
A stream of curses keeps flowing out of him.
He's chattier than I thought.
Elizabeth, did you hear anything?
No.

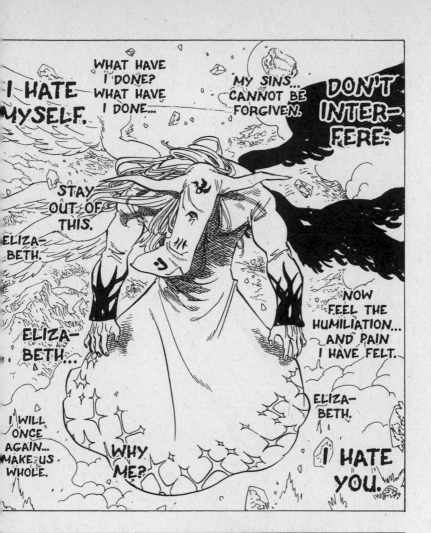

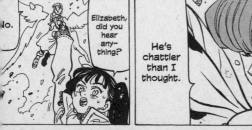

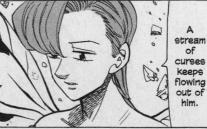

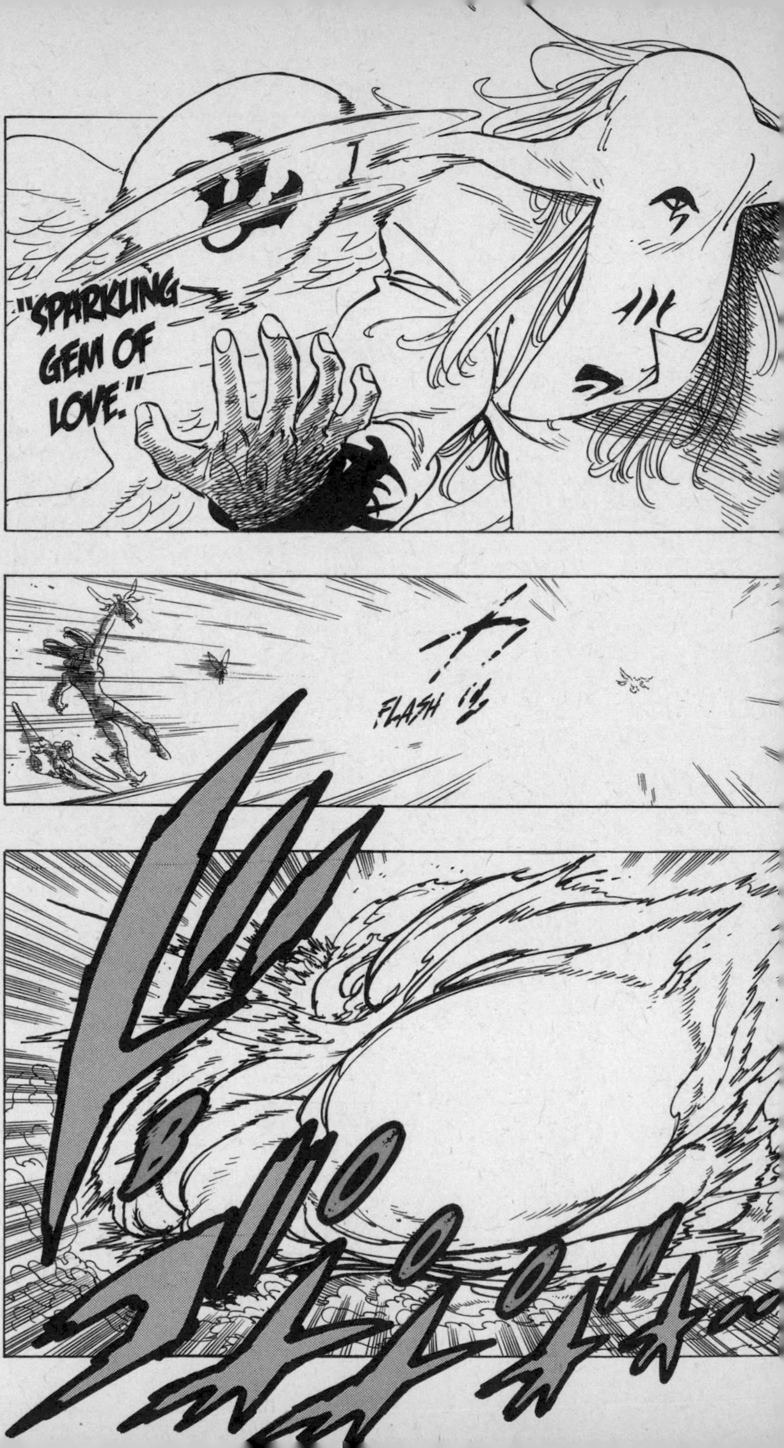
"SPARKLING GEM OF LOVE."
FLASH

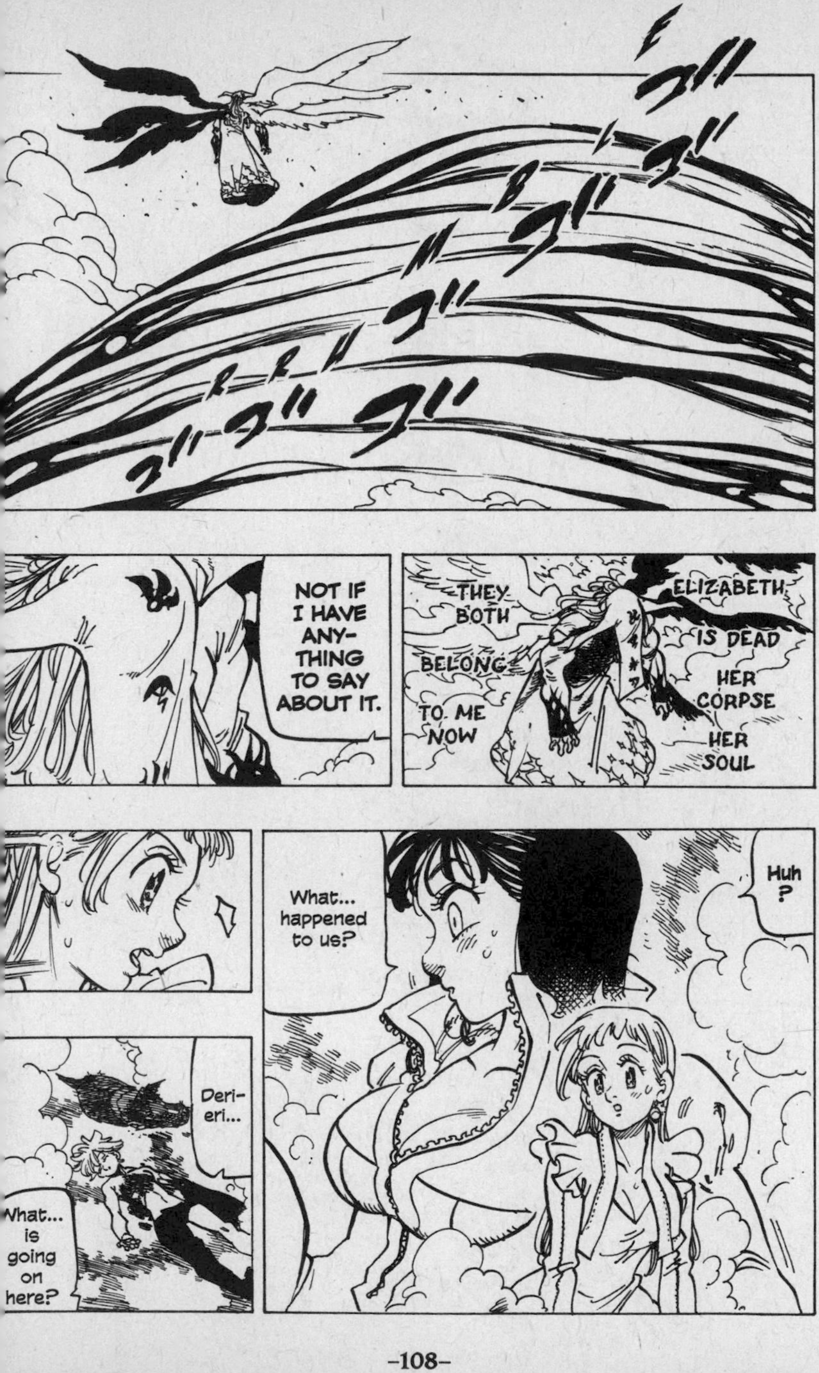
RRUMBLE
ELIZABETH IS DEAD
HER CORPSE
HER SOUL
THEY BOTH
BELONG
TO ME NOW
NOT IF I HAVE ANY-THING TO SAY ABOUT IT.
Huh?
What... happened to us?
Deri-eri...
What... is going on here?

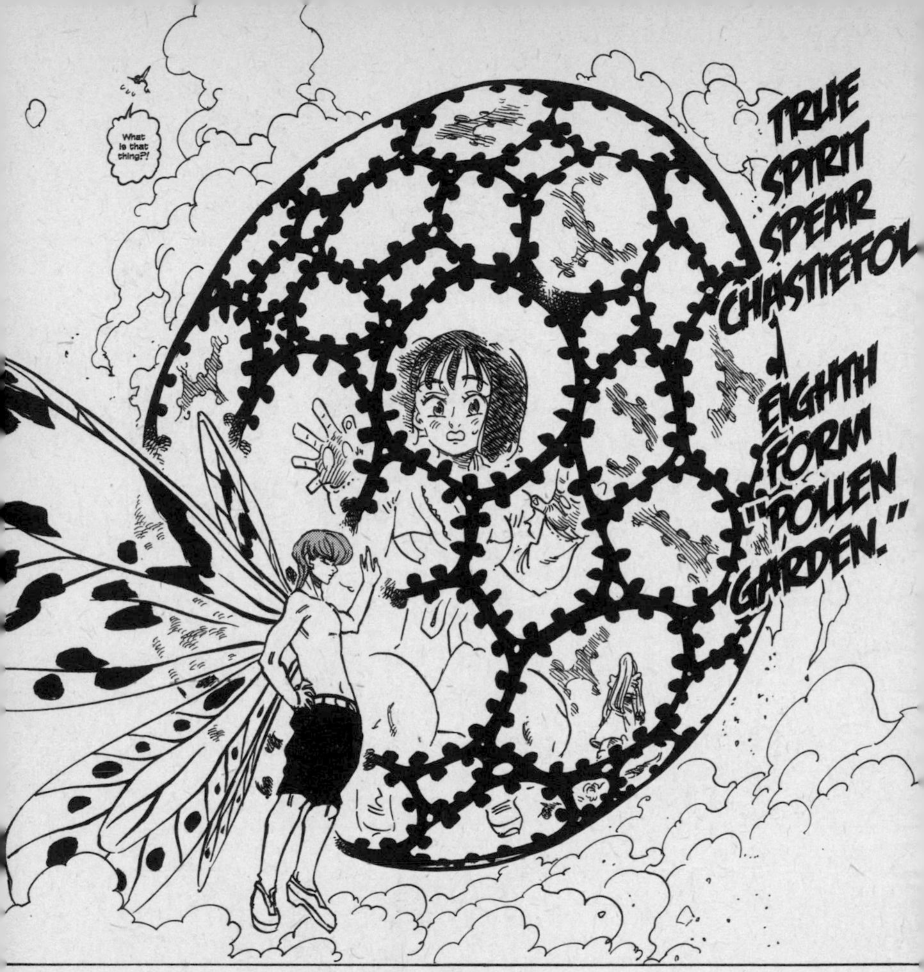
What is that thing?!
TRUE SPIRIT SPEAR CHASTIEFOL
EIGHTH FORM "POLLEN GARDEN."

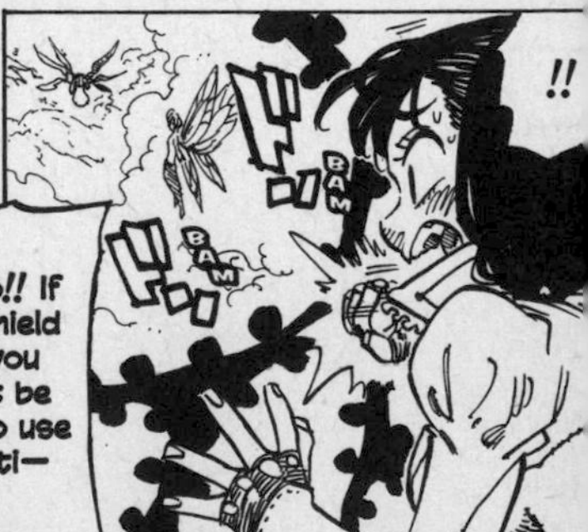
!!
BAM
BAM

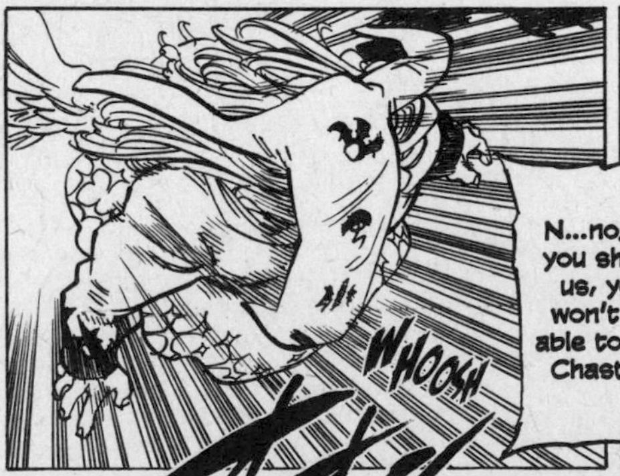
N...no!! If you shield us, you won't be able to use Chasti—
WHOOSH

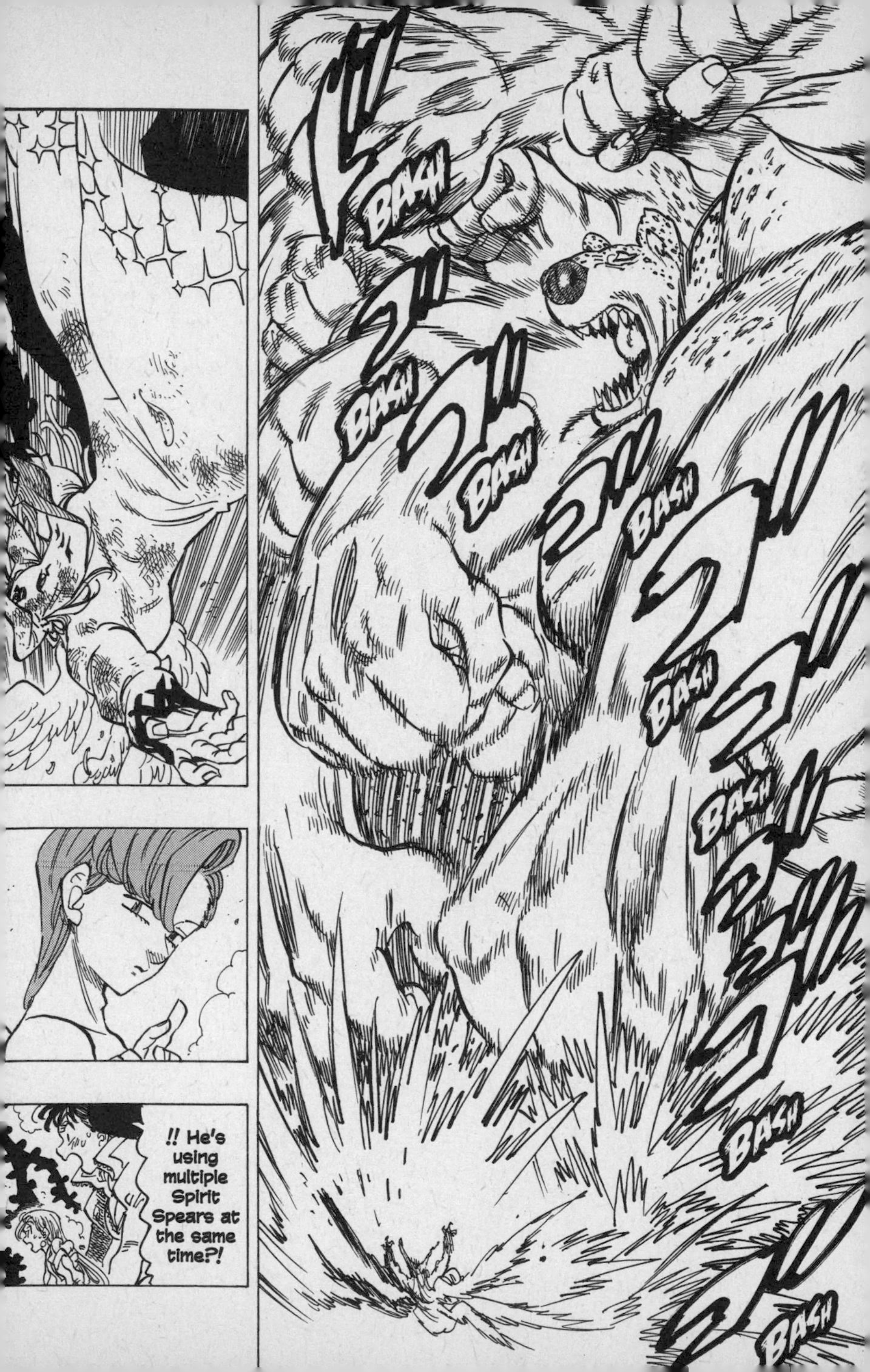
BASH
BASH
BASH
BASH
BASH
BASH
BASH
BASH
!! He's using multiple Spirit Spears at the same time?!

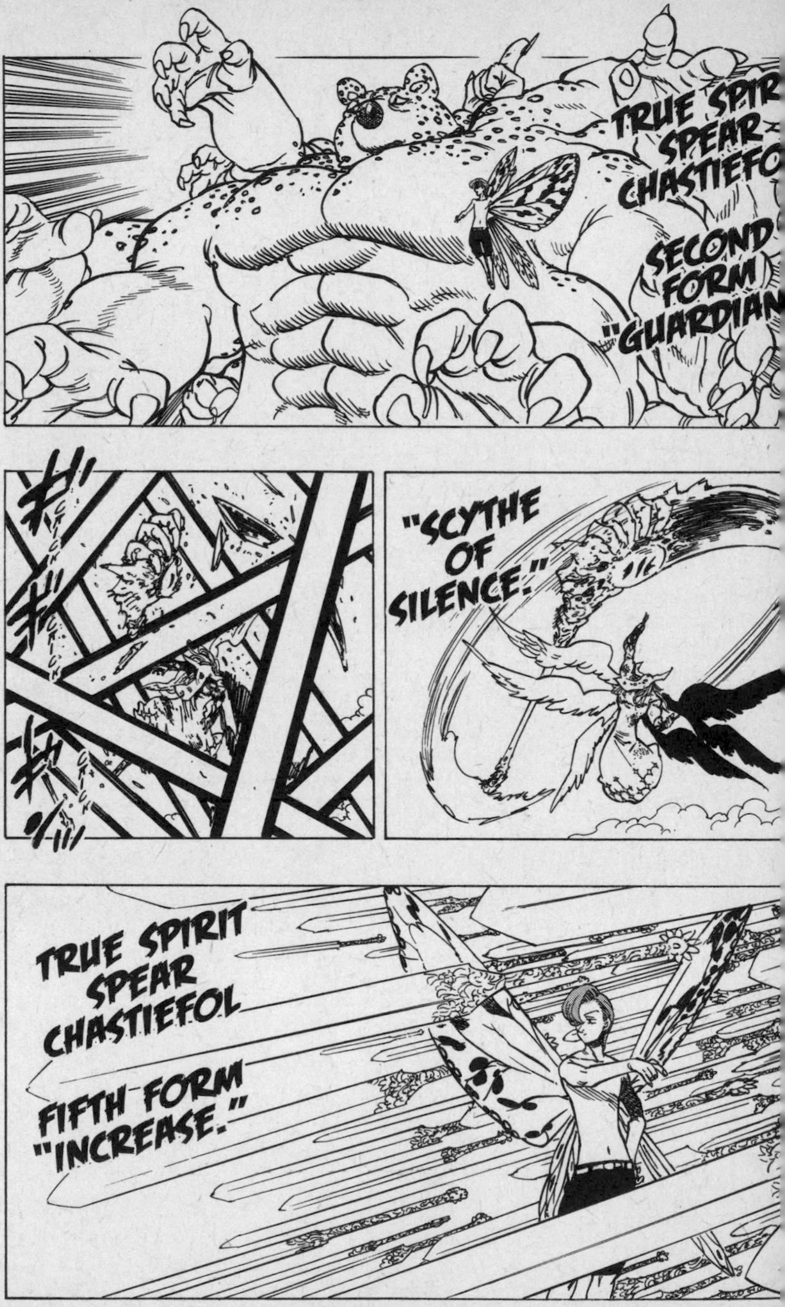
TRUE SPIR
SPEAR
CHASTIEFO
SECOND
FORM
"GUARDIAN
"SCYTHE OF SILENCE."
TRUE SPIRIT SPEAR CHASTIEFOL
FIFTH FORM "INCREASE."

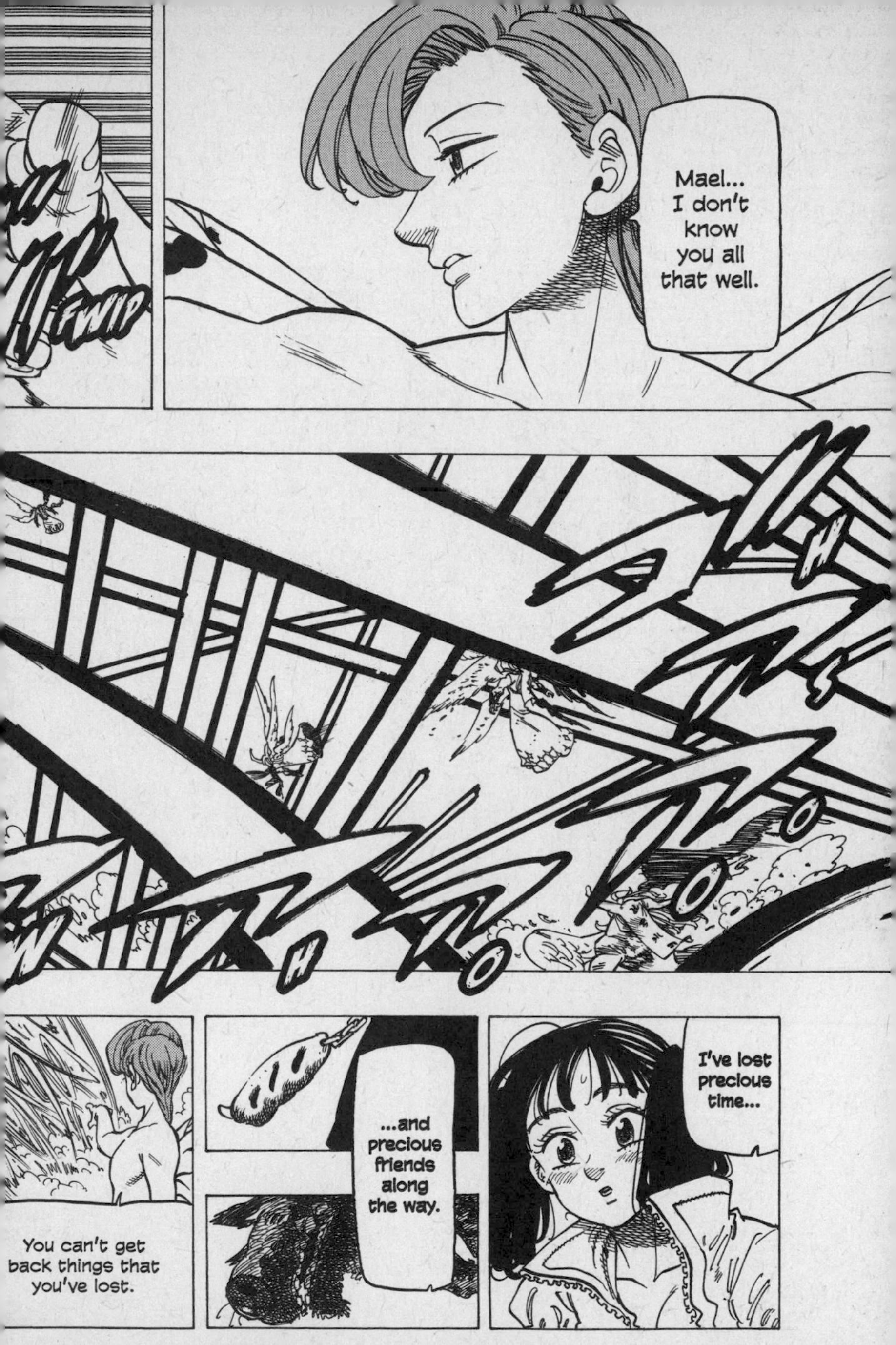
Mael... I don't know you all that well.
FWIP
I've lost precious time...
...and precious friends along the way.
You can't get back things that you've lost.

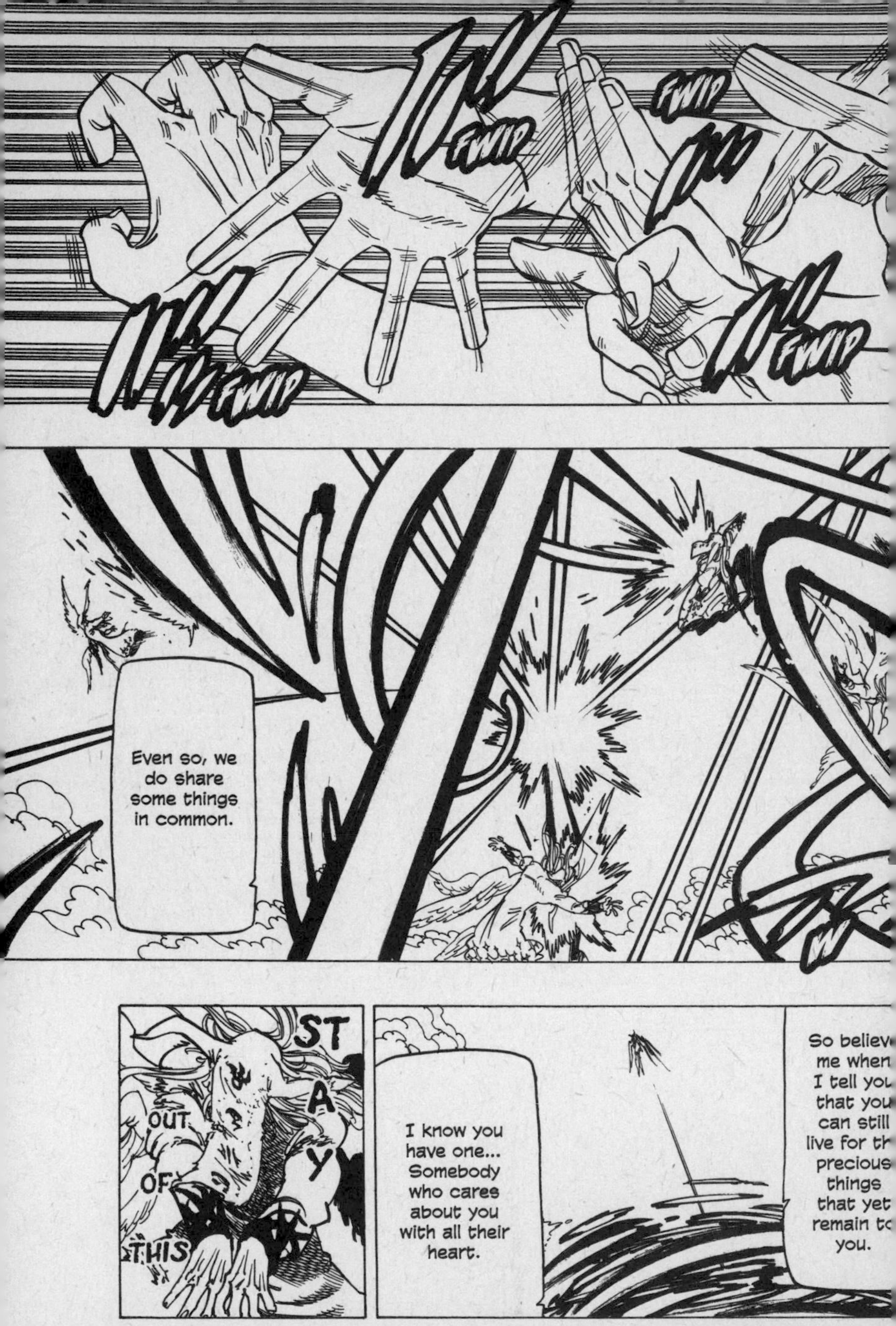
FWIP
FWIP
FWIP
FWIP
Even so, we do share some things in common.
So believe me when I tell you that you can still live for the precious things that yet remain to you.
I know you have one... Somebody who cares about you with all their heart.
STAY OUT OF THIS

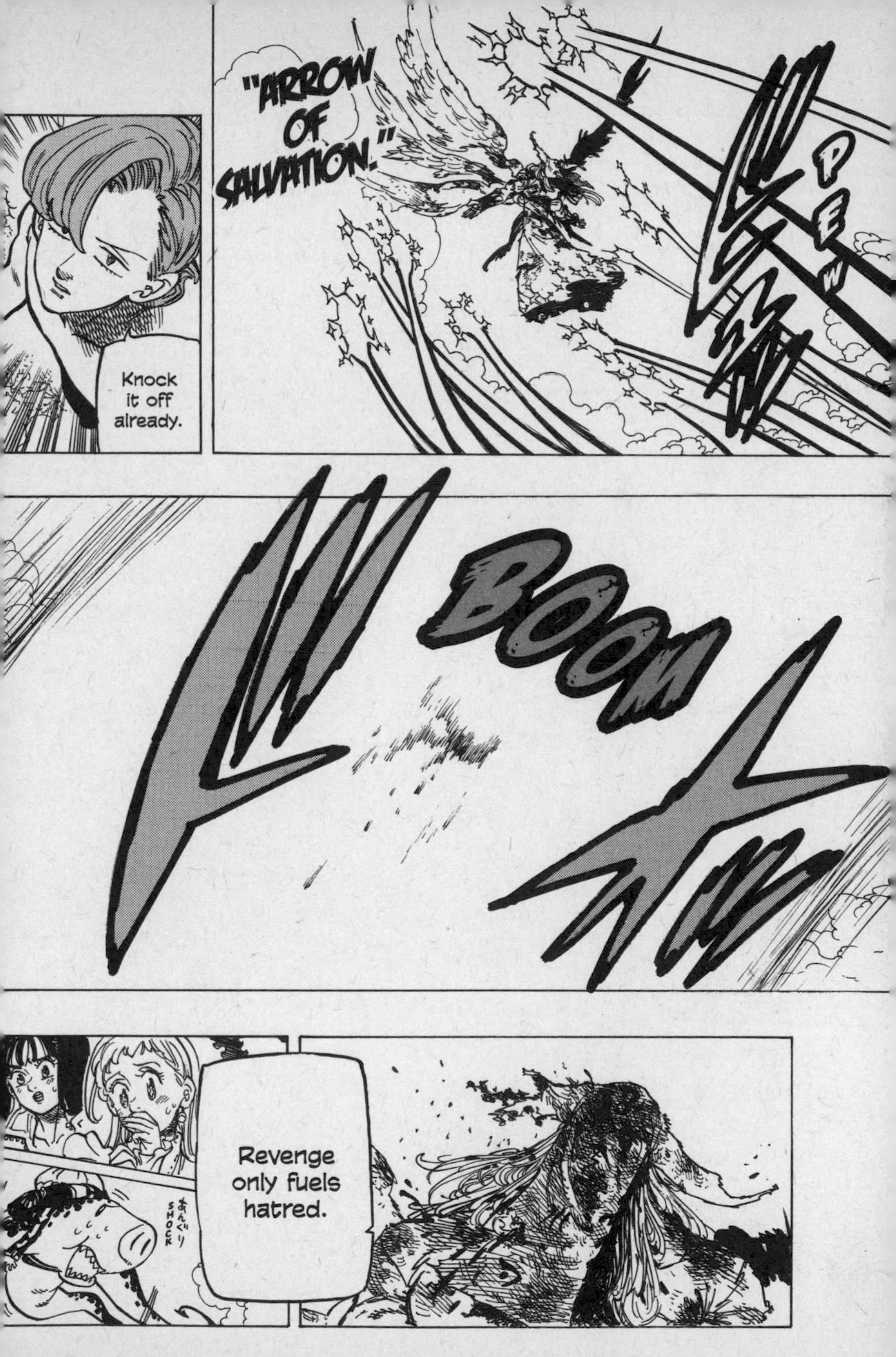
"ARROW OF SALVATION."
PEW
Knock it off already.
BOOM
Revenge only fuels hatred.
SHOCK

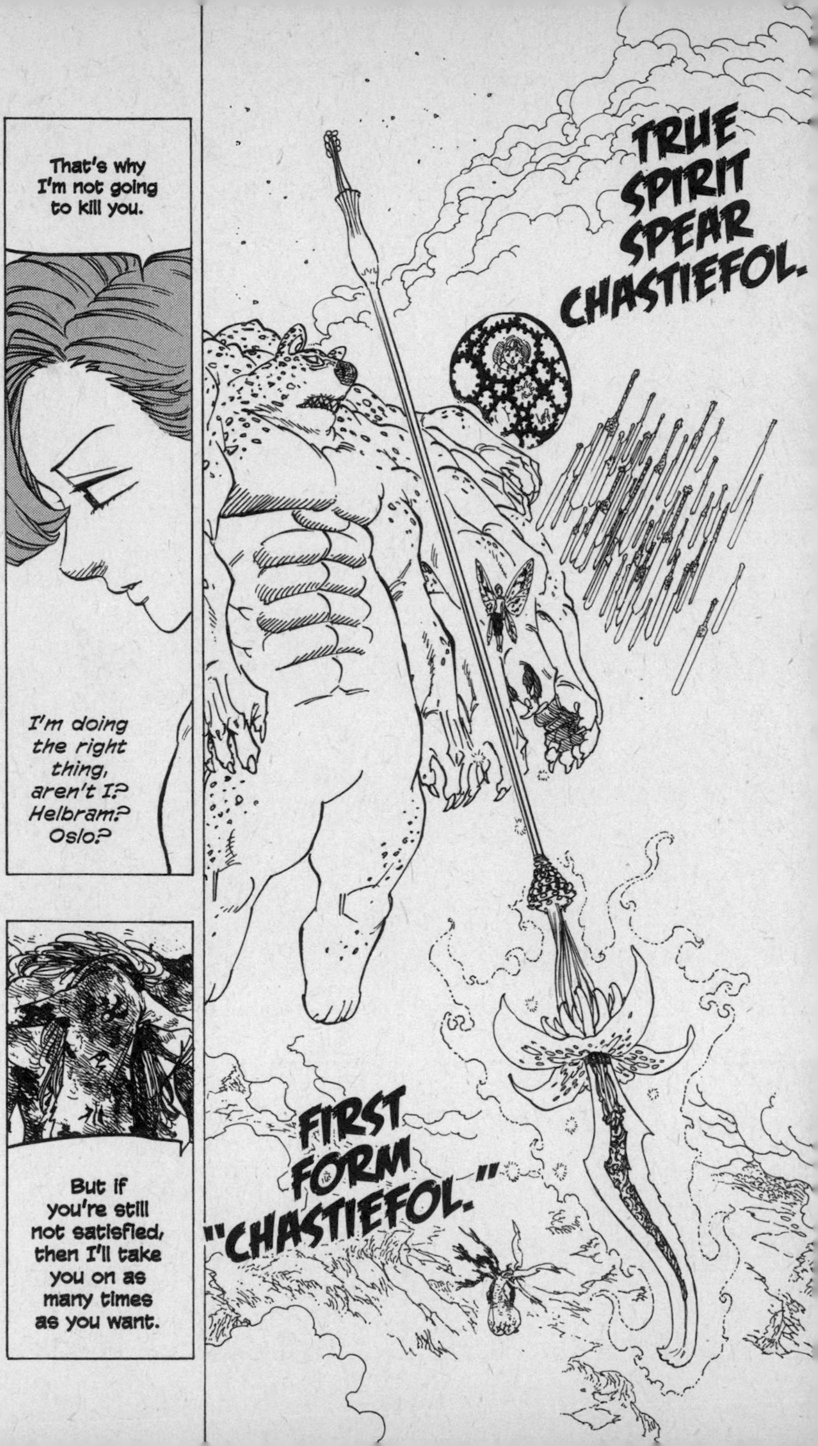

That's why I'm not going to kill you.
I'm doing the right thing, aren't I? Helbram? Oslo?
But if you're still not satisfied, then I'll take you on as many times as you want.
TRUE SPIRIT SPEAR CHASTIEFOL.
FIRST FORM "CHASTIEFOL."

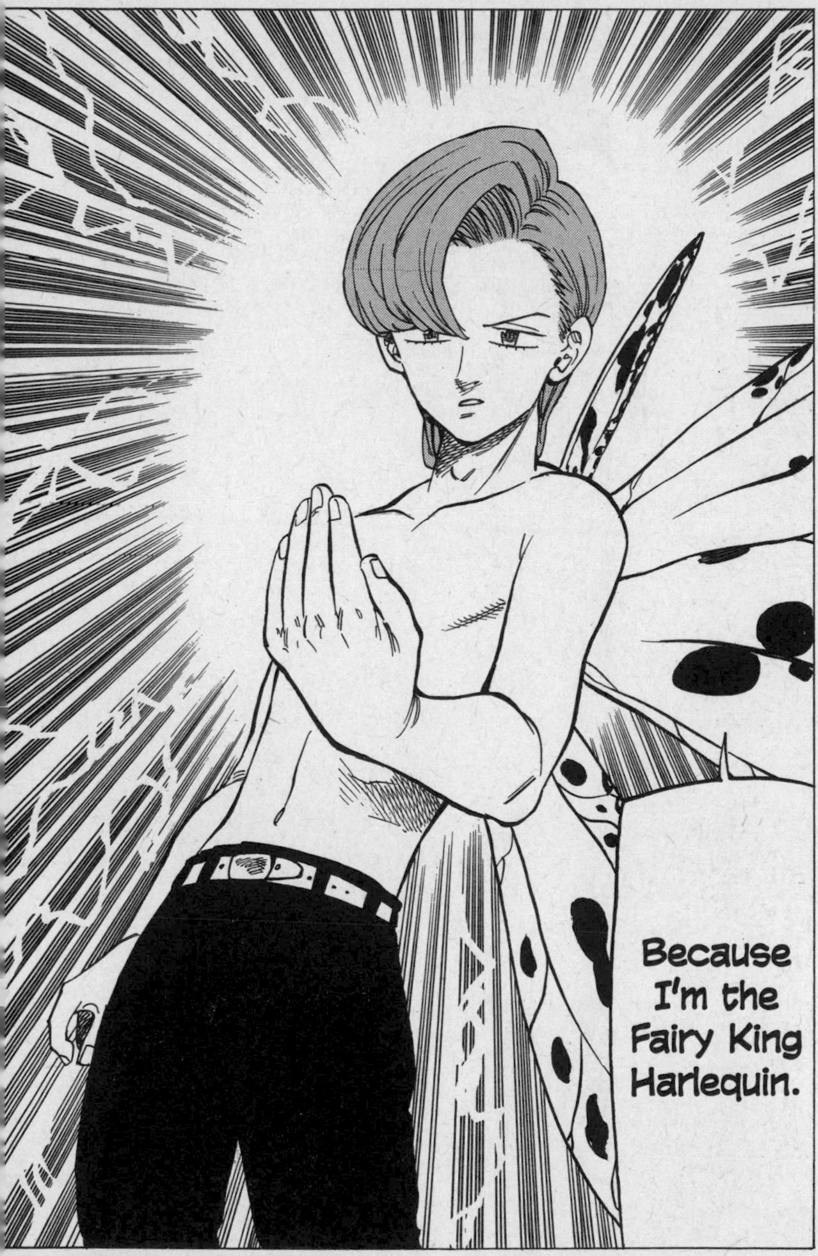
Because I'm the Fairy King Harlequin.

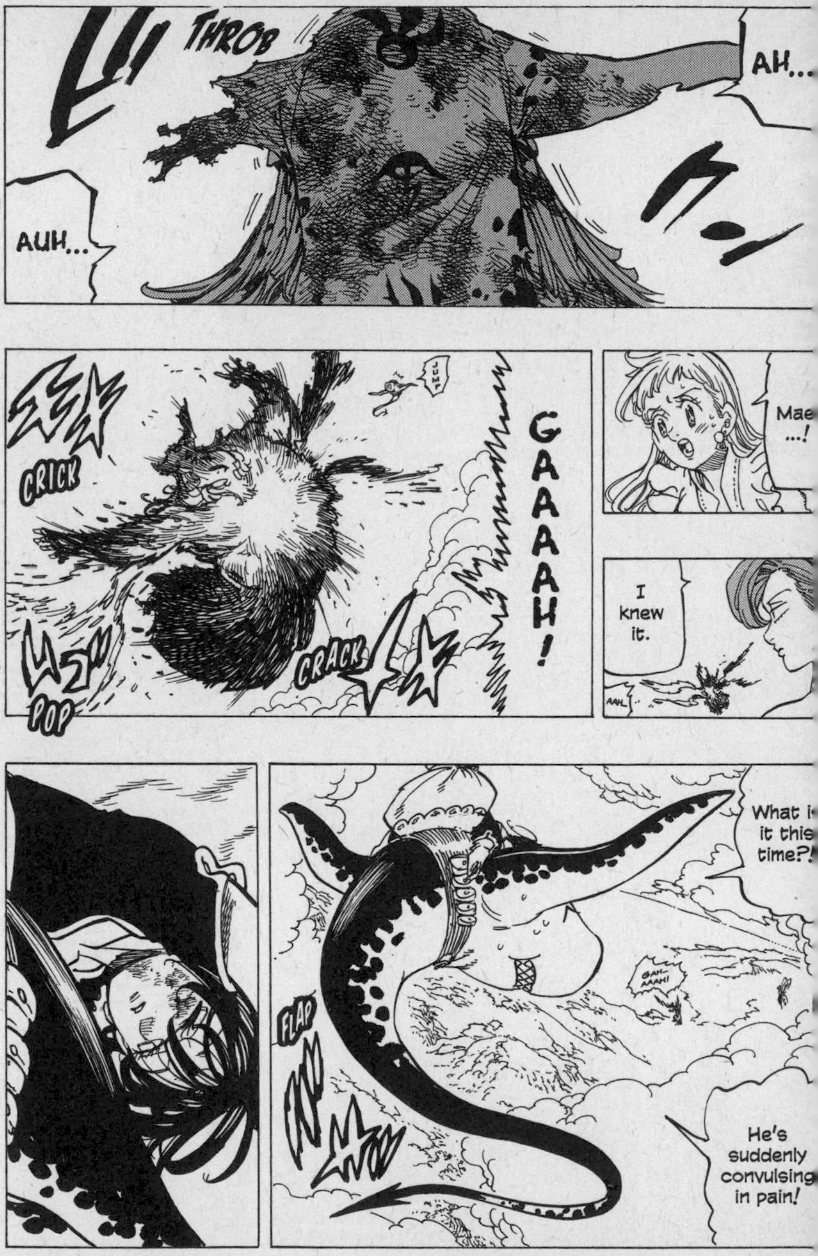
AH...
THROB
AUH...
Mae ...!
I knew it.
AAH
GAAAAAH!
JUMP
CRICK
CRACK
POP
What i
it this
time?!
He's suddenly convulsing in pain!
GAH-AAAH!
FLAP

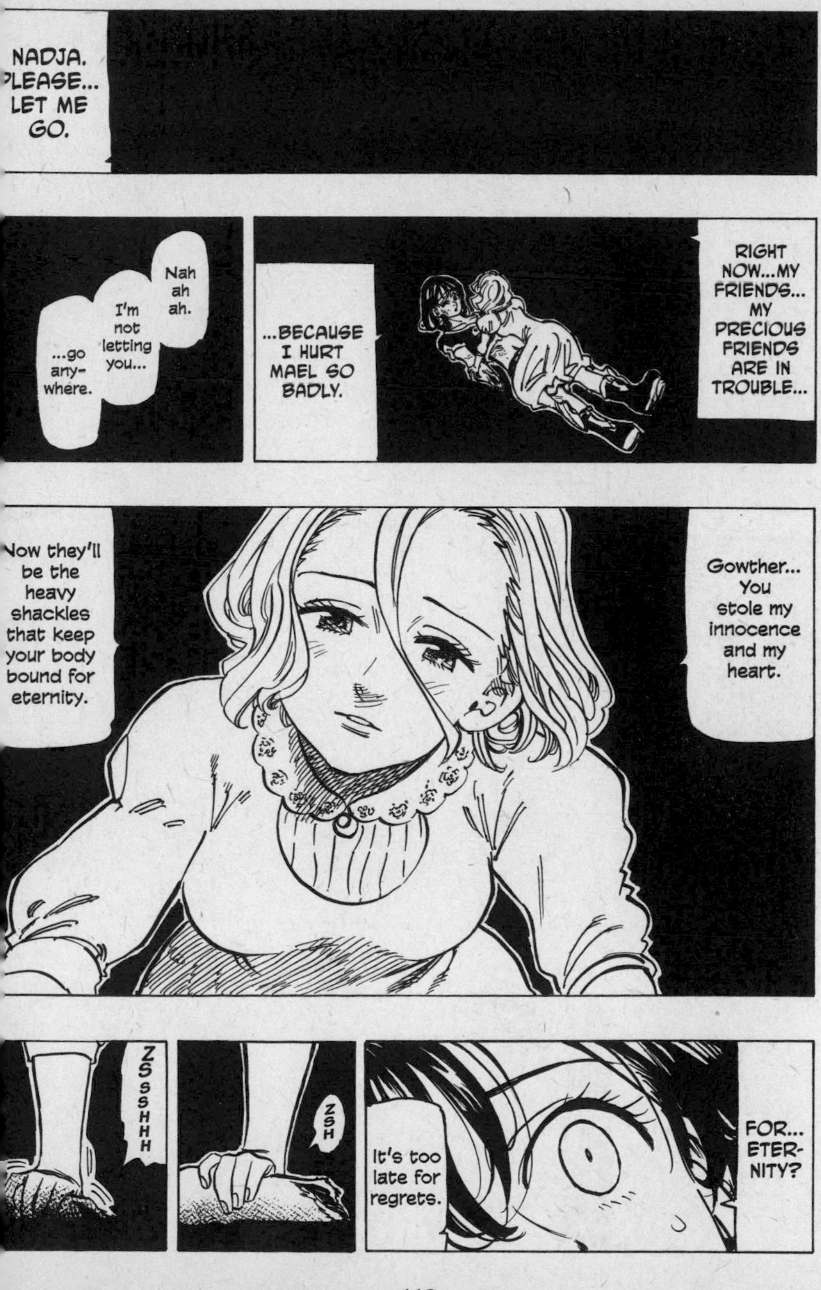
NADJA. PLEASE... LET ME GO.
RIGHT NOW...MY FRIENDS... MY PRECIOUS FRIENDS ARE IN TROUBLE...
...BECAUSE I HURT MAEL SO BADLY.
Nah ah ah.
I'm not letting you...
...go anywhere.
Gowther... You stole my innocence and my heart.
Now they'll be the heavy shackles that keep your body bound for eternity.
FOR... ETERNITY?
It's too late for regrets.
ZSH
ZSSHHH

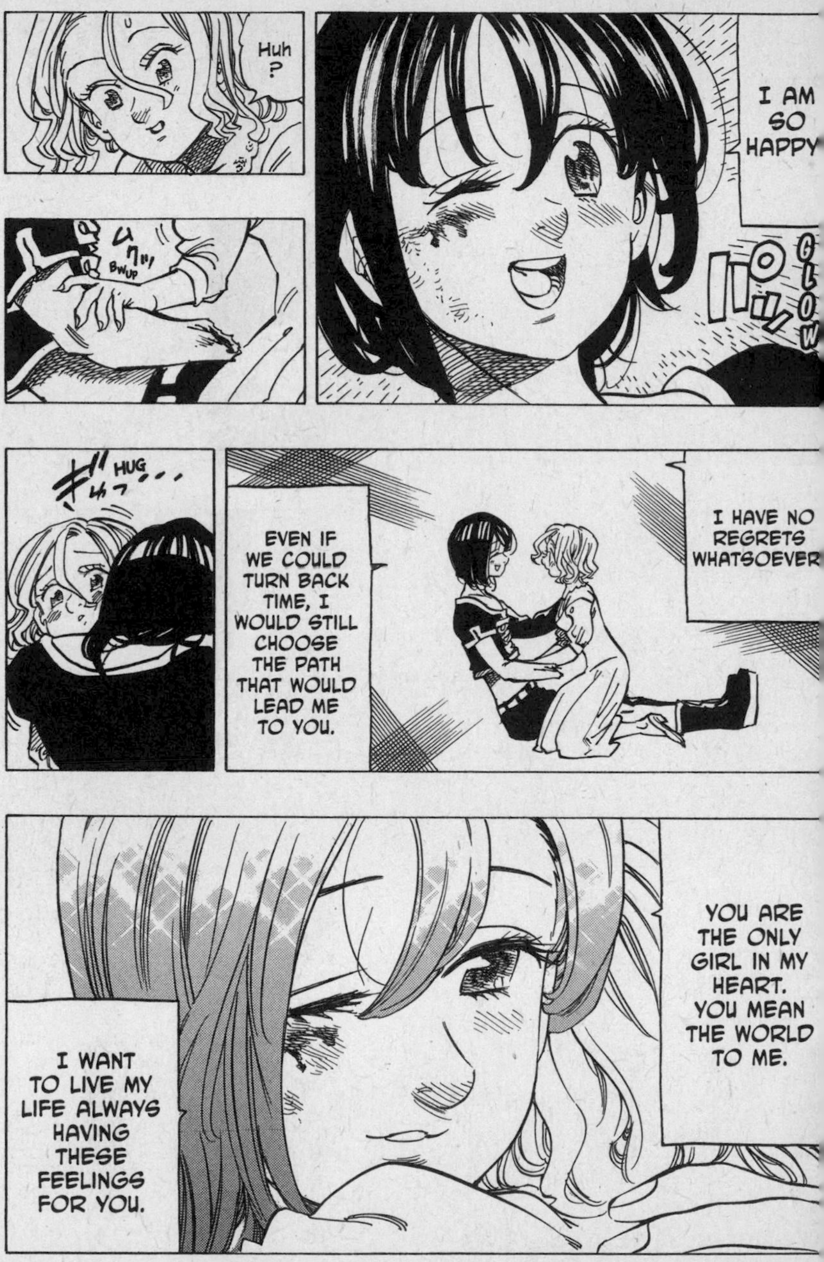
I AM SO HAPPY
GLOW
Huh?
BWUP
I HAVE NO REGRETS WHATSOEVER
EVEN IF WE COULD TURN BACK TIME, I WOULD STILL CHOOSE THE PATH THAT WOULD LEAD ME TO YOU.
HUG
YOU ARE THE ONLY GIRL IN MY HEART. YOU MEAN THE WORLD TO ME.
I WANT TO LIVE MY LIFE ALWAYS HAVING THESE FEELINGS FOR YOU.

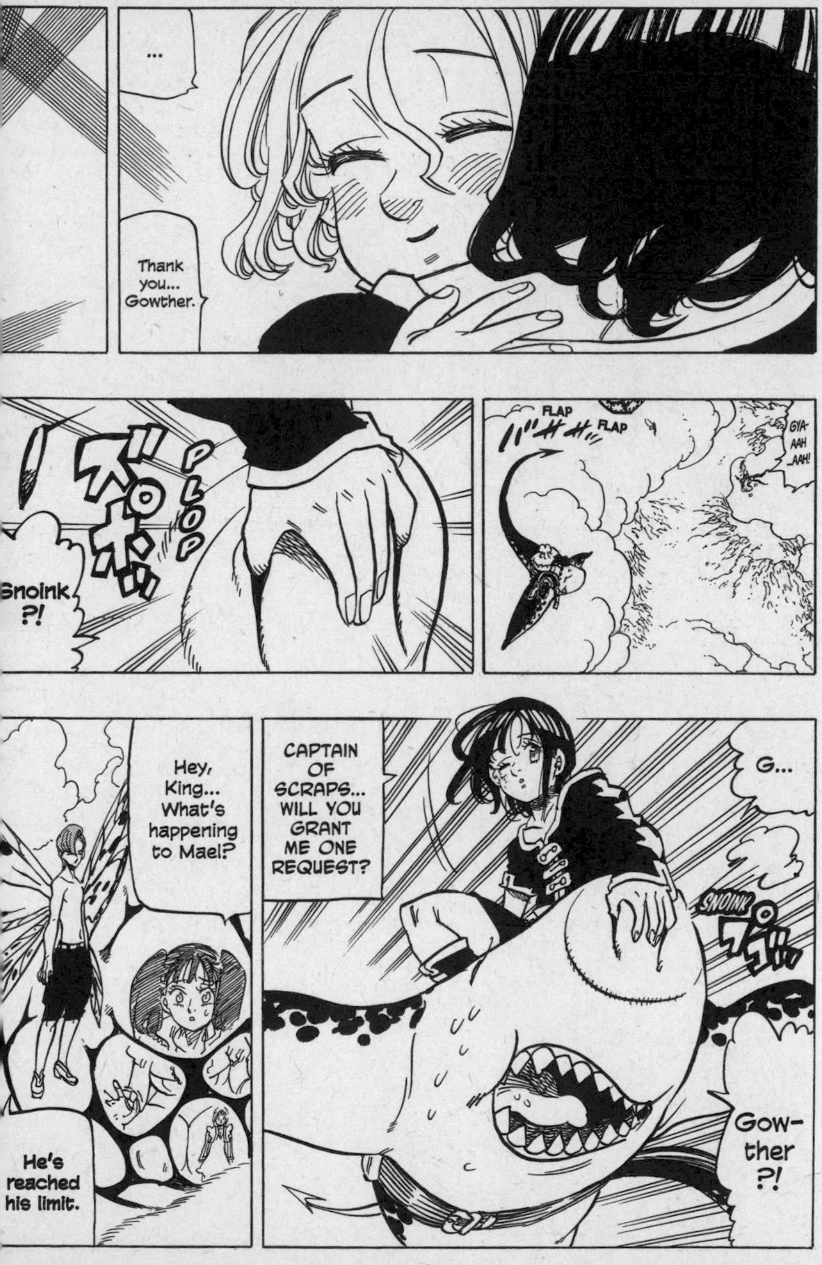
...
Thank you... Gowther.
GYAAAH!
FLAP
FLAP
PLOP
Snoink?!
G...
CAPTAIN OF SCRAPS... WILL YOU GRANT ME ONE REQUEST?
SNOINK
Gow-ther?!
Hey, King... What's happening to Mael?
He's reached his limit.

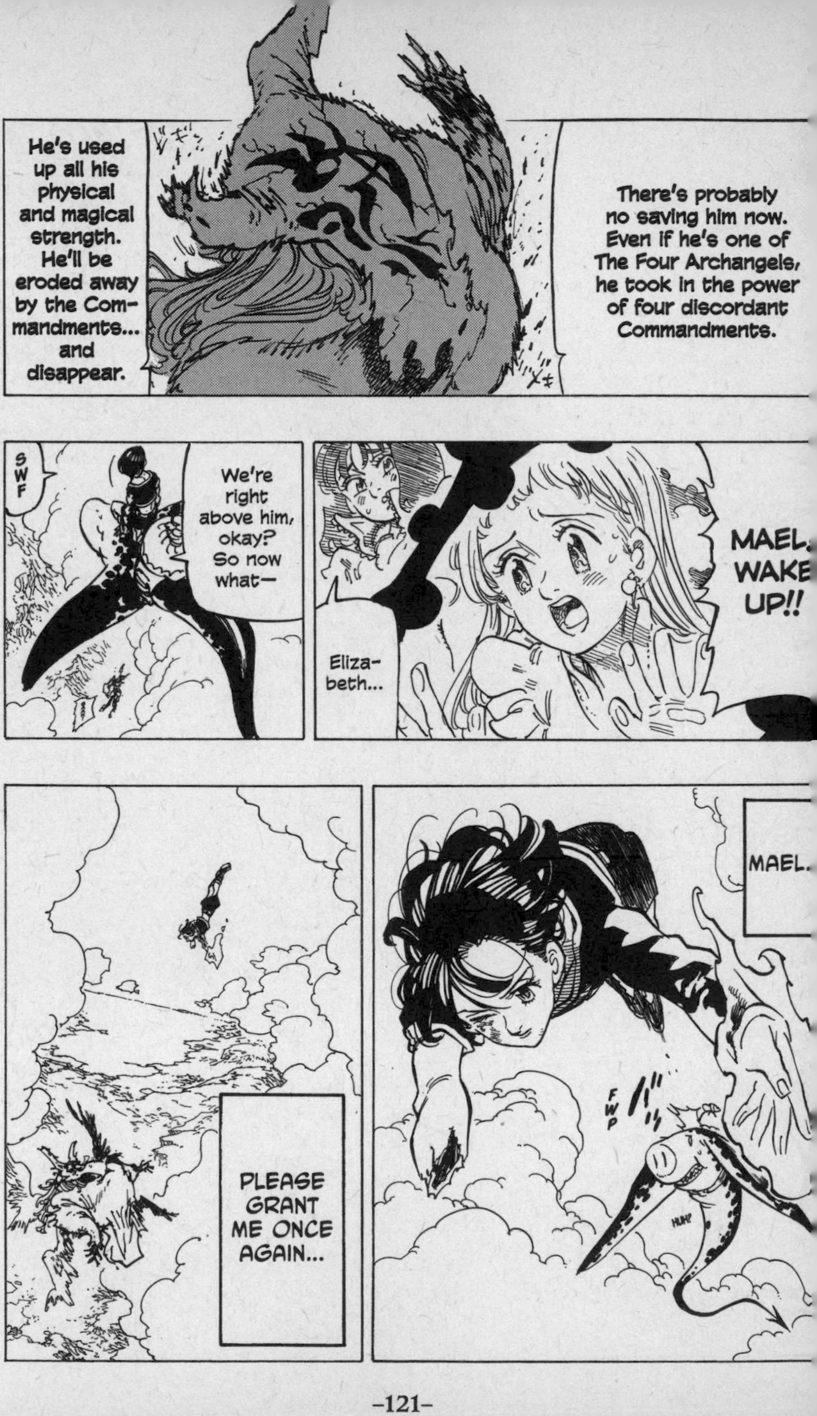
There's probably no saving him now. Even if he's one of The Four Archangels, he took in the power of four discordant Commandments.
He's used up all his physical and magical strength. He'll be eroded away by the Commandments... and disappear.
MAEL, WAKE UP!!
Eliza-beth...
We're right above him, okay? So now what—
SWF
MAEL.
FWP
HUH?
PLEASE GRANT ME ONCE AGAIN...

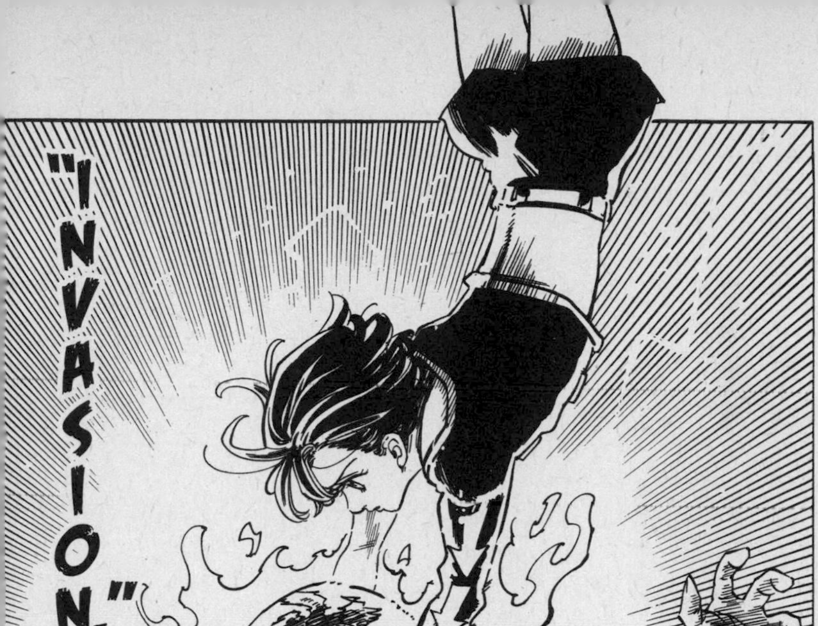
...THE CHANCE TO SAVE YOU!
"INVASION."

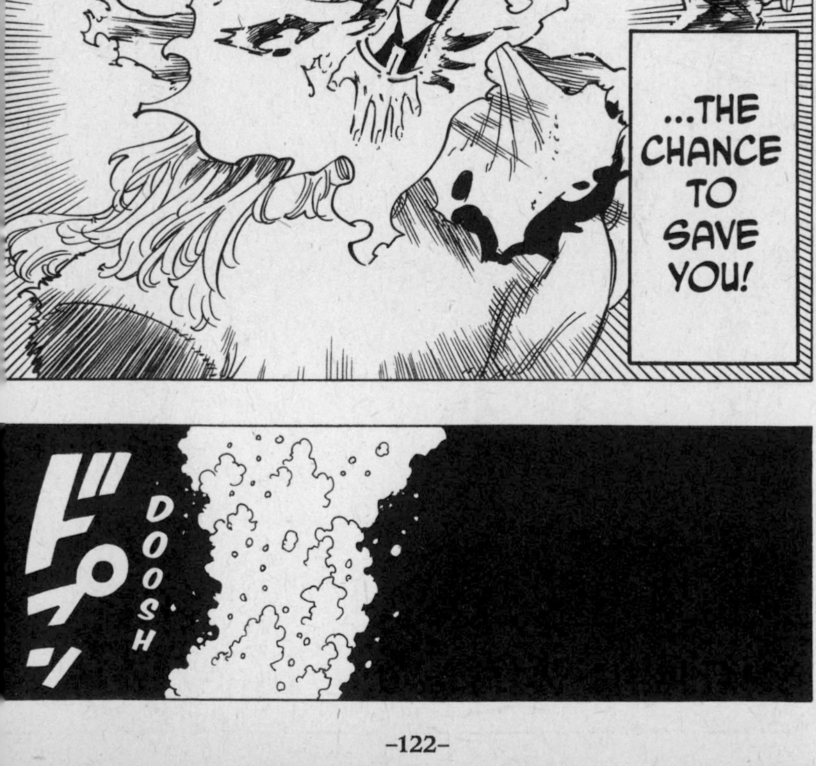
DOOSH

Chapter 282 - Gowther vs. Mae

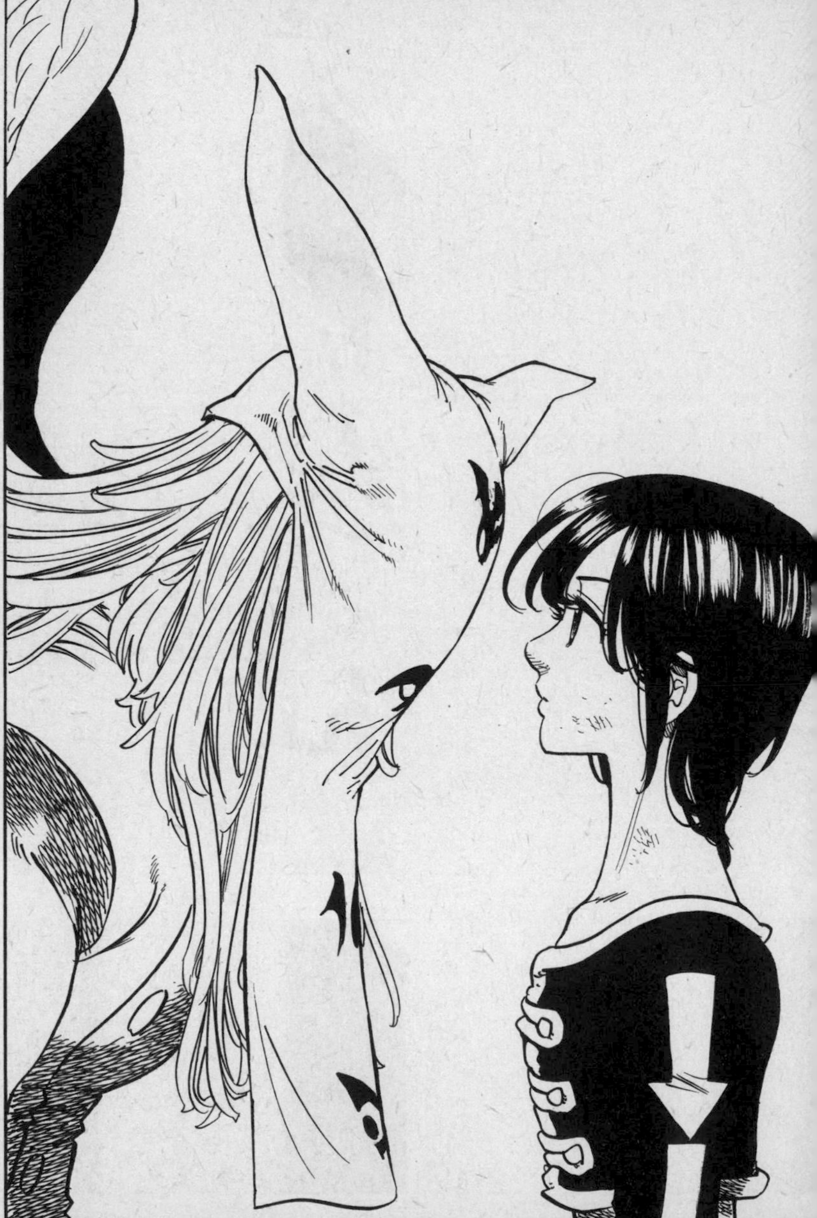

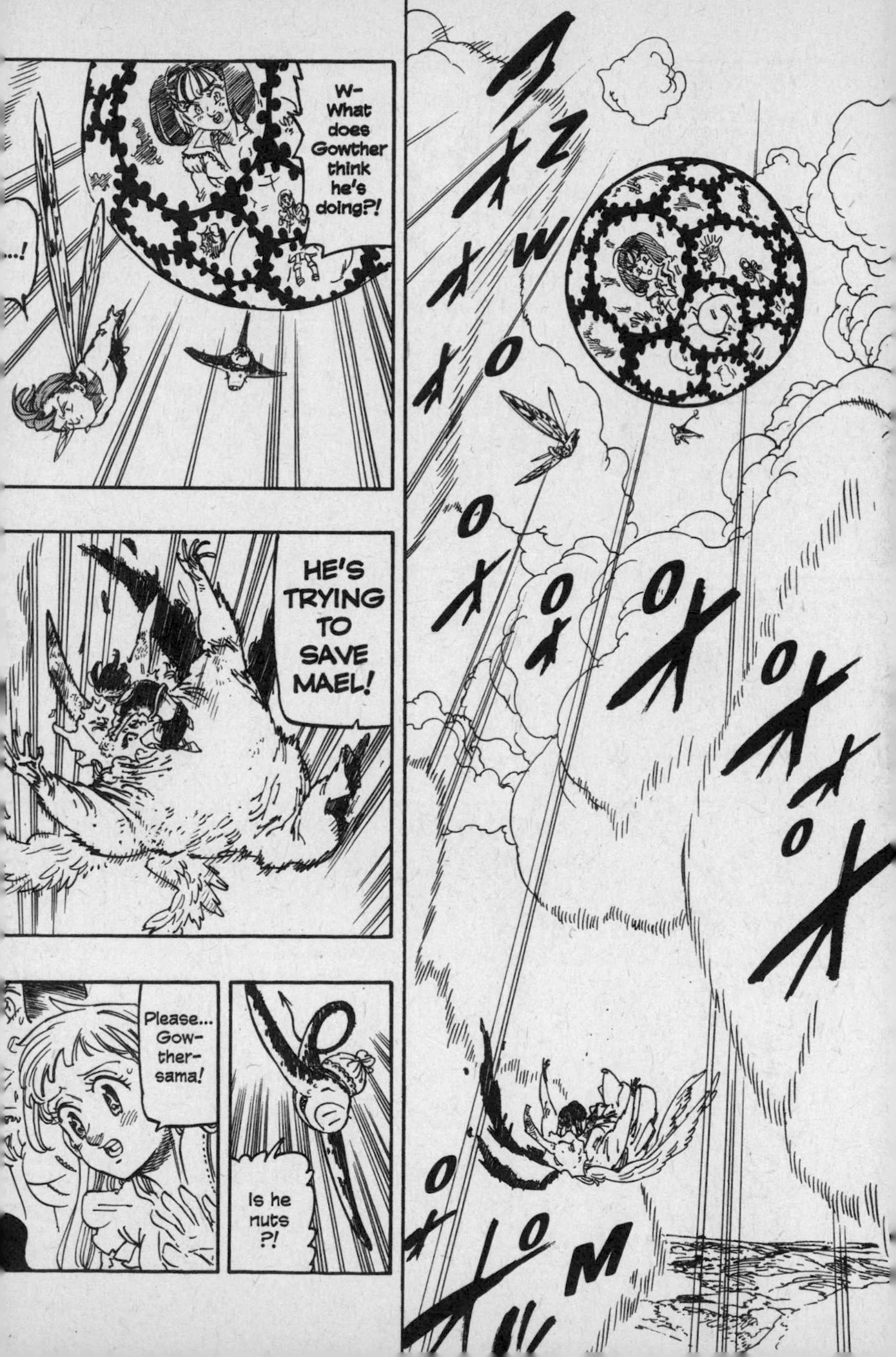
W-What does Gowther think he's doing?!
...!
HE'S TRYING TO SAVE MAEL!
Is he nuts?!
Please... Gow-ther-sama!

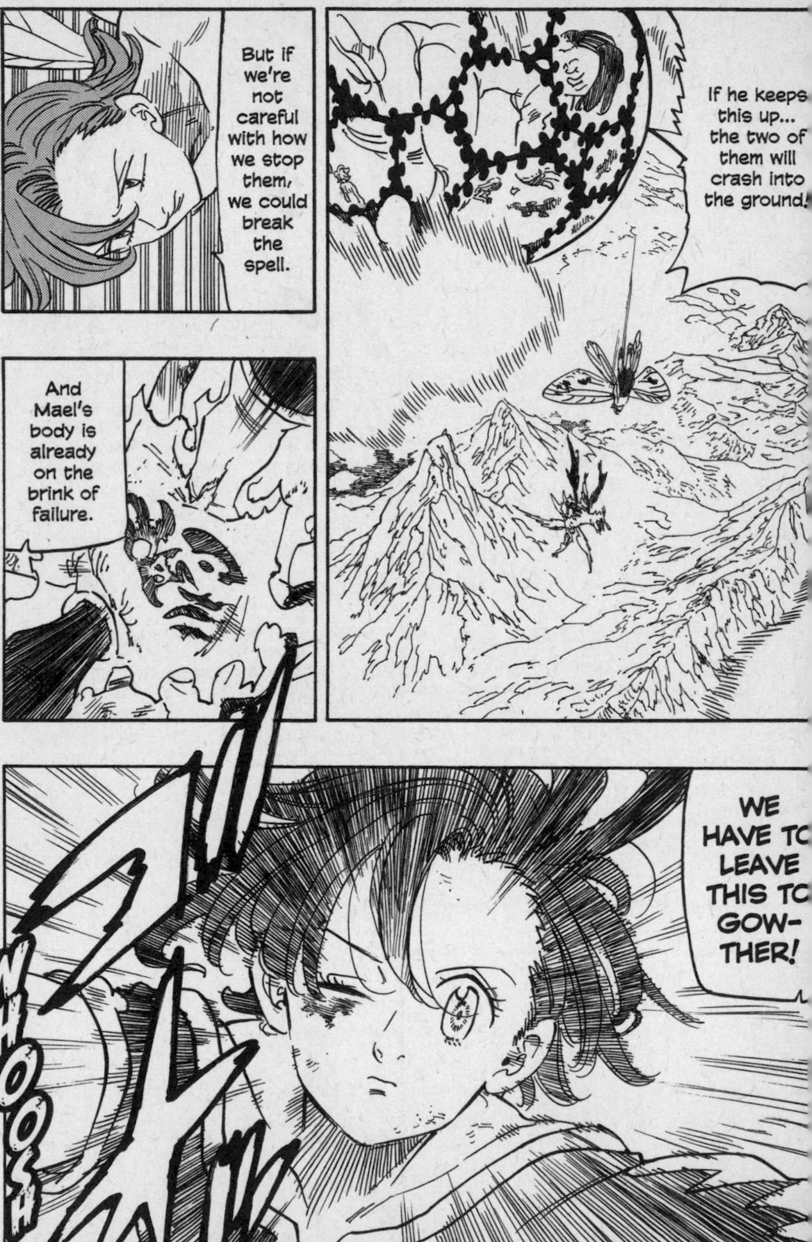

If he keeps this up... the two of them will crash into the ground!
But if we're not careful with how we stop them, we could break the spell.
And Mael's body is already on the brink of failure.
WE HAVE TO LEAVE THIS TO GOW-THER!
WHOOOSH

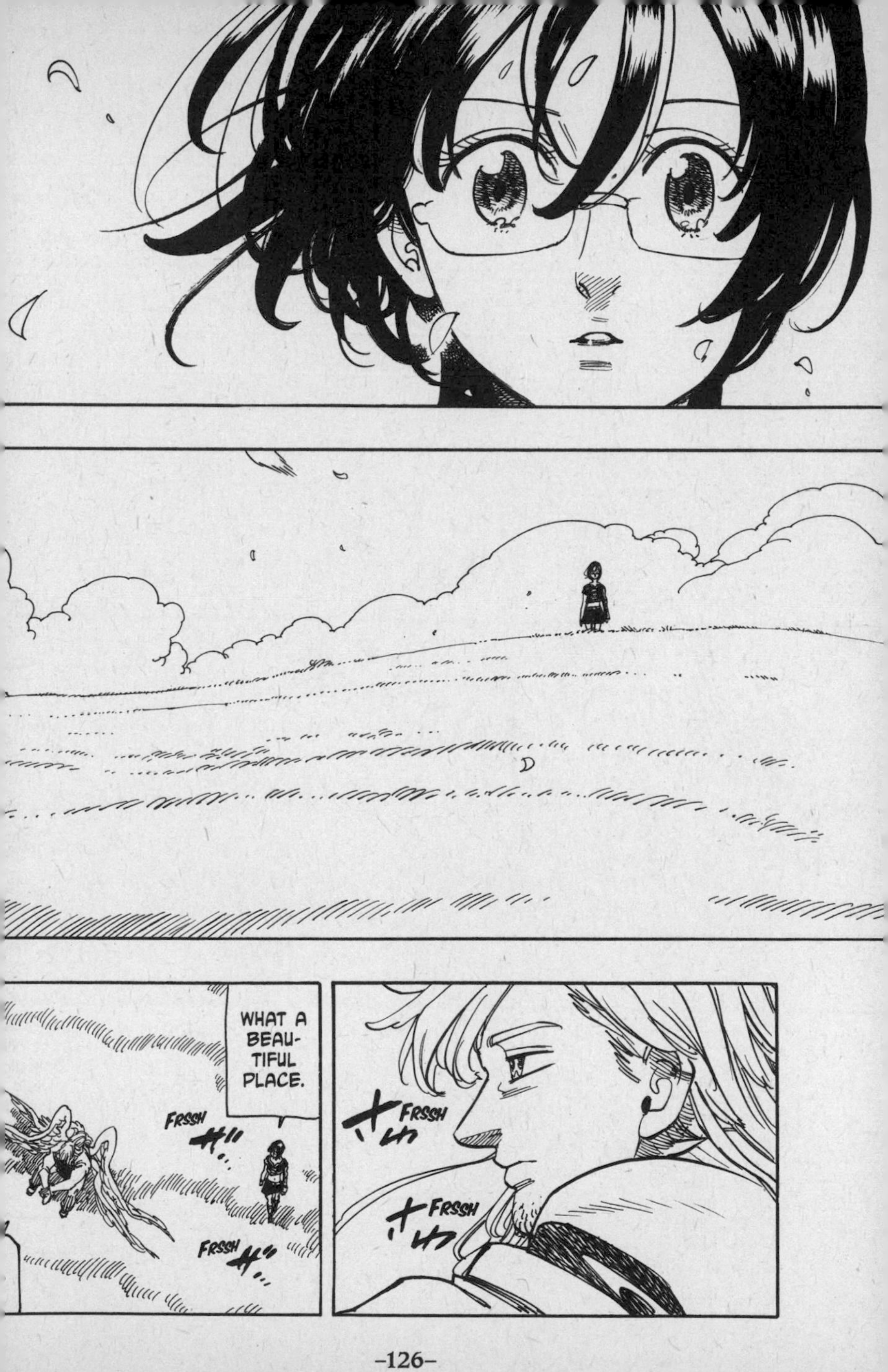
FRSSH
FRSSH
WHAT A BEAU-TIFUL PLACE.
FRSSH
FRSSH

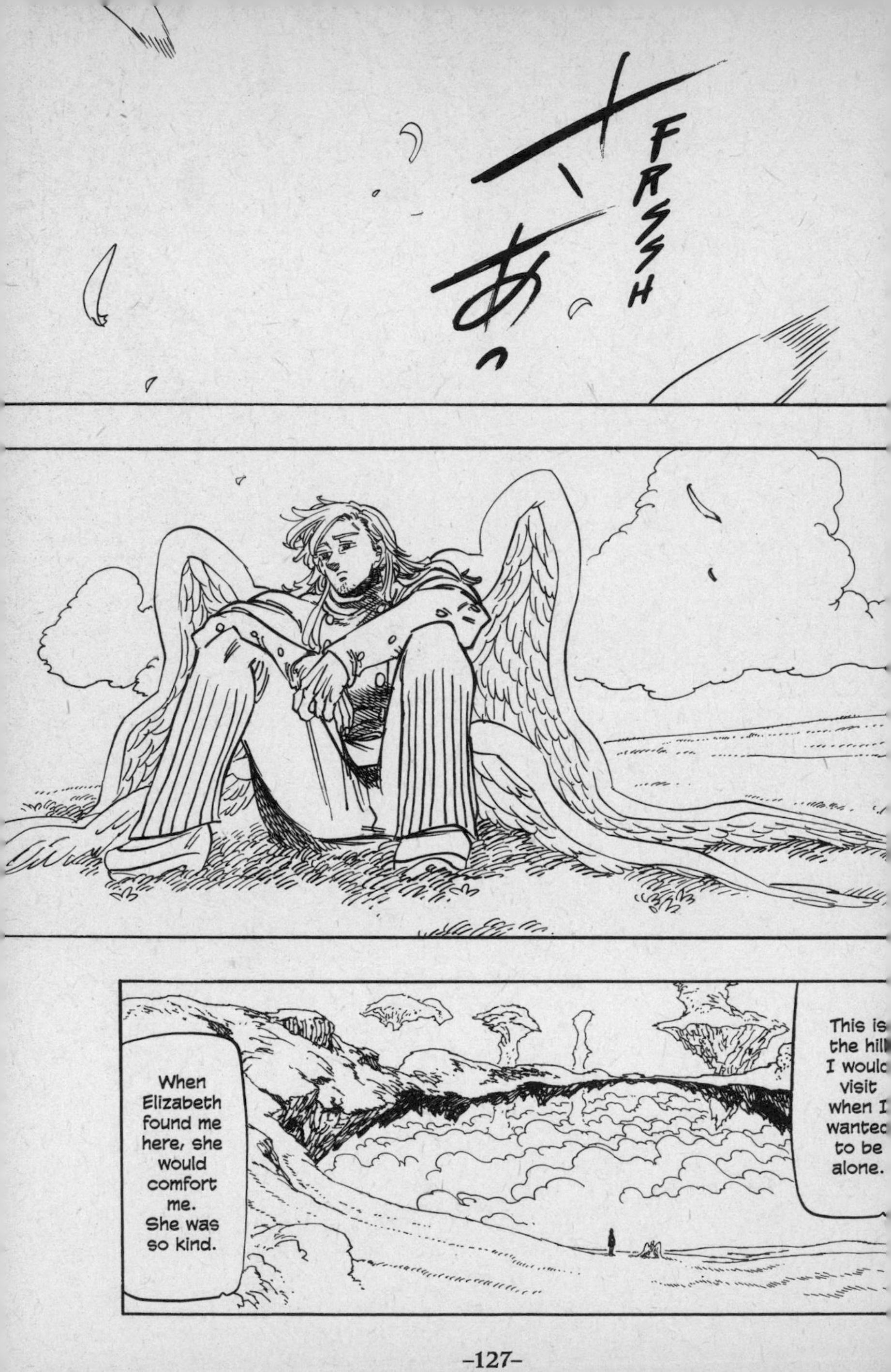
FRSSH
This is the hill I would visit when I wanted to be alone.
When Elizabeth found me here, she would comfort me. She was so kind.

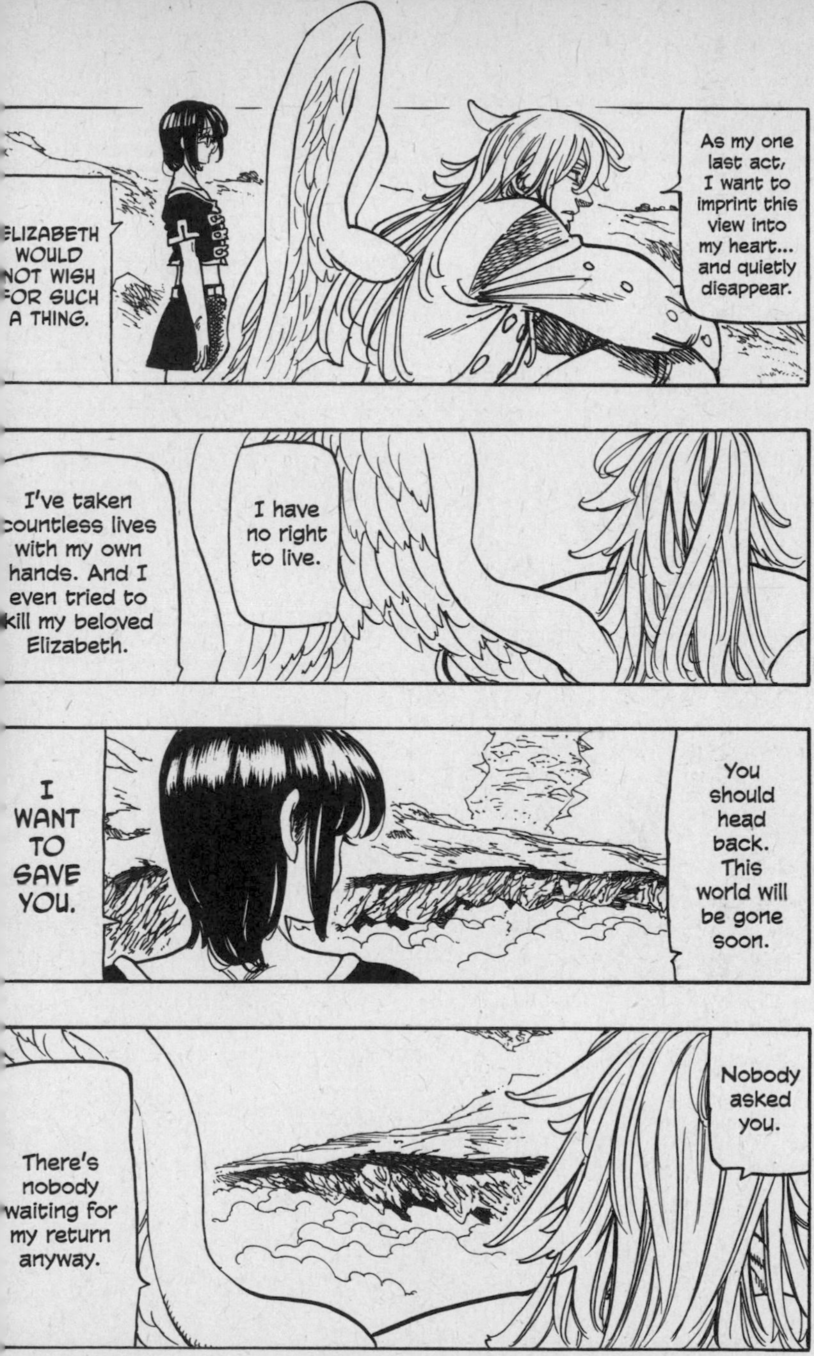
As my one last act, I want to imprint this view into my heart... and quietly disappear.
ELIZABETH WOULD NOT WISH FOR SUCH A THING.
I have no right to live.
I've taken countless lives with my own hands. And I even tried to kill my beloved Elizabeth.
You should head back. This world will be gone soon.
I WANT TO SAVE YOU.
Nobody asked you.
There's nobody waiting for my return anyway.

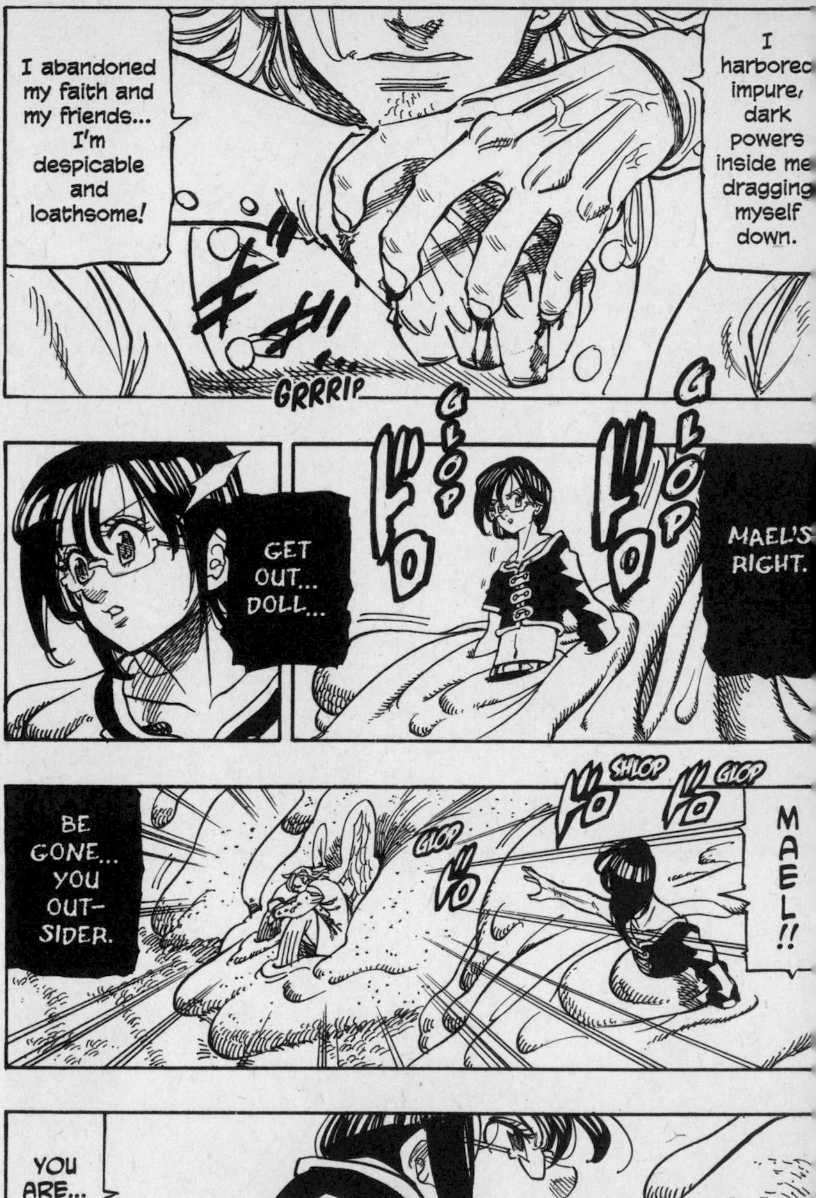
I harbored impure, dark powers inside me dragging myself down.
I abandoned my faith and my friends... I'm despicable and loathsome!
GRRRIP
GLOP
GLOP
MAEL'S RIGHT.
GET OUT... DOLL...
MAEL!!
GLOP
SHLOP
GLOP
BE GONE... YOU OUT-SIDER.
YOU ARE...

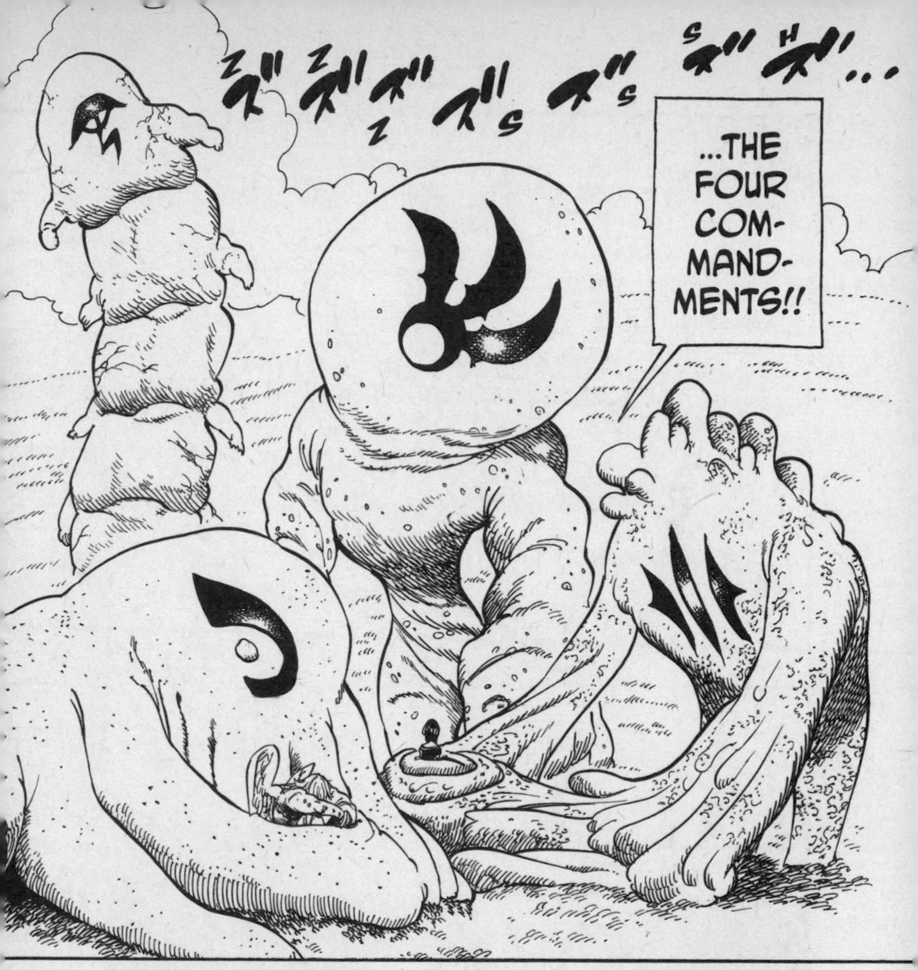
...THE FOUR COMMANDMENTS!!

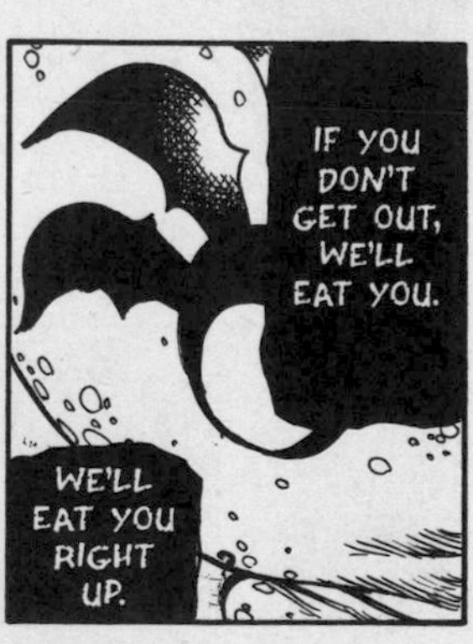
IF YOU DON'T GET OUT, WE'LL EAT YOU.
WE'LL EAT YOU RIGHT UP.

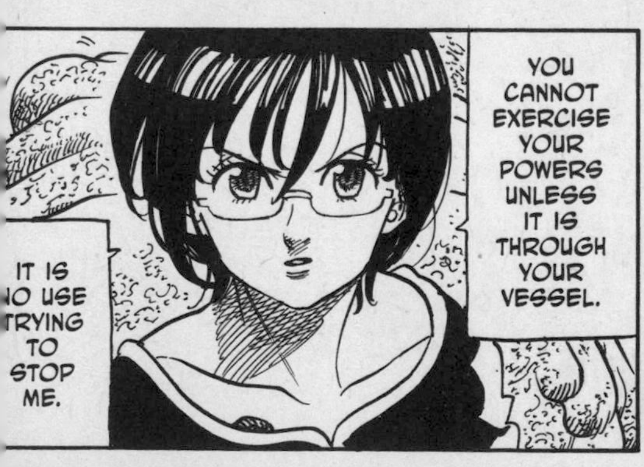
YOU CANNOT EXERCISE YOUR POWERS UNLESS IT IS THROUGH YOUR VESSEL.
IT IS O USE RYING TO STOP ME.

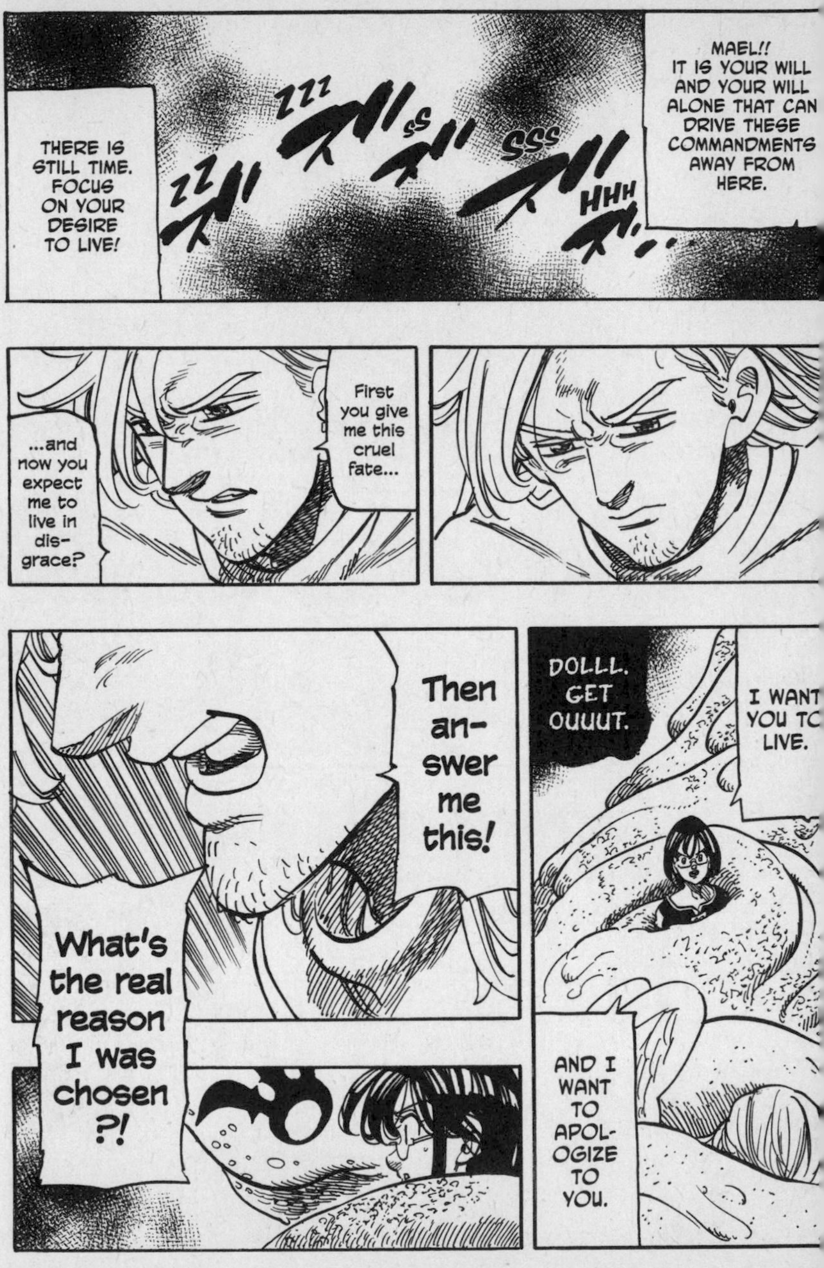
MAEL!! IT IS YOUR WILL AND YOUR WILL ALONE THAT CAN DRIVE THESE COMMANDMENTS AWAY FROM HERE.
HHH
SSS
ss
ZZZ
ZZZ
THERE IS STILL TIME. FOCUS ON YOUR DESIRE TO LIVE!
First you give me this cruel fate...
...and now you expect me to live in dis-grace?
I WANT YOU TO LIVE.
DOLLL. GET OUUUT.
AND I WANT TO APOL-OGIZE TO YOU.
Then an-swer me this!
What's the real reason I was chosen?!

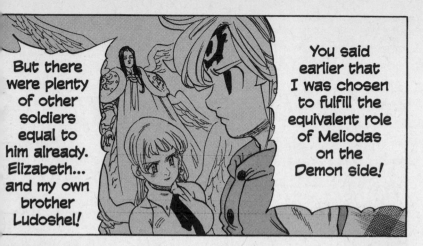

You said earlier that I was chosen to fulfill the equivalent role of Meliodas on the Demon side!
But there were plenty of other soldiers equal to him already. Elizabeth... and my own brother Ludoshel!
And yet you chose me. Why is that?
Why?
THE ONE WHO CHOSE YOU...
.WAS MY CREATOR GOWTHER.
IF THESE ARE YOUR MEMORIES...
...THEN YOU MUST REMEMBER MY FACE.
What?
WOOOOO

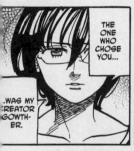

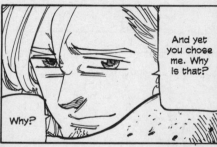

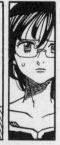

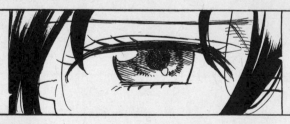

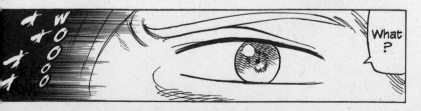

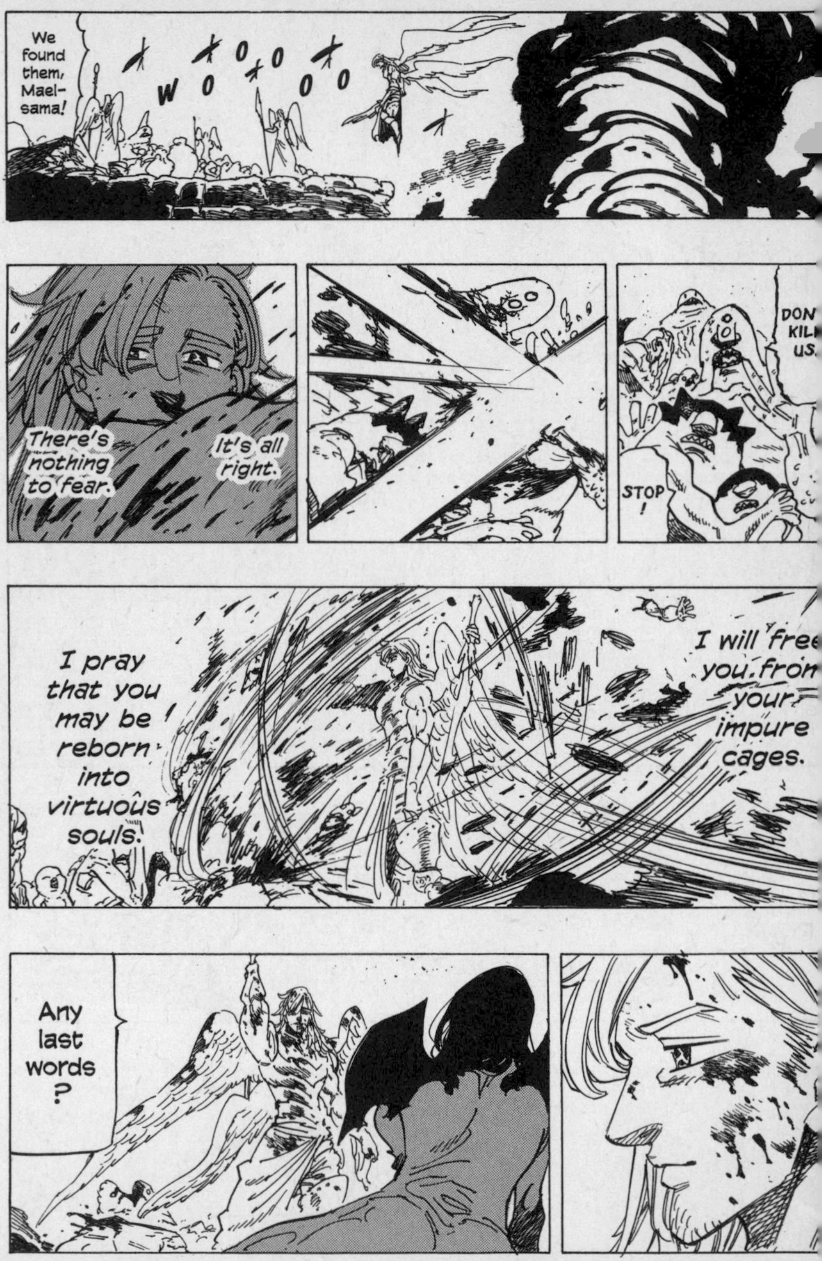
We found them, Mael-sama!
WOOOOO
DON
KIL
US.
STOP!
It's all right.
There's nothing to fear.
I will free you from your impure cages.
I pray that you may be reborn into virtuous souls.
Any last words?

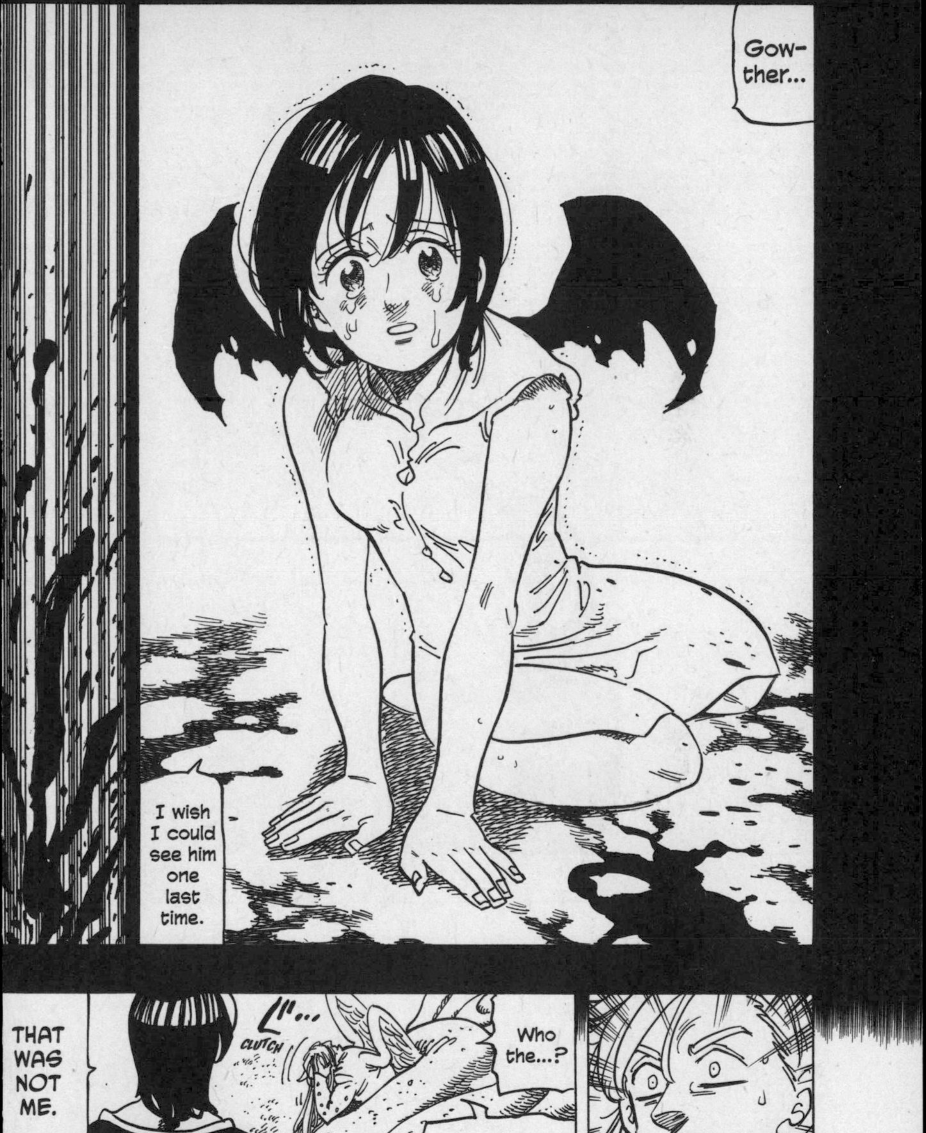
Gow-ther...
I wish I could see him one last time.
Who the...?
CLUTCH
She looked just like you, Gowther.
THAT WAS NOT ME.

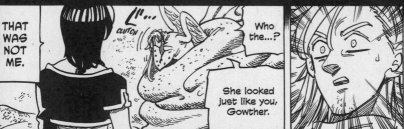

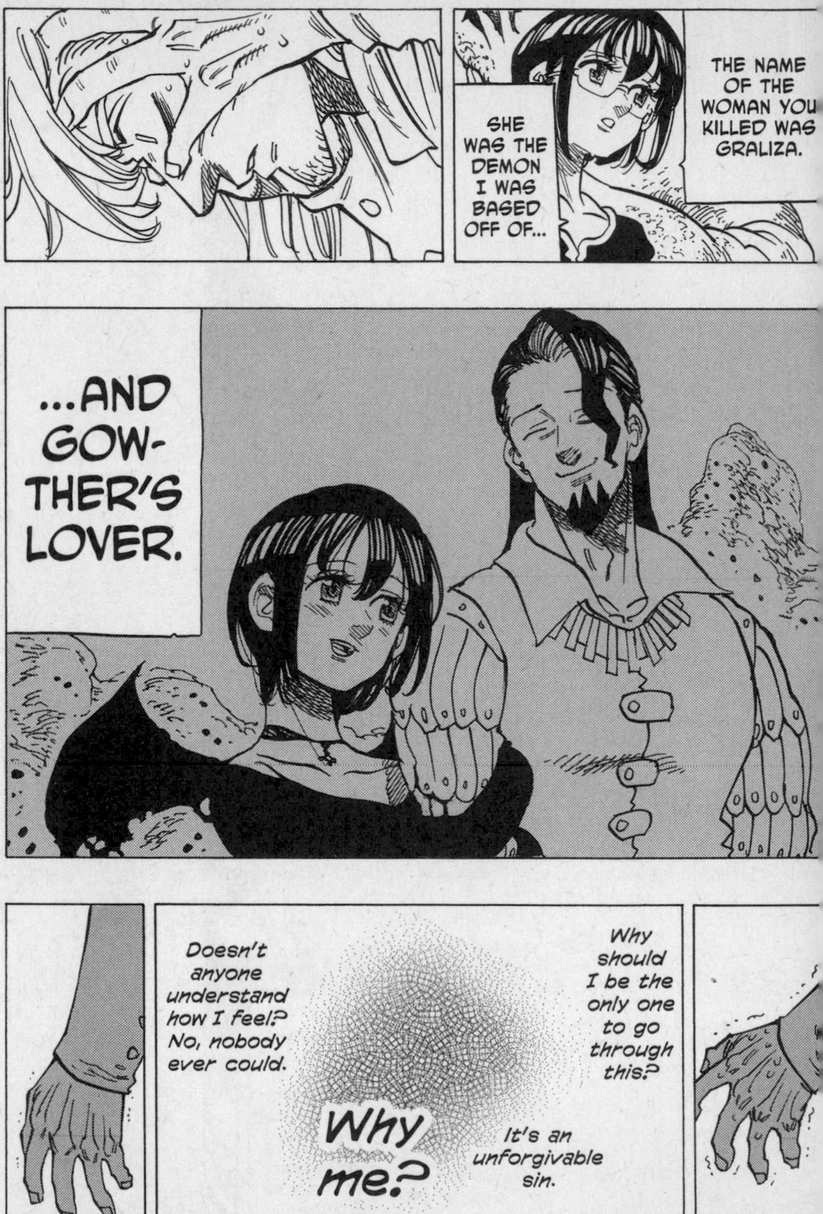
THE NAME OF THE WOMAN YOU KILLED WAS GRALIZA.
SHE WAS THE DEMON I WAS BASED OFF OF...
...AND GOW-THER'S LOVER.
Why should I be the only one to go through this?
It's an unforgivable sin.
Why me?
Doesn't anyone understand how I feel? No, nobody ever could.

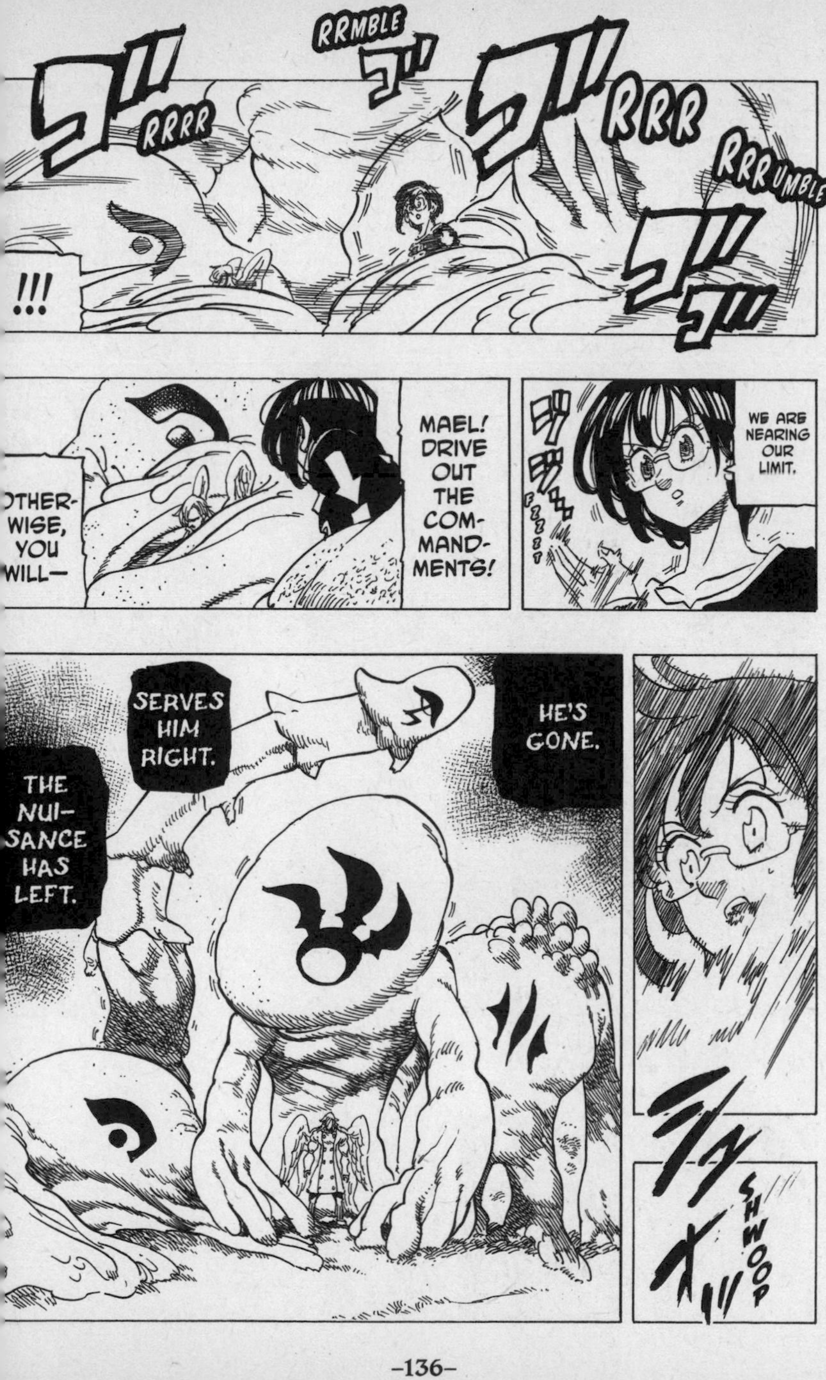
RRRUMBLE
RRR
RRMBLE
RRRR
!!!
WE ARE NEARING OUR LIMIT.
FZZZT
MAEL! DRIVE OUT THE COMMANDMENTS!
OTHERWISE, YOU WILL—
SHWOOP
HE'S GONE.
SERVES HIM RIGHT.
THE NUISANCE HAS LEFT.

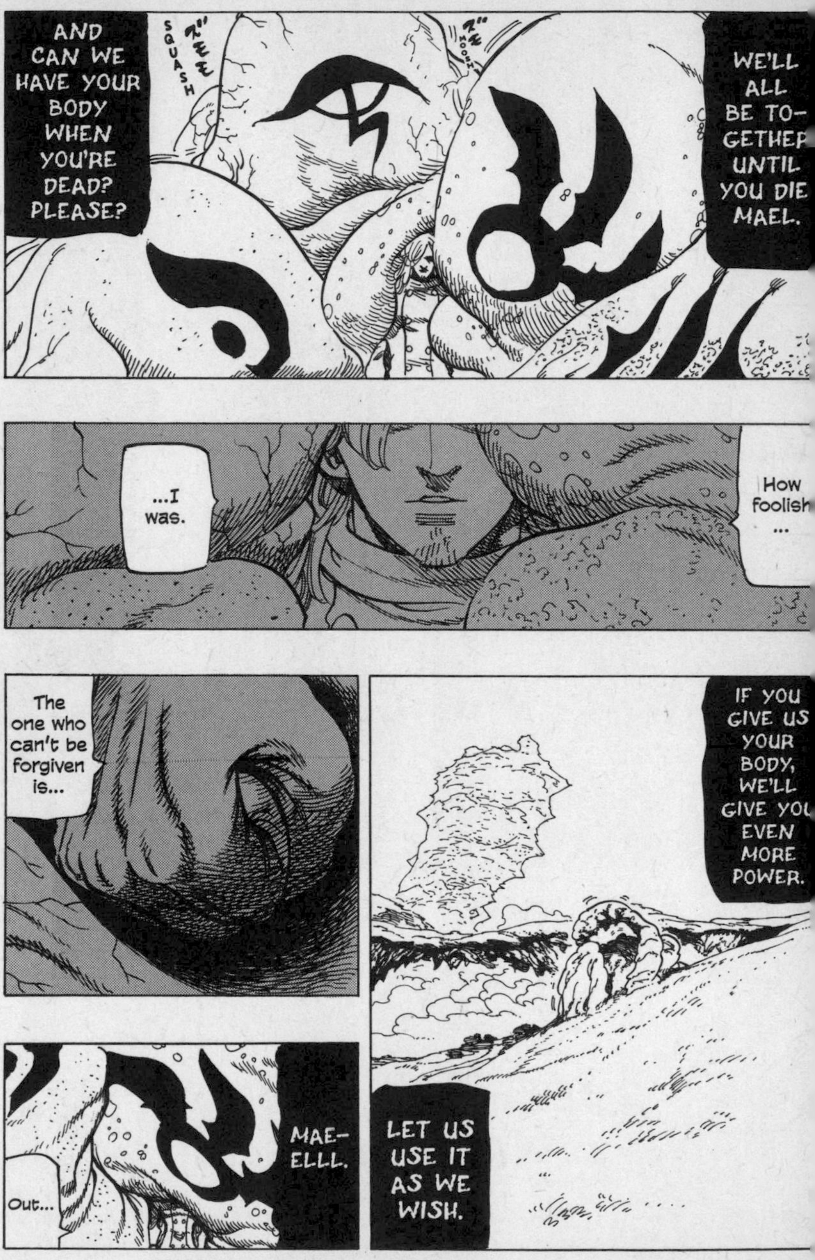
WE'LL ALL BE TO-GETHER UNTIL YOU DIE MAEL.
MOOSH
SQUASH
AND CAN WE HAVE YOUR BODY WHEN YOU'RE DEAD? PLEASE?
How foolish...
...I was.
IF YOU GIVE US YOUR BODY, WE'LL GIVE YOU EVEN MORE POWER.
LET US USE IT AS WE WISH.
The one who can't be forgiven is...
MAE-ELLL.
Out...

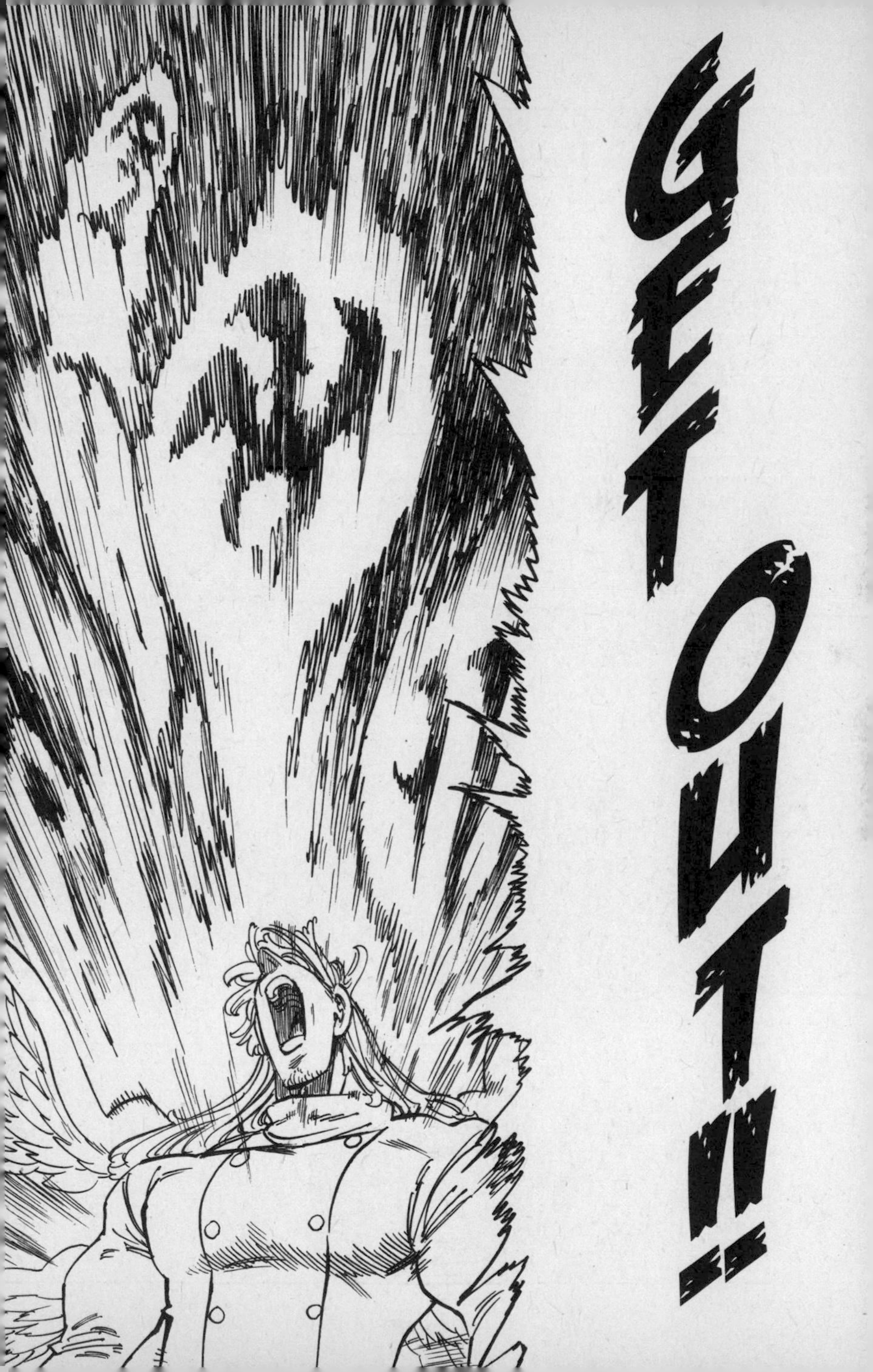
GET OUT!!

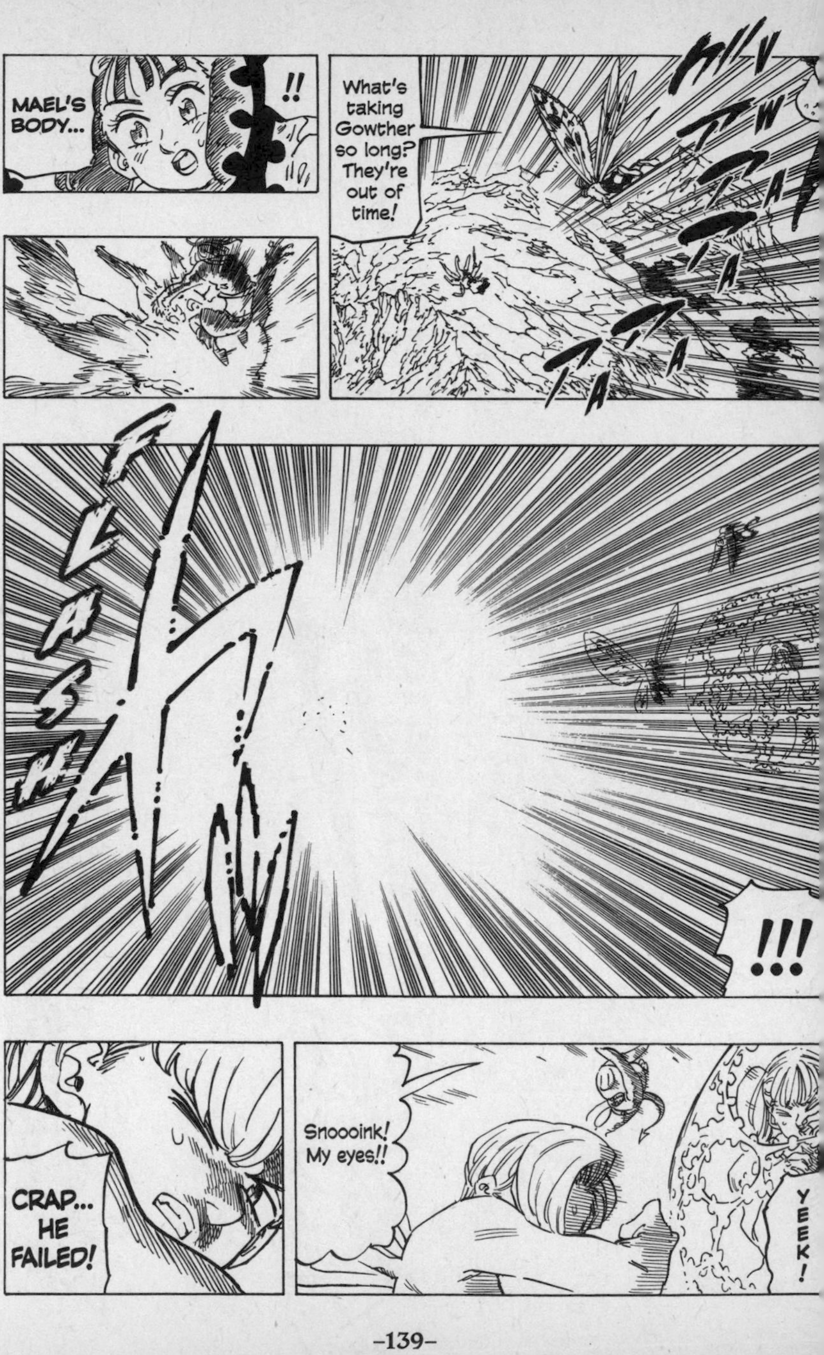
What's taking Gowther so long? They're out of time!
MAEL'S BODY...
!!
!!!
Snoooink! My eyes!!
YEEK!
CRAP... HE FAILED!

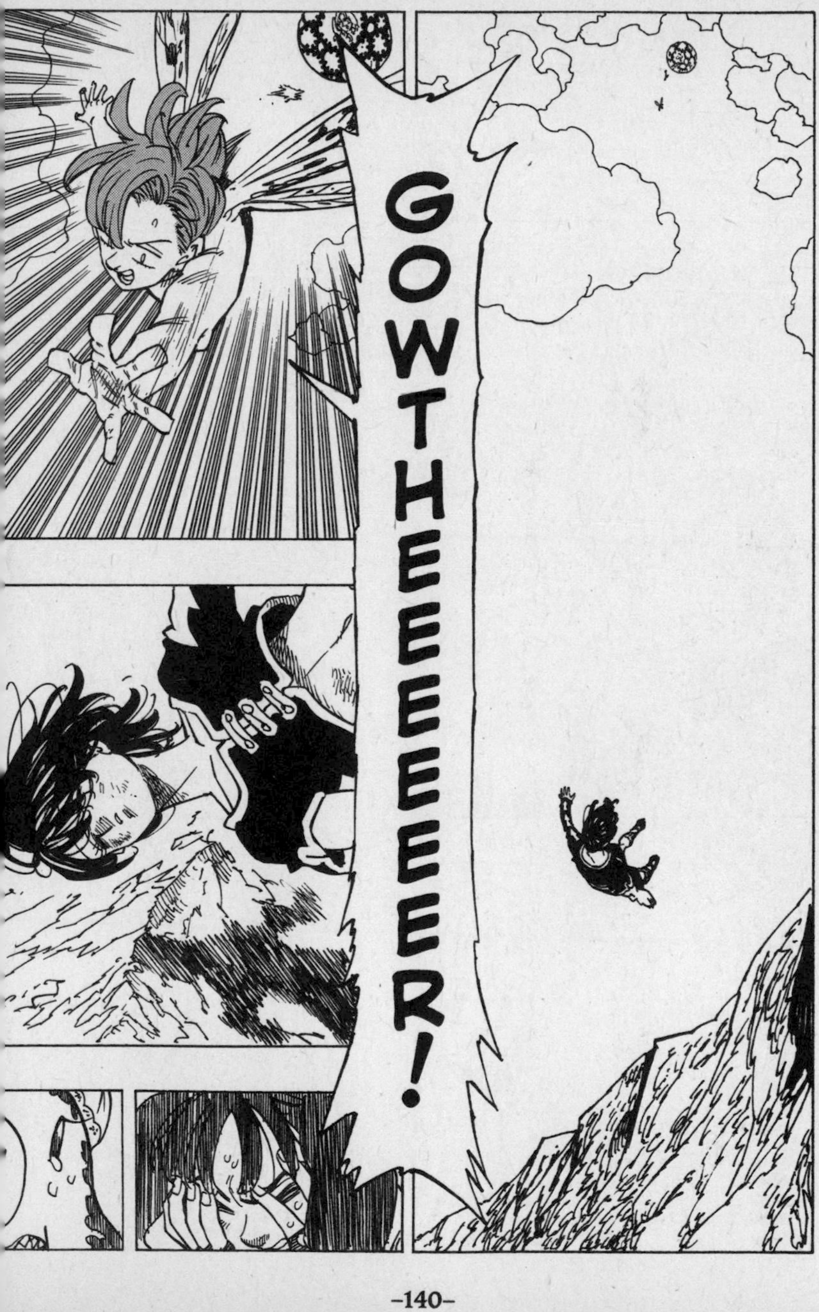
GOWTHEEEEEER!

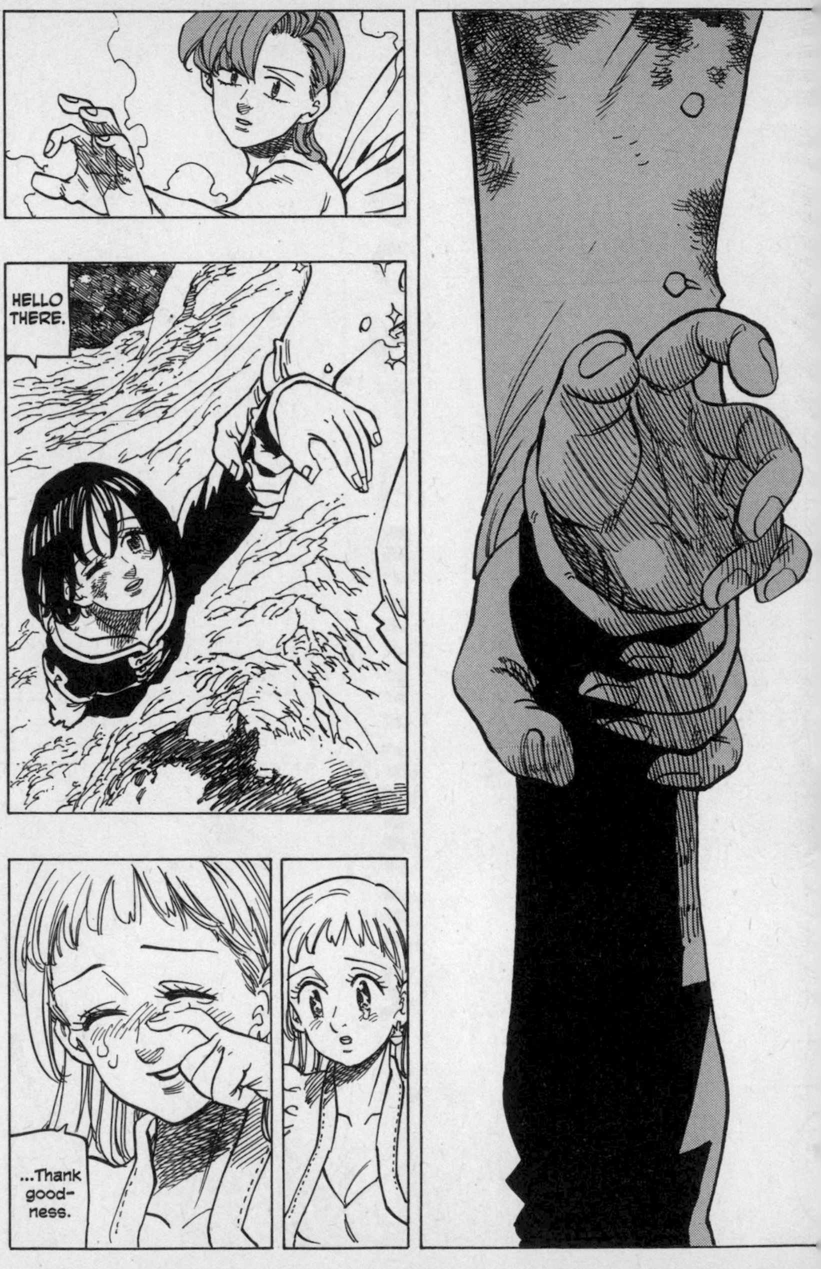
HELLO THERE.
...Thank goodness.

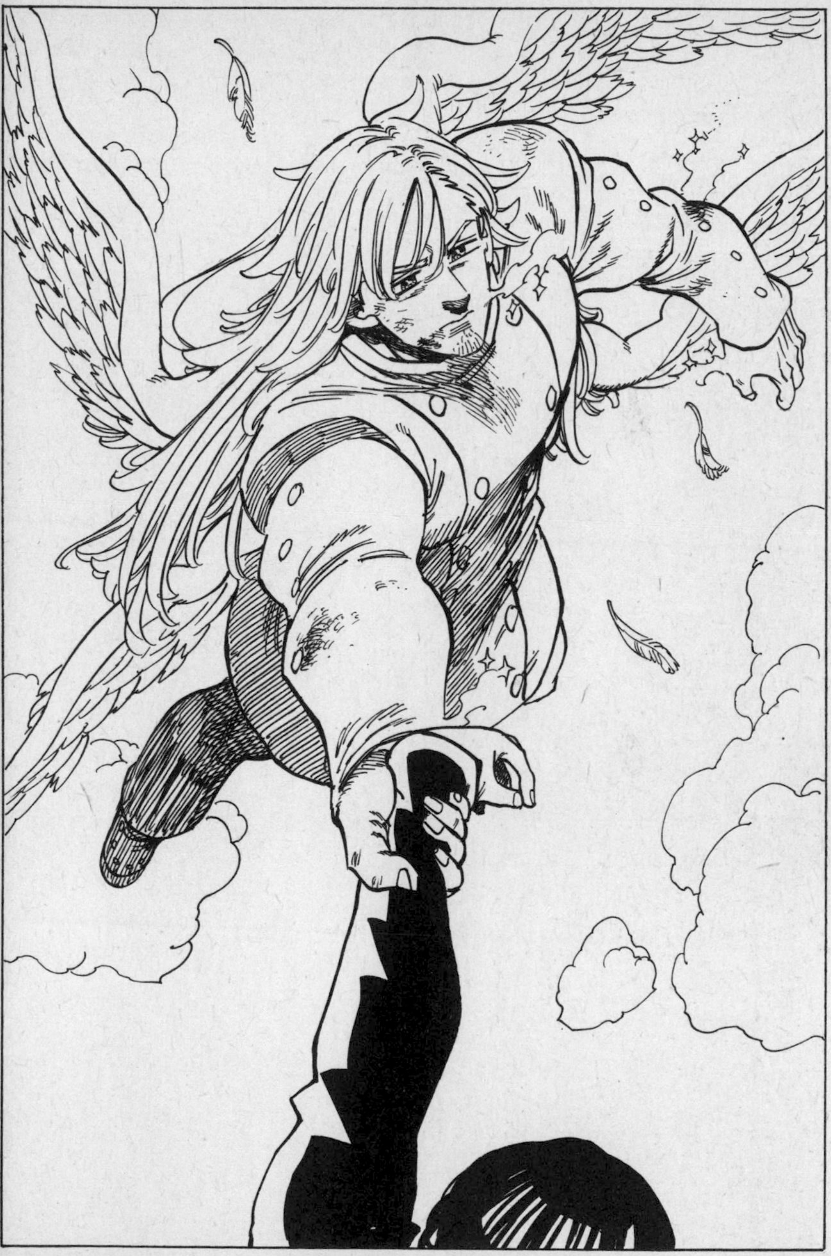

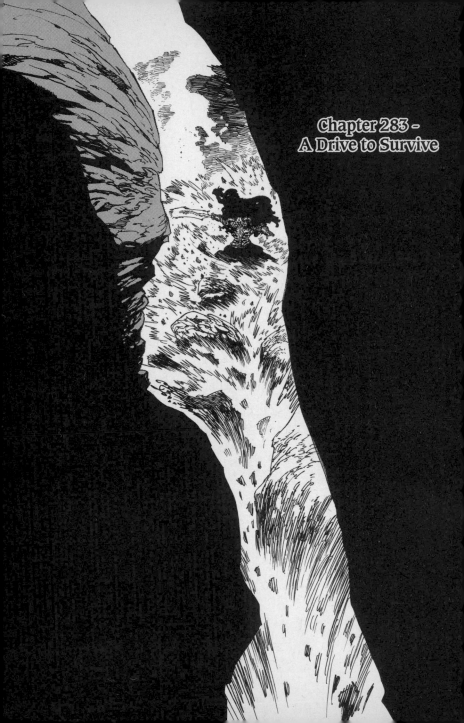

Chapter 283 –
A Drive to Survive

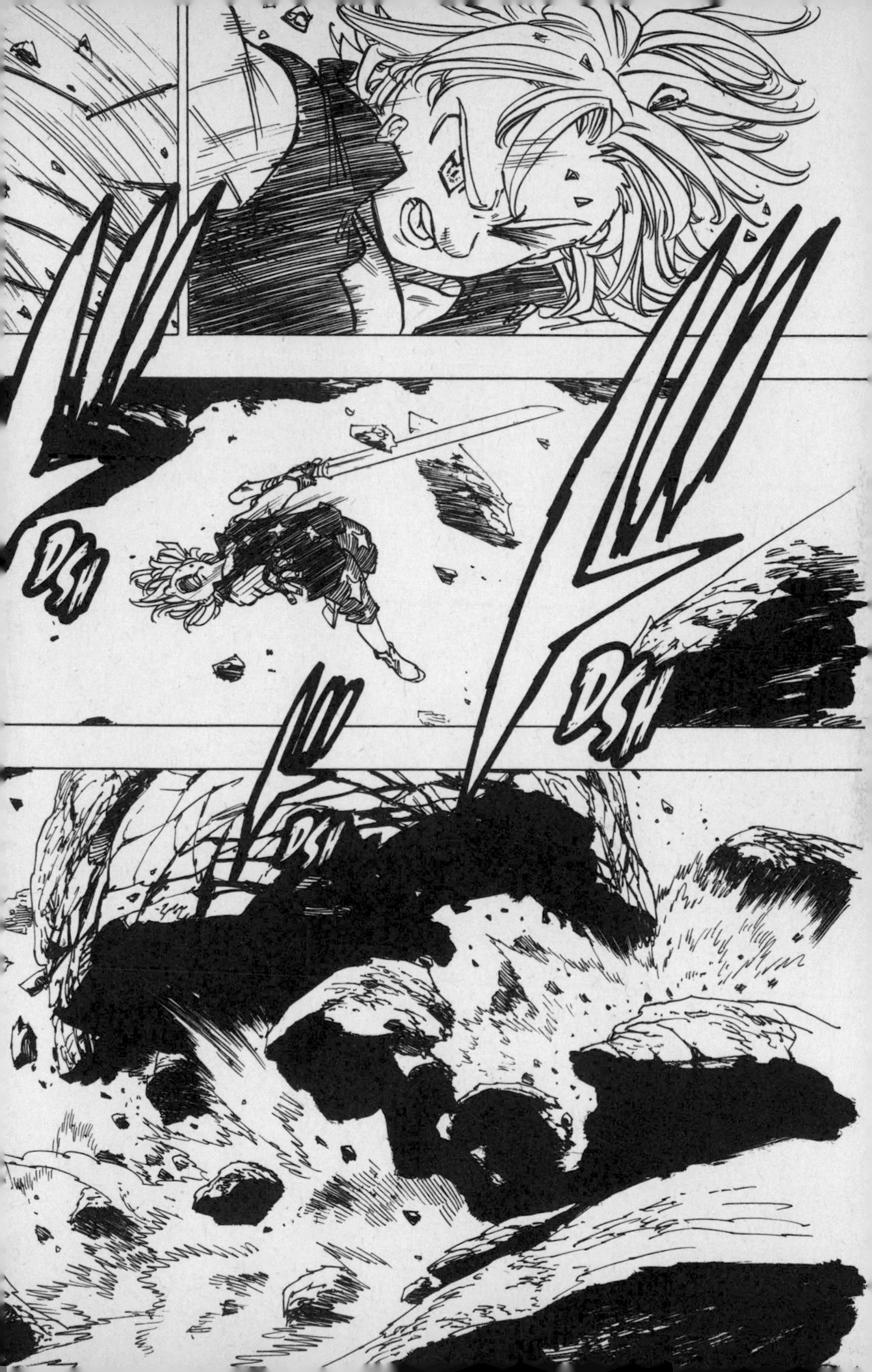
DSH
DSH
DSH

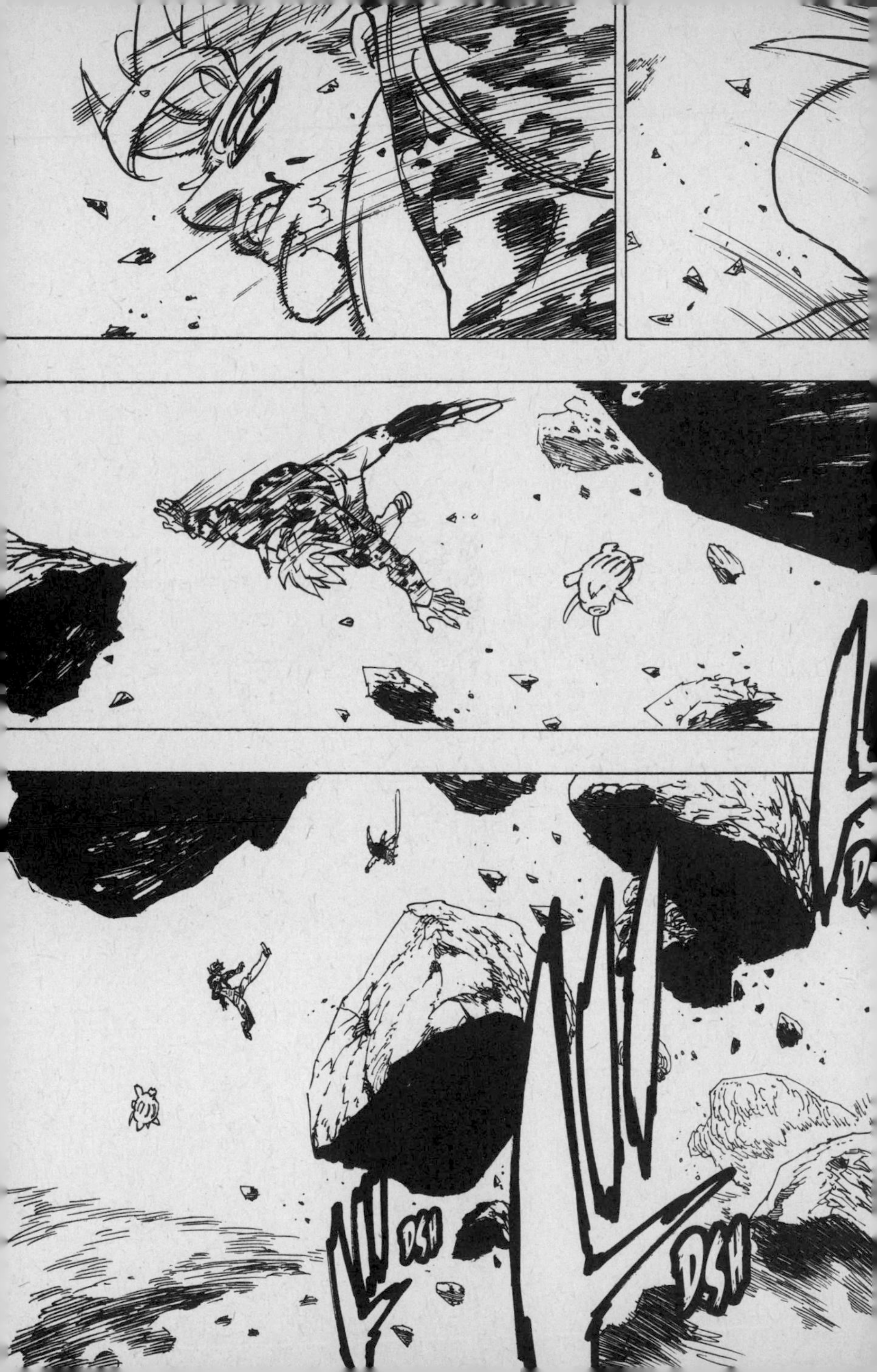
DSH
DSH

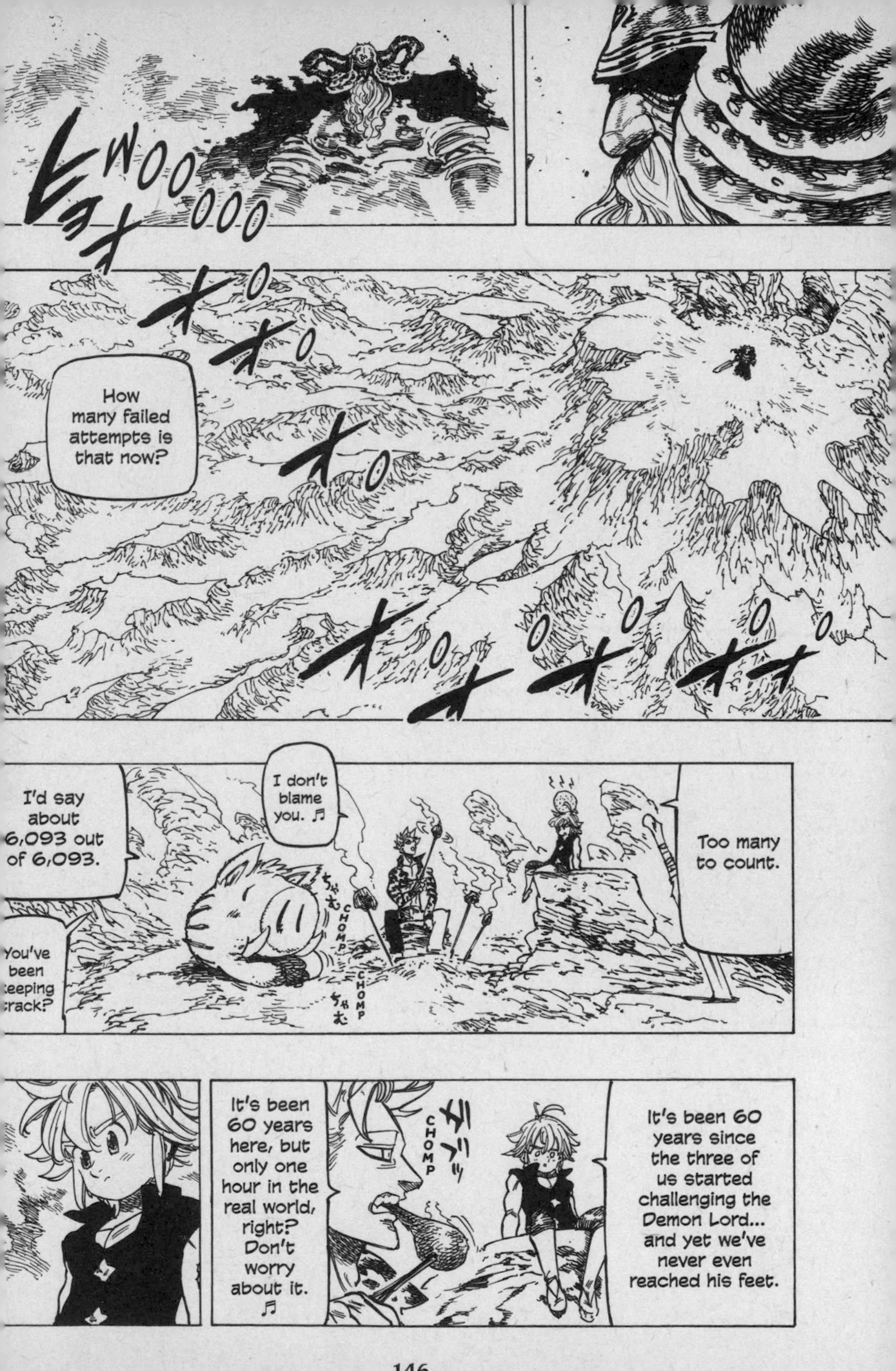
WOOOOOOOOOOOOOOO
How many failed attempts is that now?
Too many to count.
I don't blame you. ♫
I'd say about 6,093 out of 6,093.
You've been eeping rack?
CHOMP
CHOMP
It's been 60 years since the three of us started challenging the Demon Lord... and yet we've never even reached his feet.
CHOMP
It's been 60 years here, but only one hour in the real world, right? Don't worry about it. ♫

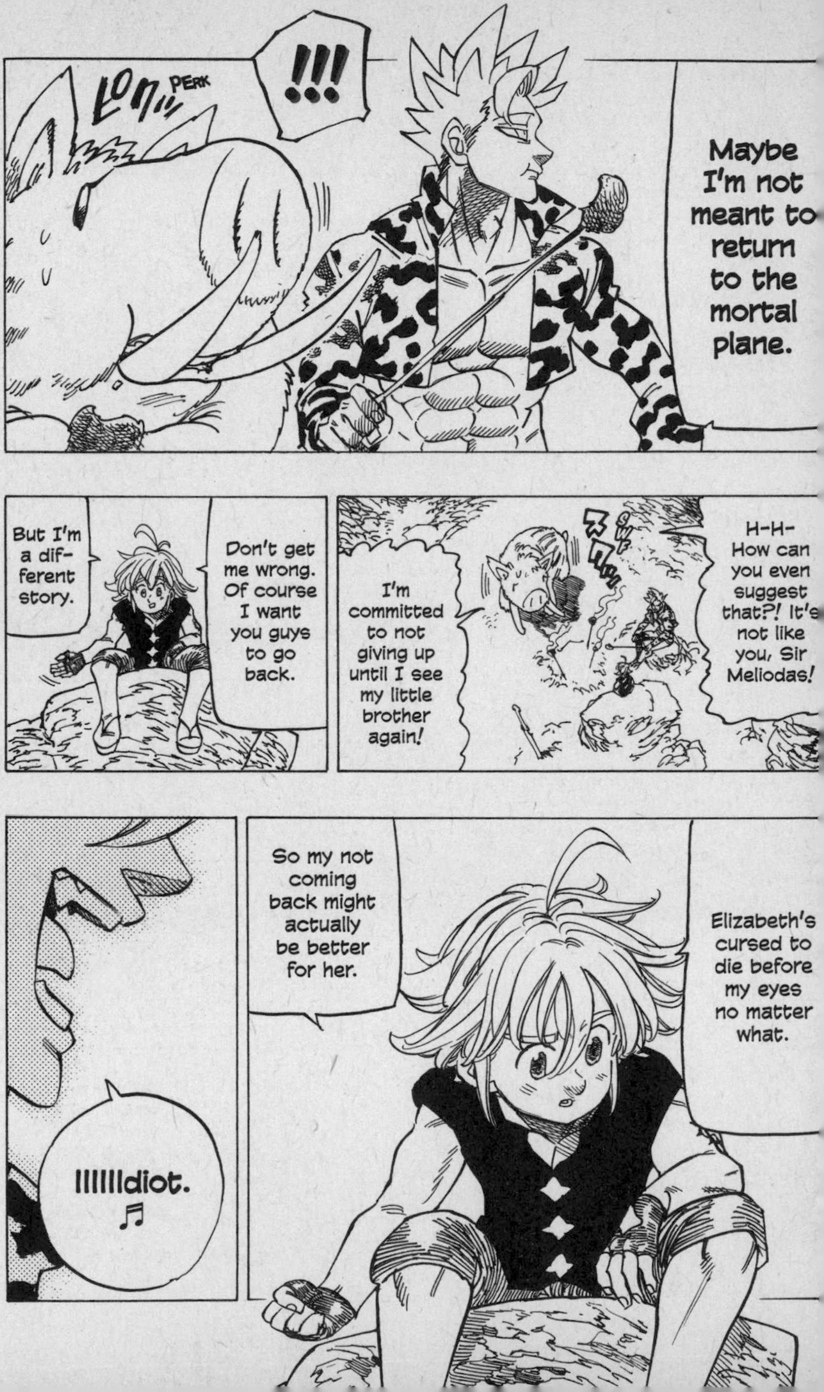

Maybe I'm not meant to return to the mortal plane.
!!!
PERK
H-H-How can you even suggest that?! It's not like you, Sir Meliodas!
I'm committed to not giving up until I see my little brother again!
Don't get me wrong. Of course I want you guys to go back.
But I'm a different story.
Elizabeth's cursed to die before my eyes no matter what.
So my not coming back might actually be better for her.
IIIIIIdiot. ♫

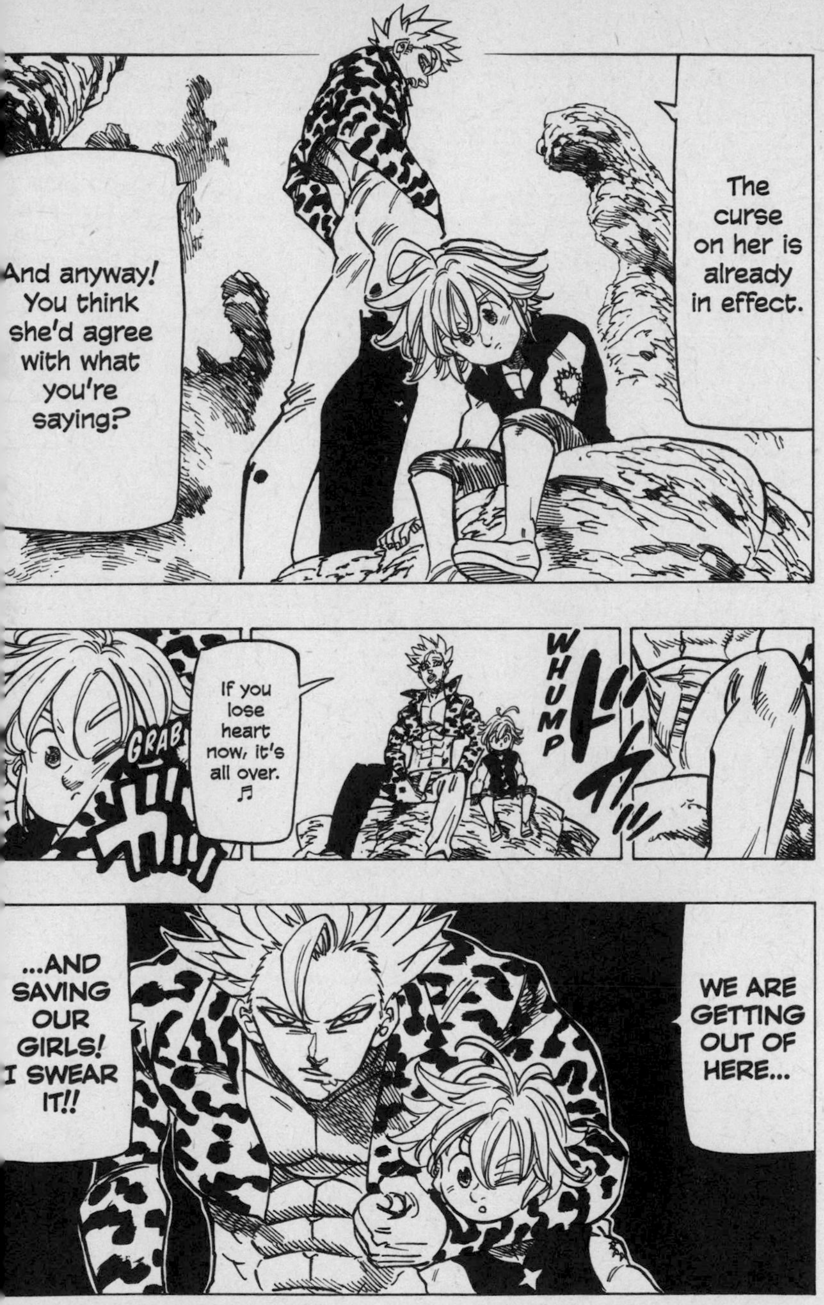
The curse on her is already in effect.
And anyway! You think she'd agree with what you're saying?
WHUMP
If you lose heart now, it's all over. ♬
GRAB
WE ARE GETTING OUT OF HERE...
...AND SAVING OUR GIRLS! I SWEAR IT!!

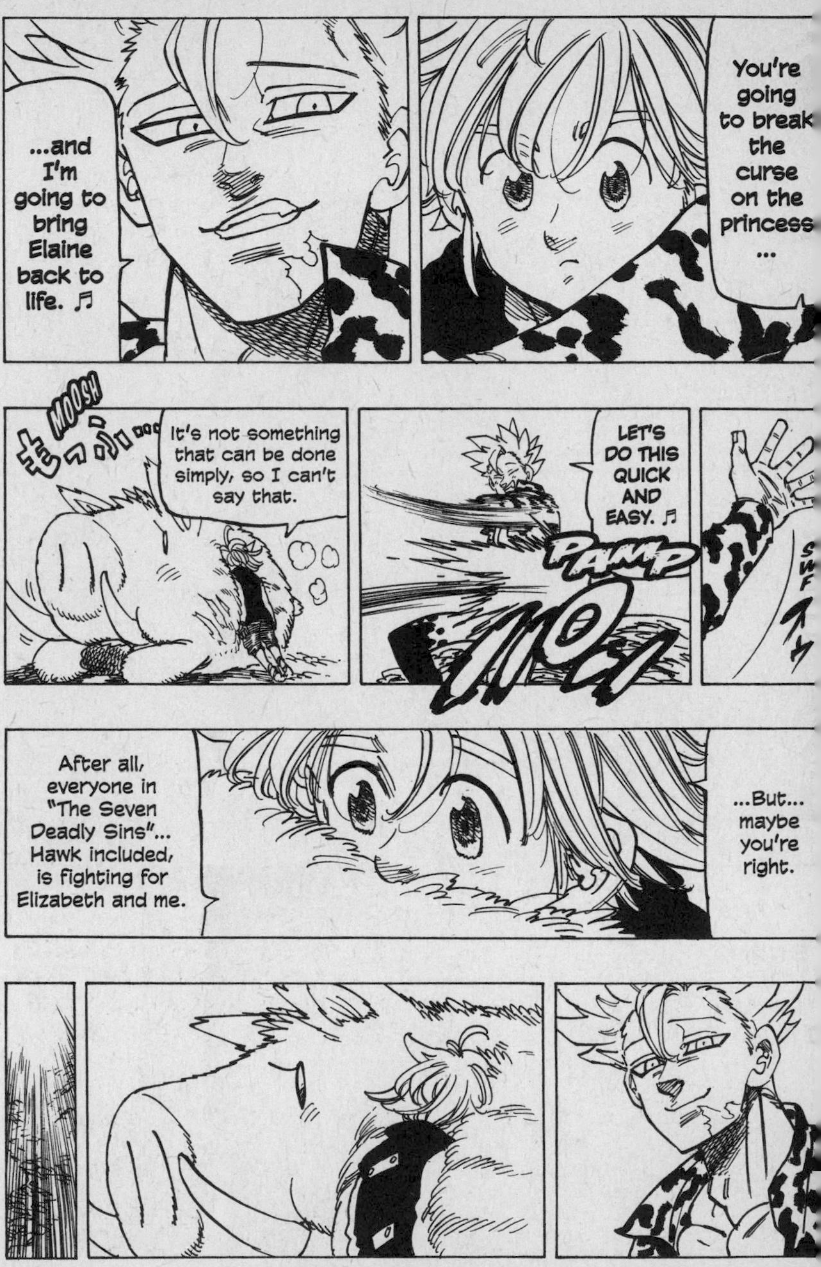
You're going to break the curse on the princess ...
...and I'm going to bring Elaine back to life. ♫
SWF
LET'S DO THIS QUICK AND EASY. ♫
PAMP
MOOSH
It's not something that can be done simply, so I can't say that.
...But... maybe you're right.
After all, everyone in "The Seven Deadly Sins"... Hawk included, is fighting for Elizabeth and me.

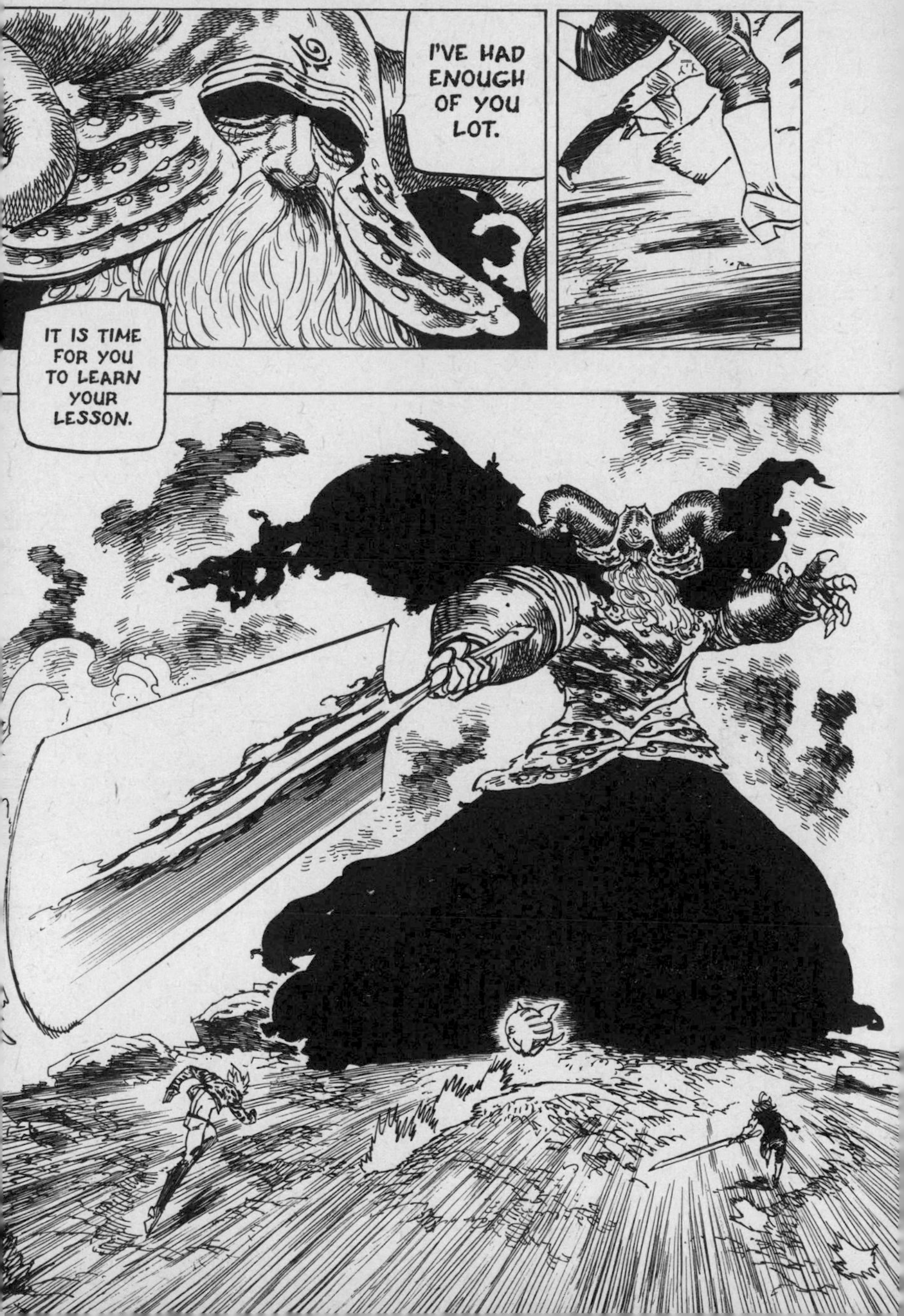
I'VE HAD ENOUGH OF YOU LOT.
IT IS TIME FOR YOU TO LEARN YOUR LESSON.

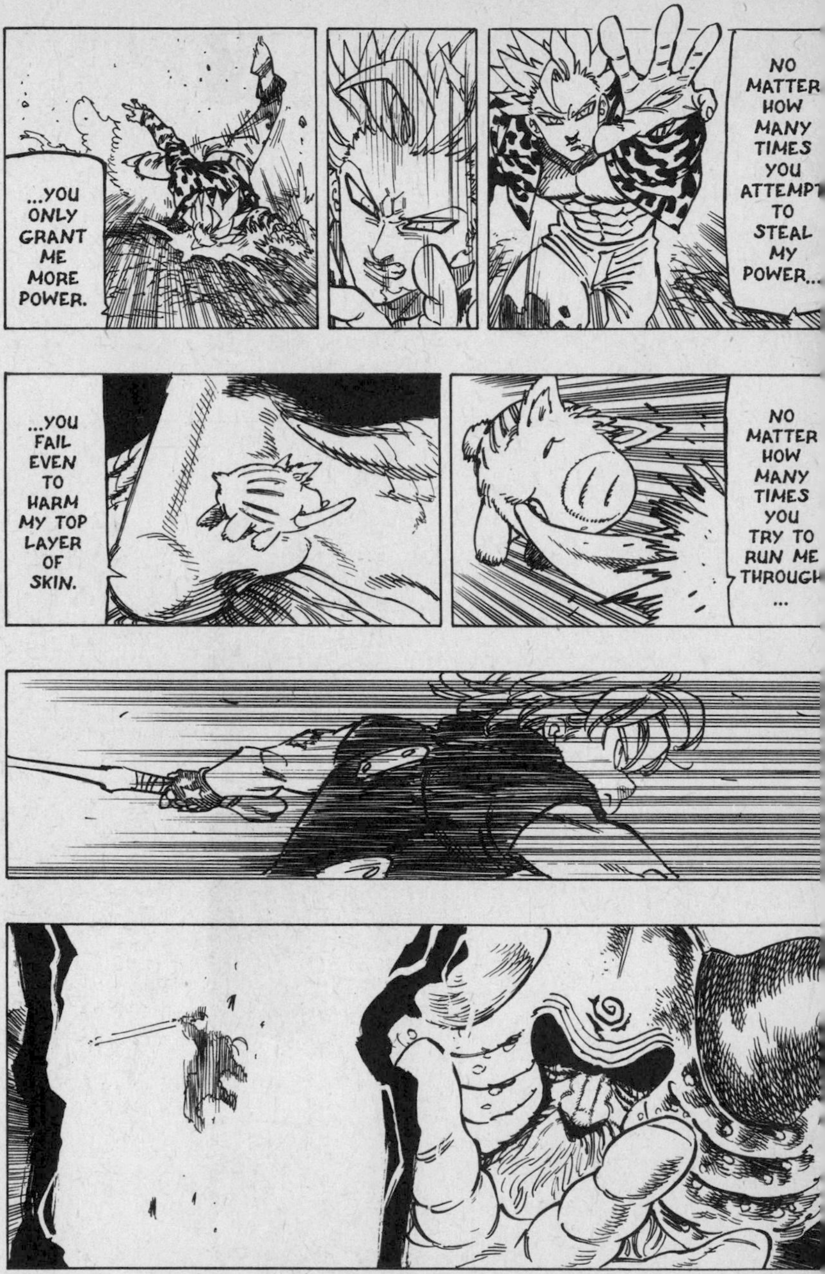
NO MATTER HOW MANY TIMES YOU ATTEMPT TO STEAL MY POWER...
...YOU ONLY GRANT ME MORE POWER.
NO MATTER HOW MANY TIMES YOU TRY TO RUN ME THROUGH ...
...YOU FAIL EVEN TO HARM MY TOP LAYER OF SKIN.

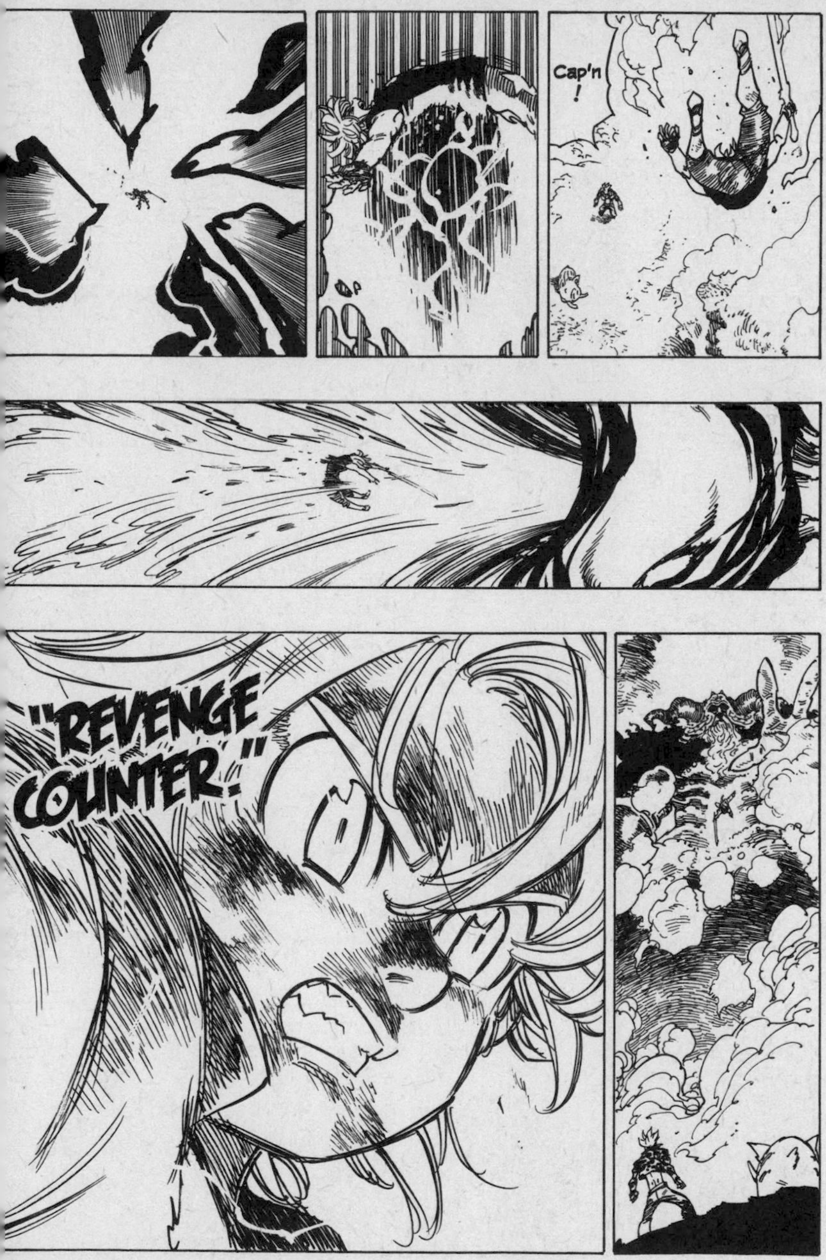
Cap'n
!
"REVENGE COUNTER."

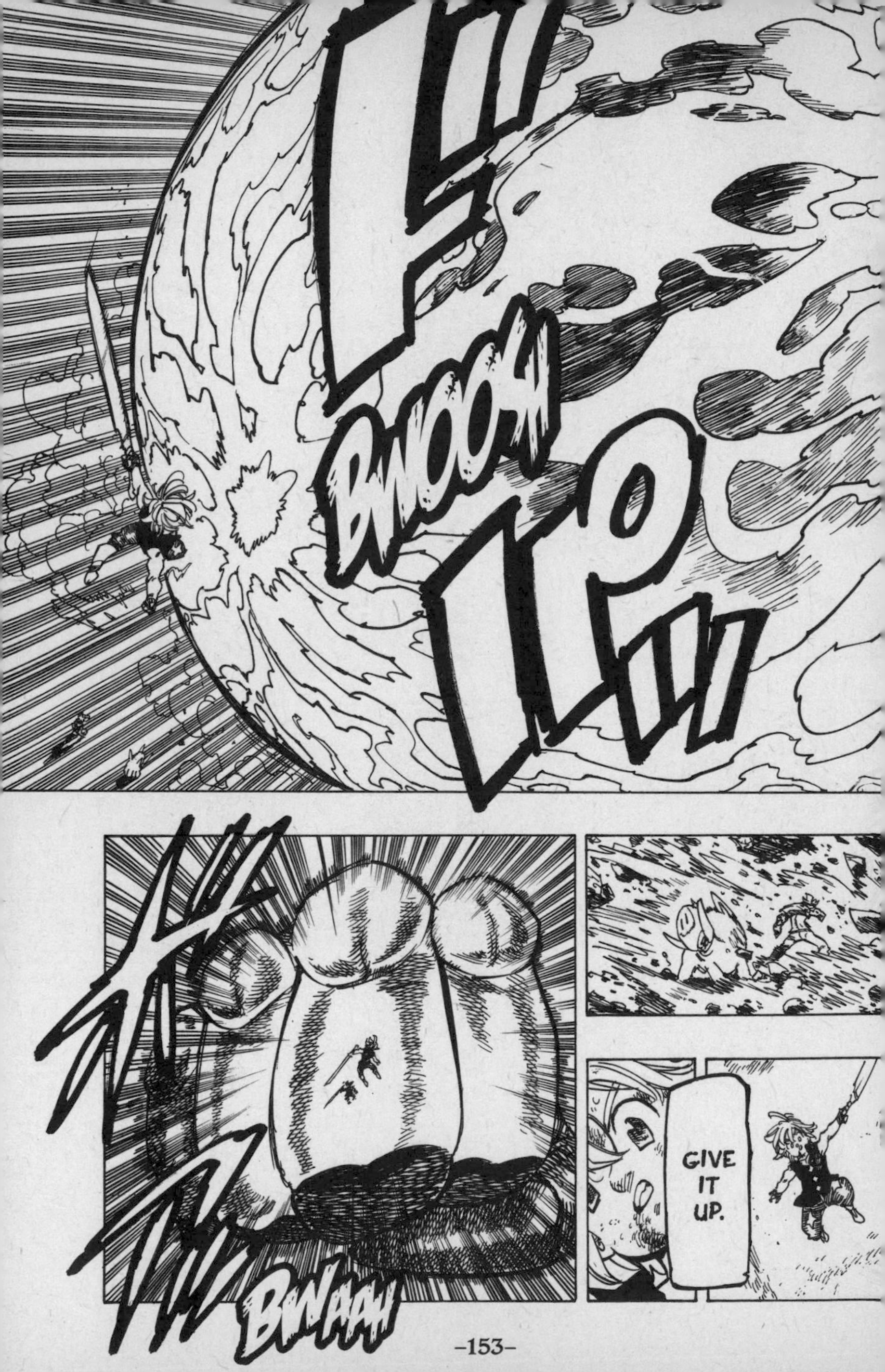
BWOOM
GIVE IT UP.
BWAAH

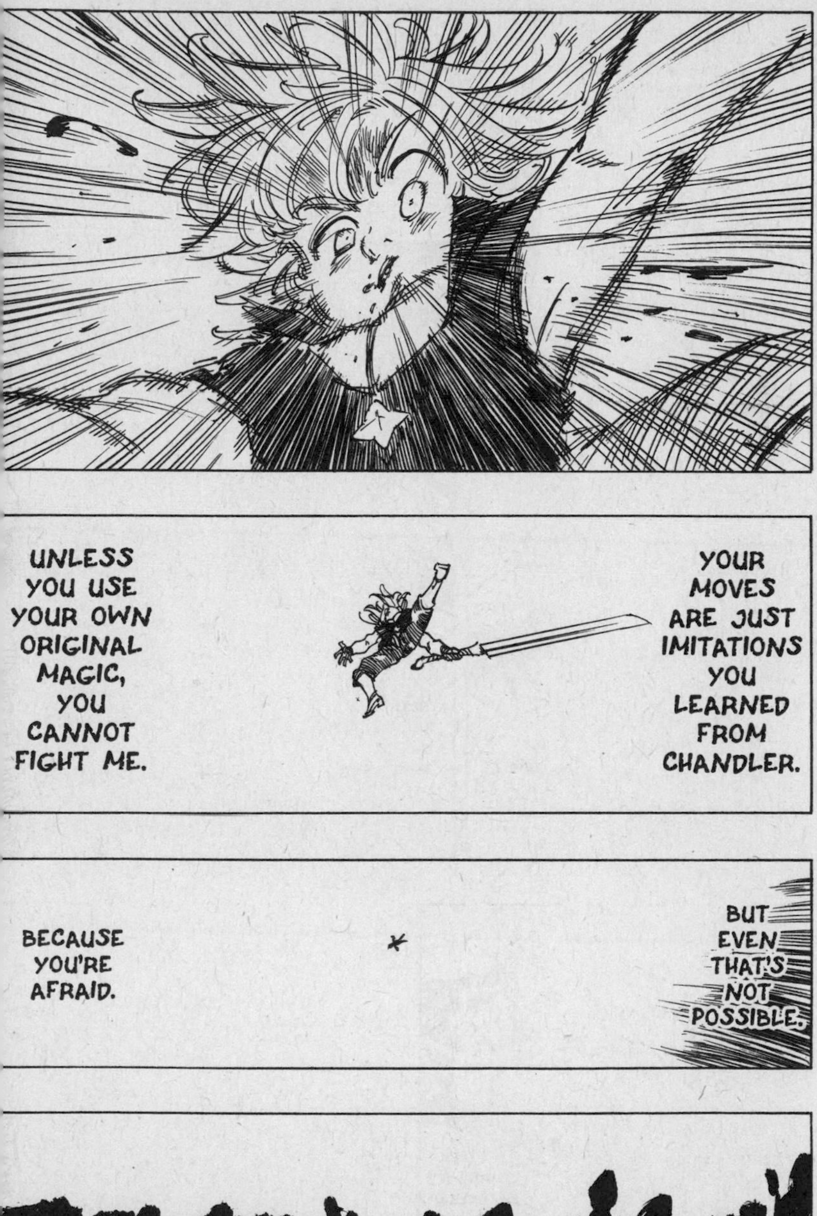
YOUR MOVES ARE JUST IMITATIONS YOU LEARNED FROM CHANDLER.
UNLESS YOU USE YOUR OWN ORIGINAL MAGIC, YOU CANNOT FIGHT ME.
BUT EVEN THAT'S NOT POSSIBLE.
BECAUSE YOU'RE AFRAID.

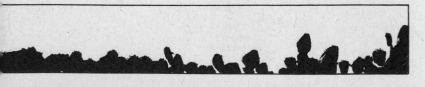

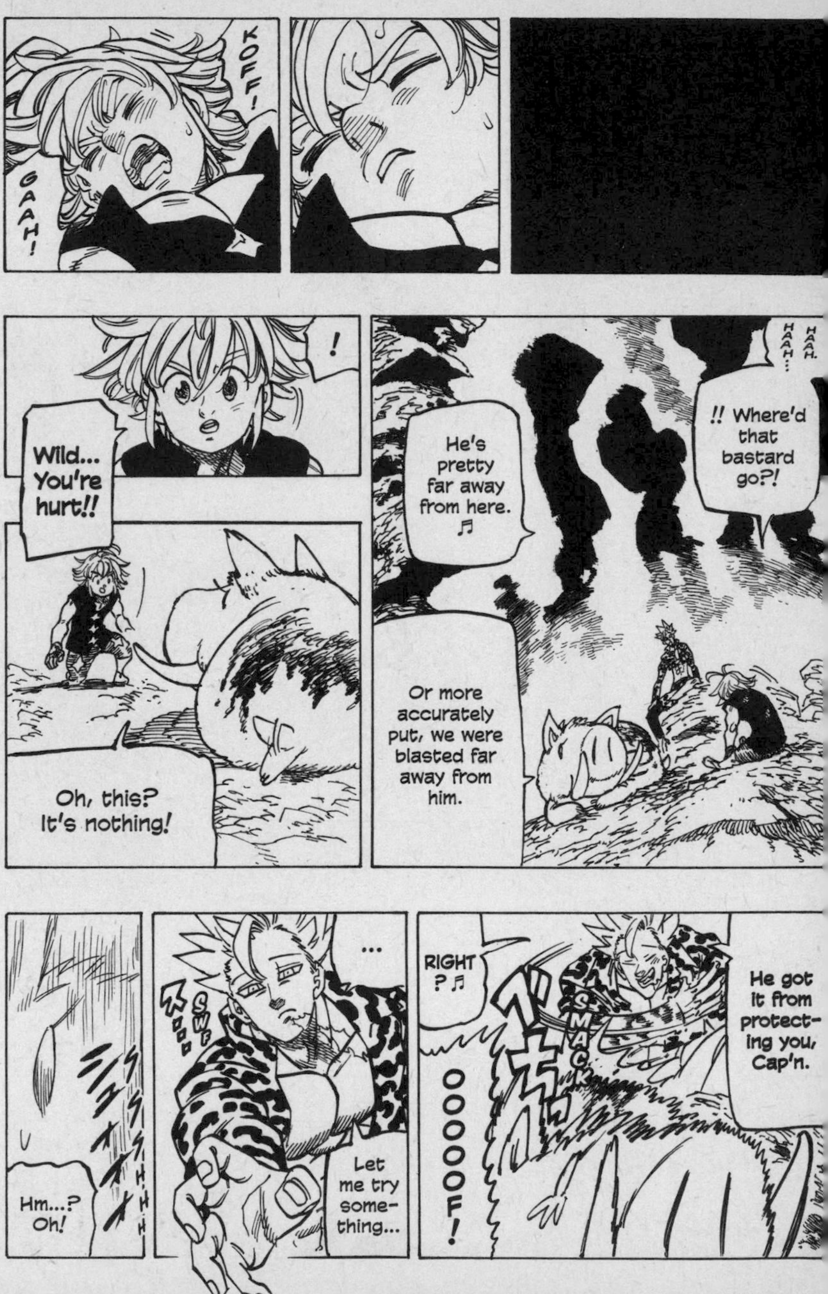
KOFF!
GAAAH!
HAAH... HAAH.
!! Where'd that bastard go?!
He's pretty far away from here. ♬
Or more accurately put, we were blasted far away from him.
!
Wild... You're hurt!!
Oh, this? It's nothing!
He got it from protecting you, Cap'n.
RIGHT? ♬
SMACK
OOOOOOF!
...
SWF
Let me try something...
SSSHHHH
Hm...? Oh!

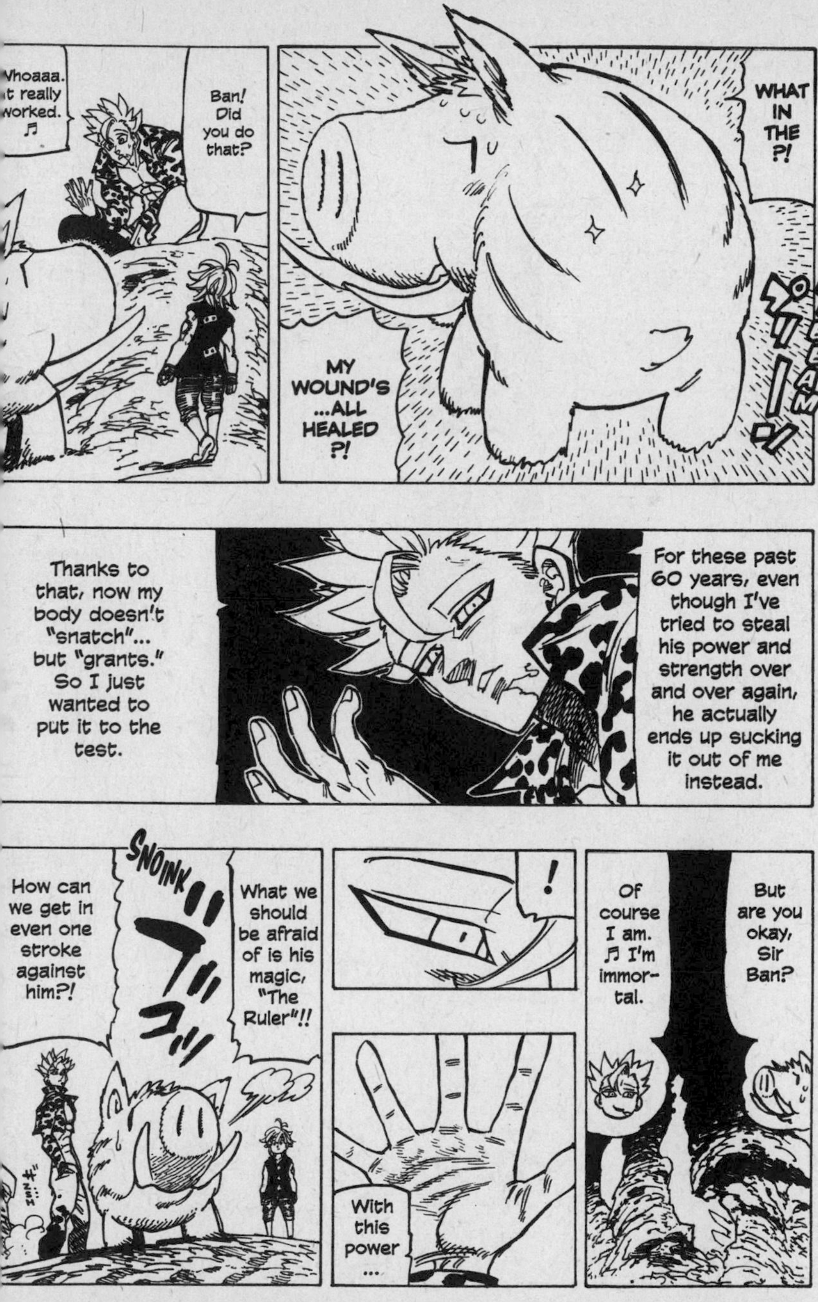
WHAT IN THE ?!
GLEEEAM!
MY WOUND'S ...ALL HEALED ?!
Ban! Did you do that?
Whoaaa. It really worked. ♫
For these past 60 years, even though I've tried to steal his power and strength over and over again, he actually ends up sucking it out of me instead.
Thanks to that, now my body doesn't "snatch"... but "grants." So I just wanted to put it to the test.
But are you okay, Sir Ban?
Of course I am. ♫ I'm immortal.
!
With this power ...
What we should be afraid of is his magic, "The Ruler"!!
SNOINK
How can we get in even one stroke against him?!

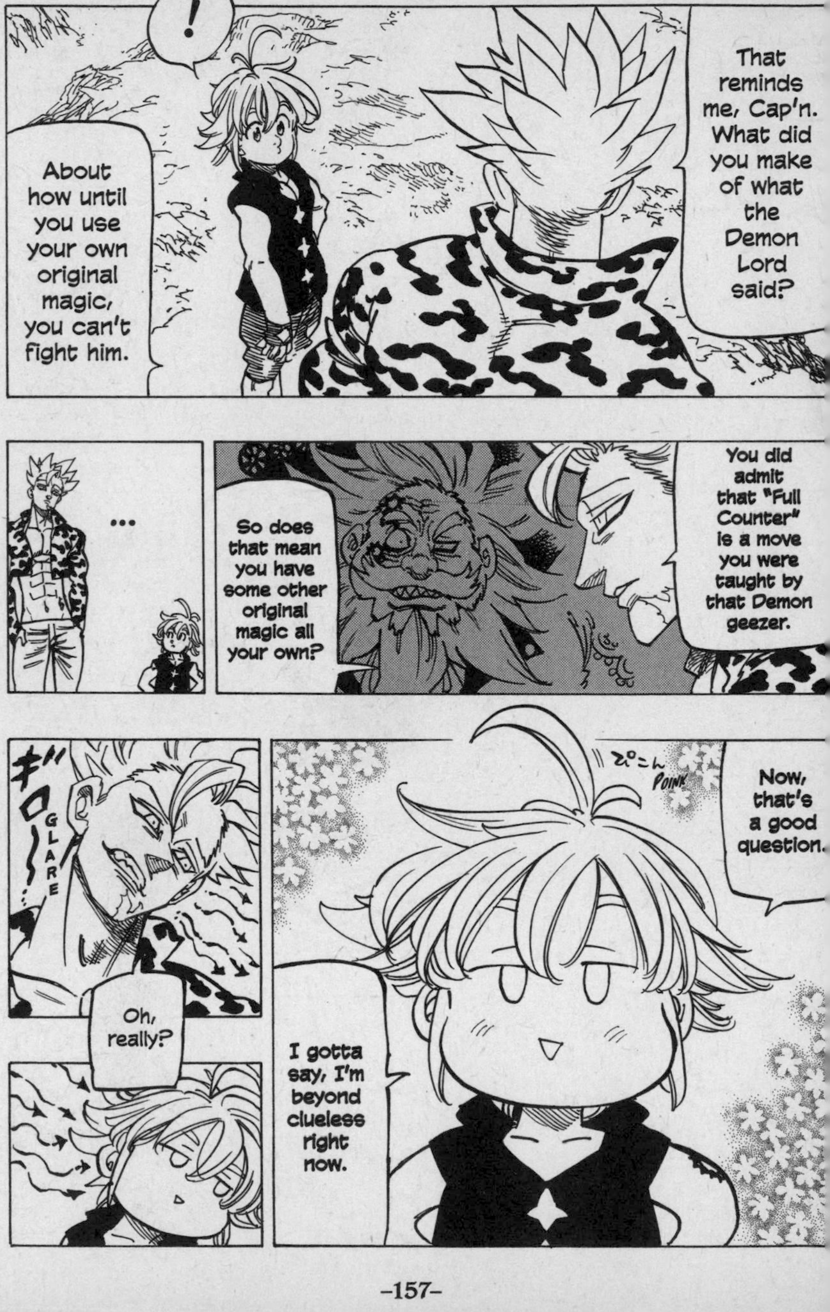
That reminds me, Cap'n. What did you make of what the Demon Lord said?
!
About how until you use your own original magic, you can't fight him.
You did admit that "Full Counter" is a move you were taught by that Demon geezer.
So does that mean you have some other original magic all your own?
...
ぴこん POINK
Now, that's a good question.
I gotta say, I'm beyond clueless right now.
ギロ GLARE
Oh, really?

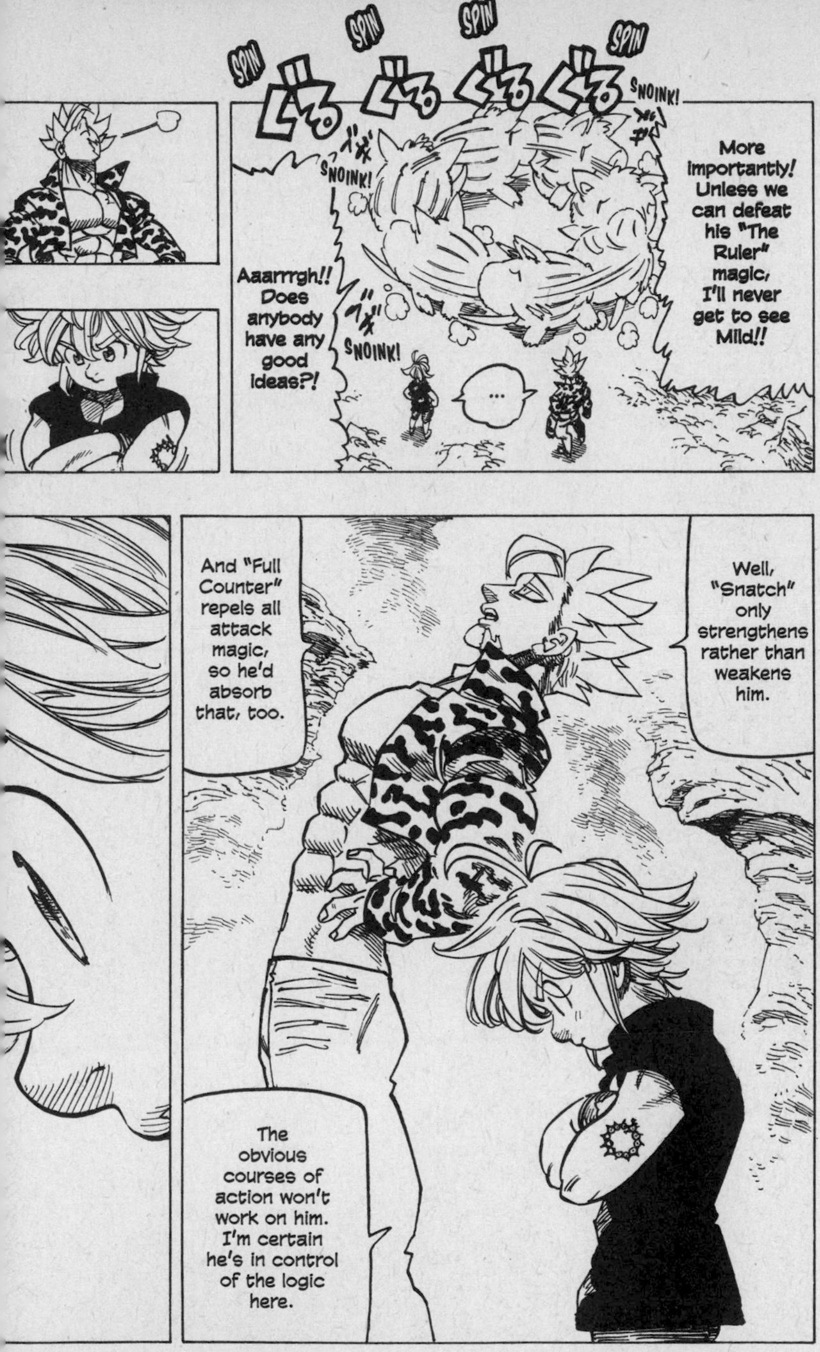
SPIN
SPIN
SPIN
SPIN
SNOINK!
More importantly! Unless we can defeat his "The Ruler" magic, I'll never get to see Mild!!
SNOINK!
Aaarrrgh!! Does anybody have any good ideas?!
SNOINK!
...
Well, "Snatch" only strengthens rather than weakens him.
And "Full Counter" repels all attack magic, so he'd absorb that, too.
The obvious courses of action won't work on him. I'm certain he's in control of the logic here.

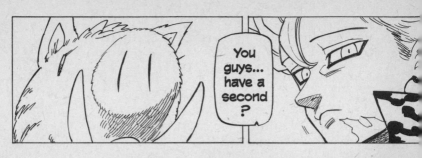

You guys... have a second?

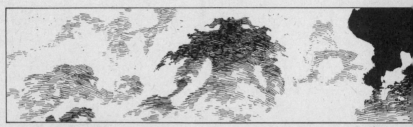

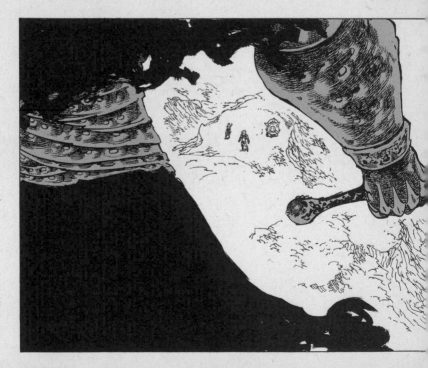

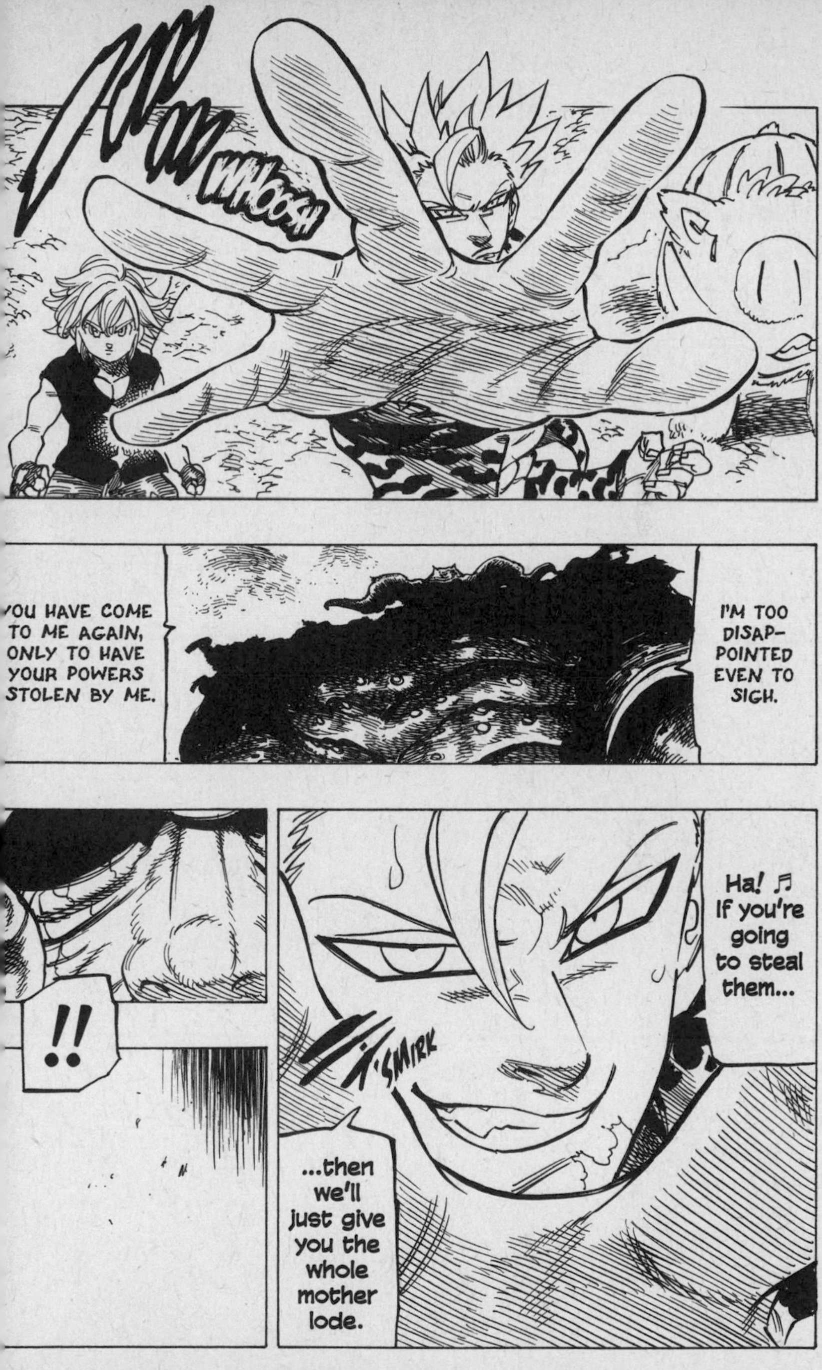
WHOOSH
I'M TOO DISAPPOINTED EVEN TO SIGH.
YOU HAVE COME TO ME AGAIN, ONLY TO HAVE YOUR POWERS STOLEN BY ME.
Ha! ♫ If you're going to steal them...
SMIRK
...then we'll just give you the whole mother lode.
!!

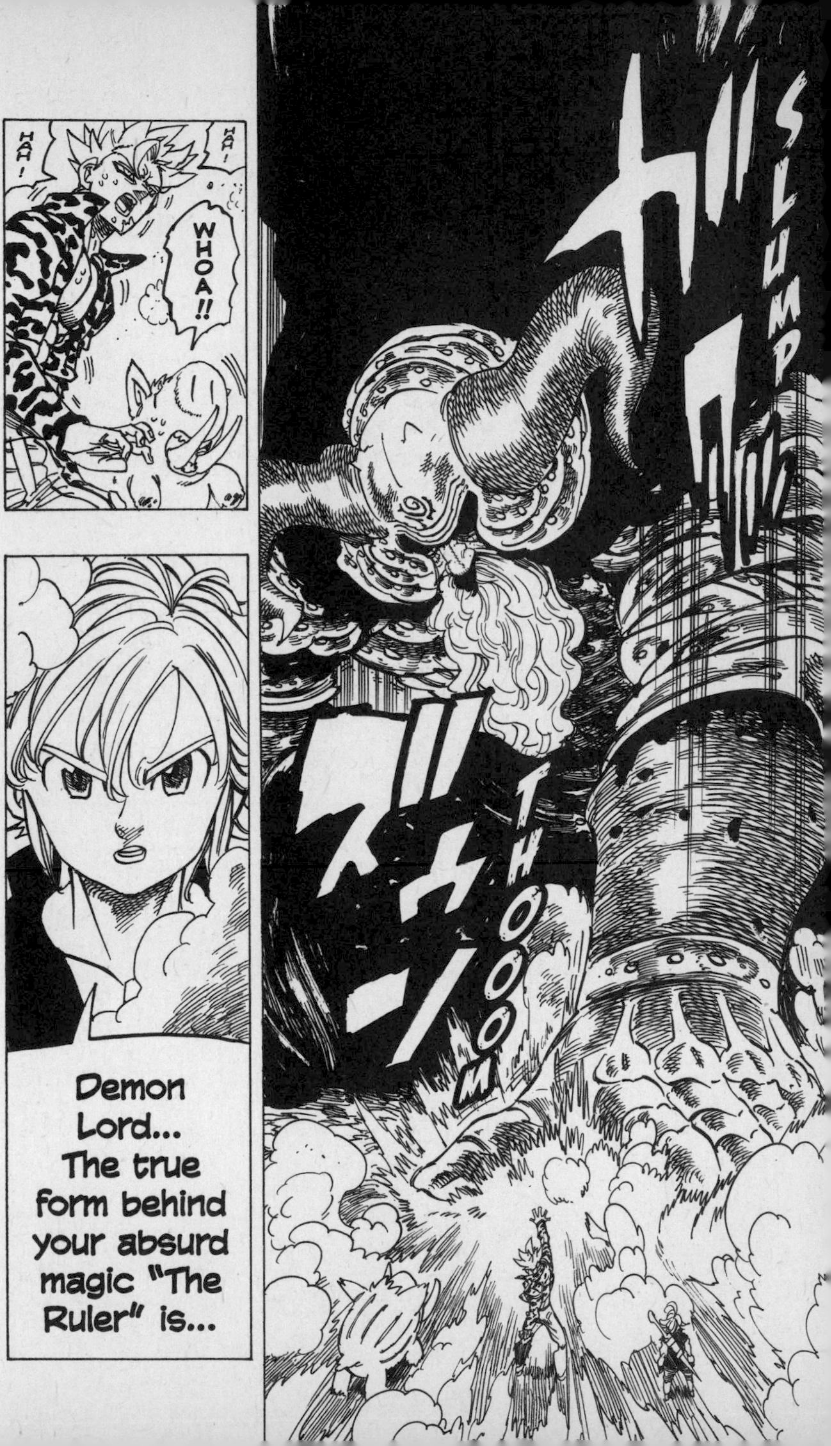
SLUMP
THOOOOM
HAH!
HAH!
WHOA!!
Demon Lord... The true form behind your absurd magic "The Ruler" is...

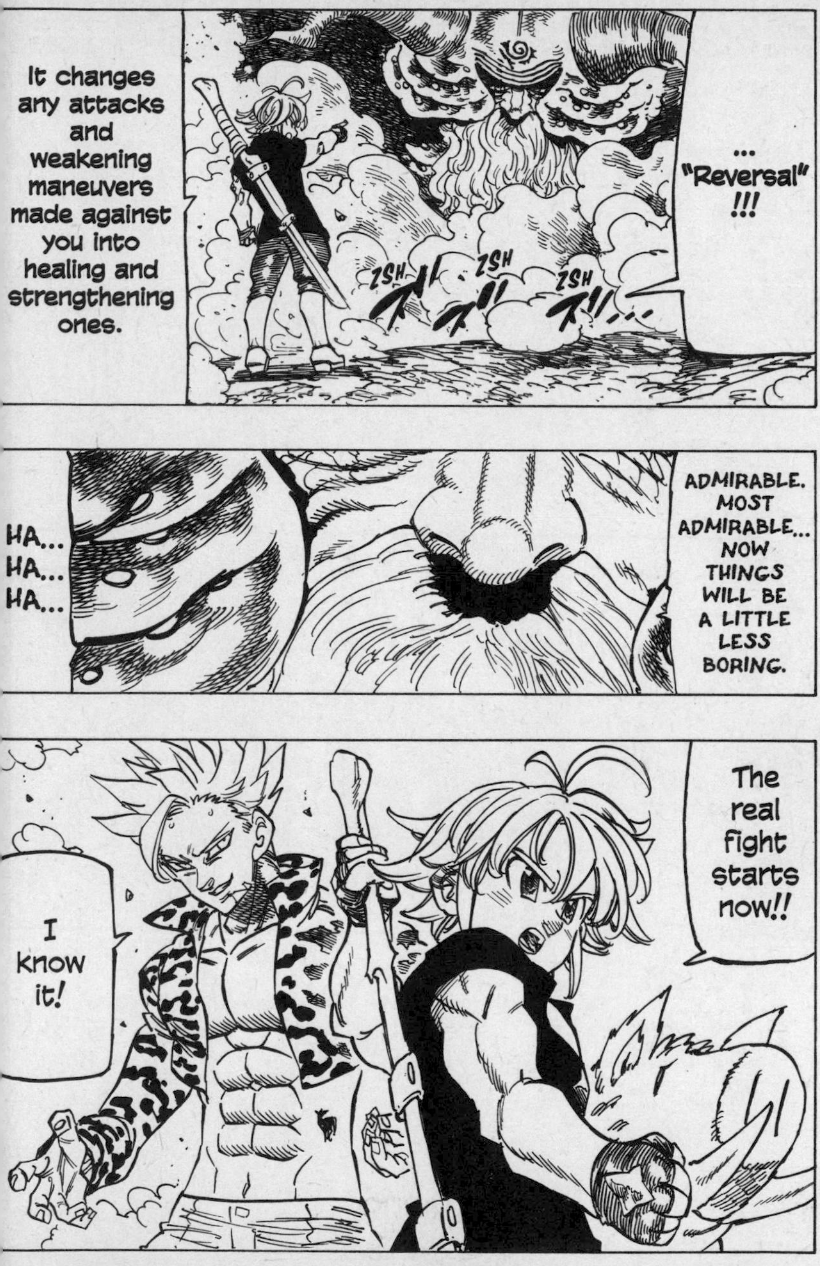
... "Reversal" !!!
ZSH ZSH ZSH
It changes any attacks and weakening maneuvers made against you into healing and strengthening ones.
ADMIRABLE. MOST ADMIRABLE... NOW THINGS WILL BE A LITTLE LESS BORING.
HA... HA... HA...
The real fight starts now!!
I know it!

Chapter 284 - The Doorway to Hope

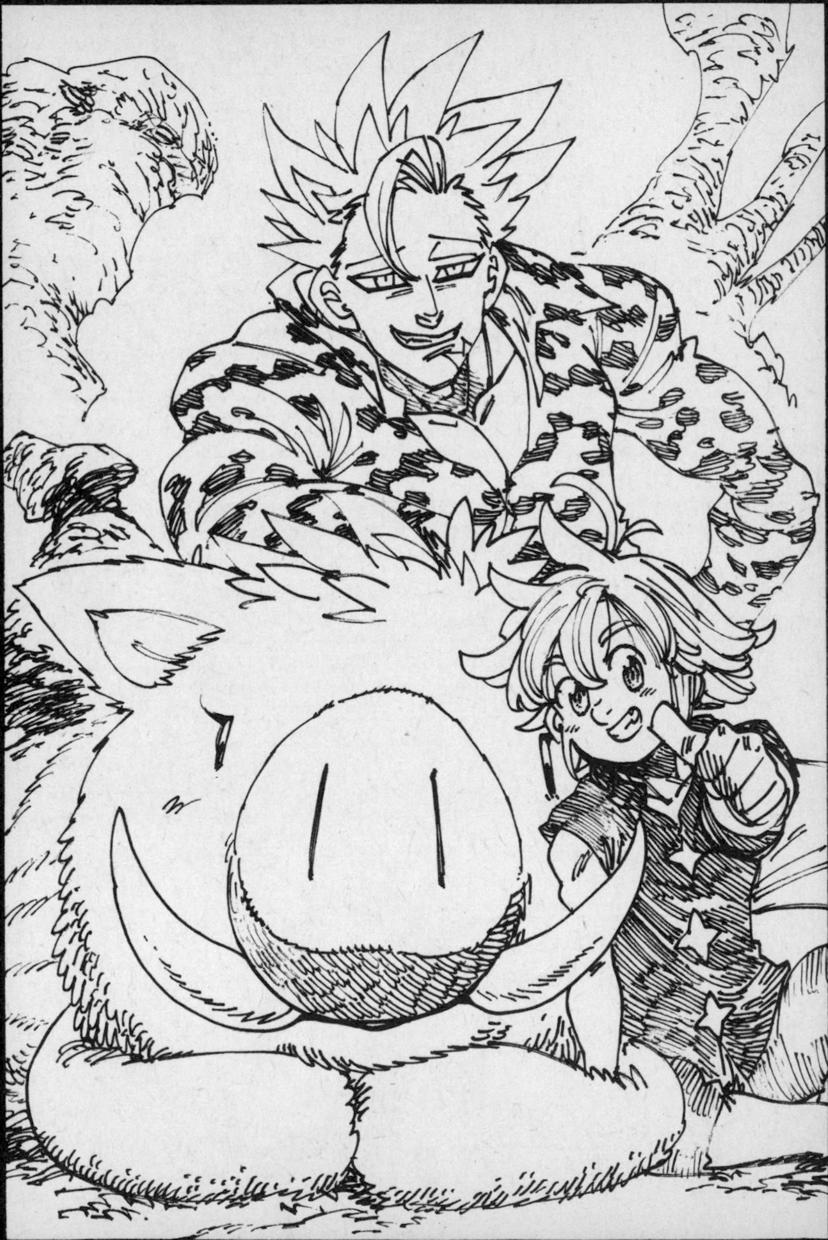

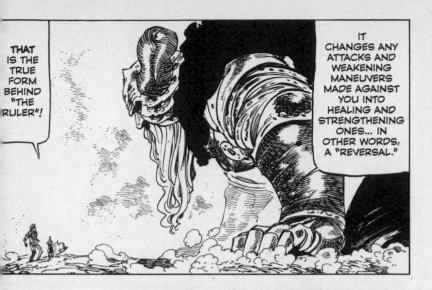

IT CHANGES ANY ATTACKS AND WEAKENING MANEUVERS MADE AGAINST YOU INTO HEALING AND STRENGTHENING ONES... IN OTHER WORDS, A "REVERSAL."
THAT IS THE TRUE FORM BEHIND "THE RULER"!
MELIODAS... OR RATHER, THE ESSENCE OF MY SON'S EMOTIONS.
I WILL NEVER LET YOU RETURN TO THE MORTAL PLANE.
THEN WE'LL FORCE OUR WAY THROUGH!!

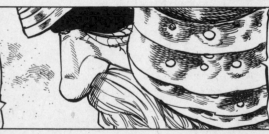

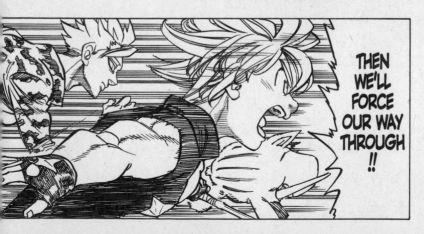

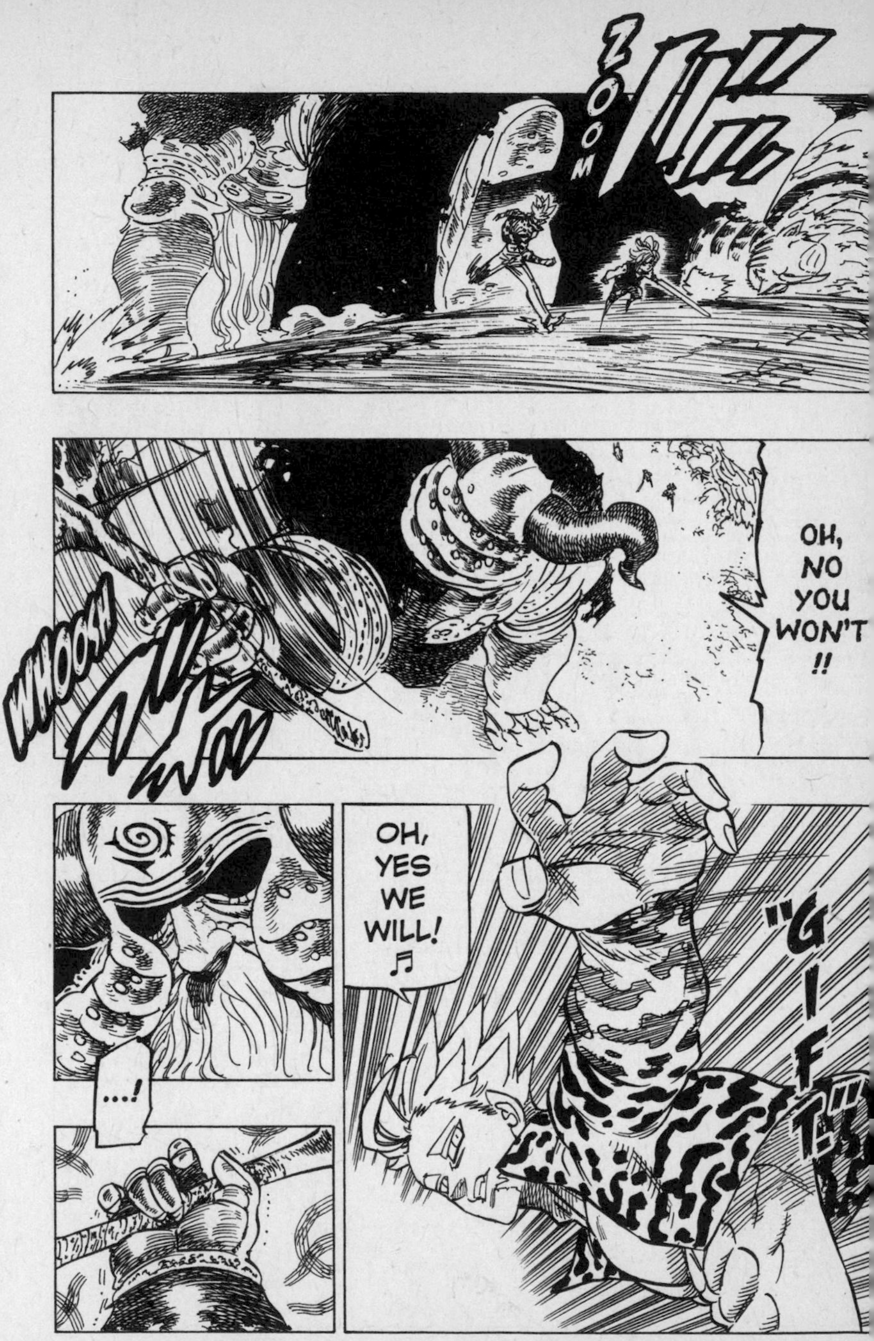
ZOOM
OH, NO YOU WON'T!!
WHOOSH
"GIFT"
OH, YES WE WILL! ♫
...!

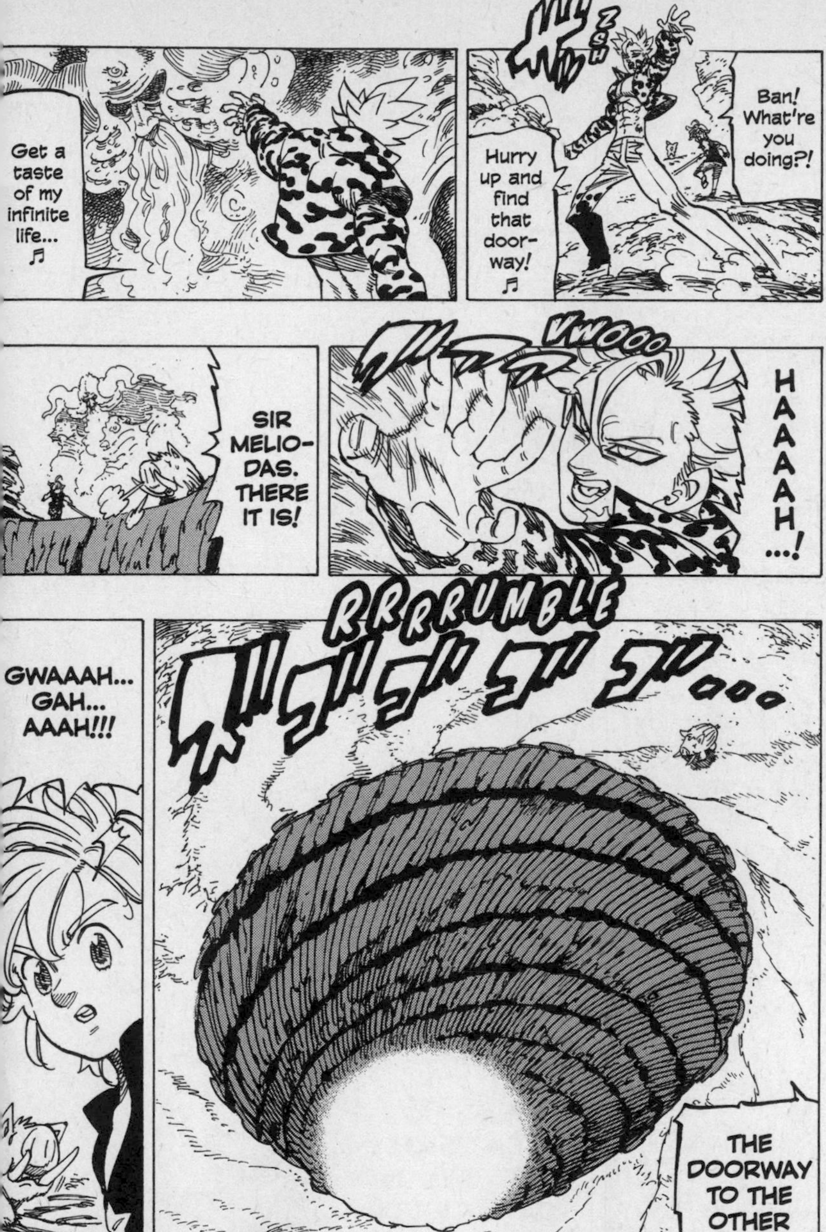
Ban! What're you doing?!
ZSH
Hurry up and find that doorway! ♬
Get a taste of my infinite life... ♬
VWOOO
HAAAAH...!
SIR MELIODAS. THERE IT IS!
RRRRUMBLE
THE DOORWAY TO THE OTHER SIDE!
GWAAAH... GAH... AAAH!!!

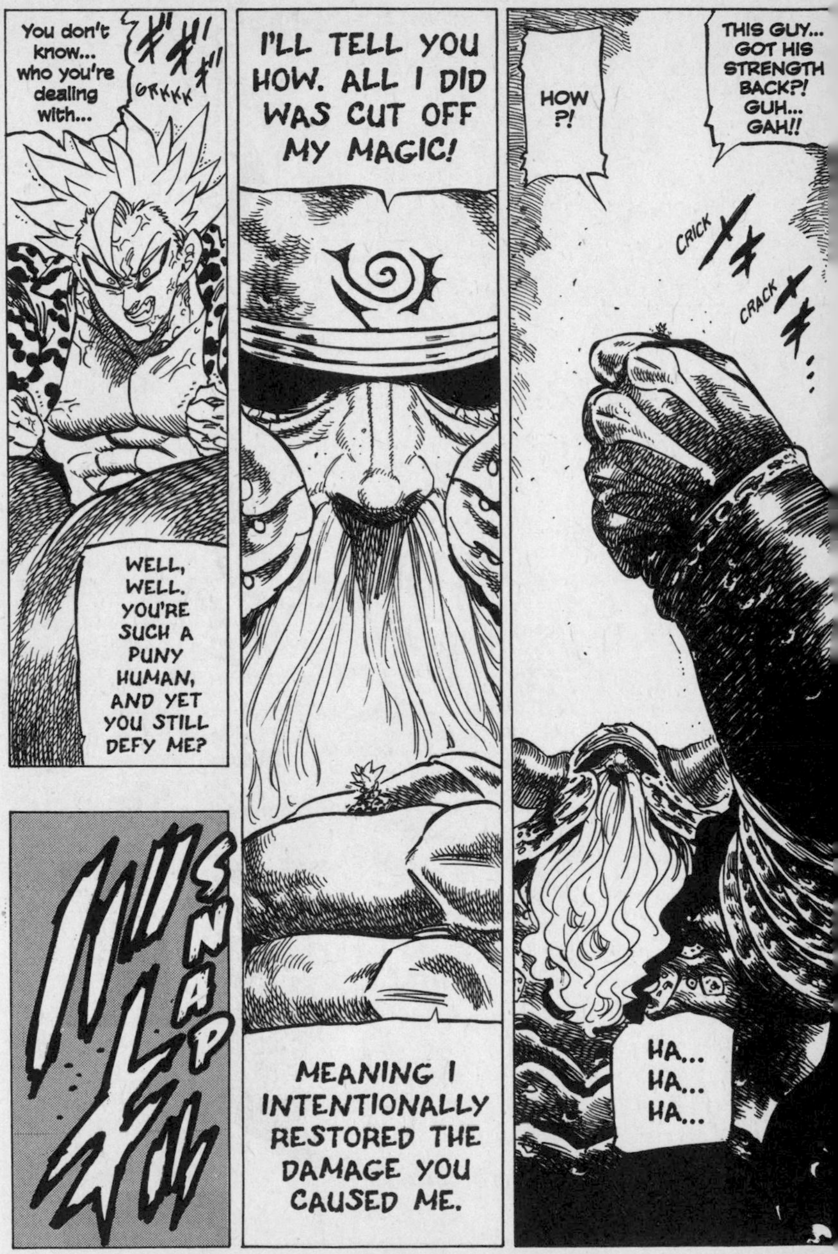
THIS GUY... GOT HIS STRENGTH BACK?! GUH... GAH!!
HOW ?!
CRICK
CRACK
HA... HA... HA...
I'LL TELL YOU HOW. ALL I DID WAS CUT OFF MY MAGIC!
MEANING I INTENTIONALLY RESTORED THE DAMAGE YOU CAUSED ME.
GRKKK
You don't know... who you're dealing with...
WELL, WELL. YOU'RE SUCH A PUNY HUMAN, AND YET YOU STILL DEFY ME?
SNAP

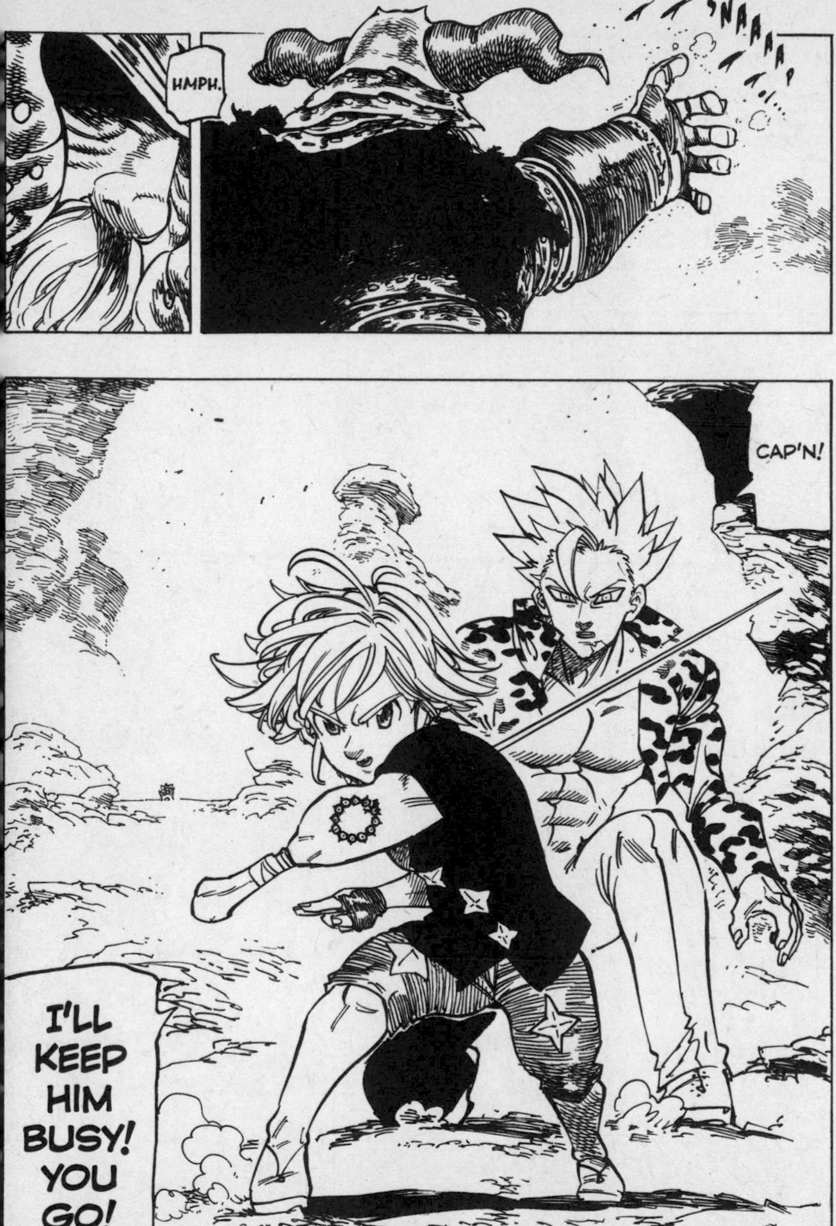
SNAAAAP
HMPH.
CAP'N!
I'LL KEEP HIM BUSY! YOU GO!

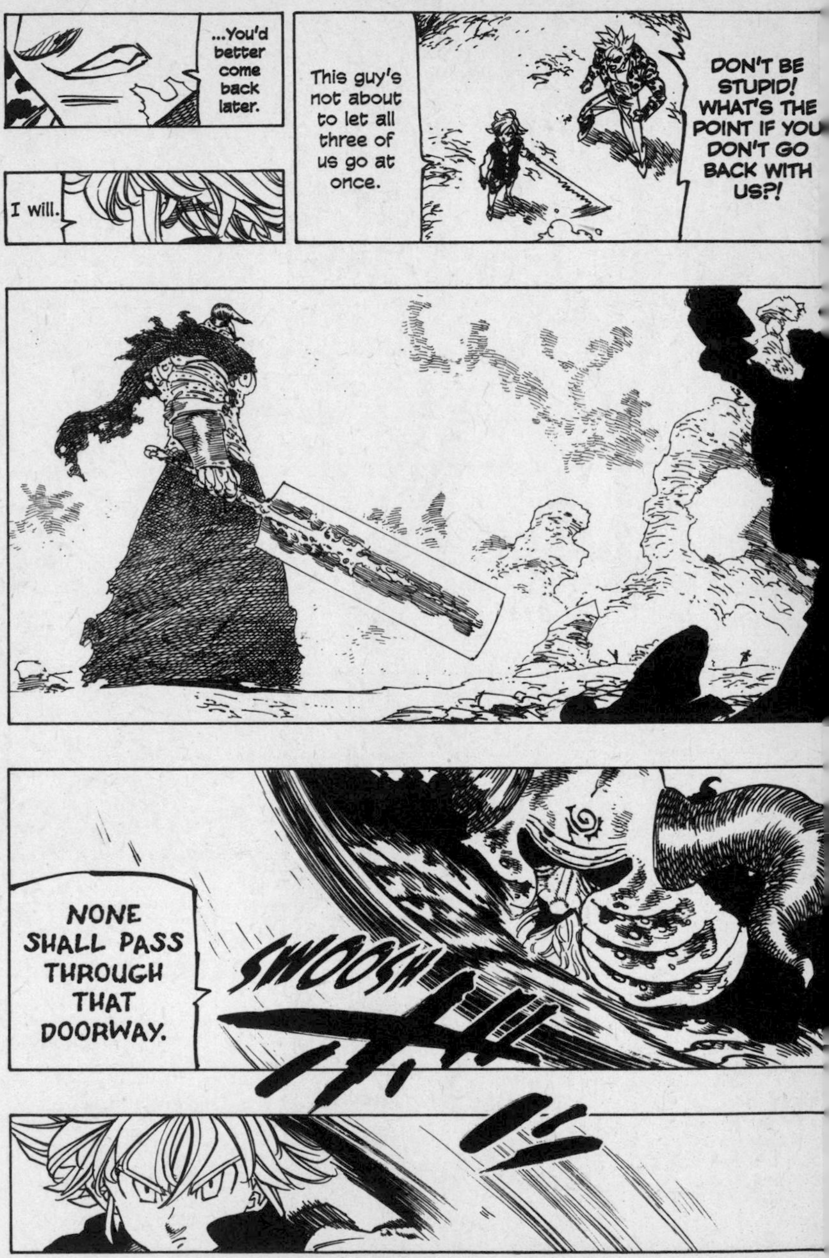
DON'T BE STUPID! WHAT'S THE POINT IF YOU DON'T GO BACK WITH US?!
This guy's not about to let all three of us go at once.
...You'd better come back later.
I will.
NONE SHALL PASS THROUGH THAT DOORWAY.
SWOOSH

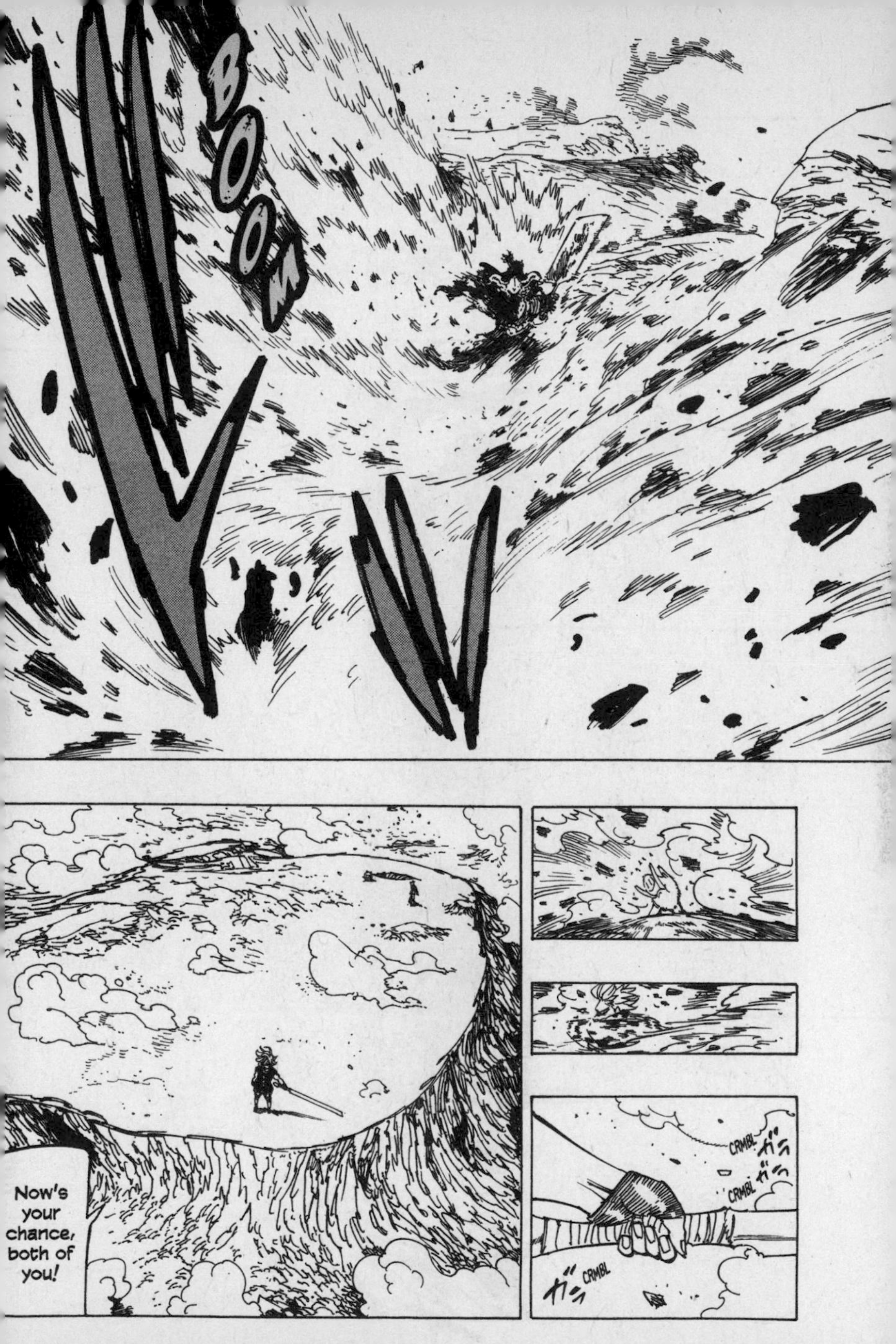
BOOOM
Now's your chance, both of you!
CRMBL
CRMBL
CRMBL

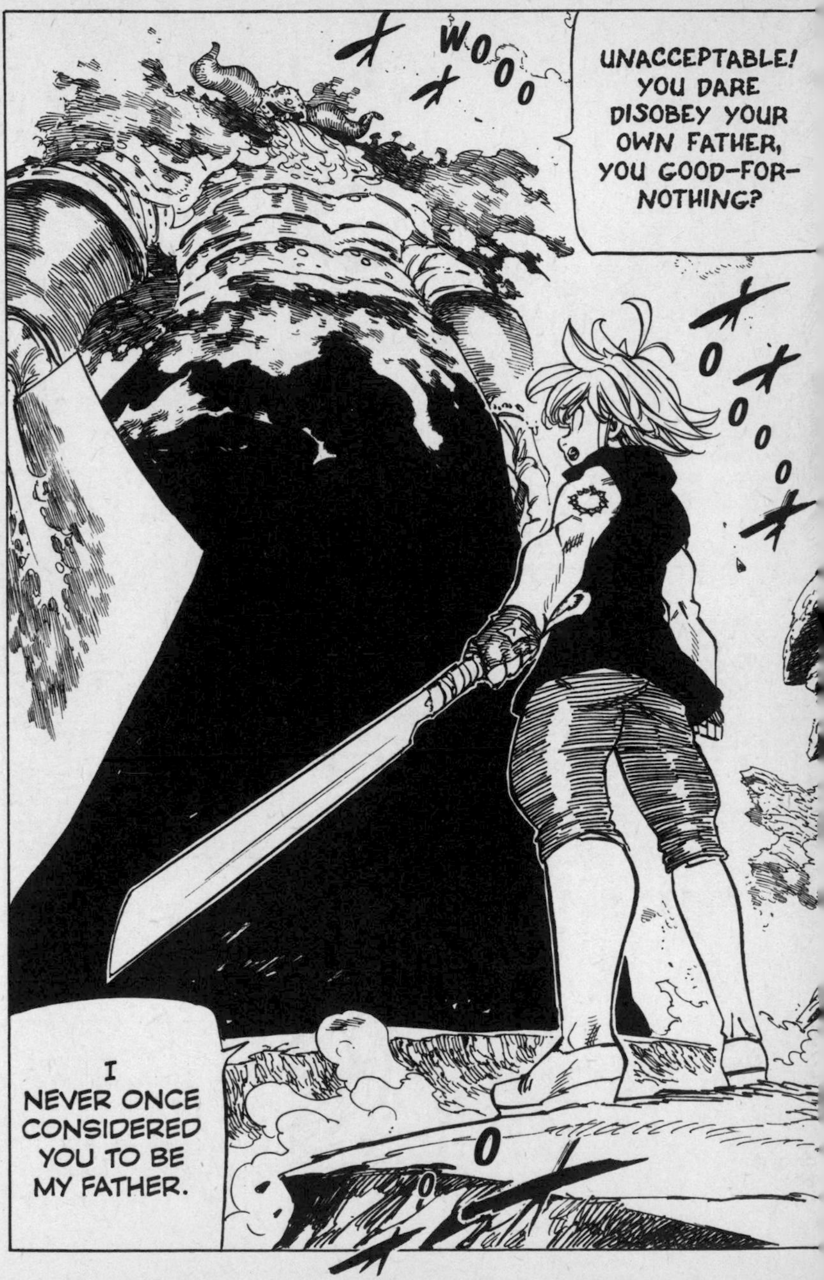
WOOOO
UNACCEPTABLE! YOU DARE DISOBEY YOUR OWN FATHER, YOU GOOD-FOR-NOTHING?
OOOOO
I NEVER ONCE CONSIDERED YOU TO BE MY FATHER.
O
O

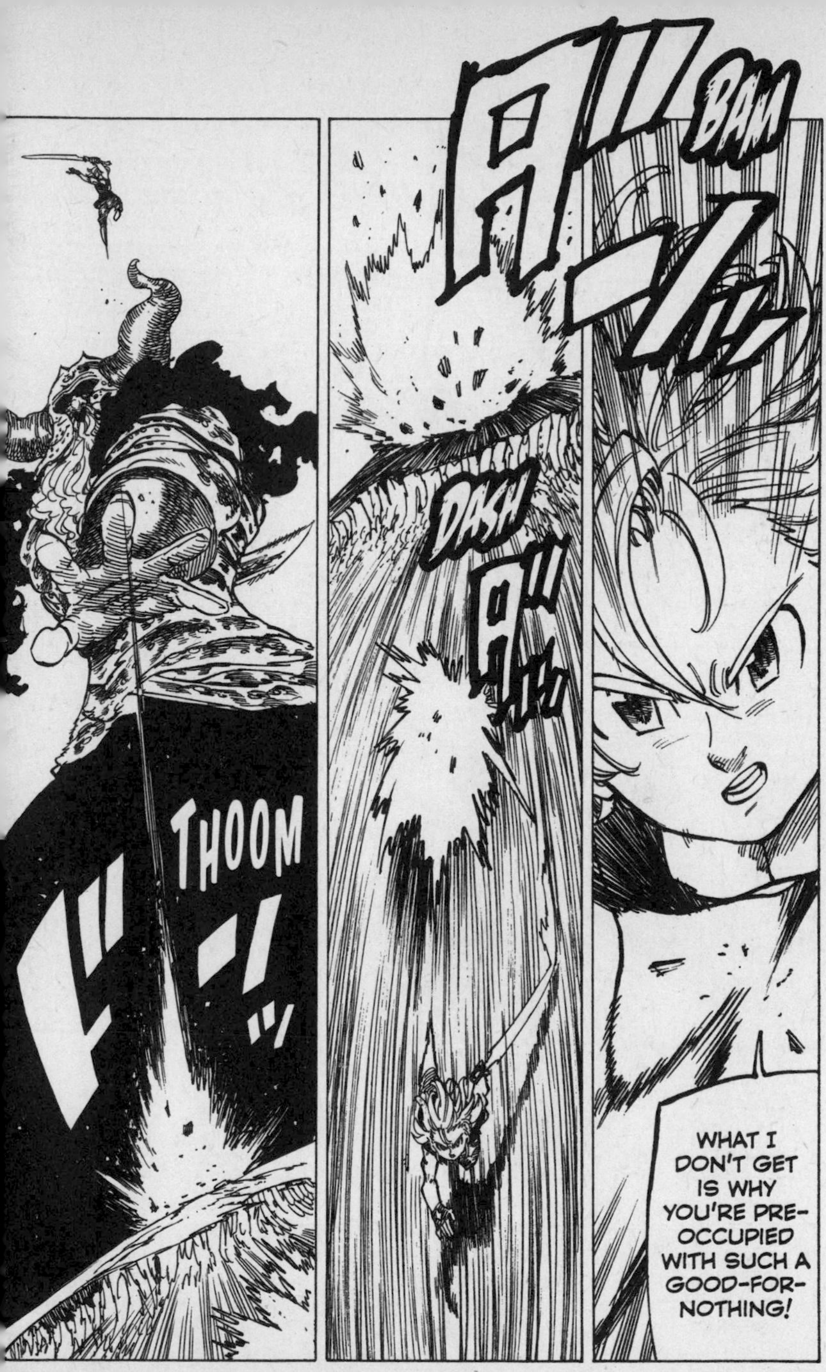
BAM
WHAT I DON'T GET IS WHY YOU'RE PRE-OCCUPIED WITH SUCH A GOOD-FOR-NOTHING!
DASH
THOOM

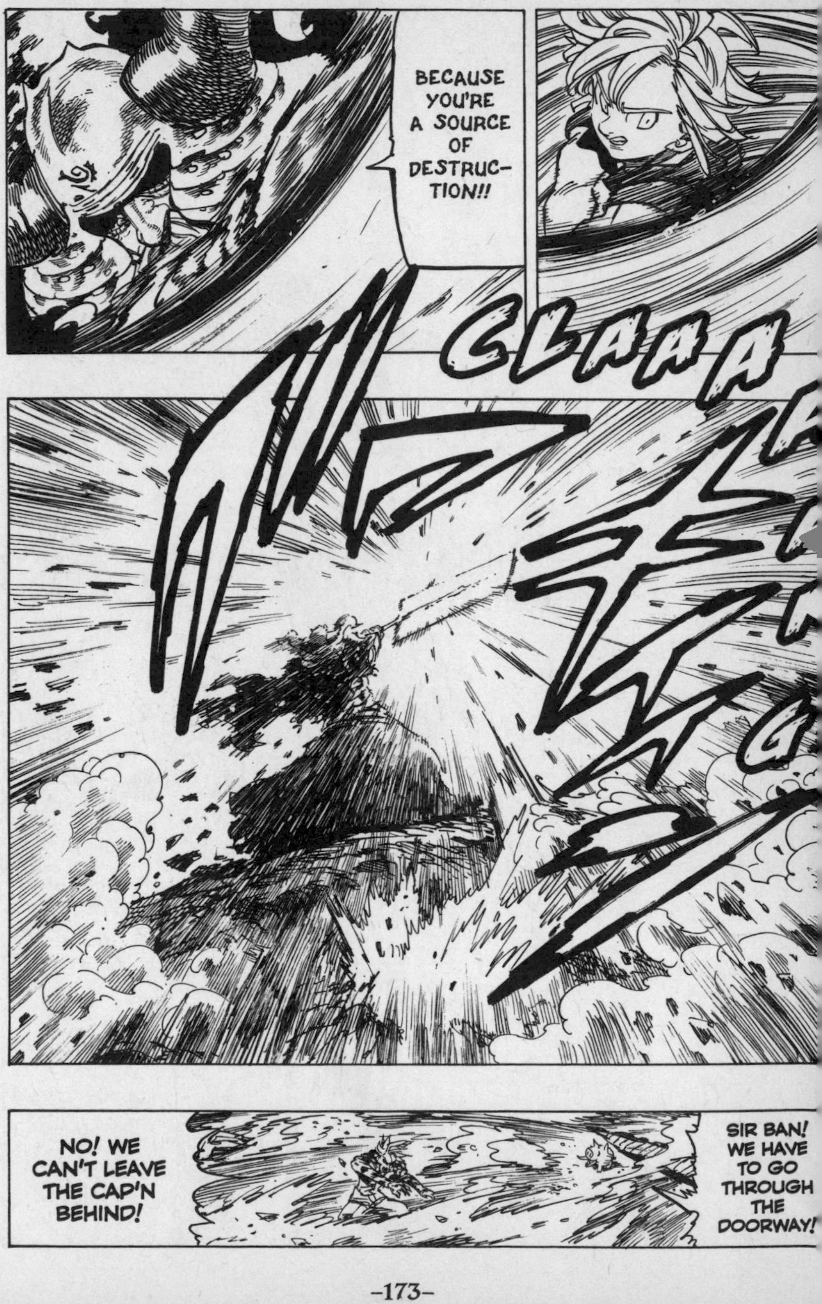
BECAUSE YOU'RE A SOURCE OF DESTRUCTION!!
CLAAAA
SIR BAN! WE HAVE TO GO THROUGH THE DOORWAY!
NO! WE CAN'T LEAVE THE CAP'N BEHIND!

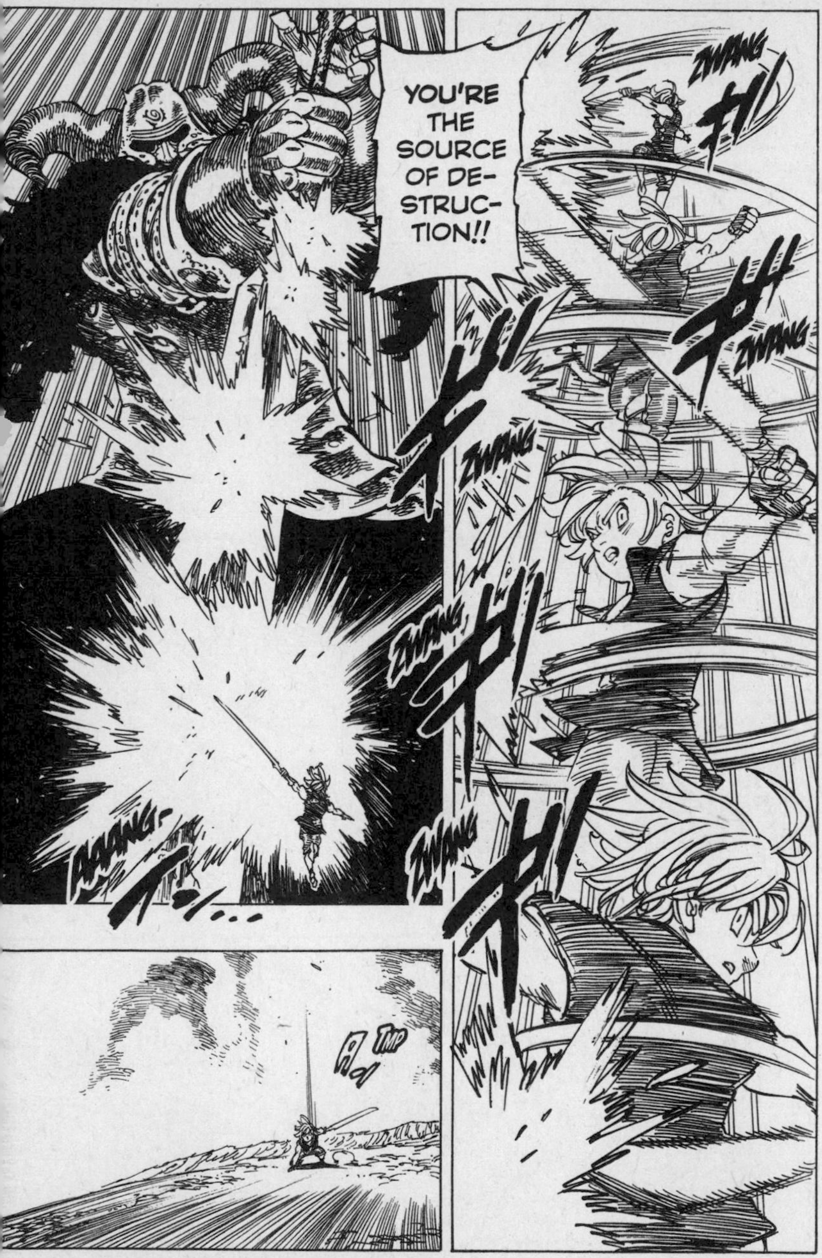
ZWANG
ZWANG
ZWANG
ZWANG
ZWANG
YOU'RE THE SOURCE OF DE- STRUCTION!!
TMP

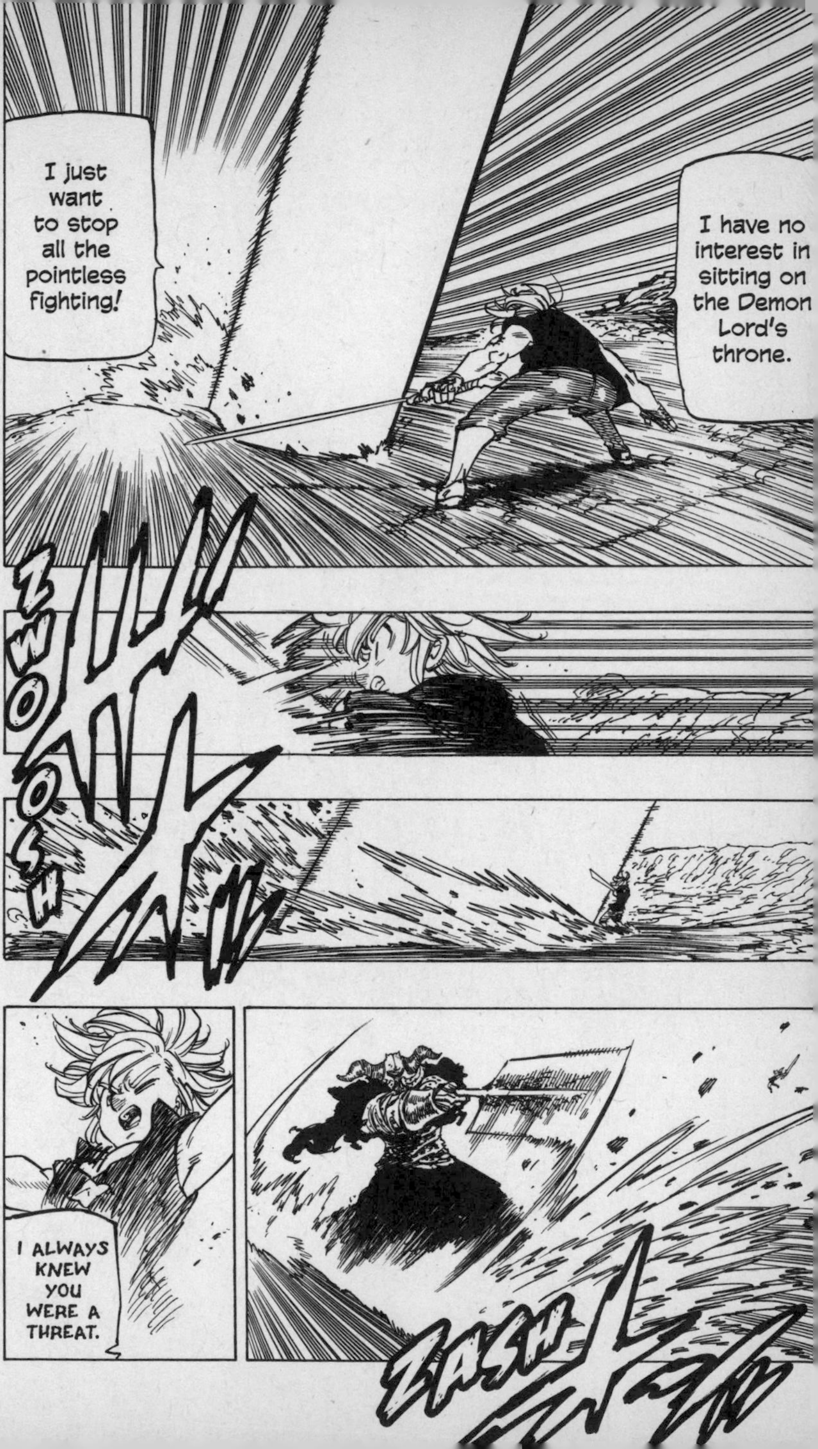

I have no interest in sitting on the Demon Lord's throne.
I just want to stop all the pointless fighting!
ZWOOOSH
ZASH
I ALWAYS KNEW YOU WERE A THREAT.

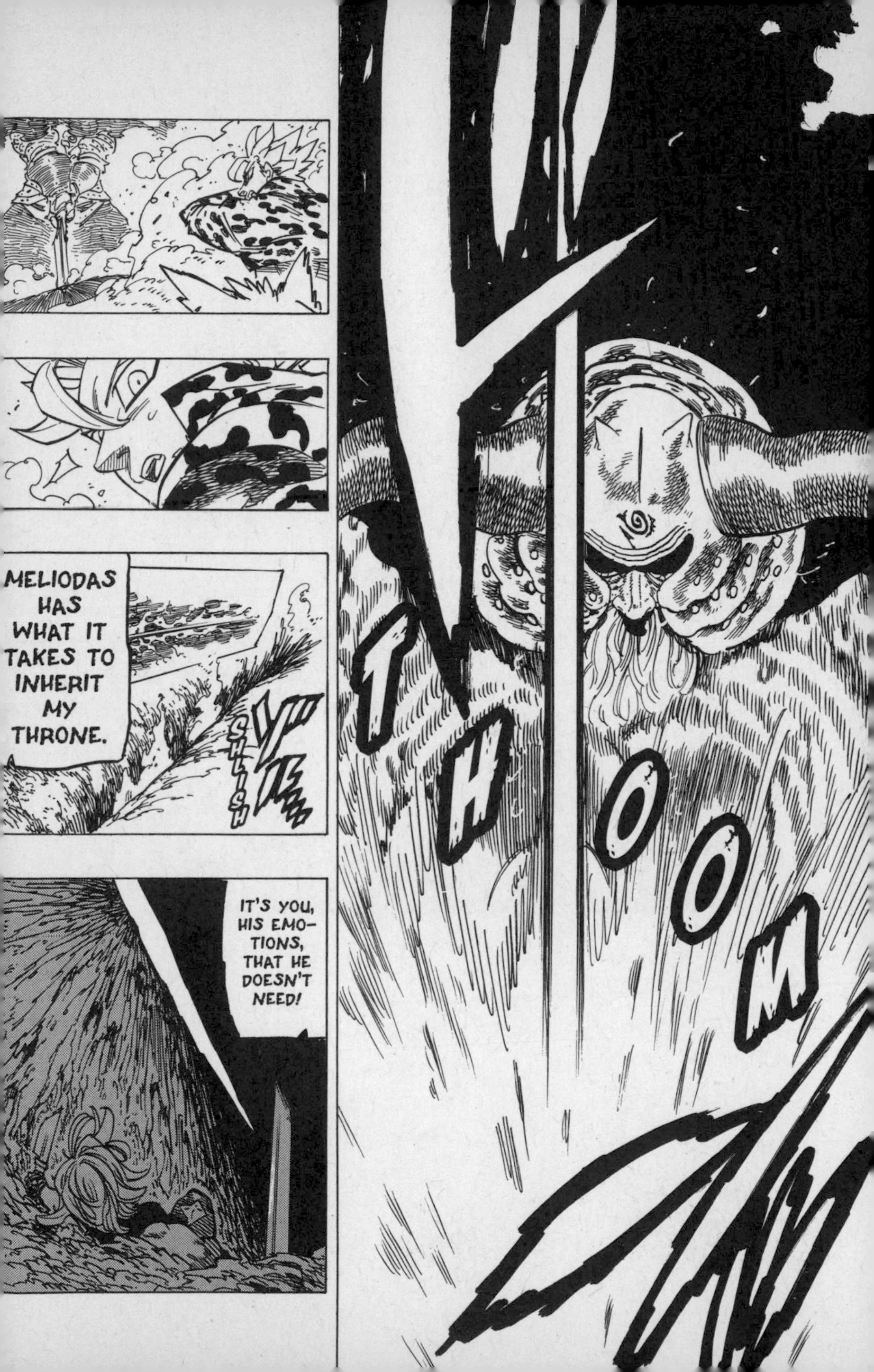
THOOM
MELIODAS HAS WHAT IT TAKES TO INHERIT MY THRONE.
SHLISH
IT'S YOU, HIS EMOTIONS, THAT HE DOESN'T NEED!

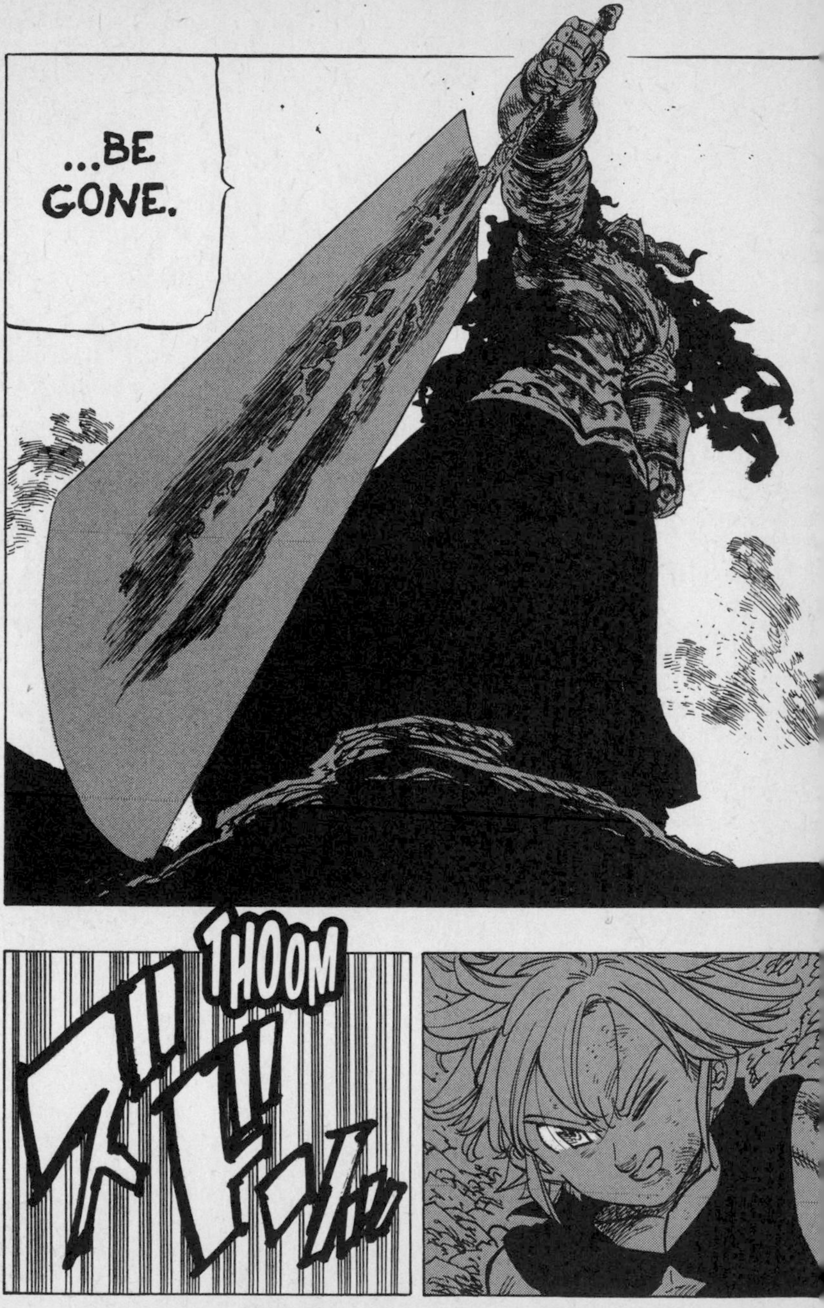
...BE GONE.
THOOM

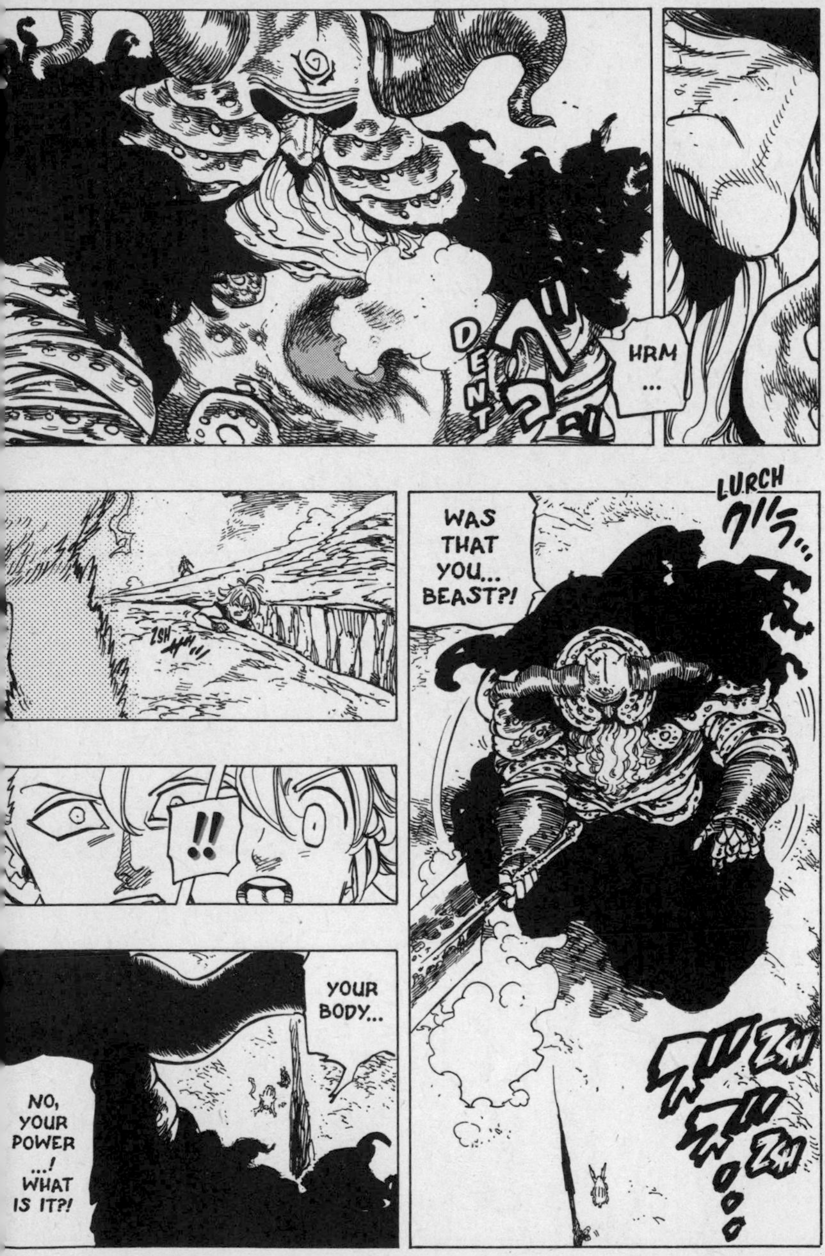
HRM
...
DENT
WAS THAT YOU... BEAST?!
LURCH
ZSH
!!
YOUR BODY...
NO, YOUR POWER ...! WHAT IS IT?!
ZSH
ZSH

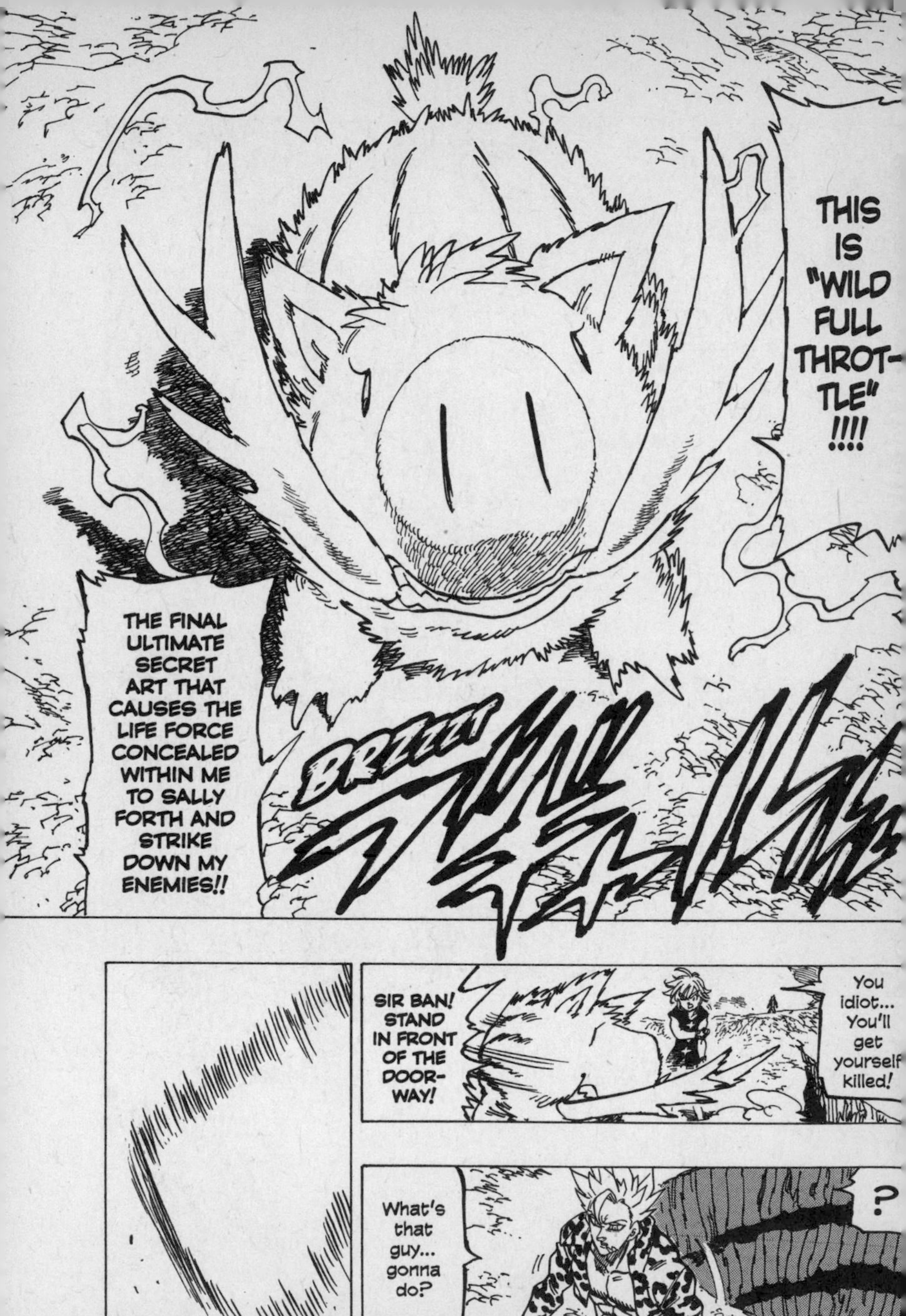
THIS IS "WILD FULL THROT-TLE"!!!!
BRZZZT
THE FINAL ULTIMATE SECRET ART THAT CAUSES THE LIFE FORCE CONCEALED WITHIN ME TO SALLY FORTH AND STRIKE DOWN MY ENEMIES!!
You idiot... You'll get yourself killed!
SIR BAN! STAND IN FRONT OF THE DOOR-WAY!
?
What's that guy... gonna do?

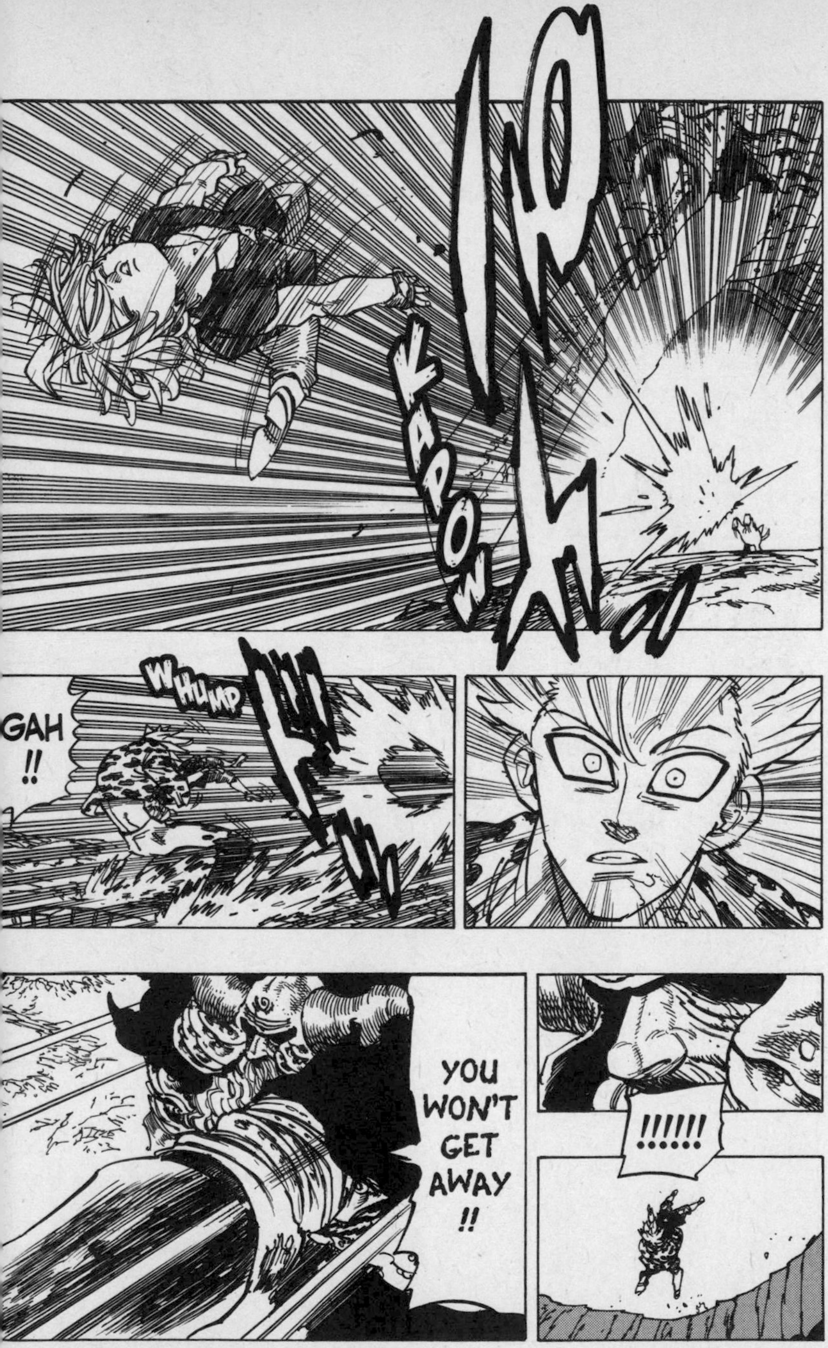
KAPOW
WHUMP
GAH!!
!!!!!!
YOU WON'T GET AWAY!!

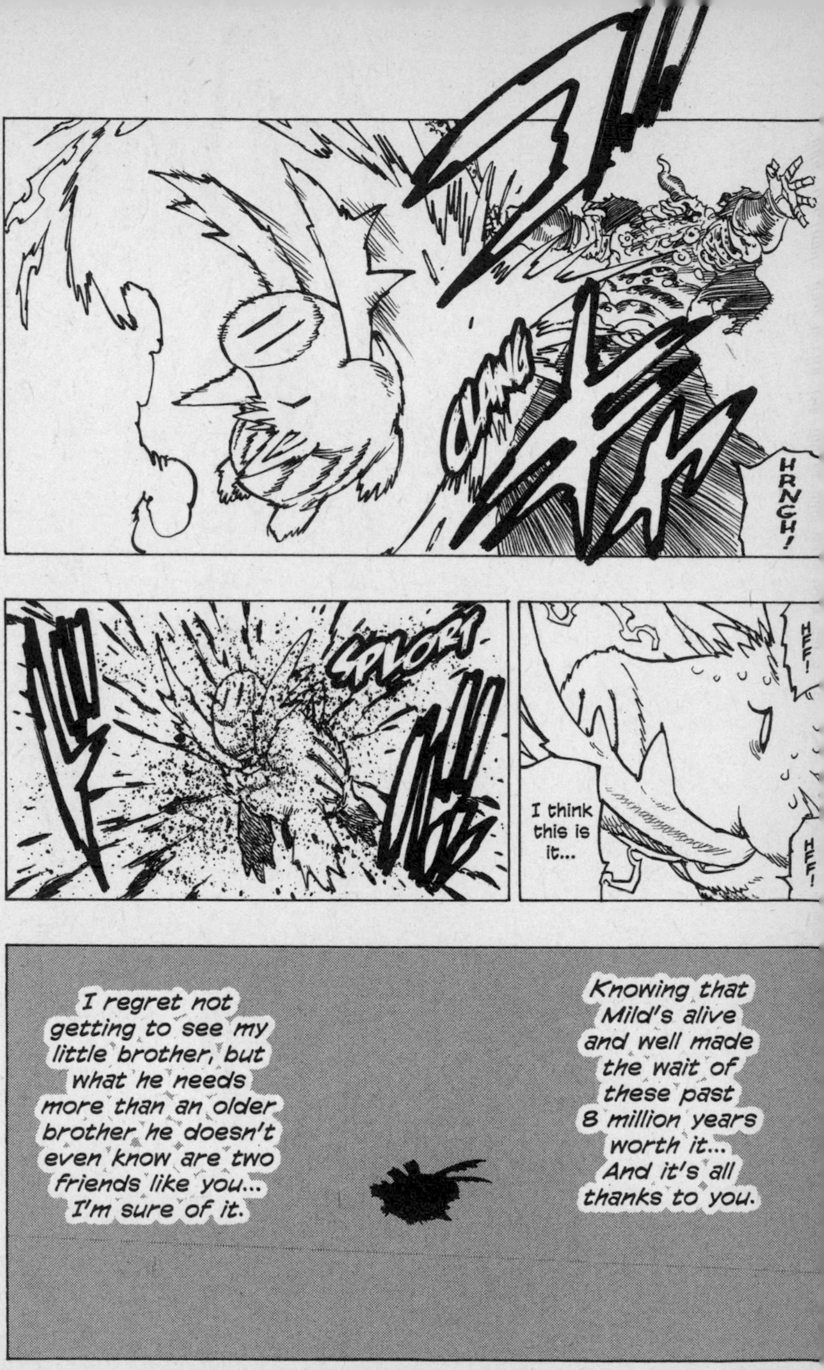
HRNGH!
CLANG
HEF!
HEF!
I think this is it...
SPLORT
Knowing that Mild's alive and well made the wait of these past 8 million years worth it... And it's all thanks to you.
I regret not getting to see my little brother, but what he needs more than an older brother he doesn't even know are two friends like you... I'm sure of it.

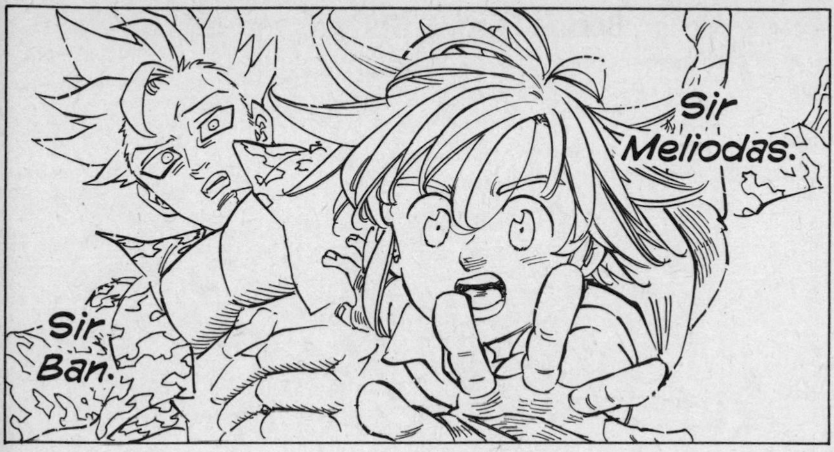
Sir Meliodas.
Sir Ban.

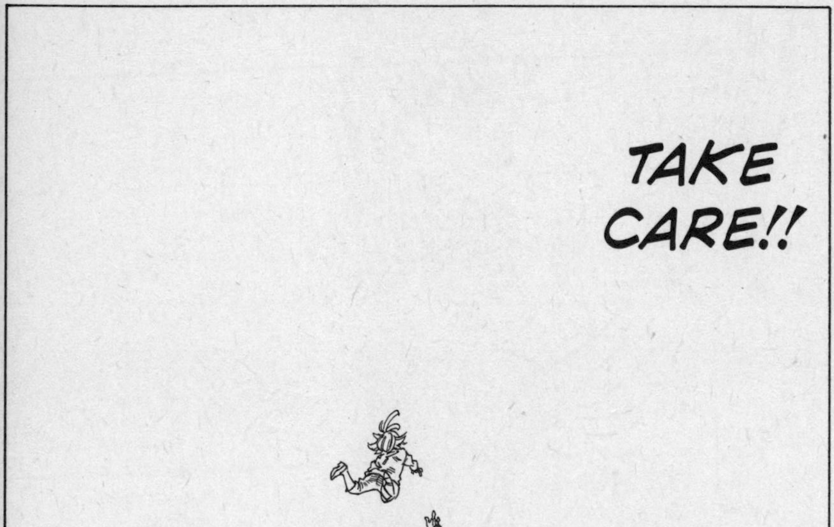
TAKE CARE!!

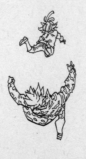

To Be Continued in Volume 35...

Bonus Story - Showdown at High Noon

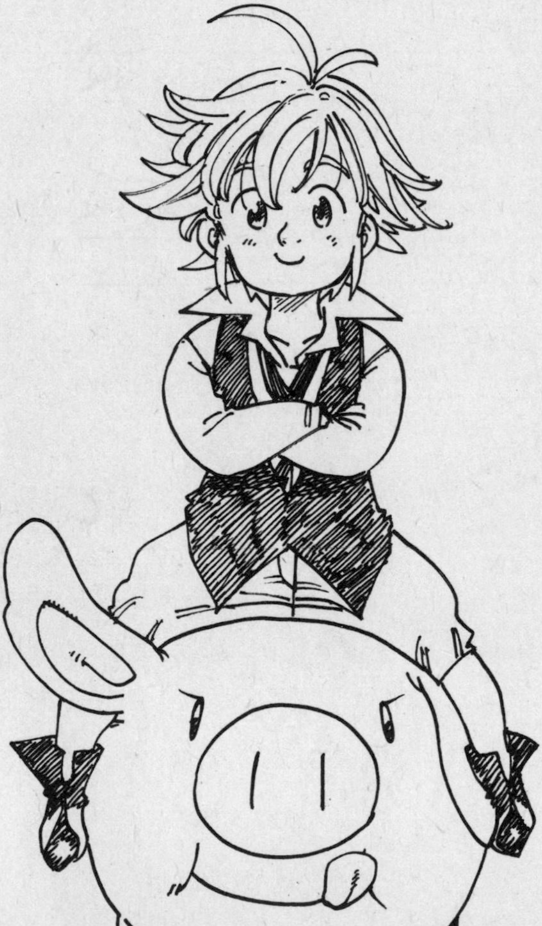

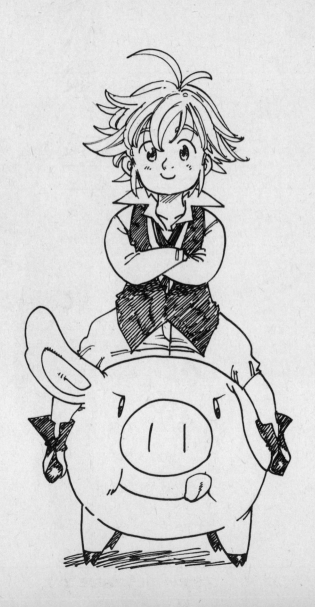

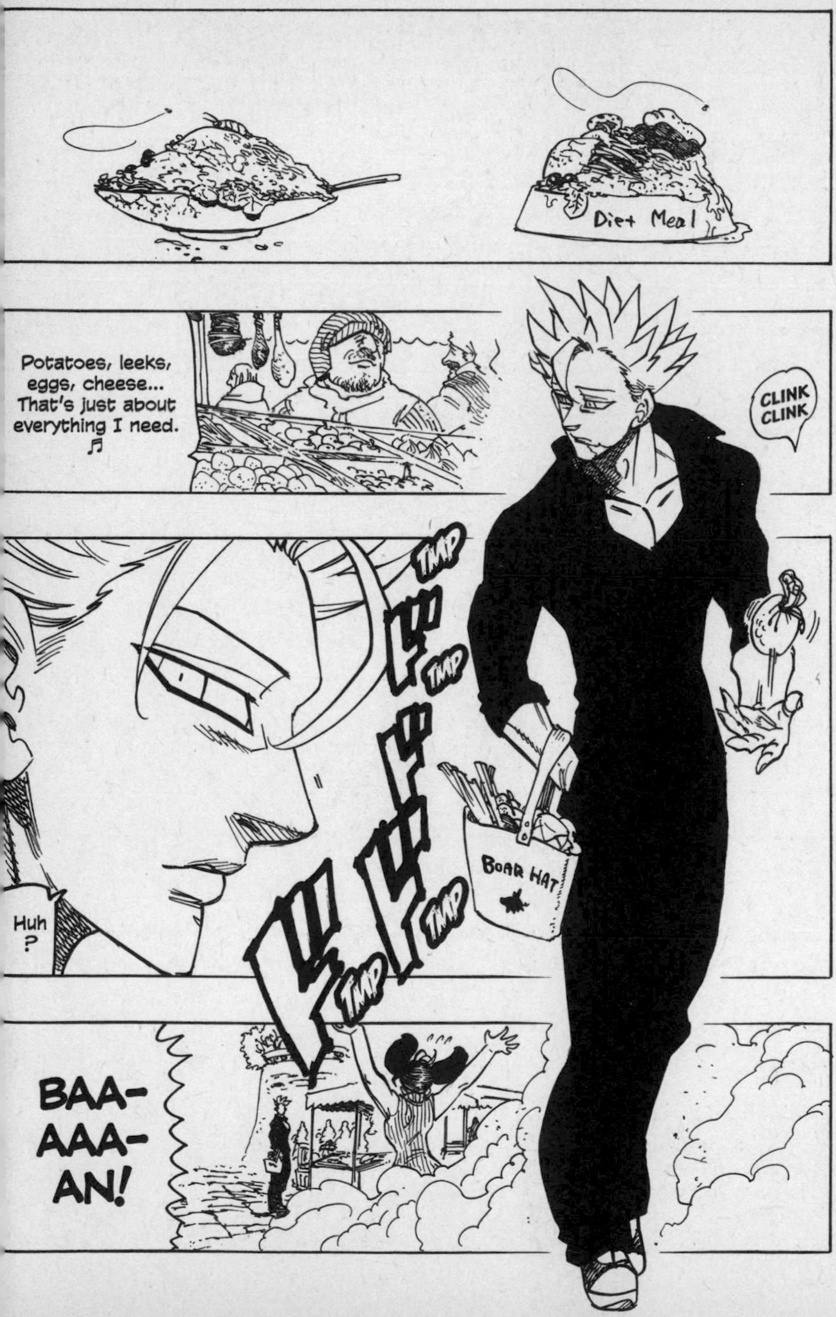
Diet Meal
CLINK CLINK
Potatoes, leeks, eggs, cheese... That's just about everything I need. ♫
TMP TMP TMP TMP
BOAR HAT
Huh?
BAA-AAA-AN!

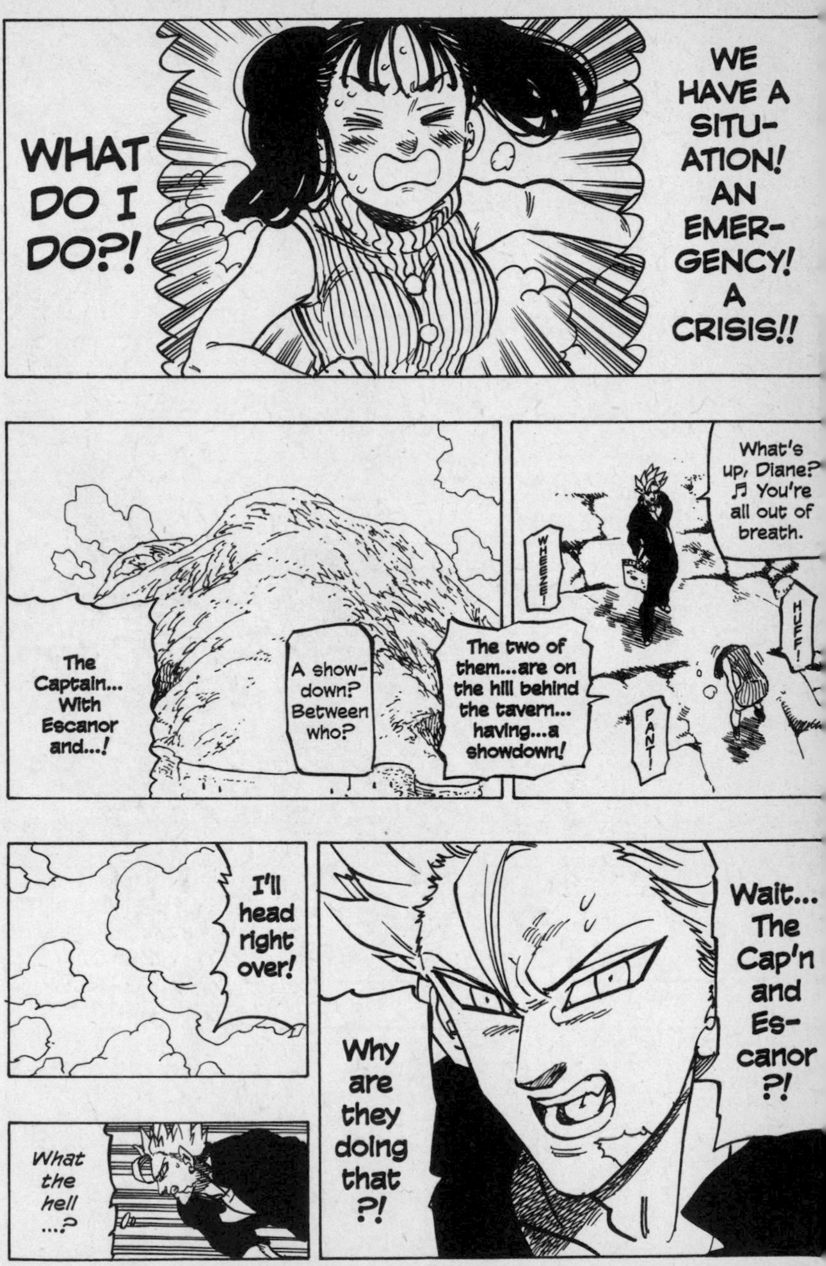
WE HAVE A SITUATION! AN EMERGENCY! A CRISIS!!
WHAT DO I DO?!
What's up, Diane? ♫ You're all out of breath.
WHEEZE!
HUFF!
PANT!
The two of them...are on the hill behind the tavern... having...a showdown!
A showdown? Between who?
The Captain... With Escanor and...!
Wait... The Cap'n and Escanor?!
Why are they doing that?!
I'll head right over!
What the hell ...?

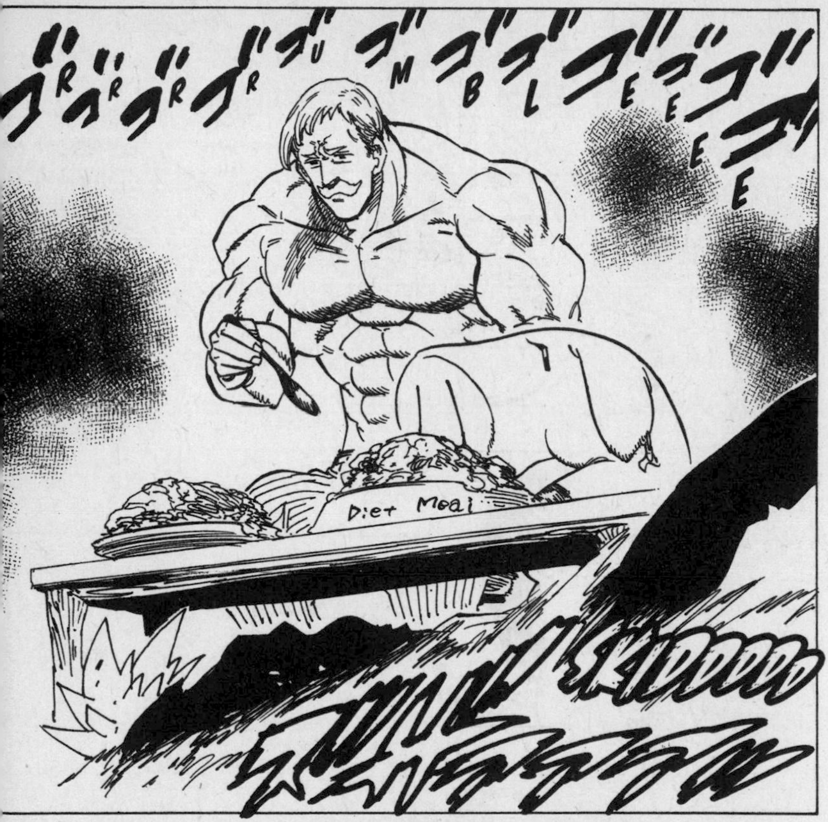
RRRRUMBLEEEE
Diet Meal
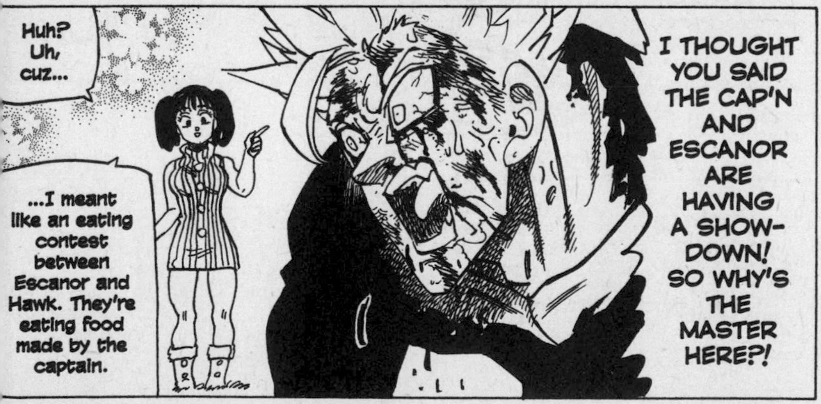
I THOUGHT YOU SAID THE CAP'N AND ESCANOR ARE HAVING A SHOW-DOWN! SO WHY'S THE MASTER HERE?!
Huh? Uh, cuz...
...I meant like an eating contest between Escanor and Hawk. They're eating food made by the captain.

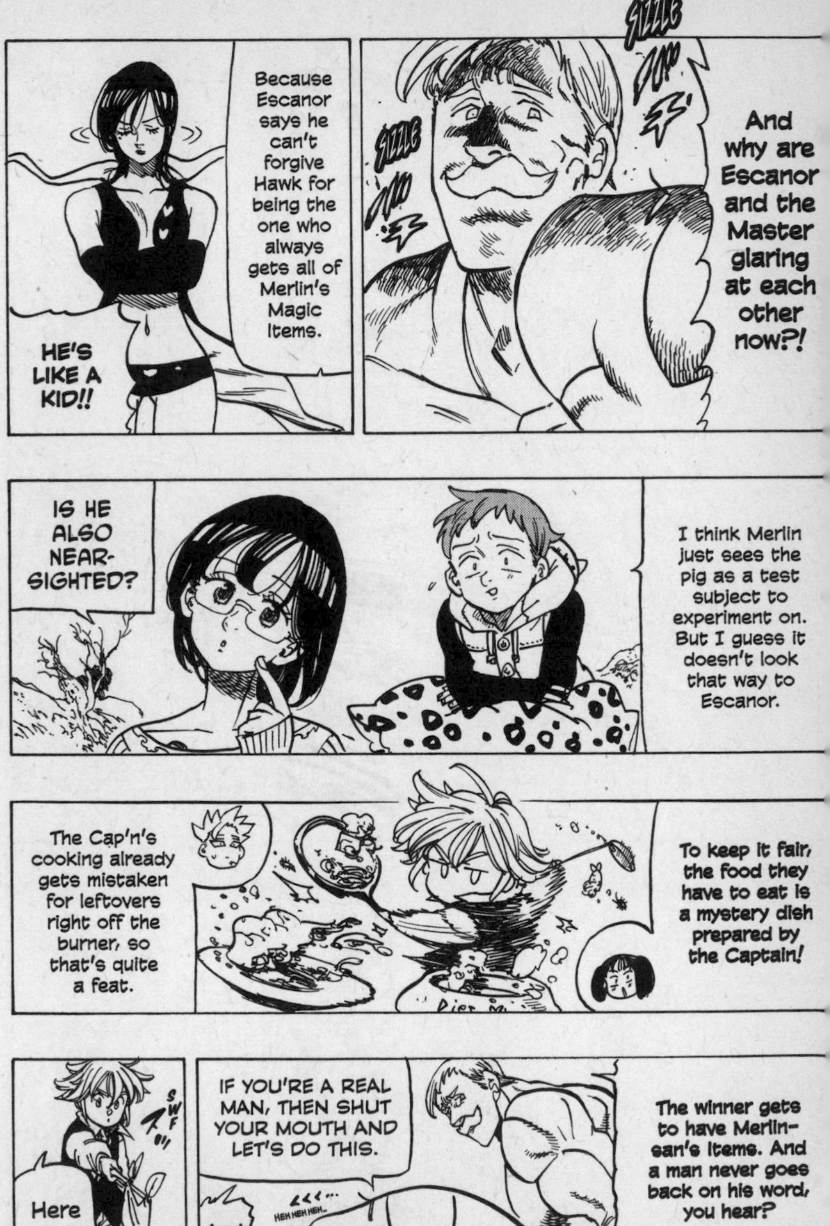
SIZZLE
SIZZLE
And why are Escanor and the Master glaring at each other now?!
Because Escanor says he can't forgive Hawk for being the one who always gets all of Merlin's Magic Items.
HE'S LIKE A KID!!
I think Merlin just sees the pig as a test subject to experiment on. But I guess it doesn't look that way to Escanor.
IS HE ALSO NEAR-SIGHTED?
To keep it fair, the food they have to eat is a mystery dish prepared by the Captain!
The Cap'n's cooking already gets mistaken for leftovers right off the burner, so that's quite a feat.
The winner gets to have Merlin-san's Items. And a man never goes back on his word, you hear?
IF YOU'RE A REAL MAN, THEN SHUT YOUR MOUTH AND LET'S DO THIS.
HEH HEH HEH...
Augh ...!
SWF
Here goes.

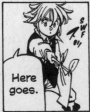

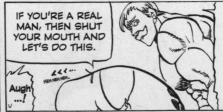

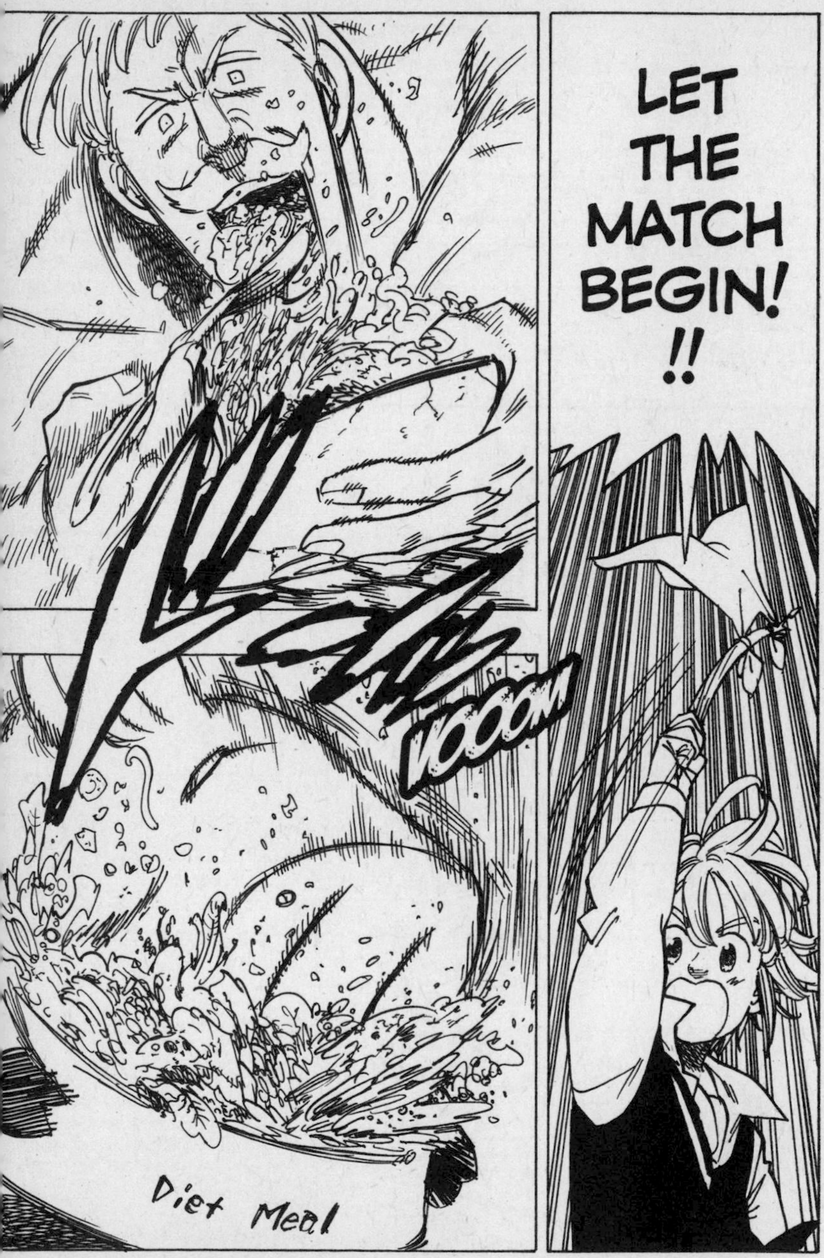
LET THE MATCH BEGIN!!!
VOOOM
Diet Meal

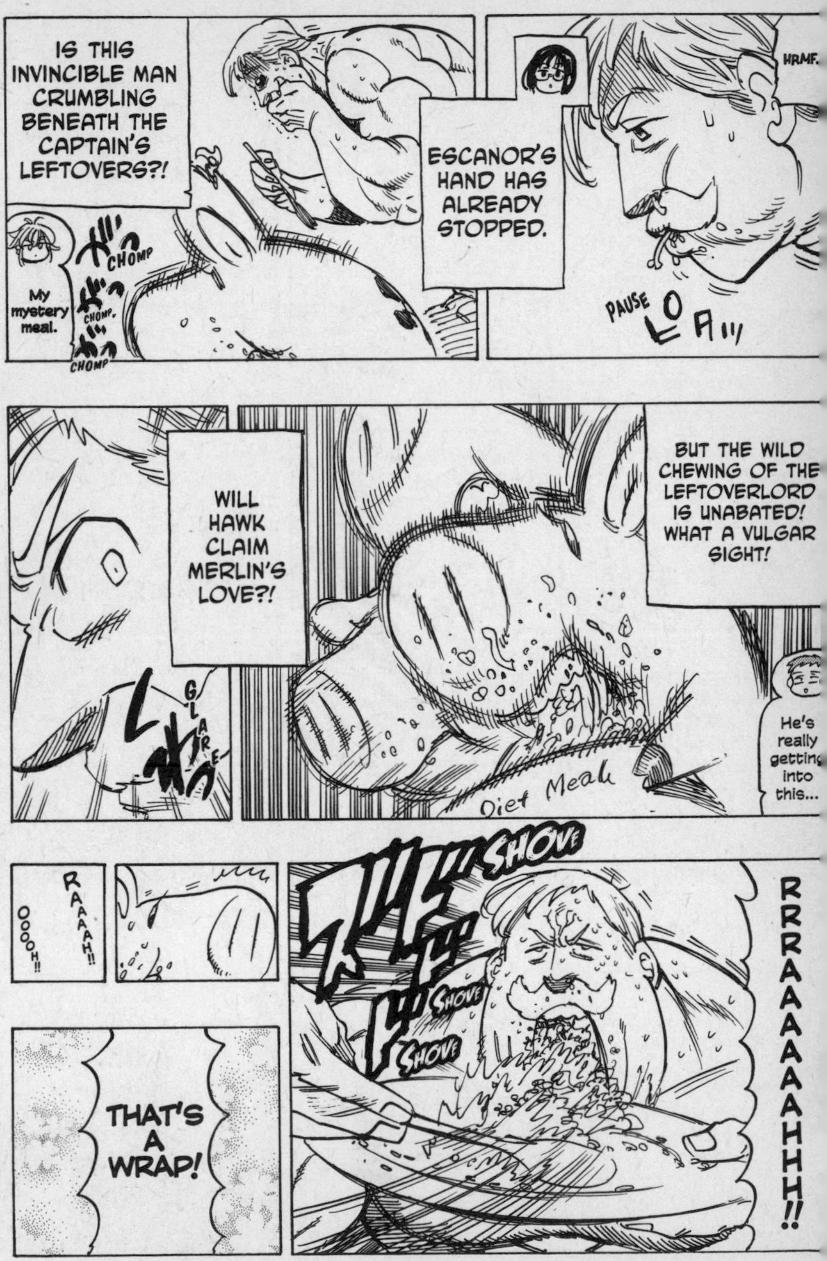
HRMF.
ESCANOR'S HAND HAS ALREADY STOPPED.
PAUSE
IS THIS INVINCIBLE MAN CRUMBLING BENEATH THE CAPTAIN'S LEFTOVERS?!
CHOMP
CHOMP
CHOMP
My mystery meal.
BUT THE WILD CHEWING OF THE LEFTOVERLORD IS UNABATED! WHAT A VULGAR SIGHT!
He's really getting into this...
Diet Meals
WILL HAWK CLAIM MERLIN'S LOVE?!
GLARE
RRRAAAAAAAHHH!!
SHOVE
SHOVE
SHOVE
RAAAAH!!
OOOOH!!
THAT'S A WRAP!

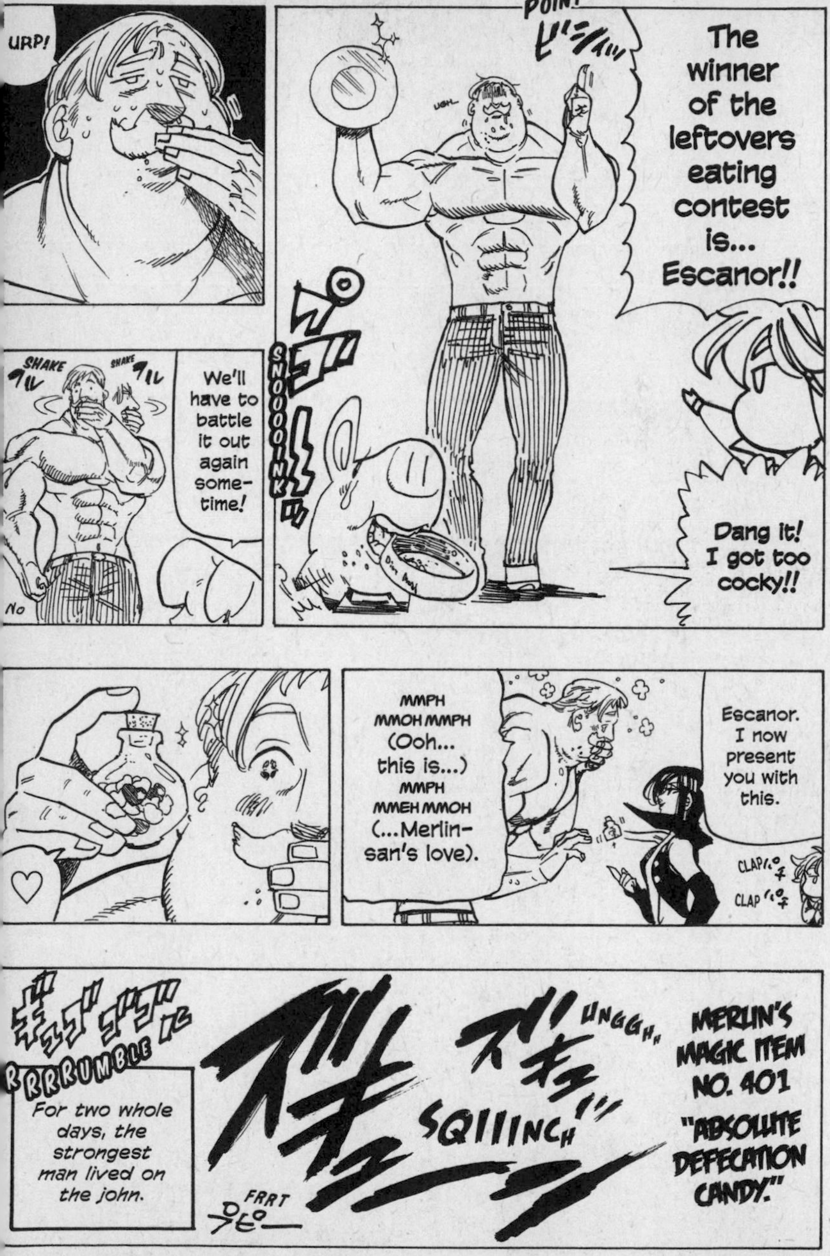
POINT
The winner of the leftovers eating contest is... Escanor!!
UGH
SNOOOOOINK
Dang it! I got too cocky!!
URP!
SHAKE
SHAKE
We'll have to battle it out again sometime!
Escanor. I now present you with this.
MMPH MMOH MMPH (Ooh... this is...) MMPH MMEH MMOH (...Merlin-san's love).
CLAP
CLAP
MERLIN'S MAGIC ITEM NO. 401 "ABSOLUTE DEFECATION CANDY."
UNGGH
SQIIINCH
FRRT
RRRUMBLE
For two whole days, the strongest man lived on the john.

THE END

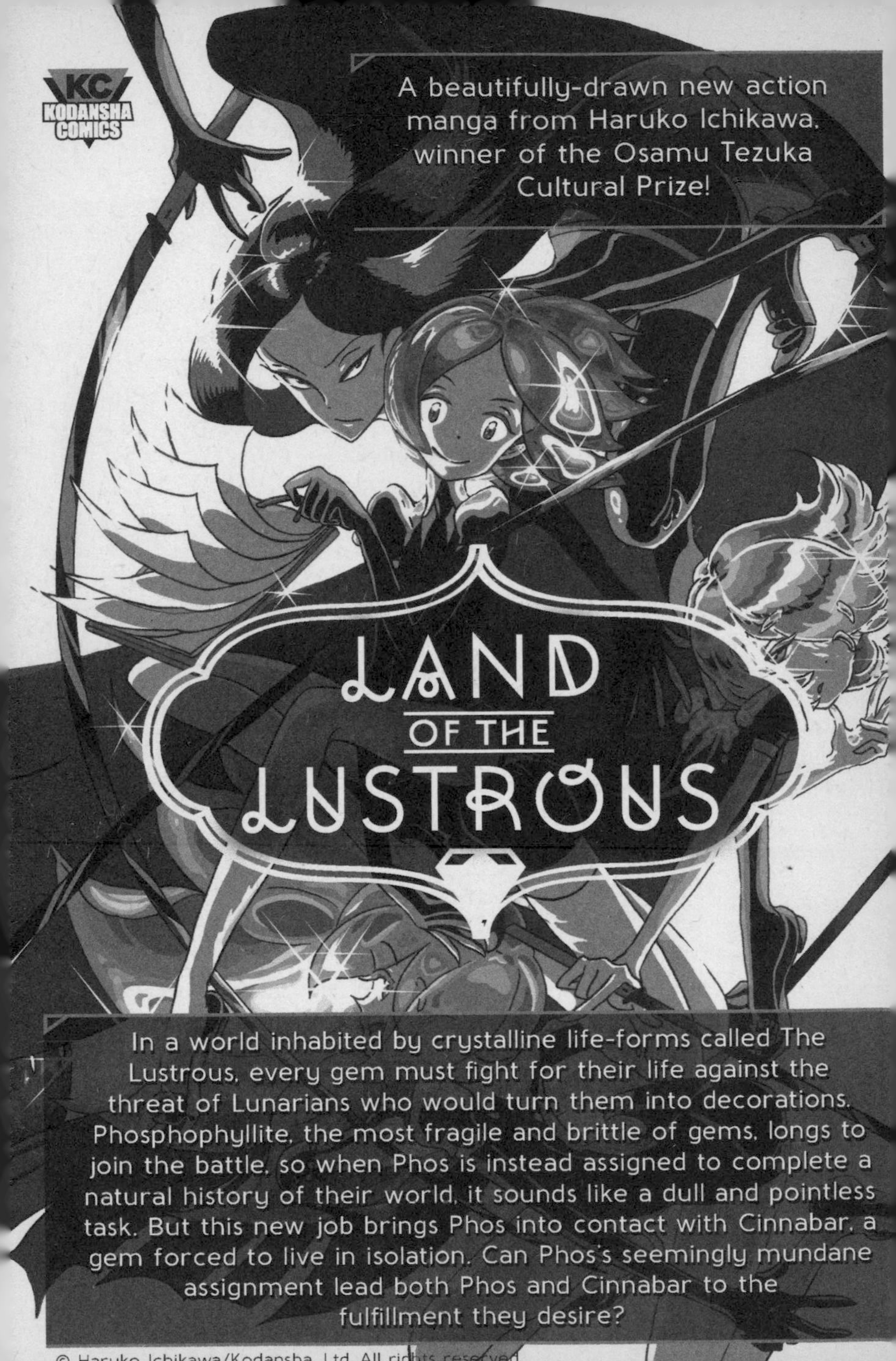
KC KODANSHA COMICS
A beautifully-drawn new action manga from Haruko Ichikawa, winner of the Osamu Tezuka Cultural Prize!
LAND OF THE LUSTROUS
In a world inhabited by crystalline life-forms called The Lustrous, every gem must fight for their life against the threat of Lunarians who would turn them into decorations. Phosphophyllite, the most fragile and brittle of gems, longs to join the battle, so when Phos is instead assigned to complete a natural history of their world, it sounds like a dull and pointless task. But this new job brings Phos into contact with Cinnabar, a gem forced to live in isolation. Can Phos's seemingly mundane assignment lead both Phos and Cinnabar to the fulfillment they desire?

The Seven Deadly Sins volume 34 is a work of fiction. Names, characters, places, and incidents are the products of the author's imagination or are used fictitiously. Any resemblance to actual events, locales, or persons, living or dead, is entirely coincidental.

A Kodansha Comics Trade Paperback Original.

Published in the United States by Kodansha Comics, an imprint of Kodansha USA Publishing, LLC, New York.

Publication rights for this English edition arranged through Kodansha Ltd., Tokyo.

First published in Japan in 2018 by Kodansha Ltd., Tokyo.

ISBN 978-1-63236-872-0

Printed in the United States of America.

www.kodanshacomics.com

9 8 7 6 5 4 3 2 1

Translation: Christine Dashiell
Lettering: James Dashiell
Kodansha Comics edition cover design: Phil Balsman